UNDERSTANDING MAYA INSCRIPTIONS
A HIEROGLYPH HANDBOOK

2nd edition

DEDICATION

We dedicate this book to Chris Jones, whose Maya
hieroglyph workshops at the early Maya Weekends at Penn
sparked our interest in glyphs; to Linda Schele, whose
inspirational annual Workshops and Advanced Seminars at
Austin hooked us securely; to Ben Leaf, who as mentor of
the Philadelphia Maya hieroglyph study group, has
provided us with a continuing challenge to delve ever
deeper into glyph studies; and to Elin Danien, who through
the wonderful Maya Weekends at Penn she has created, has
provided us (and many others) with the opportunity to
learn about the latest important developments in the fast
moving world of Maya studies.

UNDERSTANDING MAYA INSCRIPTIONS
A HIEROGLYPH HANDBOOK

2nd edition

by
John F. Harris
and
Stephen K. Stearns

Published by

The University of Pennsylvania Museum
of Archaeology and Anthropology
Philadelphia
1997

Library of Congress Cataloging-in-Publication Data

Harris, John F. (John Ferguson)
    Understanding Maya inscriptions : a hieroglyph handbook / by John F. Harris and Stephen K. Stearns. --
2nd ed.
        p.   cm.
    Includes bibliographical references (p.).
    ISBN 0-924171-41-3 (pbk.)
    1. Maya languages--Writing--Handbooks, manuals, etc.
I. Stearns, Stephen K. II. Title.
F1435.3.W75H37 1996
497'.415-dc20   96-4454
                                                                                    CIP

Copyright © 1997
The University of Pennsylvania Museum
of Archaeology and Anthropology
Printed in the United States of America

This second edition incorporates revised editions of the earlier publications: *Understanding Maya Inscriptions: A Hieroglyph Handbook* 1992, *New and Recent Maya Hieroglyph Readings: A Supplement to Understanding Maya Inscriptions* 1993, and *A Resource Bibliography for the Decipherment of Maya Hieroglyphs and New Maya Hieroglyph Readings* 1994.

2nd edition 1997

TABLE OF CONTENTS

FOREWORD
TO THE SECOND EDITION

Scholarly understandings of ancient Maya civilization have grown at an extremely rapid pace in the past few decades, but, in recent years, no part of Maya studies has matched the increase in knowledge logged by epigraphic research. The rate of this growth is witnessed by the fact that John F. Harris' and Stephen K. Stearns' highly useful *Understanding Maya Inscriptions: A Hieroglyph Handbook,* which was originally published in 1992, had a *Supplement* published just on year later and a second supplement with an expanded *Resource Bibliography* the year after that. Now, only five years after the first edition and three years after the second supplement, the authors found that a completely revised edition combining all three original editions was necessary. And if the current trajectory of growth holds to its present path—and there is every indication that it will for the near future—then we should not be surprised if the authors hear a call for a new edition in a few years!

This outstanding publication is just one example of the importance that Maya studies holds to the University of Pennsylvania Museum and the commitment that the Museum has made in this area both in the past and the present. Today, the ongoing research of Dr. Robert Sharer, the Shoemaker Professor and Curator of the American Section, and his students, along with David Sedat, Research Associate in the American Section, at the great site of Copan, Honduras; the research of Dr. Wendy Ashmore, Associate Curator of Maya Archaeology in the American Section, and her students in the settlement around Xunantunich, Belize; the continuing of Dr. Chris Jones, Research Specialist in the American Section, on the publications of the Tikal and Quirigua Projects; and my own work on the publications of the Sayil Archaeological Project (I also hold the title of Curator of Mesoamerican Archaeology in the American Section), as well as the continuing labor of our Curator Emeritus, Dr. William R. Coe, on the final reports of the Tikal Project, all show the tremendous strength and interest of the Museum in the study of the ancient Maya. In addition, the Museum's highly successful Maya Weekends, now in their fifteenth year, continue to thrive under the very energetic and creative leadership of Elin Danien. Finally, the very active Pre-Columbian Society, which grew out of the early Maya Weekends, is made up of a number of devoted members who provide many of the hieroglyphic workshops that highlight not only the Maya Weekends but regular activities of the Society throughout the year.

I could go on, but I hope that it is clear that the University of Pennsylvania Museum is exceedingly proud of being a center and haven for the study of the Pre-Columbian Maya world. Its publication of this new edition of *Understanding Maya Inscriptions* is just one more indication of the role it is pleased to be able to play in the advancement of Maya studies and the bringing together of professional and amateur enthusiasts alike in this important endeavor.

Jeremy A. Sabloff
The Charles K. Williams II Director

PREFACE
TO THE SECOND EDITION

When the first edition of *Understanding Maya Inscriptions* was published in 1992, we hoped that it would be useful to both amateurs and professionals, and it has more than fulfilled our expectations. *Understanding* has been adopted as the primary text in Maya epigraphy courses at colleges and universities throughout the country, and is one of the principal references for the ever growing number of amateur epigraphy groups. That first edition was followed by annual supplements with new readings and a comprehensive bibliography.

The increasing pace of discovery makes any attempt to be "complete" in this field of study almost impossible. Today, with the underlying principles of Maya hieroglyphic inscriptions well understood, new decipherments come virtually more rapidly than our ability to absorb and communicate the information. We would seem to be in the position of the sorcerer's apprentice who, having mastered the spell that would create brooms, was unable to stop them, and had to fend off an ever increasing army of straw-tipped poles!

Clearly, it was time for a new edition that would incorporate all the advances made during the past three years. Through their skill, talent, and enthusiasm, John Harris and Steve Stearns once again make even the most complex material clear and understandable. In their efforts they have been helped by and have drawn on the work of many scholars whose contributions are acknowledged throughout the text. This greatly expanded second edition includes the material in the first edition and its supplements, adds new decipherments, new calendric information, and an imposing bibliography. Most of the breakthroughs of the past four years are presented here. But make no mistake. The growth of knowledge in this field is so rapid that there are readings, interpretations, and discoveries that have been made since this manuscript went to the printer, and are being made even as you read this. It is my fond hope that the use of this book may lead to ever more discoveries.

I would like to acknowledge the great debt owed to the members of University Museum Publications who labored so diligently to produce this volume: Tobia Worth, Zoanna Carrol, Toni Montague, and Karen Vellucci.

Elin Danien
Maya Weekend Coordinator

FOREWORD
TO THE FIRST EDITION
OF *UNDERSTANDING MAYA INSCRIPTIONS*

This present volume continues a long-standing dedication of the University of Pennsylvania to the decipherment of Maya hieroglyphic writing. This began with Daniel Garrison Brinton, Professor of American Archaeology and Linguistics, who published both the first copy of Diego de Landa's 1566 Maya alphabet (*American Historical Magazine*, 1870) and the first Maya hieroglyphics textbook, *A Primer of Mayan Hieroglyphics*, in 1895. His enthusiastic remarks in the Primer about the numerical discoveries of Forstemann and his criticisms of the phonetic "decipherments" of Brasseur, Le Plongeon, Cresson, de la Rochefoucauld and Thomas, were influential in drawing American scholars away from phonetics and toward the more fruitful calendric portions of newly discovered texts.

The death of Brinton in 1899 began a thirty-year hiatus in Maya studies at the University, which ended finally with the arrival of J. Alden Mason and his student Linton Satterthwaite and the beginning of excavations at Piedras Negras. Out of this fieldwork in the 1930s came not only the architectural reports and calendric studies of Satterthwaite but the 1960 decipherment of Maya historical texts by a former field assistant, Tatiana Proskouriakoff. Excavations at Caracol, Tikal and Quirigua during the 1950s, 60s and 70s elevated the University into the top rank of Mayanist institutions, attracting students such as myself who were interested in both field excavation and decipherment.

The annual Maya Weekends at the University of Pennsylvania began in 1983 with the expressed goals of disseminating the new decipherments to the general public and of attracting amateur talent to the continuing work. I wrote a workbook for the session, calling it *Deciphering Maya Hieroglyphs* and revising it in 1984 in a second edition. Out of the first weekend was born the Pre-Columbian Society at The University Museum, a group dedicated to sponsoring monthly lectures and decipherment work groups. Members of the glyph group have led workshops at the Maya Weekends since its second year.

The old workbook has gotten out of date as our knowledge of calendrics and historical events has led to decipherment of the syllabic glyphs and the grammar. I had wanted to revise it and add the new discoveries, but had been unwilling to take time from excavation reports. When John Harris asked me if I wanted to join him and Steve Stearns in a revision, I suggested that they go ahead and write it. I had seen and been impressed by Steve's workbook for his Beginner's Workshop on Maya Calendrics and knew that John had developed an excellent understanding of the new epigraphic work. This new volume carries on the spirit of Daniel Brinton and of myself in reaching out from academic studies to the untapped reservoir of energy in people who have hardly heard of Maya hieroglyphics, making them realize that they too might make a lasting contribution to such an esoteric field.

Christopher Jones
Research Specialist
American Section
The University of Pennsylvania Museum

PREFACE
TO THE FIRST EDITION
OF *UNDERSTANDING MAYA INSCRIPTIONS*

This volume is the culmination of ten years of programs at The University of Pennsylvania Museum designed to inform and involve the public in current work in deciphering ancient Maya hieroglyphic inscriptions. The Maya Weekend at The University of Pennsylvania Museum of Archaeology and Anthropology began auspiciously in 1983, with 125 participants who spent two days with Christopher Jones as he took them through the intricacies of the Maya writing system. Chris, an archaeologist and epigrapher whose seminal work includes the first recognition of "parentage" glyphs (Jones 1977) communicated his enthusiasm and excitement to this audience, who very clearly wanted more of the same! The program has developed and changed over the years, in response to participants' requests and the constantly growing insights into the content of the inscriptions, until now the annual Maya Weekend features more than a score of experts who lecture on current Maya archeology and lead over a dozen workshops in glyph decipherment for an audience that numbers more than five hundred devotees.

At the first Maya Weekend, a few people began the discussions that led to the formation of the Pre-Columbian Society at the University Museum, a nonprofessional organization with monthly lectures on Americanist archaeology, preceded by three hours of intensive work by a growing number of "glyphies" who travel from as far away as Williamstown, Mass., and Washington, D.C., to take part in these monthly seminars. Over the years, some of the glyph group participants have achieved significant levels of understanding, made discoveries of their own, and contributed to the general fund of knowledge of Maya hieroglyphic inscriptions.

Among those inspired by Chris Jones during the first Maya Weekend were John Harris and Steve Stearns, the authors of this volume. As mainstays of the Pre-Columbian Society glyph group, they continually delve ever farther into the mysteries of Maya inscriptions. Their ability to explain the complexities of Maya writing has been honed through the monthly PCS workshops, where individual texts are gnawed over until their meanings are revealed or, at least, suggested; their participation as workshop leaders at the Maya Weekends and at other glyph workshops; their experience as students and as tutors, answering the endless questions of those, like me, whose quest sometimes exceeds their capacity to understand. Participants in their classes and workshops have lauded Harris and Stearns for their ability to illustrate some of the more esoteric aspects of the inscriptions.

For some time Chris Jones and I had discussed a new edition of his *Deciphering Maya Hieroglyphs* (1984), sorely in need of updating. We wanted to incorporate not only the latest glyph readings, but also the new approach to the languages(s) used in the inscriptions, the phonetic nature of the glyphs, and the techniques of structural analysis used to ferret out their meanings. We wanted to utilize the current orthography, which in some cases was quite different from the more familiar spellings of the past. Chris was unable to take on this assignment; he was involved in the publication of his fieldwork and was loath to commit the necessary time.

It was my deeply felt conviction that the new book should be designed to stand on its own. As with other glyph workbooks, the previous volume had been written for use in tandem with the Maya Weekend workshops. The new volume, it was hoped, would function as a self-teaching tool for the uninitiated but eager proto-Mayanist. With such a goal, the choice of authors was clear. Fortunately, John and Steve agreed to take on the job. They divided the work, with Steve writing the first two chapters, and John the rest; they wrote separately, exchanged manuscripts, edited each other, commented, rewrote, and finished it all in time for the publication to coincide the tenth annual Maya Weekend! I am forever in their debt.

Unlike many other academic disciplines, the field of Maya hieroglyphic decipherment welcomes the presence of the non-professional. This acceptance by Mayanists of large numbers of nonacademics—amateurs whose interest is nurtured, whose scholarship is respected, and whose findings are given credence—

can be traced to a small group of epigraphers who invite public participation and encourage the nonacademic investigator. Among these mentoring scholars are Kathryn Josserand and Nicholas Hopkins, now headquartered in Florida, who conduct workshops throughout the United States; Peter Mathews, who offers workshops in Cleveland; and Tom Jones, with a program in California.

But foremost in creating the growing public interest in glyph decipherment is the annual workshop conducted by Linda Schele in Austin, Texas. Over the past sixteen years, Linda has clarified the mystery of Maya glyphs for thousands of people who have attended her lectures and spent untold hours concentrating on previously unread inscriptions in and attempt to prize out their meanings. Linda's charismatic personality and exhilarating platform manner have inspired more enthusiasts, and laid the foundation for more glyph readings, than any other individual Mayanist.

Today, where once only a mere handful of scholars pored over the glyphs in dedicated and oft-times fruitless study, there are dozens whose brilliant deductions build on painstaking investigation to produce a body of work that may soon reveal the entire history of the Maya as it was recorded by their scribes.

This situation exists because a few scholars reached out to the public with an inclusive embrace that invited all who were interested to attend, to question, to strive, and to contribute to the bubbling pot of Maya hieroglyph studies. This book, written by two men whose professional lives are far removed from academia, exemplifies the close cooperation between professional and amateur in the field of Maya epigraphy.

Here, then, is the result of that collaboration: a book that can teach you how to read the ancient Maya inscriptions. It uses the latest methods of structural analysis, illustrates the traditional techniques for computing Maya calendrics, introduces the currently acceptable orthography, proved syllabary and syntax, suggests new readings and presents previous interpretations. In short, a book to put you on the path of an intellectual adventurer whose fascination never ends.

We hope these pages meet with the approval of "glyphies" everywhere. The intent is to help the neophyte, and yet to be of value to those more knowledgeable. Let us hear from you—with your questions, your comments, and, perhaps, your new reading of the inscriptions. That, finally, is what this book is about: encouraging fresh legions in the service of hieroglyph decipherment.

Elin Danien
Maya Weekend Coordinator

1

An Overview of Maya Writing

Introduction

Many people are familiar with Egyptian hieroglyphs. They are usually encountered in an early grade in books, movies, and world history classes. Simple in shape, many are immediately recognizable objects, both animate and inanimate. Maya hieroglyphs, however, are more intimidating. Many are abstract shapes along with strange images of people and animals. Further, Maya artists and scribes seemed to have had an aversion to blank space; to European-oriented minds, their iconography and their writing seem to overflow with details difficult to absorb at a glance.

Take a look at Figure 1:1. What do you see?

Most people quickly see heads—usually in profile facing to the left. Most of the heads seem to represent creatures having both human and animal characteristics. The hands are also easy to recognize. Look at the hand in the lower-right corner, position F9 if you use the coordinates printed along the top and left edges of the drawing. Assume that you're looking at the back of a right hand. The gesture is awkward but not impossible. It's similar to the gesture at F4. The hand at E3 (a left hand this time) is holding an open-mouthed face. And there is another hand at A6; this one looks quite natural. At least one graduate student has written a dissertation on the various hands and hand gestures that show up in Maya writing.

Now, a slightly harder exercise: Do you see anything that is repeated? Certainly many of the left-facing profiles are candidates. But, if you look carefully, you'll see that there are several profiles that are clearly different from one another. It might help to remember that you're looking at the equivalent of handwriting, not printed matter. Don't expect everything to be as consistent as the typeface used in this book. Allow for the same variability usually present in

any person's writing. Look at positions A8 and D6. They're the same glyph. Both have the same dominant element with small circles across the top and a curlicue in the lower left corner. This dominant element rests on two crescents with two dots between them; it is adjacent to the hook-shaped object partially enclosing three circles on the right. A9 and C3 are also the same glyph even though the profile heads are somewhat different.

It's important to spend a bit of time looking at this drawing because, for most beginners, there's far too much to absorb with a quick look. Some epigraphers (those who study writing systems) joke that Maya glyphs resemble a plate of spaghetti! We've been looking at Maya glyphs for over fifteen years and are amazed at the things we still miss on the first look.

What you've been looking at (Fig. 1:1) is a drawing of an inscription found on a carved limestone monument from a site called Piedras Negras ("Black Stones" in Spanish; unfortunately, we're not certain what the Maya called it). The University Museum did a lot of work at this site in the 1930s. Compare the real thing to the drawing and you'll be glad someone had the time and energy (and talent!) to do the drawing. Most sculpted limestone left in the jungles of Mexico or Central America for 1400 years has suffered substantial deterioration.

Maya writing shows up on a lot of things:

❑ Carved limestone monuments shaped somewhat like tombstones (which they were not), set into the ground. Archaeologists call them stelae (singular: stela). Some are as tall as 35 feet.

❑ Carved lintels over doorways leading into Maya buildings, usually of stone or wood. Because of the architectural techniques used by the Maya, their building walls were quite thick, allowing for lots of space for inscriptions on lintels.

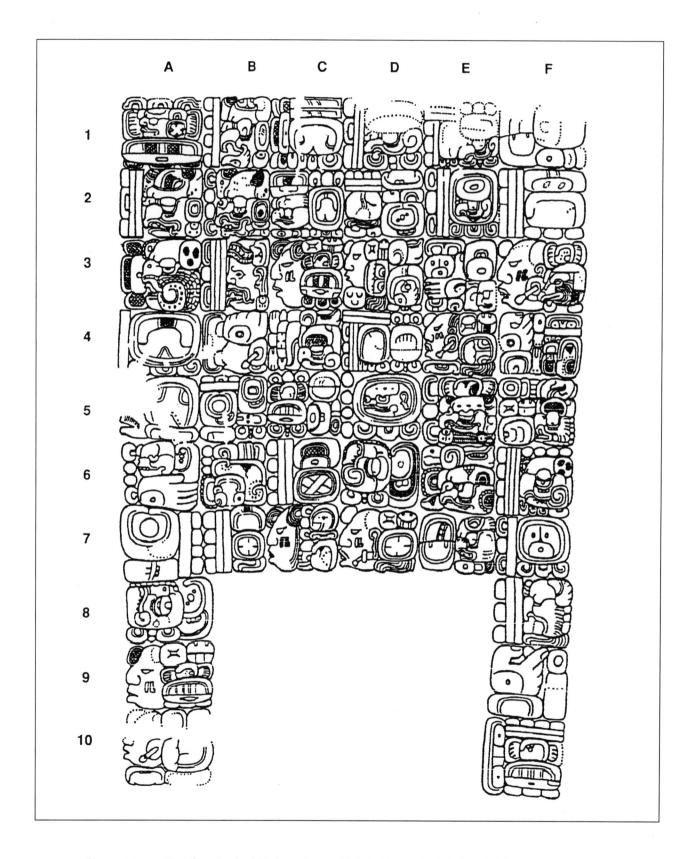

Figure 1:1.   Text from back of Piedras Negras Stela 3 (Drawn by Linda Schele).

❑ Staiways.
❑ Pounded bark paper, folded accordion style into a codex or book. Only four are known to have survived.
❑ Painted walls of caves and tombs.
❑ Painted or incised pottery.
❑ Small, portable objects, such as carved bone, jade, and shell.

The longest texts occur on stelae, lintels, and stairways because there is more space on which the scribe could work. We'll concentrate on inscriptions from these media because they're the easiest for beginners, and they are a wonderful source of information about Classic Maya history and worldview.

The Piedras Negras monument you've just looked at is referred to by archaeologists and epigraphers as Stela 3. We can use it to make generalizations about the reading order of Maya glyphs. Imagine drawing two sets of lines intersecting at right angles on the drawing so that they form a grid. Think of each cell of the grid as enclosing one glyph block which corresponds to the squarish elements at the coordinates on the drawing: A1, A2, A3, etc. Glyph block F9, for example, contains that awkward hand along with other elements below and to the right. (Fig. 1:2).

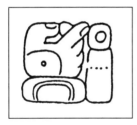

Figure 1:2.   Glyph block F9 of Piedras Negras Stela 3.

Most inscriptions begin in the upper left and are read downward in pairs. Thus you would read Stela 3 (Fig. 1:1) starting with glyph block A1, then B1, then A2, then B2, then A3, etc. When you reach glyph block B7, you have a choice. The context dictates that A8 is next, followed by A9 and A10. You then go back to the top and continue reading in pairs: C1, D1; C2, D2; C7, D7; E1, F1; E7, F7; F8, F9 and F10. This order is more logical if you know that the "dangling" glyph blocks A8, A9, A10 and F8, F9, F10 frame the portrait of a woman: she's just not shown in this drawing.

Epigraphers working with the Maya script have identified about eight hundred distinct glyphs. By most scholarly definitions, they form the basis of a true writing system. While so many glyphs may seem daunting, prospective students should know that many have only a few (some only one) known occurrences. Scholars estimate that at any point in time, only two to three hundred glyphs were in use.

To gain a good understanding of Maya hieroglyphs, one must have an elementary understanding of spoken language. As we shall soon point out, decipherment of the glyphs was impeded during the first half of this century because linguistics was ignored by most scholars. Although we are unable to impart enough information in an elementary text to make you linguistics experts, some basics will be useful.

The smallest meaningful linguistic unit is called a *morpheme*. In the spoken version of a language, a morpheme is represented by one or more sounds. Consider, for instance, the word *undoable*. It consists of three morphemes: *un-*, *do-*, and *-able*. The *morphology* of a language relates to the various linguistic units and the rules by which they are combined into words. The English word *birds* can be morphologically characterized as the noun *bird* and the plural ending *-s*. A language's *syntax* establishes relations needed to construct sentences.

A *logograph* is a unit of writing, roughly equivalent to our concept of a word. A *pictograph* is a special kind of logograph; its written form actually resembles what it represents. Thus, one of the Maya glyphs for jaguar appears to be a feline. All pictographs are logographs; the reverse is not true. Glyph blocks generally contain a prominent *main sign*, often accompanied by several smaller units called *affixes*. Depending upon their placement with respect to the main sign, an affix can be a prefix, a superfix, a postfix, or a subfix. A glyph block containing two or more signs may also be referred to as a *collocation* (for examples, see Fig. 1:3).

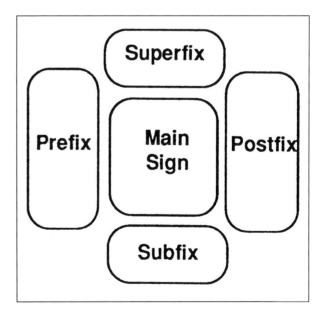

Figure 1:3.   A collocation is a glyph block containing a main sign and an affix which may be a prefix, superfix, postfix or subfix.

The reading order of glyph blocks is similar to that of the texts: left to right and top to bottom. The main sign usually contains the primary semantic information. Think of the affixes as modifiers that help resolve certain ambiguities in the writing system. Both the main signs and the affixes are collectively called *graphemes*. A morpheme may be represented by either a single grapheme or a combination of them.

Sometimes a glyph block contains more than one main sign. The simplest case is when the two main signs (and their related affixes) are reduced in size and combined in one glyph block. For example, the left half of Block C2 on Piedras Negras Stela 3 is referred to as C2a, the right as C2b. Less frequently, two main signs will be rendered with one overlapping the other. This is called *conflation*. Finally, one main sign (or easily identifiable portions) may be incorporated into another main sign; this is called *infixing*.

A language can be analyzed in a number of different ways. A phonetic approach is to break it into a basic set of sounds. The smallest distinguishable unit of sound is called a *phoneme*. Languages can have from about twenty to over eighty phonemes. In Mayan languages, most phonemes comprise consonant-vowel combinations, usually referred to as CV units or just CV. Any language can be broken down

into a set of phonemes. Such a set for a written language is called a *syllabary*. Figure 3.8 shows such a syllabary for the Maya hieroglyphic script. Obviously, such a chart is a dynamic entity; it's constantly being added to and revised. The syllabary is used by searching down the left side for the desired consonant and then scanning across that row for the appropriate vowel. For example, the CV sound *ba* could be represented by any one of three glyphs (Figure 1:4.)

Figure 1:4.   Any of these three signs could be used to represent the C-V sound ba.

Consider the Maya word for jaguar in the Yucatec dialect: *balam*. (Yucatec is spoken by Maya living in the northern and eastern parts of the Yucatan Peninsula.) The CV units of balam would be written as *ba-la-ma*. Because most Maya words end in a consonant, the final vowel is dropped. One

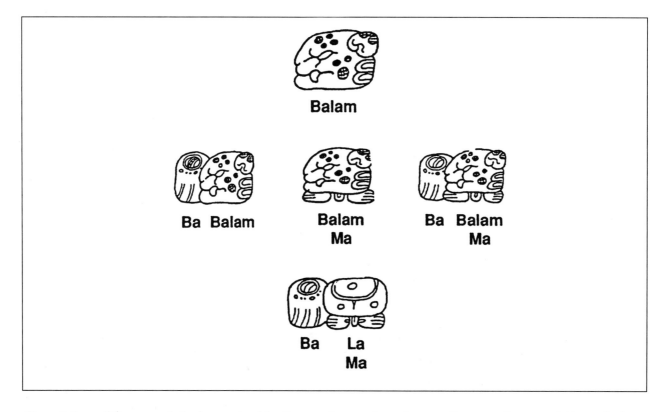

Figure 1:5.   Often several glyphs can stand for the same logograph or phoneme; these are all representations of balam.

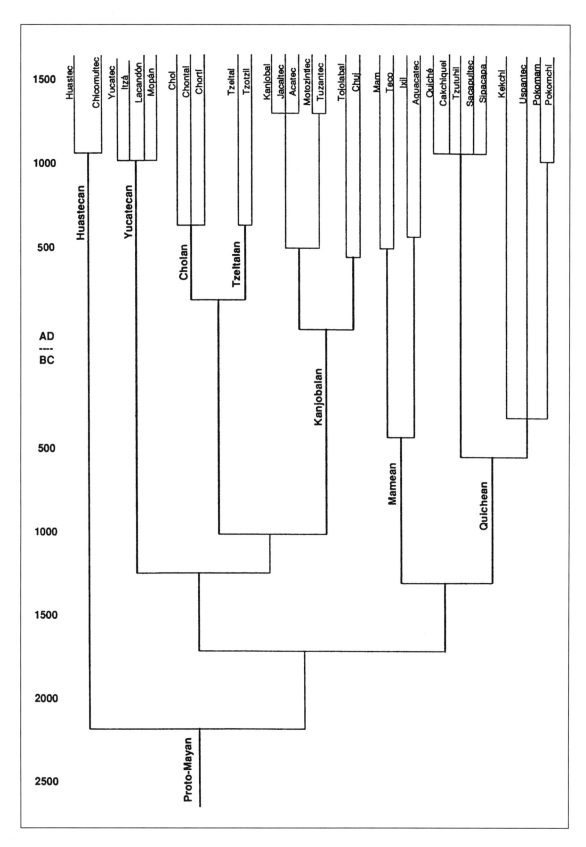

Figure 1:6.   Mayan language family tree (after Henderson 1981:fig. 5).

difficulty epigraphers have contended with is the Maya use of substitution sets. Simply put, several glyphs may substitute for the same logograph or phoneme; for example, there are five ways to represent *balam* (Fig 1:5).

The first is a logographic representation. The next three combine the logograph with one or two phonetic components. When used this way, the phonetic component is referred to as a *phonetic complement*. Scholars speculate that phonetic complements function as a clue to the reader that this glyph represents a balam (jaguar) rather than some other feline inhabitant of the Maya world. The last example is the purely phonetic spelling of balam.

A close examination of the syllabary in Chapter 3 reveals some CV combinations that may be unfamiliar to English speakers. Examples include *ch'a* and *t'o*. Soundwise, these are quite distinct from *cha* and *to*. *Ch'* and *t'* are referred to by linguists as glottalized consonants. In producing glottalized sounds, a speaker's vocal air passage is momentarily blocked, cutting off outward air flow and resulting in a small, explosive burst of sound. There's no equivalent in English, although some combinations of words approximate a glottal sound; the *t'o* sound is similar to that produced by saying fa*t* o*pal.

Many of the significant breakthroughs made in deciphering Maya hieroglyphs in the last twenty-five years are due to the collaboration of scholars in the fields of epigraphy, art history, and linguistics. Today, there are over two and a half million speakers of languages that have evolved from the one represented in the glyphic script. Thus, linguists' understanding of modern Maya dialects, grammars, and syntax has contributed significantly to understanding the ancient writing system.

Mayan languages have evolved from a "prototype" language, the ancestor of all modern dialects. The chart in Figure 1:6 (see following page) illustrates one accepted theory of this evolution. There is general agreement that the Maya who wrote the texts spoke dialects of either Cholan or Yucatec. There is less agreement on how these speakers interacted and influenced the writing system. Nevertheless, modern studies of both Yucatec and Chol have yielded important advances in glyph studies. The map in Figure 1:7 shows the approximate distribution of languages during the Classic period of Maya civilization (roughly A.D. 250–900).

One attribute of the writing system discovered through linguistic studies has to do with an almost playful use of homonyms. Until the homonym concept was understood, this feature of the writing system caused some confusion in the early attempts at decipherment. The Maya words for the number *four* and the reptile *snake* sound alike. Thus, a Maya scribe wishing to represent the number *four* could choose to use the head of a snake instead of

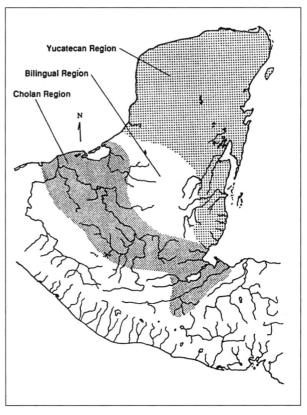

Figure 1:7.   Approximate distribution of languages during the Classic Period (after Schele and Freidel 1990: fig. 1.2).

the more common form of representing numbers with a bar-and-dot numeration system.

Numbers were among the first glyphs to be recognized and deciphered. Our number system is based on the number 10. Thus we represent the number five hundred twenty-seven as 527. This, of course, recalls the "placeholder" concept we learned in grade school:

$$527 = (5 \times 10 \times 10) + (2 \times 10) + (7 \times 1)$$

The Maya based their number system on 20 (a base 20 numerical system is called *vigesimal*; see Chapter 2). Thus, the same number 527 would be thought of by a Maya as:

$$527 = (1 \times 20 \times 20) + (6 \times 20) + (7 \times 1)$$

The Maya used a bar-and-dot notation system to represent numbers. A bar has the value of 5 while a dot represents 1. Most examples of numbers standing alone occur in the codices. More commonly, a number serves as a coefficient for a unit of time; we'll get to that shortly. Figure 1:8 shows how 527 would be written in a vigesimal system using bars and dots.

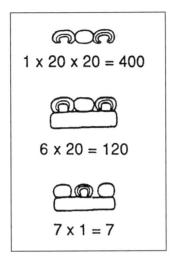

1 x 20 x 20 = 400

6 x 20 = 120

7 x 1 = 7

Figure 1:8.   Representation of 527 in a vigesimal system using bars and dots.

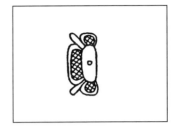

Figure 1:9.   A Maya sign for zero.

Note that the Maya use a vertical format to indicate place notation, with the largest unit at the top. The little incomplete circles adjacent to the dots are fillers.[1] They aptly illustrate the Maya's seeming compulsion to fill all available space.

A special character is used to represent zero. The most common form is a trilobed, crosshatched glyph (Fig 1:9). Sometimes an object resembling a shell is used instead.

In addition to the bar-and-dot system, the numbers *0–19* can also be represented by head variants (Appendix A). There is great variety in the head variants, each having one or more diagnostic features that identify it. For example, the headdress worn by the head variant for the number *5* contains the *tun* sign, which is highly distinctive. So is the axe in the eye for the number *6*. Also, note that the head variants for 0–13 are unique. Those for 14–19 are the same as those for 4–9 except that the former include the fleshless lower jawbone that characterizes the numeral *10*. The lower numbers, on the other hand, have a normal jaw.

A further complication is the occasional use of full-figure glyphs to represent numbers. Similar to the head variants, a number is depicted with a representation of a complete figure of a human or animal. For example, Figure 1:10 shows three ways to represent the number *5*.

The familiar bar is easy. The distinguishing characteristic for both the head variant and the full-figure glyphs is the headdress. Before moving on to the next chapter, be sure you fully understand the numeration system.

A LITTLE HISTORY

In 1549, thirty years after Cortes' landing in the New World, a Franciscan priest named Diego de Landa arrived in the newly founded city of Merida on the Yucatan peninsula. He was a severe, narrow-minded man who rose rapidly in the church hierarchy. In July 1562, he convened an *auto-de-fe* in the small Maya community of Mani. There, he continued his well-known efforts to root out heretics and combat idolatry by burning several bark paper books known today as codices.[2]

As Landa's harsh treatment of the natives continued, criticism of his methods grew. He was finally summoned back to Spain to explain his conduct to church officials. Preparations were made to censure him, and he spent the next eleven years in

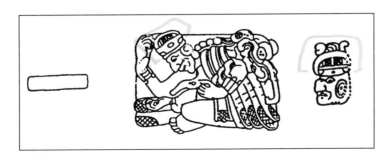

Figure 1:10.   Three different ways of representing the number 5.

Spain defending himself against various charges. During this time, he wrote an extensive document describing the people and conditions he encountered in and around Merida. It was entitled *Relación de las Cosas de Yucatan* (*Account of the Things of Yucatan*). It promptly disappeared into the archives at Seville and has not been seen in modern times. In 1863, however, an incomplete copy of Landa's *Relación* was found. It is available in several modern translations (the best known is that by Tozzer [1941]) and makes fascinating reading for anyone interested in the Maya. Eventually Landa was cleared of the charges against him and returned to Mexico. He later was appointed Bishop of Merida and lived to a ripe old age.

Landa's *Relación* has provided Mayanists with an invaluable source detailing life at the onset of the Colonial period. His explanation of the calendar system accompanied by his drawings of the day and month glyphs (see Chapter 2) provided scholars with the key to reconstructing the calendrical portion of the inscriptions. His so-called alphabet (see Fig. 3.1 and Chapter 3), however, did not provide the necessary key for deciphering the non-calendrical parts of the inscriptions until it was shown that it was not an alphabet *per se*, but rather a syllabary. Looking back on Landa's method, it is easy to see how this confusion arose. His main informant, Antonio Gaspar Chi, was a Yucatec speaker who had some knowledge of Spanish. When Landa began to question him about the writing system, he simply asked Antonio how to "spell" various common words. For instance, Landa inquired about the Maya word for lasso. Landa knew that the word was *le* (pronounced lay) and it is likely he asked, "Cómo se escribe ele-e: le?" ("How is l-e: le written?"). What Antonio heard in Landa's Castilian Spanish was a request to "spell" four Maya syllables: *e* (pronounced ay, rhymes with hay), *le* (lay), *e*, and *le*. What Landa wanted was the Maya word for lasso, so he spelled it (in Spanish: ele-e), then said it (*le*). Both men were confused but Antonio responded by writing what appears in Figure 1:11.

Antonio gave Landa exactly what he asked for--the "spelling" of the four sounds Landa asked about: e, le, e, and le. Clearly the first and third glyphs are the same; so are the second and fourth. Landa, however, interpreted the response not as syllabic in nature but as alphabetic.

Next Landa asked Antonio to spell the word for water: *ha* in Maya. This time he apparently just spelled the word in Spanish; he didn't repeat the word itself as he did with *le*. He would have said: *"Cómo se escribe hache-a?—hache"* being the Spanish word for the letter *h* and *a*, Spanish for the letter *a*. Again Antonio replied exactly to what he was asked: he gave the three signs for the sounds he heard: a-che-a. To give Landa as much useful information as he could, Antonio gave him two different versions for the *a* sound (Fig. 1:12). Antonio also conflated the first two glyphs—that is, he overlapped one with the other when he wrote them.

Landa pressed on. He asked Antonio to write anything he wanted. By this time, poor Antonio was growing tired of this game. His reply is illustrated in Figure 1:13.

These five glyphs represent the sounds for *ma-i-na-k'a-ti*—Yucatec for "I don't want to." Poor Antonio had had it! And his frustration was dutifully recorded by Landa for all future scholars.

Twentieth-century scholars vainly tried to apply the Landa "alphabet" to the decipherment problem for decades. They failed because they assumed the writing system was alphabetic like English or Spanish. It was not until Yurii Knorozov's pioneering work in the 1950s (see below) that the phonetic basis of the Maya writing system was established.

In the meantime, other work was underway. Landa also had discussed the "Mayan Calendar"—actually several cyclical time periods used primarily for divinatory purposes. Early scholars recognized that many of the inscriptions on stelae contained one or more references to these calendrical cycles. Thus Mayan calendrics was well understood early in this century. This work gave rise to the incorrect notion that the inscriptions were concerned solely with the cyclical nature of time. In fact, a widely held view still found in some references was that ancient Maya society was composed of two classes: priests obsessed with time and peasants who provided labor and food for the priests.

This concentration on calendrics is epitomized by the work of Sylvanus Morley during the early 1900s. Morley was affiliated with the Carnegie Institute of Washington, D.C. He concentrated on finding new stelae, going so far as to post "reward" notices for information leading to new finds. He was a collector of dates—any calendrical information found on new inscriptions. He did little to analyze the remaining texts.

Figure 1:11.   Antonio Gaspar Chi's written response when asked by Landa how to write l - e: le.

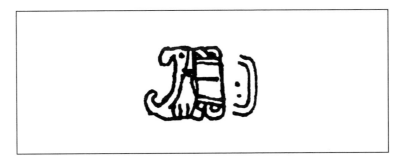

*Figure 1:12.   Glyphic representation for the Spanish letters, (H) ache-a:
the spelling of* Ha', *the Maya word for water.*

Figure 1:13.   Ma - i - na - k'a - ti: Yucatec for "I don't want to."

In 1926 the young English scholar J. Eric S. Thompson arrived on the scene. He began work with Morley, and he quickly became the preeminent Maya scholar of the time. He did extensive work with the inscriptions, developing a catalogue of glyphs that is still the standard today.[3] In his *A Catalog of Maya Hieroglyphs*, published in 1962, Thompson correlated the results of decades of work into a catalogue in which he assigned numbers to all the glyphs known up to that time. Of course, this implies that he made decisions related to the variability of representing the glyphs; in some cases, he was wrong in cataloguing glyphs under a single entry. The numbers are preceded with the letter *T* (for Thompson). He reserved the range T1–T500 for all the affixes. All non-portrait main signs were numbered T501–T999. The portraits were grouped into T1000–T1299. Finally, he reserved anything higher than T1299 for "glyphs of uncertain delineation or dubious origin."

Thompson had a significant impact on the scholars of his day. His views on the nature of inscriptions (as dealing solely with calendrical information) and on the nature of the writing system itself (as a rebus system with no significant phonetic elements) strongly influenced the course of Maya studies, especially epigraphy, for decades.

In 1952, Yurii Knorozov, a Russian, published a paper in which he proposed that Maya hieroglyphic writing was based on a mixed system composed of full-word signs (logographic elements) combined with syllabic signs. Thompson led the vast majority of Maya scholars in summarily rejecting Knorozov's proposal. (This may have stemmed in part from Cold War tensions and competition between the United States and the Soviet Union.) A few younger scholars—David Kelley, Michael Coe, and Floyd Lounsbury—accepted Knorozov's hypothesis and went on to confirm the phonetic basis for the Maya writing system. Thompson, however, never accepted these new concepts.

In the 1960s, Tatiana Proskouriakoff, an art historian at Harvard, published the results of her studies of stelae texts from the site of Piedras Negras. While working at the site with a University of Pennsylvania Museum expedition, she recognized that groups of stelae seemed physically positioned to be associated with specific buildings. Upon examining the texts of each group, she found that their range of dates approximated a human lifetime. Further, she found examples of the same glyph appearing in each stelae group. One such glyph was always associated with the earliest date in the group. A different glyph was found in several groups and occurred ten to twenty years after the earliest date. Another glyph common to many groups was associated with the latest date in each group. Proskouriakoff hypothesized that the stelae texts contained information about historical events in the lives of Piedras Negras personages. Further, she proposed, the unknown glyphs represented events in these people's lives, with the earliest date/event glyph in a group representing the person's birth. (This event glyph was described as an "upended frog"—one must use imagination to see the frog although the glyph itself is quite distinctive!) The latest date/event glyph, then, was proposed as the person's death, while intermediate dates perhaps represented important events in the subjects' lives.

Although he never did accept phoneticism, Thompson (1971) finally did admit that he had been wrong about the historical content of Maya inscriptions. The further interpretation of non-calendric material in the inscriptions became possible only when phoneticism was acknowledged as a basic attribute of Maya hieroglyphic writing (see Chapter 3).

In December 1973, a small conference was held at the Maya site of Palenque; it was called the *Primera Mesa Redonda de Palenque.* The main participants included a new generation of Maya epigraphers—David Kelley and Floyd Lounsbury as well as Peter Mathews and Linda Schele. In retrospect, this conference was the beginning of a new era in the understanding of Maya texts. The participants developed the approaches that serve to this day as the basic methodologies in use in glyphic decipherment.

NOTES

1. Fillers that are 1300 years old and weathered by centuries of exposure to the elements can look a lot like the numeric dots. This can impede decipherment. When working with a drawing of a Maya inscription, be aware that some bar and dot numbers may not be as drawn. If an inconsistency surfaces, an examination of a photo of the original text may be necessary.

2. The four codices that have survived to our time contain what appear to be almanacs, perhaps used to determine agricultural cycles as well as to predict astronomical events. Evidence exists that implies that they were common in sixteenth-century Maya civilization. Had more survived, it is likely that scholars would have a wider view of Maya society because the codex texts are quite different from those found on stelae and portable objects.

3. Several people are at work to improve glyph-cataloguing methods. Internet-connected readers may want to point their Web browser to The Mayan Epigraphic Database Project @ http://jefferson.village.virginia.edu/med/medwww.html.

2

CALENDRICS

BASIC CALENDRICS

Maya texts are filled with date references using a variety of time periods. As noted in Chapter 1, the calendrical information in the inscriptions was among the earliest to be deciphered. Because this information constitutes a significant portion of all texts, any study of the glyphs must begin with calendrics.

Let's think about our Gregorian calendar. A desk calendar would show the Saturday date of this year's Maya Weekend as follows (Fig. 2:1):

April						1997	
S	M	T	W	T	F	S	**12**
		1	2	3	4	5	
6	7	8	9	10	11	12	
13	14	15	16	17	18	19	
20	21	22	23	24	25	26	
27	28	29	30				

102	**Saturday, April 12**	263

Figure 2:1. Page from desk calendar showing April 12, 1997.

Today is Saturday, April 12, 1997. It's also the sixth day of the week. It's the twelfth day of the fourth month. It's the 102nd day of the year (there are 263 days left in this year). Hence, we are quite comfortable describing any specific date in a variety of ways. So were the Maya. There is nothing complex about Maya calendrics. What gives people difficulty are the different cycles that must be manipulated. Most people give no conscious thought to mentally manipulating our seven-day weeks; 28-, 30-, or 31-day months; 365-day years; or centuries of 100 years. We do have to concentrate to handle leap months and years, however.

If I remind you that today is Saturday and ask what day of the week falls 16 days from now, most people easily respond with Monday. They do not count 16 days into the future. Instead, most recognize that 16 days is 2 weeks plus 2 days, or 2 Saturdays in the future plus 2 days: Monday. Similarly, 71 days from now is Sunday. 143 days from now is Tuesday. The same principle applies to Maya calendrics, except that their cycles were based on different multiples of time. A Maya scribe familiar with calendrics would write the date April 12 1997 using glyphs (Fig. 2:2).

Like our calendar, the Maya calendar operated in terms of both a series of cycles of varying lengths and a linear system that could pinpoint a date in time absolutely. In the above example, three different systems for recording the date are used. The first method, the Long Count (LC), pinpoints a date based on a linear progression of time. The other two methods, the 260-day *tzolk'in* and the 365-day *haab*, involve cyclic time.

To become comfortable with these cycles and to understand how to manipulate them, it's necessary to review a little basic math. Think back to grade school when you first learned how to divide two numbers. At first, the problems were simple because they "came out even": $12 \div 4 = 3$ or $15 \div 3 = 5$. Then things got more complicated when remainders were introduced: $16 \div 7 = 2$, R2.

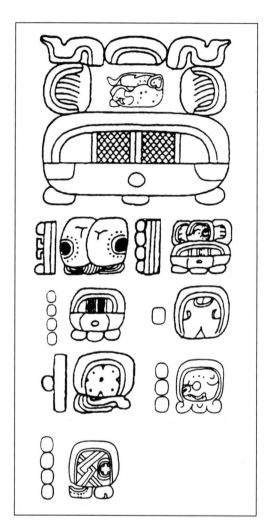

Figure 2:2.   Initial Series representation for April 12, 1997.

Keeping remainders in mind, let's return to the "What day is it 16 days from Saturday?" question. Most people answer that by *unconsciously* dividing 16 by 7 (days in a week) and adding the remainder, 2 days, to Saturday, giving Monday.

Knowing this, we can now (with the help of pencil and paper) determine that, if today is Saturday, 1200 days from now is a Tuesday (1200 ÷ 7 = 171, R3). We'll return to this concept when we start working with the 260-day *tzolk'in* and the 365-day *haab*.

Now, let's review one last bit of arithmetic: factors. For example: 12 = 2 × 2 × 3, or 30 = 2 × 3 × 5. The *factors* of 12 are 2, 2 and 3. The *factors* of 30 are 2, 3, and 5. The numbers 12 and 30 have common factors of 2 and 3. We'll also return to this concept shortly.

Now we're ready to delve into the Maya cal-

endar. You may be aware that the Maya referred to days using both names and numbers. Because we're just beginning, however, we won't make things harder by using the Maya names—not just yet. But this does raise an important point: While we refer to a day as Saturday, the Maya used both a name *and* a number. It did not make sense to them to refer to a day with just the name or just the number—both had to be specified.

Let's now devise a cycle similar, in principle, to the Maya's 260-day *tzolk'in*. Let's use three day numbers and four day names to designate our days. We'll use the day names A, B, C, and D and the day numbers 1, 2, and 3. We'll combine these day names and numbers in the following way:

1A 2B 3C 1D 2A 3B 1C 2D 3A 1B 2C 3D 1A...

The first day is 1A, the second, 2B, then 3C, 1D, and so on. Eventually we get back to 1A and repeat the sequence. The repeat occurs after twelve distinct day number/day name combinations. Note that with four day names and three day numbers, 12 = 4 × 3.

Now consider the same four day names, but let's use only two (instead of three) day numbers:

1A 2B 1C 2D 1A...

In this case, there are only four distinct day number/day name combinations. One might have expected there to be eight (= 4 × 2). However, remember factors. In the first example, 4 (= 2 × 2) and 3 (= 3 × 1) have no common factors. Thus, there are twelve day number/day name combinations. In the second example, 4 (= 2 × 2) and 2 (= 2 × 1) have a common factor. This must be taken into account in the following manner: 4 = (4 × 2) ÷ 2

People who remember algebra will recognize this as a problem in combinations and permutations. Fortunately, one does not have to understand the math to make use of the following general formula: C = n × m / (a × b × c...) where:

C = the number of distinct day number / day name combinations
n = the number of day numbers
m = the number of day names
a, b, c = the factors common to *both* n and m

With this as background, we may now tackle the real Maya 260-day *tzolk'in* cycle. This cycle has twenty day names. These names vary among Mayan languages, but most scholars make use of the Yucatec names. (We've made use of the currently accepted orthography.). Samples of the glyphic representations of the following day names are found in Appendix B:

Imix	Chuwen
Ik'	Eb
Ak'bal	Ben
K'an	Ix
Chikchan	Men
Kimi	Kib
Manik'	Kaban
Lamat	Etz'nab
Muluk	Kawak
Ok	Ahaw

The Maya combined these day names with thirteen day numbers, ranging from 1 to 13. Thus, a cycle would be:

1 Imix, 2 Ik', 3 Ak'bal...13 Ben, 1 Ix...7 Ahaw, 8 Imix, 9 Ik'...

Remember: the first day is 1 *Imix*; referring to that day as simply Imix makes no sense to a Maya. Now, how many distinct days are there with 13 day numbers and 20 day names? Referring back to our combination formula:

$$n = 13 (= 13 \times 1)$$
$$m = 20 (= 2 \times 2 \times 5)$$

a,b,c do not exist as there are no common factors

Then, $C = 13 \times 20 = 260$

From the Maya point of view, there are 260 different days in the *tzolk'in* cycle. Anthropologists have documented that this cycle is still in use today in Maya communities in the highlands of Guatemala. It is used by shamans for divinatory purposes to assist local townspeople in making important decisions regarding business ventures, marriages, journeys, and so on. An excellent description of this divination process is included in the book *Time and the Highland Maya*, by Barbara Tedlock (1992).

The next important cycle we must understand consists of 365 days and is called the *haab*; some older books refer to it as the "vague year." It consists of 18 months of 20 days plus one last month of 5 days. The names of the months (again, in Yucatec) are:

Pohp	Sak
Wo	Keh
Sip	Mak
Sotz'	K'ank'in
Tzek (or Sek)	Muwan
Xul	Pax
Yaxk'in	K'ayab
Mol	Kumk'u
Ch'en	Wayeb
Yax	

Samples of the glyphic representations of these month names are found in Appendix C. The last month, *Wayeb*, comes at the end of the Maya year and was considered an unlucky time. Decisions were put off during this time; travel was avoided; any child born during *Wayeb* often was stigmatized for life.

Like day names, the month names do not stand alone but are accompanied by a numeric coefficient (month number). The month numbers do not work like the day numbers, however. The Maya attached considerable significance to the *completion* of several time periods, including months. As one month ended, the next was considered to be "seated." In the inscriptions, a special glyph signifying the "seating" of a month (the same glyph was used for the seating of a ruler) was used to designate the completion of one month and the beginning of another (Fig. 2:3). Thus the last day of, say, *Pohp*, is designated the seating of *Wo*. The first day of *Wo* is given the month number 1 and is referred to as 1 *Wo*.

Figure 2:3.   One version of the seating glyph.

The next days are designated 2 *Wo*, 3 *Wo*, 4 *Wo*...19 *Wo*. The last day of the month *Wo* is called the seating of *Sip*. Epigraphers have adopted the convention of using the number 0 for the seating glyph. (This is somewhat confusing to the uninitiated as it implies that 0 *Wo* is the first day of the month *Wo*. Actually, it's the last day of the month *Pohp*.)

Because the *haab* cycle is 365 days long, it approximates a solar year. According to Landa (Tozzer 1941) the Maya year begins on the first day of *Pohp*. The dates progress as follows:

1 Pohp, 2 Pohp...19 Pohp, 0 Wo
1 Wo, 2 Wo...19 Wo, 0 Sip
1 Sip...0 Sotz'
1 K'ayab...0 Kumk'u
1 Kumk'u, 2 Kumk'u...19 Kumk'u, 0 Wayeb
1 Wayeb, 2 Wayeb, 3 Wayeb, 4 Wayeb, 0 Pohp

The Maya were not content with just these two cycles. At some point early in Maya history, they locked the *tzolk'in* and *haab* cycles together into a greater cycle, which is usually referred to as the Calendar Round (CR). This was done by associating the day position 4 *Ahaw* in the *tzolk'in* with the month position 8 *Kumk'u* in the *haab*. The resulting date, 4 *Ahaw* 8 *Kumk'u*, is associated with the creation of the current world in which the Maya live. Thus, any day is completely specified by giving both its *tzolk'in* and *haab* designations:

> 4 Ahaw 8 Kumk'u
> 5 Imix 9 Kumk'u
> 6 Ik' 10 Kumk'u

What comes next? You are correct if you answered 7 *Ak'bal* 11 *Kumk'u.*

There are examples throughout the corpus of Maya inscriptions in which a date was specified using either the *tzolk'in* alone or the *haab* alone. The more common approach, however, was to specify fully the day, using the Calendar Round. Looking back at the inscription for the date Saturday, April 12, 1997, you should identify the Calendar Round for that day as 3 *Kimi* 4 *Pohp* (Fig. 2:4).

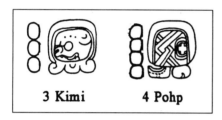

3 Kimi   4 Pohp

Figure 2:4.   The Calendar Round for April 12, 1997.

An important question is: How many days are there in a Calendar Round cycle? Remember the *tzolk'in* has 260 days and the *haab* has 365. These values can be factored as follows:

$$260 = 2 \times 2 \times 5 \times 13 \text{ and } 365 = 5 \times 73$$

Note that 5 is the common factor. By dividing the total number of days (260 × 365) by 5, we arrive at the total number of days in a CR:

$$260 \times 365 / 5 = 18,980$$

Thus, 18,980 days must pass between each occurrence of a specific Calendar Round date. This amounts to about 52 years.

Because the *tzolk'in* and *haab* have common factors, not every possible combination of the two can occur in a Calendar Round. This is evident from the fact that we divided by 5. As the two meshed cycles progress, certain day names always occur with the same group of month numbers (Table 2:1). This fact is often helpful in deciphering an eroded date when the month number (often referred to as the coefficient of the month) or the day name is illegible.

This principle is illustrated by examining a

TABLE 2:1 Day Name: Month Number Conversions	
If the day name is:	Then the month number must be:
Imix, Kimi, Chuwen. or Kib	4, 9, 14, or 19
Ik', Manik', Eb, Kaban	0, 5, 10, or 15
Ak'bal, Lamat, Ben, Etz'nab	1, 6, 11, or 16
K'an, Muluk, Ix, Kawak	2, 7, 12, or 17
Chikchan, Ok, Men, Ahaw	3, 8, 13, or 18

portion of Stela 22 from the site of Naranjo in the northeast Petén region of Guatemala (Fig. 2:5)

Comparing the glyph block at E4 with the sample day name glyphs in Appendix B reveals that this is clearly the day 9 *Manik'* of the *tzolk'in.* One is then tempted to assume that the following glyph, at F4, is the *haab* portion of the Calendar Round. Our table of day name/month number dependencies, however, shows that, for a day name *Manik',* the month number must be 0, 5, 10, or 15. The coefficient on the eroded glyph at F4 is none of these; it looks like 9. Therefore, we must look elsewhere for a *haab* month having one of the required four coefficients. In fact, we find the seating glyph, representing the coefficient 0, still well preserved at E6. The complete Calendar Round for the first date on Naranjo Stela 22 is 9 *Manik'* 0 *K'ayab.*

In each of the two examples we've examined so far, there have been several glyphs *before* the Calendar Round that we're now able to recognize. These glyphs specify the date in the Maya Long Count.

Whereas the *tzolk'in* and *haab* are repeating cycles of 260 and 365 days, the Long Count represents a linear count of days from a mythical starting point in prehistoric time. Many texts begin with a Long Count; this is usually preceded by a glyph called the Initial Series Introducing Glyph (ISIG). Early scholars working with calendrics quickly recognized Long Count dates in the inscriptions and referred to the first such date as the Initial Series. This date is usually followed by something called the Supplementary (or Secondary) Series; more about this later.

The ISIG is often an oversized glyph occupying two or more glyph blocks, as in the example for April 12, 1997 (see Fig. 2:2). On the Naranjo Stela 22, however, the text begins with an eroded ISIG that occupies only a single glyph block. The ISIG has one variable element within it. This is framed by two comb-like elements and is referred to as the "patron of the month." Each ISIG has a unique patron element placed within it depending upon the *haab* date with which the Long Count is associated. Samples of

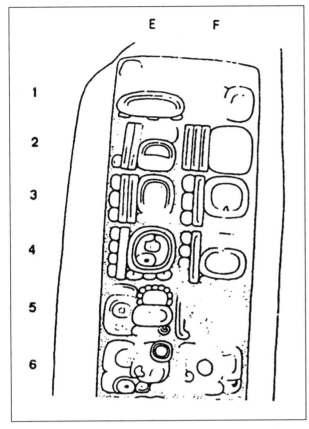

Figure 2:5. Partial text from Naranjo Stela 22 (drawn by Ian Graham).

these patrons are shown in Appendix D. The patrons come in handy when the *haab* sign is eroded; if the ISIG is visible, then the *haab* month can be determined by its patron.

Following the ISIG is the Long Count date itself, usually consisting of five glyphs, each with a coefficient. Each glyph represents a period of time based, with one exception, on the *vigesimal* system (base 20). These are usually arranged in descending order as follows:

> 1 bak'tun = 144,000 Days (or 20 k'atuns)
> 1 k'atun = 7200 Days (or 20 tuns)
> 1 tun = 360 Days (or 18 winals, the Base 20 exception)
> 1 winal = 20 Days (or 20 k'ins)
> 1 k'in = 1 Day

Although this is the order in which the components of the Long Count are usually written, it is simpler to discuss them in the opposite order.

One should think of these five components of the Long Count in terms of the odometer of an automobile. The *k'in* is in the lowest position—just like the tenths-of-a-mile on the odometer. Next

comes the *winal*, then the *tun*, and so on. The *k'in* represents a count of days; *k'in* means day or sun in Yucatec. The *k'in* coefficient varies from 0 to 19. After twenty days, the coefficient changes from 19 back to 0 and the *winal* coefficient is increased by 1—again, just like an odometer. Thus, 1 *winal* represents twenty days—like a twenty-day month. The *winal* coefficients vary from 0 to 17. After 18 *winals*, when the winal coefficient flips from 17 back to 0, a period of 360 days has passed. The *tun* and *k'atun* coefficients vary from 0 to 19, just like the *k'in*. The *bak'tun* coefficient varies from 0 to 13.

Take another look at the Maya version of April 12, 1997 (Fig. 2:2). The Initial Series Introducing Glyph (ISIG) is followed by the five Long Count glyphs with their coefficients. Make sure you're conversant with reading order and bar-and-dot notation by writing down Arabic numbers for the Long Count:

> _____ bak'tuns
> _____ k'atuns
> _____ tuns
> _____ winals
> _____ k'ins

By convention, epigraphers write Long Count dates in descending order (*bak'tun, k'atun...*) with the coefficients separated by periods. Thus, the Long Count for April 12, 1997 would be written

12.19.4.1.6

This represents a count of days from a mythological starting point: the Long Count's zero date. The number of days is $(12 \times 144,000) + (19 \times 7200) + (4 \times 360) + (1 \times 20) + (6 \times 1)$ or 1,866,266 days since the Long Count began.

Our Western minds would assume that the Long Count began on 0.0.0.0.0. The Maya mind again thinks in terms of completion of a previous *bak'tun* period before the zero date. Thus the Long Count of the next-to-last day of the prior period was written as

12.19.19.17.19

Adding one day results in

13.0.0.0.0

to signify the completion of the 13th *bak'tun*. Because there are only 13 *bak'tuns* in the cycle, the next day would be written as

0.0.0.0.1

This signifies the beginning of a new era, in which the *bak'tun* coefficient returns to 0.

The Maya merged the Long Count and the Calendar Round together for all time by telling us that 13.0.0.0.0 fell on 4 *Ahaw* 8 *Kumk'u.* This means that each Long Count date can be equated with one and only one Calendar Round date:

13.0.0.0.0	4 Ahaw 8 Kumk'u
0.0.0.0.1	5 Imix 9 Kumk'u
0.0.0.0.2	6 Ik' 10 Kumk'u
0.0.0.0.3	7 Ak'bal 11 Kumk'u
.	
.	
12.19.4.1.6	3 Kimi 4 Pohp

The correlation of Long Count dates with our Gregorian calendar has always been of interest to archaeologists; such a correlation would help date both archaeological strata and portable objects found in excavations. Morley and Thompson, as well as others, worked to identify a specific relation between the two calendars. Although there are many clues, especially in Landa's *Relación,* no single correlation meets all the requirements the clues impose.

During the early years of the twentieth century, Herbert Spinden proposed one such correlation, which bears his name. It was accepted for many years. Then Thompson, in conjunction with J. Martínez Hernandez and J. T. Goodman, proposed another correlation that was approximately 260 years later than Spinden's. Now most Mayanists accept the accuracy of the G-M-T (Goodman-Martínez-Thompson) correlation as agreeing more closely with the archaeological and inscriptional data than that proposed by Spinden. This G-M-T correlation has been refined to such a point that today there is agreement to within three days.

The correlation is specified in the form of a number, or constant, associated with yet another calendar. Astronomers date celestial events using the Julian Day Number (JDN). Like the Long Count, the JDN is a count of days, in this case, from noon on New Year's Day 4713 B.C. (To be even more specific, it was noon in the ancient city of Babylon.) This first day was Julian day number 0. At noon the following day, the JDN became 1, then 2, 3, and so on. All Maya scholars are in agreement that JDN 0 predates the 13.0.0.0.0 Long Count that ushered in the current Maya age. (According to Maya folklore, there were other worlds with dates in eras *prior* to 13.0.0.0.0.) Therefore, any correlation constant is the number of days that must be added to JDN 0 to reach the day corresponding to the Long Count 13.0.0.0.0.

Epigraphers and archaeologists are about evenly split today on using the correlation constants 584,283 or 584,285. We have chosen to use the 584,285 correlation in this book. With it, the Long Count base date 13.0.0.0.0 corresponds to a Grego-rian date of August 13, 3114 B.C. Note that this is well before the earliest-known Maya settlements in Mesoamerica.

There is additional information contained in the calendrical portion of hieroglyphic texts. As noted above, many inscriptions begin with an ISIG followed by a Long Count followed by the Supplementary (or Secondary or Lunar) Series. The Supplementary Series provides information about lunar phenomena and certain deities. The commonly used designations of the Supplementary Series are confusing. Morley was the first to study them and assigned them the letters A through G; but, when read in the inscriptions, they are usually found in reverse order (G through A). Later studies added three more glyphs to the series, designated X, Y, and Z. A Supplementary Series with all glyphs present (rare!) would read:

G F Z Y E D C X B A

The first two, G and F, refer to a set of patron deities and the headdresses they wore. The deities are frequently referred to as the Lords of the Night, drawing on Mexica (Aztec) sources. There were nine Lords of the Night and each ruled for one day in a rotating cycle. Archaeologists have given these deities the sterile designations of G1, G2, G3...G9. Thus we have a nine-day cycle associated with the Lords of the Night. Recognizing the glyph naming the ruling Lord allows for confirmation of the date, because there is a correlation between dates and the nine-day series. Appendix E illustrates several examples of the glyphs representing these nine Lords.

Paired (or conflated) with Glyph G is Glyph F, associated with a deity called the Jester God, often represented iconographically on the headband of royalty (Fig. 2:6).

Figure 2.6   One form of Glyph F.

Glyphs Z and Y seem to designate a cycle of seven, but more work is required to understand their function completely (Yasugi and Saito 1991).

Glyphs E and D combine to indicate the age of the moon during the current lunation (Fig. 2:7). (A lunation is approximately 29.5 days long.) Think of these glyphs as meaning "N days after the moon arrived." Different sites seemed to start counting at different times. Some began at new moon, while oth-

Figure 2:7   Glyphs E and D of the Lunar Series.

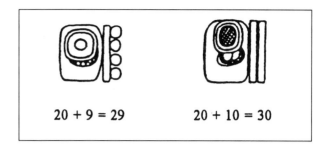

20 + 9 = 29   20 + 10 = 30

Figure 2:10.   Examples of Glyph A of the Lunar Series.

ers waited for the appearance of the first crescent after new moon.

Glyph C identifies the current lunation in a series of six (Fig. 2:8). Bar-and-dot representations of the numbers 2 through 6 are used, but the number 1 has not been found. Instead, where a 1 would be expected, the phonetic equivalent of "first" is used. The head in this glyph is variable while the flat hand is verbal. (See Schele, Grube and Fahsen 1992).

Figure 2:8   Glyph C of the Lunar Series.

Glyphs X and B are related to the above-mentioned lunation series (Fig. 2:9). It is believed that the Maya named each lunation; Glyph X gave information on the name of the current lunation. At least thirteen forms of Glyph X (lunation names) are known. Glyph B is verbal in nature, it literally reads "it is named" (u k'aba).

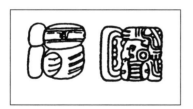

Figure 2:9   An example of Glyphs X and B of the Lunar Series.

Glyph A tells us how long the current lunation is, either 29 or 30 days (Fig. 2:10). As far as is known, the Maya did not use fractions. Hence, they identified the length of a lunation as either 29 or 30 days. By alternating between the two, they could approximate the actual length of 29.5 days.

The last cycle we'll discuss is called the 819-Day Count. It apparently had some ritual significance, which will be more apparent after its description. It is a repeating cycle of four periods (or quadrants) of 819 days and is cited in several inscriptions appearing on carved monuments and pottery, and in the codices. Its exact significance is unclear, but it may have specified the periodic reenactment of some action originally performed by the Maya gods. Thus, every 819 days, the Maya elite may have performed some specific ritual.

Epigraphers and Maya calendar buffs have long been fascinated by the fact that

$$819 = 13 \times 9 \times 7$$

It is thus tantalizing to hypothesize that the 819-Day Count is in some manner a combination of three other cycles: the thirteen day numbers of the tzolk'in, the 9 Lords of the Night, and some as yet poorly understood seven-day cycle, perhaps that of the Supplementary Series glyphs Z and Y.

There are fifteen known inscriptions containing an 819-Day Count. Most often, the 819-Day Count is introduced by a Distance Number, which links a Long Count to an earlier date, called the 819-Day Count Station. This earlier date is easily recognized because it always has a tzolk'in coefficient of 1. (Note that this makes sense because 13 is a factor of 819.)

This date usually is followed by a glyph that appears to function as a verb (Fig. 2:11). Following this verb, there often appears some combination of a reference to God K (a major Maya deity), a reference to a specific cardinal direction, and a color associated with that direction.

Analysis of the fifteen known examples in regard to their colors and directions reveals an interesting pattern. Each direction is associated with a specific color, resulting in the following correspondences: Red:East, Yellow:South, Black:West, White:North. Color and directional symbolism still is found today in rituals performed in transferring local governmental control in Highland Maya communities in Guatemala.

Interestingly, the 819-Day Count and the Long Count do *not* have an obvious common starting point. (4 *Ahaw* 8 *Kumk'u*, because it does not have a *tzolk'in* coefficient of 1, is not an 819-Day Count station.) The 819-Day Count station immediately preceding 13.0.0.0.0 is 12.19.19.17.17, 1 *Kaban* 5 *Kumk'u*, which falls in the previous era.

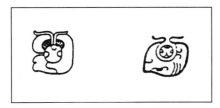

Figure 2:11   Examples of 819 Day Count verbs.

CALENDRICS MANIPULATION

At this point, you should have a basic understanding of the 260-day *tzolk'in*, the 365-day *haab*, the Long Count, the 819-Day Count, and the 9-day Lord of the Night sequence. Further, you should be comfortable with the Calendar Round combination of *tzolk'in* and *haab*, the meshing of the Calendar Round with the Long Count (at 4 *Ahaw* 8 *Kumk'u*), and the concept of correlation. Remember:

❑   Long Counts yield an absolute date, fixed in time and correlated with the Gregorian calendar. Any Long Count has one and only one Calendar Round position.

❑   Calendar Round dates, on the other hand, repeat every 52 years. Thus: each CR date corresponds to a number of different LC dates. In order to determine which LC date applies to a given CR date, some additional information is required to narrow the possibilities. In an archaeological context, such data include stylistic forms, architectural styles, and relation to other events for which a Long Count is known.

Now we'll spend a little time learning to manipulate Maya dates. There are two classes of problems: computing a Calendar Round (CR) when the Long Count (LC) is known and computing a set of LCs that match a CR. Most people working with the inscriptions have access to computer or calculator programs that significantly simplify what we're about to learn. It is important, however, that anyone with a serious interest in pursuing Maya epigraphy understand the principles about to be described.

We'll begin by computing a CR when the LC is known. This process involves determining how many days have elapsed between some base date and the LC date. In principle, this is exactly like

answering the question "What day is it sixteen days from Saturday?" At first, however, working with intervals of thirteen and 365 days is much more confusing than working with the familiar week of seven days.

Appendix F contains a set of five tables, which will simplify the arithmetic we must do. These tables were originally devised by Dr. Linton Satterthwaite, Jr., and were included in Chris Jones' (1984) hieroglyph workbook.

Table F:1 shows the relationship between the *tzolk'in* day name and the *k'in* position in the Long Count. Because there are twenty day names and twenty different possible coefficients for the *k'in*, a specific coefficient always maps to a specific day name. Thus, if the Long Count *k'in* coefficient is 8, the day name *must* be *Lamat*. In an eroded text where the Long Count is illegible, if the day name is *Ahaw*, then the *k'in* coefficient *must* be 0. Using Table F:1, one can *always* immediately identify the day name in a Calendar Round when the Long Count *k'in* coefficient is known.

Table F:2 shows how many days have elapsed in the *haab* at the seating of each month name. The two columns on the right give the same information, one in Long Count notation (*tuns*, *winals*, *k'ins* with leading zeros omitted) and another in our decimal notation. For example, 0 *Yax* is the 180th day of the *haab*; this represents 0 *tuns*, 9 *winals*, and 0 *k'ins* (0.9.0). In using this table, it is often necessary to interpolate to obtain intermediate values. For instance, to determine the *haab* position for 11 *Yax*, we would look up 0 *Yax* (180) and add eleven days, yielding 191 (0.9.11).

Table F:3 is simply a reference showing the Calendar Rounds corresponding to several *bak'tun* completion Long Counts. The first, of course, is the beginning of the current era: 13.0.0.0.0. Most dated texts have a *bak'tun* coefficient of 9 so the 9.0.0.0.0 CR is used most of the time as a base date. This table is a starting point for doing LC to CR date manipulations.

Table F:4 is a table of remainders. There are five pairs of columns, corresponding to the five place holders of the LC (*bak'tuns*, *k'atuns*, etc.) Each pair shows the remainders that result from dividing the chosen time period by 13 and 365 days. For instance, consider the entries for 10 *bak'tuns*. Remember that 10 *bak'tuns* represent (10 × 144,000) days or a total of 1,440,000 days. Dividing 1,440,000 by 13 results in a quotient of 110,769 with a remainder of 3. Dividing the same number by 365 gives 3945 with a remainder of 75. Hence, the entries in the remainders table for 10 *bak'tuns* are 3 and 75.

Table F:5 is multipurpose. The second column, labeled Vague Yrs (vague because a true solar year is 365.2425 days long), lists various multiples of 365-day periods. The leftmost column shows the number of Calendar Rounds equivalent to the vague years, given in the second column; vague years less than 52 represent a fractional CR. The third column, labeled Long Count 20, converts the number of years in the vague years column into LC notation. The *k'in* position of the LC represents the remainder when dividing the number of days by 20. Finally, the rightmost column gives another remainder, this time for a divisor of 13. The row with the arrow represents one Calendar Round (52 vague years), or 0.2.12.13.0 days. As you recall, one CR equals 18,980 days, which yields a remainder of 0 when divided by either 20 or 13.

We will now use these tables to determine a CR date from a specific LC date. We'll use the LC date found on Stela 21 from Tikal:

$$9.15.3.6.8$$

Remember that the Calendar Round is composed of both a *tzolk'in* and a *haab*; we have four components to derive: the day number, day name, month number, and month name. We'll follow a three-step process to accomplish this.

❑ STEP 1　Using Table F:1, we can immediately identify the day name, given that the *k'in* coefficient is 8. This corresponds to a day name of *Lamat*.

Using Table F:3, we choose the nearest *previous* base date (9.0.0.0.0 8 *Ahaw* 13 *Keh*) and subtract it from our Long Count. This gives the difference in *k'atuns*, *tuns*, *winals*, and *k'ins* between our two dates.

9.	15.	3.	6.	8
9.	0.	0.	0.	0　(8 *Ahaw* 13 *Keh*)
	15.	3.	6.	8

Thus, the difference is equivalent to 15 *k'atuns*, 3 *tuns*, 6 *winals*, and 8 *k'ins*.

❑ STEP 2　Using Table F:4, we can divide these time periods by both 13 and 365 to determine the resulting remainders. We usually construct a simple tabular listing, with the appropriate entries from Table F:4, then add the two sets of remainders:

	13	365
15 *k'atuns*	9	325
3 *tuns*	1	350
6 *winals*	3	120
8 *k'ins*	8	8
	21	803

❑ STEP 3　What we're about to do is related to the "What day is it sixteen days from Saturday?" question. To answer that, we divided 16 by 7 (days in a week) and added the remainder, 2 days, to Saturday, giving Monday.

We're going to apply the same principle to find both the day number (ranging from 1 to 13) and the *haab* (a 365 day cycle). The *tzolk'in* for our base date is 8 *Ahaw*. We already know the day name for our LC is *Lamat* (from Step 1). What we must determine is what the day number is after 15 *k'atuns*, 3 *tuns*, 6 *winals*, and 8 *k'ins* have elapsed. The remainders table we constructed in Step 2 tells us. Under the column labeled 13, we have the remainders; their sum is 21. This implies that after this particular amount of time, the day number has advanced by 21 days. We must add 21 to our base-date day number, 8.

$$8 + 21 = 29$$

Remember, however, that day numbers vary from 1 to 13. Our number exceeds 13. Thus we must do one more remainder operation:

$$29 \div 13 = 2 \text{ R}3$$

The remainder, 3, is the day number which accompanies *Lamat* for our Long Count. We're halfway there: the *tzolk'in* for 9.15.3.6.8 is 3 *Lamat*.

Now, in principle, we do the same thing for the *haab*. The difference is that the entire *haab* is a single 365-day cycle. First we must determine where in that cycle our base date *haab*, 13 *Keh*, falls. For this, we consult Table 2. 0 *Keh* is 220 days into the cycle. Then 13 *Keh* must be 13 days later, or 233 days into the cycle. Using the remainders found in Step 2, we know that the *haab* cycle has increased by 803 days from 13 *Keh*.

$$233 + 803 = 1036$$

As with the *tzolk'in*, this number exceeds the 365-day cycle boundary for the *haab* so another remainder operation is called for:

$$1036 \div 365 = 2 \text{ R}306$$

We now use Table F:2 in reverse, noting that position 300 corresponds to 0 *Pax*. Therefore, position 306 must be 6 *Pax*.

We've done it! The Calendar Round for 9.15.3.6.8 is:

3 Lamat 6 Pax

Many people find the preceding a bit confusing. We're convinced that one must actually work through the tables and do the arithmetic in order to understand the principles involved. Therefore, let's do another Long Count to Calendar Round problem.

The inscription on Stela 24 from the site of Naranjo in the northeast Petén has the following LC date:

9.12.10.5.12

Fill in the blanks in the following example to determine the corresponding Calendar Round.

❏ STEP 1   Use Table F:3 to find the immediately preceding base date LC and CR. Write them below. Then subtract the base date from the Naranjo St. 24 LC.

9   12.   10.   5.   12

___   ___   ___   ___   ___

              (_ _____ __ _____)

_____

___   ___   ___   ___   ___

Use Table F:1 to determine the LC day name and write it here:

_____

❏ STEP 2   Copy the subtraction result in the blanks to the left of the *k'atuns*, *tuns*, *winals*, and *k'ins* labels. Then use Table F:4 to find the remainders for both 13- and 365-day cycles. Write them down. Add the two columns.

		13	365
_____	k'atuns	___	___
_____	tuns	___	___
_____	winals	___	___
_____	k'ins	___	___
		___	___

❏ STEP 3   Use the base 13 remainder from Step 2 and the base date *tzolk'in* to determine the LC's *tzolk'in*. Use the base 365 remainder and the base date *haab* to determine the LC's *haab*.

13   365

—   —   Base Date Positions

—   —   Remainders

_____

—   —   Sum

If the *tzolk'in* sum is greater than 13, divide it by 13 and write down the remainder. If it's equal to or less than 13, dividing by 13 will give a quotient of 0 with a remainder equal to the *tzolk'in* sum. (In other words, just use the sum.)

If the *haab* sum is greater than 365, divide it by 365 and write down the remainder. If it's equal to or less than 365, dividing by 365 will give a quotient of 0 with a remainder equal to the *haab* sum.

13   365

___ / 13 = ___ R ___   ___ / 365 = ___ R ___

The base 13 remainder is the LC day number (the day name was determined in Step 1). The base 365 sum is used with Table F:2 to determine the LC **haab** date. Write down the resultant CR:

___ _____ ___ _____

To check your work, refer to Appendix G for a solution to this problem. Also, Appendix H has one more LC to CR example for additional practice.

Now we consider the other class of calendar manipulation problems: computing a set of Long Counts for a given Calendar Round. For this, we make use of the Tun Ending Table table, found in Appendix I. At first glance, the table is confusing but, once understood, it is indispensable for problems of this type.

The *Tun* Ending Table comprises 13 columns of cells, beginning at the left, with pairs of entries in each cell. There is one additional column at the right. Remember that there is a relationship between the day name and month number in a Calendar Round. For example, the day name, *Ahaw* is always associated with a month number of 3, 8, 13, or 18. This is apparent from the rightmost column. The day number is *not* contained in the rightmost column. Possibilities for it are found in the adjoining column pairs. Each pair contains a "shorthand" notation for a Long Count date followed by a day number of a Calendar Round. For instance, consider the first row of the table. Locate the column containing:

9.0.0 8

The left entry represents 9.0.0.0.0. The right entry indicates that the day number of the Calendar Round for 9.0.0.0.0 is 8. The remainder of the CR is found in the rightmost column:

Ahaw 13 Keh

Thus, this pair of table entries tells us that the CR for 9.0.0.0.0 is 8 *Ahaw* 13 *Keh*. Now look at the next pair of entries immediately below this one:

.1 4

The left entry contains the next *tun* coefficient. Since this is a table of *tun* endings, this entry represents the next *tun* completion *after* the one above it. This is our shorthand notation for the Long Count date 9.0.1.0.0. The corresponding CR is then 4 *Ahaw* 8 *Keh*, read from the right entry and the rightmost column of the same row.

What is the Calendar Round for 9.17.0.0.0? Find the left table entry for 9.17.0; combine the right entry, 13, with the rightmost column in the same row, *Ahaw* 18 *Kumk'u*. Then the complete CR is 13 *Ahaw* 18 *Kumk'u*.

What is the CR for 9.10.5.0.0? First, find the entry for 9.10.0. Move down the same column five cells and find:

.5 7

Combining the right entry, 7, with the rightmost column in the row gives a Calendar Round of 7 *Ahaw* 3 *Pax*.

We also can use the table to find a Long Count date for a given Calendar Round having a day name *Ahaw*. Consider 3 *Ahaw* 3 *Keh*. Using the *Tun* Ending Table, scan down the rightmost column, looking for *Ahaw* 3 *Keh*. You'll find it in the third row. Now scan the third row for a cell having a pair of entries whose right entry is 3. It's two columns to the left of the rightmost column. The left entry in that cell is 10.2.0, which signifies a Long Count of 10.2.0.0.0; this is *one* LC (of many) for the CR 3 *Ahaw* 3 *Keh*.

To find other LCs, corresponding to particular CR dates, we make use of the fact that a CR repeats every 18,980 days (approximately 52 years). We can add or subtract this number of days from 10.2.0.0.0 to find other LCs with the same CR. To aid in this, we've provided Table F:5 with the Calculation Tables giving Long Count notations for a variety of Calendar Round multiples. For instance, one CR

(18,980 days) is equivalent to 2 *k'atuns*, 12 *tuns*, 13 *winals*, and no *k'ins*. This is written:

2.12.13.0

and you'll find it in the middle of Table F:5 with a large arrow pointing to this entry. Other multiples of CR periods are also included in Table F:5.

Now let's do a problem using these tables. The first known ruler of the site of Naranjo, Ruler I, was born on 9.4.10.8.17 and died on 9.9.2.0.4. If his accession occurred on 6 *K'an* 2 *Sip*, what was the LC date of his accession? Obviously we must find a LC date that falls between Ruler I's birth and death. Further, it's likely that he acceded during the first half of his life. Therefore, we must find a LC date that meets these conditions.

We'll make use of the Tun Ending Table. However, *tuns* end on Calendar Rounds having *Ahaw* day names and our CR is 6 *K'an* 2 *Sip*. We must therefore back up or go forward to the closest *Ahaw* date. Looking at Table F:1, we see that *K'an* is the fourth day in the day name sequence. If we back up by 4 days, we'll be at *Ahaw*. Therefore, let's subtract 4 days from both the *tzolk'in* and *haab*:

6 K'an	2 Sip
-4	-4
2 Ahaw	18 Wo

Make sure you understand how we got from 6 *K'an* to 2 *Ahaw* and from 2 *Sip* to 18 *Wo*.

Now we have a CR date with an *Ahaw* day name. Let's use the *Tun* Ending Table to find a qualifying LC date. Look in the rightmost column for *Ahaw* 18 *Wo*; it's about halfway down. Scan that row for a pair of entries with a 2 (as in 2 *Ahaw*) in the right position. It's in the seventh column from the left. The left entry in this cell is .12; this means the *tun* position of the Long Count is 12. To find the *bak'tun* and *k'atun*, scan up the column until you find *9.5.0*. One Long Count date for 2 *Ahaw* 18 *Wo* is then 9.5.12.0.0. Comparing this to Ruler I's birth and death dates, we find this LC meets our selection criteria. There's just one more thing to do. We subtracted 4 days from the original CR to get to one having a day name *Ahaw*. We must now add those 4 days back to get the Long Count date of Ruler I's accession:

9.5.12.0.0
+4
9.5.12.0.4

Let's do one more. Use the *Tun* Ending Table to verify that Ruler I's birth date, 9.4.10.8.17, corresponds to the CR, 7 *Kaban* 5 *K'ayab*.

First we must adjust the CR so that it falls on an *Ahaw* date. Table F:1 shows *Kaban* is seventeenth in the day name sequence; we must add 3 days to get to *Ahaw*.

$$7 \text{ Kaban} \quad\quad 5 \text{ K'ayab}$$
$$+3 \quad\quad\quad\quad +3$$
$$10 \text{ Ahaw} \quad\quad 8 \text{ K'ayab}$$

In the *Tun* Ending Table, we look for *Ahaw* 8 *K'ayab*. It's three-fourths of the way down. Remaining on this row, scan to the left, looking for a day number 10. We find it in the column immediately to the left of our starting point. The tun position is .5 and, looking up five rows, we can determine that the LC is 10.8.5.0.0. This is much too late for Ruler I's birth. We must subtract some number of Calendar Round multiples to find a date in the 9.4.10.0.0 range, approximately 1 *bak'tun*, 3 1/2 *k'atuns* earlier. Using Table F:5, we find that 9 Calendar Rounds corresponds to 1.3.15.9.0. Let's try subtracting that amount from 10.8.5.0.0:

$$10.\ 8.\ 5.\ 0.\ 0$$
$$-1.\ 3.\ 15.\ 9.\ 0$$
$$9.\ 4.\ 10.\ 9.\ 0$$

This date falls into our acceptable range. By subtracting the 3 days that were added initially to reach an *Ahaw* date, we arrive at the correct LC date.

$$9.\ 4.\ 10.\ 9.\ 0$$
$$-3$$
$$9.\ 4.\ 10.\ 8.17$$

This Long Count does indeed correspond to that of Ruler I's birth. Therefore, we have verified the Calendar Round. Appendix J has one more CR to LC example for practice.

DISTANCE NUMBERS

We'll begin this section with an exercise in calendrics. If the Long Count for April 12, 1997 is 12.19.4.1.6, what is the Long Count for New Year's Day, 1 January 2000?

The solution to this problem requires us to determine how many days there are between the two dates. This is not too difficult. First we must find out how many days remain in 1997. We can count days on a calendar or, remembering our previous calendar page example, refer to it. The 263 found in the lower-right corner is the number of days we want. Next, there are two full years of 365 days. One more day

brings us to 1 January 2000:

1997	263
1998	365
1999	365
1 January 2000	1
	994

Thus, 994 days after April 12, 1997 is 1 January 2000. Now we must convert this number into the Maya notation of *bak'tuns*, *k'atuns*, *tuns*, *winals*, and *k'ins*. Remembering that there are 144,000 days in a *bak'tun* and 7200 days in a *k'atun*, we can see that our number 994 is less, so there are no whole bak'tuns or k'atuns to deal with. A tun, however, is 360 days. Dividing, we have:

$$994/360 = 2 \text{ R}274$$

2 tuns with a remainder of 274 days. Dividing the remainder by 20, the number of days in a winal, gives:

$$274/20 = 13 \text{ R}14$$

13 winals with a remainder of 14 days (or k'ins). Thus we can express 1372 days as:

$$0.\ 0.\ 2.\ 13.\ 14$$

This is *not* a Long Count. That's because it does not represent a date occurring 994 days after 4 Ahaw 8 Kumk'u. Rather, it represents the number of days between two dates. Such a time span is referred to as a *Distance Number* (DN) and is usually written without leading zeros (e.g., 2.13.14).

To complete the solution to our problem, we have only to add this DN to the Long Count for April 12, 1997:

$$12.19.4.1.6$$
$$+2.13.14$$
$$12.19.6.15.0$$

This is an example of "carrying" in calendrical computations. Make sure you understand the arithmetic. For instance, 6 k'ins plus 14 k'ins is 20 k'ins, which is a winal. Thus the k'in position is 0 and we must "carry" one winal. 1 winal plus 13 winals plus the 1 winal carried is a total of 15. To the uninitiated, this is confusing. But conceptually, it's just like the way we add, carrying 10s, 100s, 1000s, and so on.

Distance Numbers are important in deciphering texts because they serve as "signposts" within Maya grammar. This topic will be explored in depth in the section on grammar. For now, it is sufficient to point out that most Maya "sentences" are introduced with a temporal phrase, which represents calendrical information. Many texts carved on stone monuments (stelae, altars, lintels) begin with a Long

Count date and (possibly) lunar calendrical data as well. Subsequent phrases are generally introduced with Distance Numbers. Remember, however, there are lots of texts that do *not* follow this model.

At this point, let's return to the first text we looked at: Piedras Negras Stela 3 (see Figs. 1:1 and Fig. 2:12). This text is a good one for beginners because it contains several "sentences" and behaves in a very regular fashion. A significant portion of the text is calendrical in nature. For now, let's concentrate on identifying those parts. Beginning at glyph block A1, you should recognize an Initial Series Introducing Glyph with a month patron of *Yaxk'in*. The next five blocks (B1, A2, B2, A3, B3) contain a Long Count date. The *tzolk'in* follows at A4. Note that the *haab* is

not next. The glyph blocks from B4 to A7 contain lunar information. Finally, at B7, we find the *haab*. The verb and subject occupy the next three blocks; we'll skip over them for now.

We encounter our first Distance Number at C1-D1. It's a good example to begin with. First of all, the writing order of time periods for DNs is the reverse of that used in the Long Count. That is, DNs begin with the *k'in* position, then follow the *winal*, *tun*, and so on. Where the Long Count almost always contains five time periods with their coefficients, the DN contains only what's needed to represent the desired count of days. In this example, there are 0 *k'ins* (note the zero sign), 10 *winals*, and 12 *tuns*. Another characteristic of DNs is the combination, or

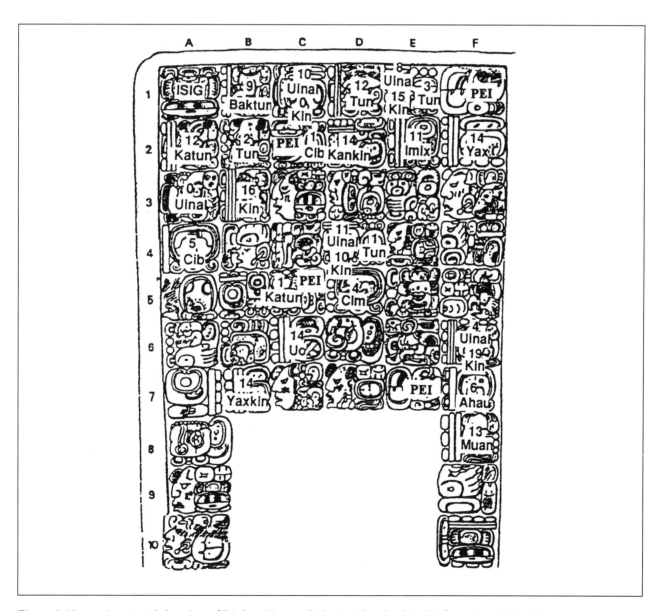

Figure 2:12   Annotated drawing of Piedras Negras Stela 3 with calendrical information indicated.

conflation, of the *k'in* and *winal* glyphs and their coefficients into a single glyph block. This occurs at C1.

The function of Distance Numbers is to link the dates of specific events (expressed by verbs, which we've skipped over so far). Our first DN links the initial Long Count, 9.12.2.0.16, 5 *Kib* 14 *Yaxk'in*, to the Calendar Round found at C2b-D2: 1 *Kib* 14 *K'ank'in*. But which date came first? The Maya scribe told us by including the glyph at C2a. It's often referred to as the Posterior Event Indicator, or PEI. A rough translation might be: "And then it happened" or "it came to pass."

Thus, we can paraphrase our text so far as: On 9.12.2.0.16, 5 *Kib* 14 *Yaxk'in*, something (expressed at A8-A10) happened. After zero *k'ins*, 10 *winals*, and 2 *tuns* it came to pass 1 *Kib* 14 *K'ank'in*.

There are several forms of the PEI; the substitution set for the main sign is large (Fig. 2:13). The Maya read this collocation as *iwal ut* ("and then it happened").

Figure 2:13   Examples of the Post Event Indicator (PEI).

As you might expect, a Distance Number can also link one date to an *earlier* one. In this case, the only difference would be that a PEI would not appear. Instead, an Anterior Event Indicator, or AEI, would be used (Fig. 2:14). Phonetically, the collocation may be read *uti* ("it had happened" or "since").

Figure 2:14.   Examples of the Anterior Event Indicator (AEI).

Finally, there is a small number of examples in which a past date is linked by a Distance Number to an event in the future. In this case a Future Event Indicator (FEI) may be used (Fig. 2:15)[1]

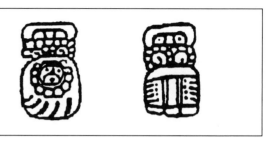

Figure 2:15.   Examples of the Future Event Indicator (FEI).

There is no requirement that the date indicators be present when Distance Numbers appear in a text. They are commonly omitted.

There are two more Distance Numbers in the text of Stela 3. All the calendrical data is indicated on Figure 2:12. Thus, of the 48 glyph blocks on Stela 3, thirty contain calendrical or lunar information. The Distance Number calculations for Stela 3 can be summarized as shown in Table 2:2.

Just as the Long Count is often preceded by the Initial Series Introducing Glyph (ISIG), so may Distance Numbers be introduced by a Distance Number Introducing Glyph (DNIG). This glyph has a variety of substitutable forms, but one of the most common has been referred to as the *hel* glyph; it probably did *not* have this pronunciation (Fig. 2:16).

A cautionary note about this glyph is required. The same glyph is used in a different context to specify an individual's position in a ruling dynasty. Thus, a ruler may be referred to as the "seventh successor" to the dynasty's founder. This could be specified by using the bar-and-dot notation for "7" as an affix to the *hel* glyph. Although the two different contexts for the glyph are usually clear, this duality can result in confusion.

Figure 2:16   Distance Number Introductory Glyph (DNIG).

CALENDRICS COMPUTER PROGRAMS

There is a great temptation to skip over the material in this chapter, thinking it's a perfect candidate for a computer program. DO NOT DO SO! Only after the calendrics concepts have been mastered should one consider the use of a computer. Until then, keep pencil and paper handy to calculate dates from distance numbers, verify long counts, and identify calendar rounds for a given LC.

NOTES

1. A reading for such a Future Event Indicator was proposed independently by Terry Kaufman and Ben Leaf, a founding member of the Pre-Columbian Society at The University of Pennsylvania Museum. It is: *ut'om* ("then it will happen").

TABLE 2:2 Distance Number Calculations for Stela 3		
9. 12. 2. 0. 16	5 *Kib* 14 *Yaxk'in*	27 June 674
+ 12. 10. 0		
9. 12.14.10.16	1 *Kib* 14 *K'ank'in*	21 Nov. 686
+ 1. 1. 11.10	(winal/k'in coefficient not in normal order)	
9. 13. 16. 4. 6	4 *Kimi* 14 *Wo*	21 Mar. 708
+ 3. 8.15	(winal/k'in coefficient not in normal order)	
9. 13.19. 13. 1	11 *Imix* 14 *Yax*	28 Aug. 711
+ 4.19		
9. 14. 0. 0. 0	6 *Ahaw* 13 *Muwan*	5 Dec. 711

3

Phoneticism and Spelling in Maya Hieroglyphic Writing

Before dealing with the workings of the Maya hieroglyphic writing system in detail, we will look at phoneticism because developments in this area have allowed the reading of many glyphic representations as Maya words. In the discussions that follow, individual components of glyph complexes will often be referred to by Thompson numbers, or "T-numbers" for short. These are numbers that J. E. S. Thompson assigned to both affixes and main signs during his pioneering studies of hieroglyphic texts (Thompson 1962). Although the system badly needs updating to include elements that Thompson neglected, or wasn't aware of, T-numbers are currently widely used.

The case for phoneticism in Maya hieroglyphic writing has been established beyond doubt.

However, this is a relatively recent development. In the early years of interest in the Maya script, there was much discussion as to the nature of the constituent symbols.[1] Brasseur de Bourbourg, who in the mid-nineteenth century discovered the long-lost Landa manuscript, which included Landa's "alphabet" (Fig. 3:1), thought that the symbols were primarily phonetic. The prevalent view held by the prolific Seler, Förstemann, Schellhas, and others, however, was that the script was largely, if not entirely, logographic and/or ideographic, with each symbol standing for a word or an idea. In 1876, de Rosny, an early supporter of the phonetic view, combined two symbols, one from the Landa alphabet, to form *kutz*, a Maya word for turkey, a reading still accepted today. The phonetic position

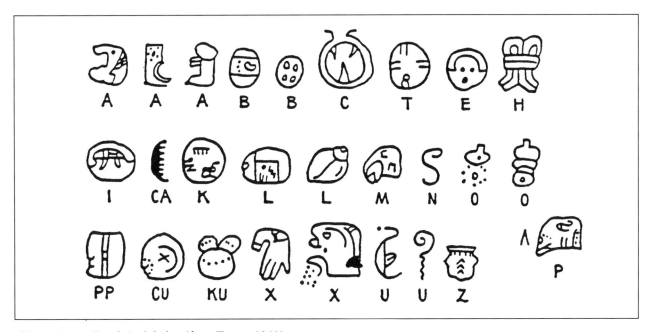

Figure 3:1   Landa's alphabet (from Tozzer 1941).

was further developed by Cyrus Thomas in several papers published in the 1880s and '90s, in which he maintained that the very existence of the Landa "alphabet" implied a major role for phonetics (Thomas 1892a, 1892b, 1893). Although he saw the Landa symbols primarily as letters, he realized that several of them must represent syllables. He also appreciated that a sign could be both ideographic and phonetic. He made many readings based upon the Landa symbols, a few of which are still valid today. By the early part of this century, however, Thomas had been so severely criticized for his proposals that he withdrew his "phonetic key" entirely (Thomas 1904). There was still latent interest in phoneticism, however, as evidenced by the summation in Sylvanus Morley's *An Introduction to the Study of Maya Hieroglyphs* (1915): "The theory now most generally accepted is that while chiefly ideographic, the glyphs are sometimes phonetic, and that although the idea of a glyphic alphabet must finally be abandoned, the phonetic use of syllables . . . must surely be recognized."

In 1933, Benjamin Whorf published a lengthy paper setting forth the "phonetic value of certain characters in Maya writing." His overall characterization of the writing system as both phonetic and syllabic, coupled with extensive use of ideographic signs, sounds rather modern. His derivations of specific phonetic values for symbols were flaw-ridden, however, and his transliteration of a passage from the Dresden Codex was so fanciful that it was extremely easy to combat his arguments regarding phoneticism. And, indeed, J. Eric Thompson did attack Whorf's idea of phoneticism fiercely, pointing out the obvious errors (Thompson, 1950). Thompson, with his gigantic stature as a Mayanist, carried the day for a time, such that even Morley, who had previously accepted a large role for phoneticism, said in his major work *The Ancient Maya* (1946): "The Maya hieroglyphic writing belongs to Class II (ideographic) above. Its characters represent ideas rather than pictures—or sounds. . . ."

The principal development, which began the irreversible path to general acceptance of phoneticism as a major component of the Maya hieroglyphic script, was a series of papers written by Yuri Knorozov that first appeared in the 1950s. Knorozov, a scholar in the Soviet Union, was an outsider to the world of the western Mayanists of the time (Knorozov 1958a, b).

This work, which first became widely available to English speakers in an article translated by Sophie Coe in *American Antiquity* (Knorozov 1958a), not only presented an extensive argument supporting the importance of phonetics, but did so in terms of a series of syllabic elements from which many Maya words could be formed. And his arguments recognized the importance of the vowel component of syllables. For example, it was known from the extant Maya languages that many words have the form C-V-C: consonant-vowel-consonant. Knorozov proposed that in hieroglyphic texts, the first syllable of a C-V-C word was represented by a C-V sign, several of which he recognized in some form in Landa's alphabet, and that the final letter of the word was represented by another C-V sign, which began with the needed consonant, and whose vowel was the same as the vowel of the first C-V syllable. As an example, to spell the word *pas* (to open), the sign for the syllable *pa* is combined with the sign for the syllable *sa*. The *a* from the *sa* is dropped in speaking the word, giving *pas* (Fig. 3:2).

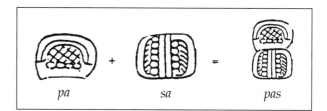

Figure 3:2   Phonetic spelling of pas.

Knorozov generated many words using this formula and he coined the term Principle of Synharmony for the requirement that the vowel of the syllable chosen for the second consonant of the C-V-C word should be the same as the vowel of the first syllable. The same process is used to produce words of two or more syllables. For example, to form the two-syllable word *bakab* (a title), three syllable signs would be chosen, *ba*, *ka*, and another *ba*, and in speaking the word, the *a* of the second *ba* is dropped to give *bakab* (Fig. 3:3).

There were at least two problems with Knorozov's work: first, he included several examples that did not follow his newly stated principle; and second, there

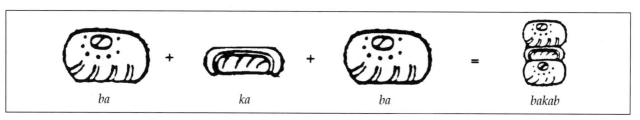

Figure 3:3   Phonetic spelling of bakab.

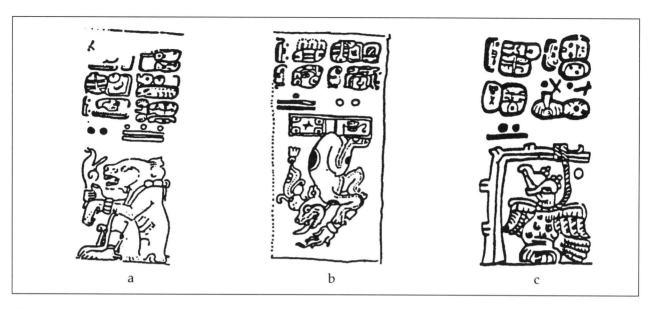

Figure 3:4   **a.** *Dresden Codex 7a;* **b.** *Dresden Codex 40b;* **c.** *Madrid Codex 91a.*

were several glaringly inconsistent proposals for sylla-ble-sound value assignments.[2] In addition, the earlier versions of the work were prefaced with Marxist dogma deprecating the previous work of Western scholars. Thompson again picked up the cudgel and by deriding the inconsistencies and errors in the work, attempted to demolish it. Consequently, Knorozov was largely ignored by Western scholarship for a time. Through the efforts of a minority of Mayanists like David Kelley, Floyd Lounsbury, and Michael Coe, how-ever, support for Knorozov's work was voiced. Many of the arguments supporting Knorozov's proposals and much additional material appeared in Kelley's *Deci-phering the Maya Script* (1976). Since that time, research by several scholars—Floyd Lounsbury, Linda Schele, Peter Mathews, David Stuart and others—has built substantially on the work begun by Knorozov. Today, it is recognized that in spite of the early errors, Knorozov's contribution was pioneering and monu-mental. Thompson, however, to his death apparently never accepted the importance of phoneticism—he maintained that the script was logographic to the end!

It is instructive to go through one of Knoro-zov's best-known examples in order to see how his method for establishing phonetic values for symbols and glyphic representations of Maya words works; it is still an important component of the investigative method used by scholars today. Some of the symbols involved are from Landa's alphabet, but the spellings would be compelling without that connection. Like the arguments presented later in this volume for estab-lishing word order in Maya hieroglyphic texts, these examples come from the codices. Codex texts offer an advantage for this kind of exercise, because they are associated with pictures to which words in the text can

clearly be related. The examples we will look at involve words for dog and turkey. Dresden Codex panels 7a and 40b (Fig. 3:4a, b) each contain a picture featuring a dog, and Madrid panel 91a (Fig. 3:4c) shows a turkey in a noose. In the texts with pictures of dogs, the positions likely to be naming the object shown contain the same pair of symbols, and Knorozov reasoned that these did indeed constitute a word for dog (other texts in the Dresden Codex containing these symbols are also associated with pictures featuring dogs). The second of the two symbols is one from Landa's list for which Knorozov proposed the syllabic value *lu*. In the panel with the picture of the turkey, the associated text contains a two symbol collocation[3] in the position expected for a word for turkey. The second symbol of this pair is the same as the first symbol in the word proposed for dog, while the first is the Landa symbol for *cu* (*ku* in modern orthography). Knorozov looked in the Maya language dictionaries for a word for dog that ended in *l* and began with the same syllable whose ini-tial consonant ended a word for turkey, which in turn started with the syllable *ku*. He came up with the words *tzul* for dog, and *kutz* for turkey (Fig. 3:5).[4] Not only were the proposed syllabic values *ku* and *lu* sup-ported and the glyphic spellings for the names of the two animals found by this exercise, but the sound value for *tzu*, a symbol not found in Landa's list, was also determined. These results illustrate an extremely important requirement for establishing a phonetic value for a symbol: the proposed value must work in contexts other than the single word for which it is ini-tially proposed. Ideally it must work in all cases where a test is possible. If it does work to form many words that make sense in a variety of contexts, the proposed phonetic value for the symbol is no doubt correct and

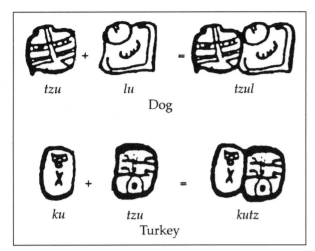

Figure 3:5   Words from the Codices for dog (tzul) and turkey (kutz).

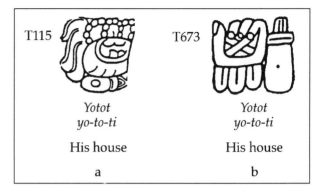

*Figure 3:7   Collocations for yotot (His House): **a.** Yaxchilan, Lintel 26, I2; **b.** Chichen Itza; Temple of the 4 Lintels, Lintel I, F4.*

is said to be "productive." The three syllabic symbols proposed here for *tzu, lu,* and *ku,* have been found to work in many contexts, and are considered to be established beyond doubt.

By this methodology, many Maya words were deciphered from glyph complexes in the codices which correlated with elements in the accompanying pictures. Some of these are shown in Figure 3:6. Each of the symbols representing the syllables in these examples occurs in many other combinations that also form known Maya words, i.e., they are "productive."[5]

The process just discussed illustrates one form of substitution. Another form of substitution, which has been of major importance in establishing phonetic readings for symbols, involves the comparison of two collocations, which by their contexts must represent the same word, but whose constituent elements are somewhat different. For example, the collocation *yotot* (his house) is written in the inscribed texts in at least two different ways (Fig. 3:7). The form shown in Figure 3:7a occurs in the texts of several sites, and the initial symbol, T115, has been shown to represent the syllable *yo* (D. Stuart 1987a). In some of the texts at Chichen Itza, the same word

appears formed with different symbols; in this case the initial symbol is T673, a hand with folded fingers and cross-bands in the palm (Fig. 3:7b). Since from the contexts the word must be the same, *yotot,* the T673 sign, which is the initial sign of this grouping, must have the same phonetic value as T115, the initial sign of the other collocation, *yo.* Several other examples have been found where this reading of T673 makes sense—i.e., it is "productive."

By the methods just outlined, many symbols have been assigned syllabic values and a sizable syllabary has been constructed (Fig. 3:8). A considerable number of blank spaces remain on the chart, but this is an active area of research, and every year several new syllable readings are established.[6]

So far in this chapter, we have considered phonetic elements, and how Knorozov and others have put them together to form words found in Maya texts. However, as you read in Chapter 1, in addition to words put together from phonetic elements, the script also contains many logographs. Logographs are signs that represent whole words; you have already seen some of these, such as *chi* (deer) (Fig. 3:6), and several glyphs for calendrical units (Chapter 2) like *k'in* (day or sun), and *k'atun* (20 *tuns*). Table 3:1 contains additional examples. We will encounter many of these terms in subsequent chapters.

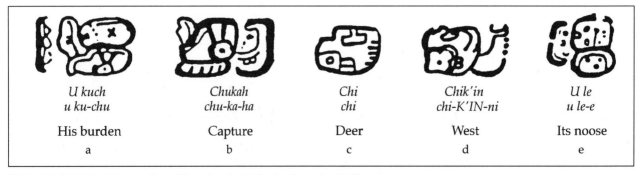

Figure 3:6   Some examples of "productive" glyphs from the Codices.

TABLE 3:1 *Logographs Representing Maya Words from Inscriptional Texts*

Balam Jaguar	*Ahaw* Lord, ruler	*Ahaw* Lord, ruler	*Pakal* Shield	*Na* Lady	*K'an* Yellow, precious
Hanab Flower	*Na* House	*Sak* White	*Tun* Year, stone	*K'al* Twenty	*Witz* Mountain
Chan Sky	*Chan* Snake	*Bak* Bone, prisoner	*Chum* Seated	*Ak'ot* To dance	*Hoy* To dedicate
Ch'ul Divine	*Nik* Flower	*Tok'* Flint	*K'in* Day, sun	*Way* Co-essence, spirit	*Way* Hole, entrance
Sih Birth	*K'awil* God K, image	*Wak* Six, raised up	*Hun* Book, codex	*Hun* One	*Nal* Place
Tan Center	*Kun* Seat	*Ek'* Black	*Ha'/Nab* Water, plaza	*Te'* Tree, wood	*K'uk'* Quetzal

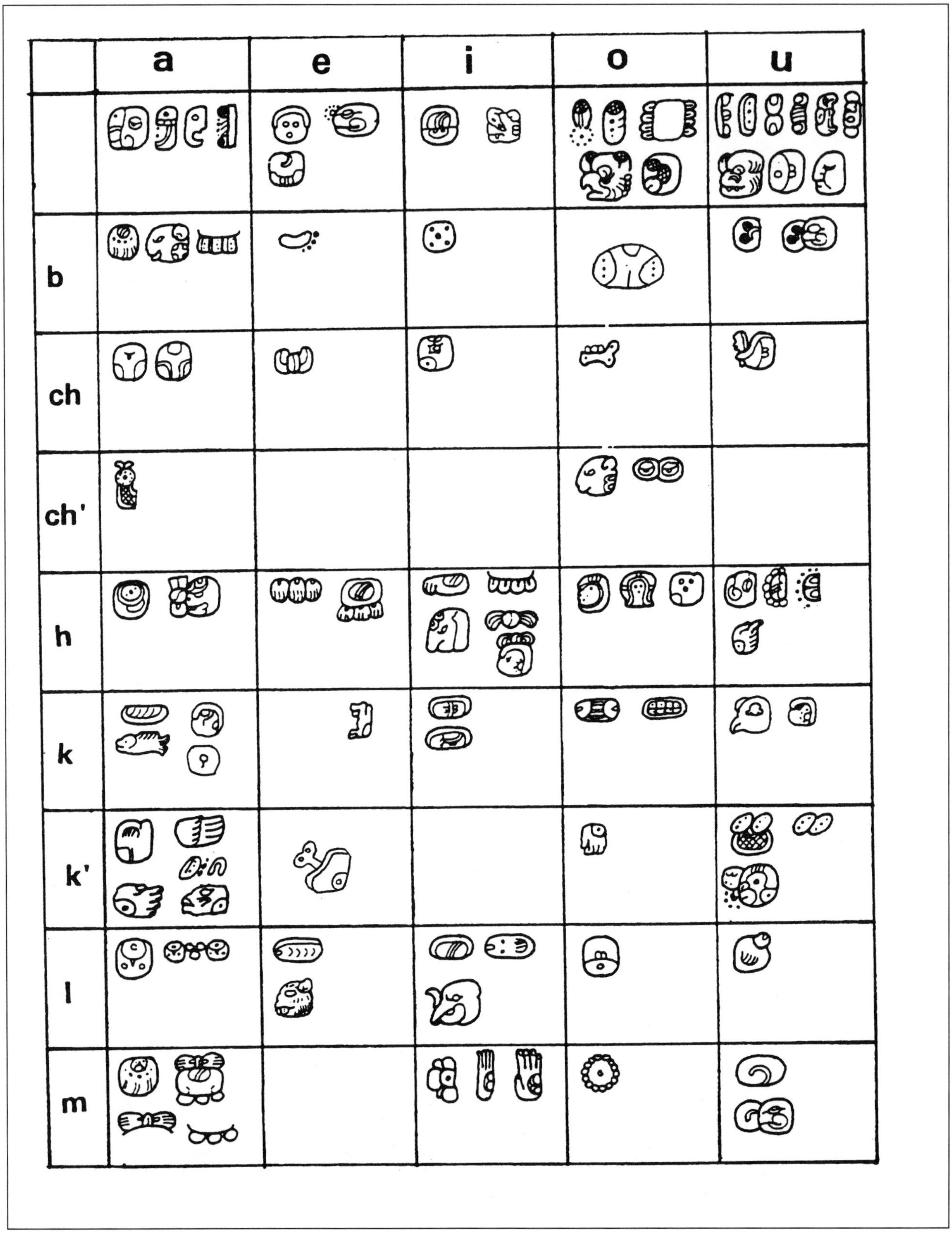

	a	e	i	o	u
b					
ch					
ch'					
h					
k					
k'					
l					
m					

Figure 3:8   A Maya syllabary (adapted from Schele and Looper 1996a).

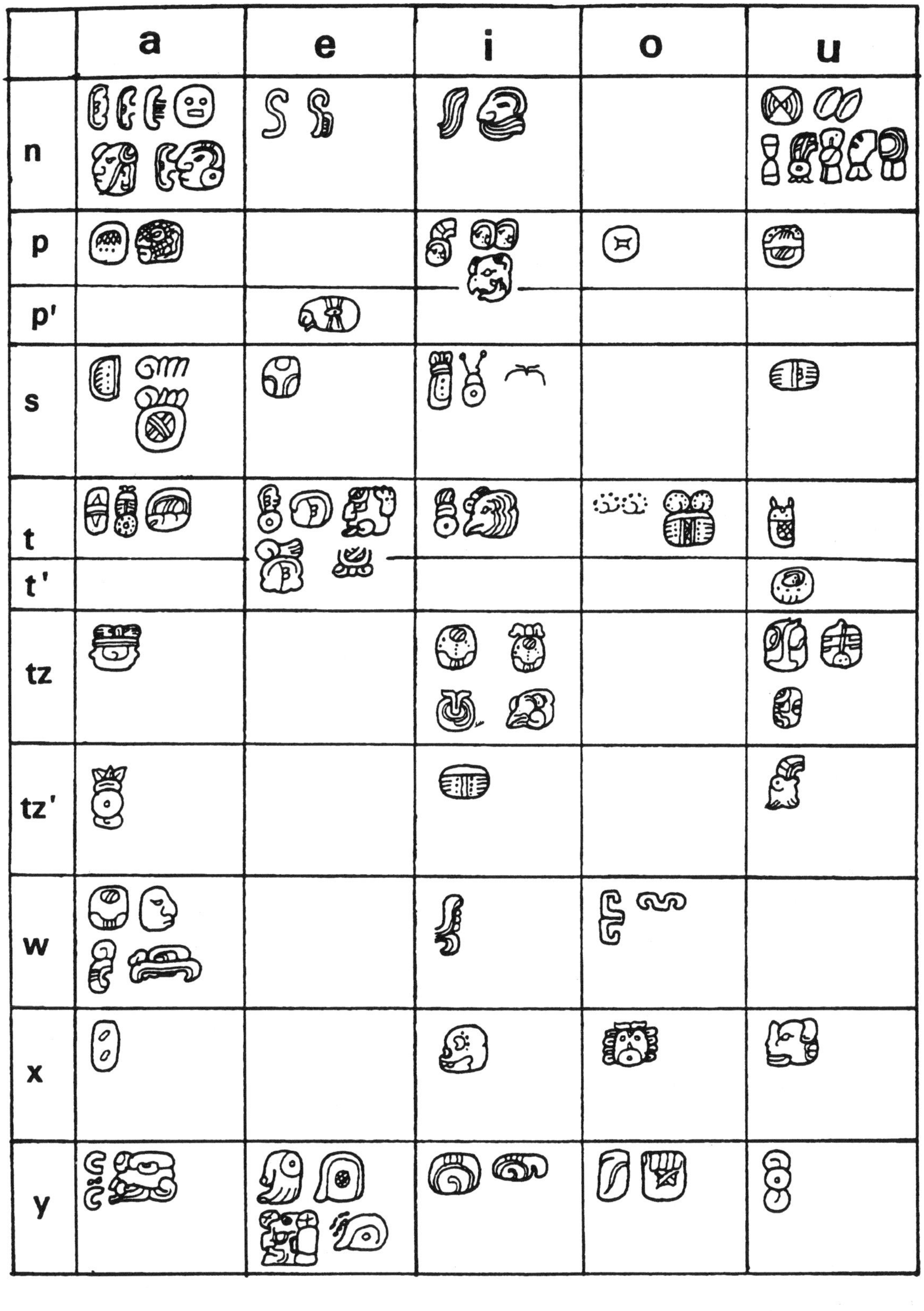

	a	e	i	o	u
n					
p					
p'					
s					
t					
t'					
tz					
tz'					
w					
x					
y					

Figure 3:8   A Maya syllabary (adapted from Schele and Looper 1996a).

There are many examples of words that can be represented by *both* phonetic spellings with syllabic signs contained in the syllabary (Fig. 3:8), and logographs. Two of the best-known examples are the words for jaguar and shield (Fig. 3:9).

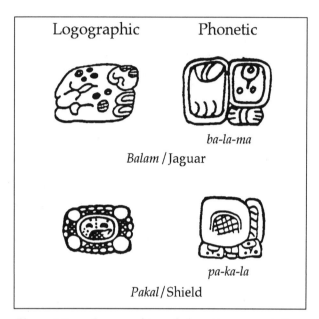

Figure 3:9   *Logographic and phonetic representations of the Maya words* balam *(jaguar) and* pakal *(shield).*

Phonetic elements are often affixed to logographs, either in front of, or at the end of, the logograph. When so positioned, they are usually serving as *phonetic complements*: they are telling the reader how a word begins or ends. For example, the logograph for *balam* (jaguar) may have a *ma* postfix to tell the reader that the word ends in *m*, or a *ba* prefix to establish that the word begins with the syllable *ba* (Fig. 3:10a, b). There is another word for jaguar, *ix* or *hix*, and there are a few examples in which the jaguar head logograph has a *hi* prefix, indicating that the word intended is *hix* rather than *balam* (Fig. 3:10c).

Although the use of symbols as phonetic complements is very common, *semantic determinatives* (devices that indicate a particular meaning for a symbol) are rare. In fact, there are only a few currently recognized examples. The most frequently occurring of these is the day sign cartouche (Chapter 2). The day signs and day names were provided by Landa, and it has since been determined that in several cases, the sign outside the cartouche has a value entirely different from the day name. A well-known example is the so-called *Kawak* sign (T528). Within the day sign cartouche, the sign stands for the day *Kawak* (Fig. 3:11a). Outside the cartouche, it can stand for the syllable *ku*, or is a logograph for the word *tun* (year or stone) (Fig.

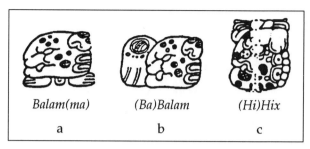

Figure 3:10   *Logographs for* jaguar *with phonetic complements.*

3:11b). Usually when representing the word *tun*, the sign has a phonetic complement, *ni*. Similarly, the "Ahaw" symbol (T533) within the day sign cartouche represents the important day *Ahaw* (Fig. 3:11c), while outside it is a logograph for the word *nik* (flower) (Fig. 3:11d). It should be pointed out that there are cases where day signs do not appear in cartouches—this is especially so in the codices. Thus, in many cases understanding the context is required to determine the function of the sign.

Another, less common semantic determinative is the headband scarf. Special headbands were donned by rulers upon accession, and they were symbols of ruling Ahaws. Several head glyphs, for example, of young men, vultures, and rodents, appear in the texts wearing headband scarves (Fig. 3:12). Semantically, the presence of the headband scarf determines that the head wearing it represents the title *Ahaw*.

Figure 3:11.   *Signs within and outside of Day Sign cartouches.*

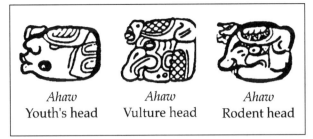

Ahaw Youth's head   *Ahaw* Vulture head   *Ahaw* Rodent head

Figure 3:12   *Heads with headband scarves representing the title Ahaw.*

A device of infrequent occurrence similar in concept to a semantic determinative consists of a pair of dots, usually positioned at the upper-left corner of a sign, which represents a command to repeat the sign to which they are attached in assembling the word(s) represented by the entire collocation. For example, in the collocation in Figure 3:13, there is a pair of dots at the upper-left corner of the sign representing the syllable *le*, indicating that *le* should be repeated. The components are thus *ti Ahaw le le*, or *ti Ahawlel*, which means "in the Ahawship." Two additional examples of signs with double dots appear in Figure 3:16, and are discussed below. (For a table with several examples of collocations containing a double-dotted sign, see Stuart and Houston 1994: fig. 57).

As mentioned above, the so-called *Kawak* sign (T528), when outside the day sign cartouche, can be both a logograph (*tun*) and a phonetic element (*ku*) (Fig. 3:14a). Another well-known main sign with analogous dual function is the "upended frog" glyph (T740), which as a logograph stands for birth, probably the Yucatec word *sih*, and as a phonetic element represents the syllable *hu* (Fig. 3:14b). There are many other main signs that can be both logographs and phonetic elements, for example, Figure 3:14c, d. There are also affixes that in addition to standing for a phonetic element can also represent a logograph. An example is T103, which as a phonetic element represents the syllable *ki*, and as a logograph stands for the word *ki*, meaning "heart" (Fig. 3:14e). Thus there is no clear-cut distinction between

the functions of main signs and affixes; both can be either logographs or phonetic syllables.

In recent years, as more and more signs have been assigned phonetic values, there has been an accelerating effort to find Maya words that match the phonetic combinations found in texts, and that make sense in the contexts in which they occur. The sources consulted for the candidate words are Maya dictionaries and word lists, some of which were compiled during Colonial times. The success of this procedure depends upon three factors: the syllabic assignments must be correct; the word must have survived into Colonial times; and the word must have been recorded in Colonial times or later. A possible problem is that the word may have survived in form and been recorded, but its meaning may have changed over the several intervening centuries between the time when the text was written and the word lists were compiled. Even with these problems, the number of successes has been encouragingly high. Of the several dictionaries currently used in this methodology, the most popular is the extensive *Diccionario Maya Cordemex* ("The Cordemex" for short; Barrera Vasquez 1980), which contains Yucatec words. Of several small Cholan dictionaries, perhaps the best known is *Diccionario Ch'ol-Espanol Espanol-Ch'ol* by Aulie and Aulie (1978). A comprehensive Cholan dictionary is eagerly awaited!

Ti Ahawlel
ti AHAW-le-le
In the Ahawship

Figure 3:13   *Use of a pair of dots as a command to double a sign.*

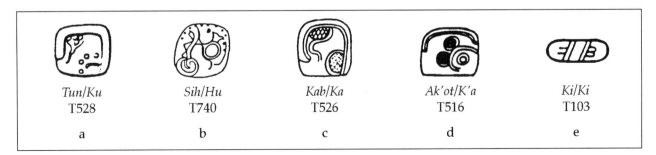

Tun/Ku T528   *Sih/Hu* T740   *Kab/Ka* T526   *Ak'ot/K'a* T516   *Ki/Ki* T103

a   b   c   d   e

Figure 3:14   *Signs serving as both logographs and phonetic elements.*

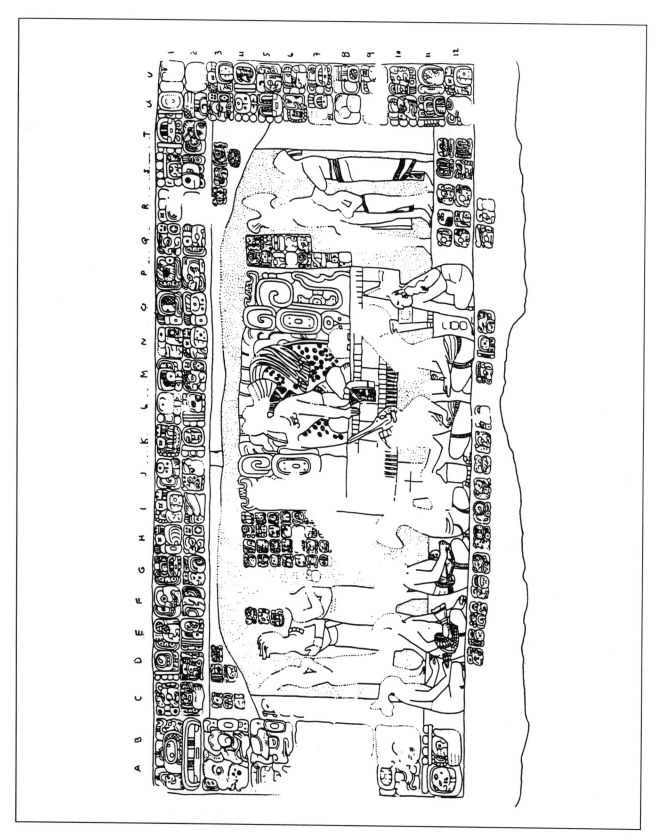

Figure 3:15   *Piedras Negras Lintel 3 (drawn by Linda Schele).*

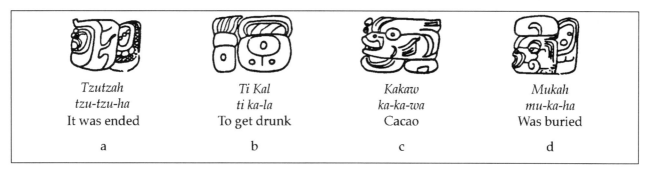

Tzutzah	*Ti Kal*	*Kakaw*	*Mukah*
tzu-tzu-ha	*ti ka-la*	*ka-ka-wa*	*mu-ka-ha*
It was ended	To get drunk	Cacao	Was buried
a	b	c	d

Figure 3:16   Collocations composed of phonetic symbols from Piedras Negras Lintel 3.

As examples of how this procedure works, let us look at several collocations from the main text of Lintel 3 of Piedras Negras (Fig. 3:15). Four words made up of phonetic symbols are shown in Figure 3:16. Figure 3:16a is the verb of the initial clause. Its main sign, T559 (variant), has been assigned the phonetic value *tzu* (see Fig. 3:8). As mentioned above, the pair of dots in the upper-left corner signifies a doubling of the syllable, hence the phonetic rendering of the main sign as it occurs here is *tzutz(u)*, or *tzutz*. The affix to the right of the main sign, T181 (*ha/ah*), is a passive verbal affix. The whole word is thus *tzutzah*. The root is *tzutz*, and is found on page 868 of the Cordemex.[7] One of its Spanish equivalents is *cerrar*, which means to close or to terminate and is consistent with the context in which the verb occurs. The clause is noting the first k'atun anniversary of Piedras Negras Ruler 4's reign, and the verb literally says that the first k'atun of his reign was closed, or was over.

The next example (Fig. 3:16b), which consists of the phonetic elements *ti*, *ka*, and *la* (T59, T25, T178, respectively), is a phrase containing the preposition *ti* followed by a verbal stem *kal*. *Kal* occurs on page 285 of the Cordemex, and among its Spanish equivalents are *hartar* and *emborrachar*, which can mean to gorge or to get drunk. These are consistent meanings for *ti kal* in the context.

The third example (Figure 3:16c), involves a doubling of a syllable as did the first example. The fish (T738) is phonetic *ka*, but the two little dots in front of the forehead of the fish indicate a doubling to give *ka ka*. The final syllable (T130) is *wa*, giving the word *kakaw(a)*, or *kakaw*, which on page 284 of the Cordemex is translated as *cacao*. This is a logical meaning in the context because it follows the phrase about gorging/getting drunk. Ruler 4 was probably drinking fermented chocolate!

The last example (Figure 3:16d) contains the syllables *mu*, *ka*, and *ha/ah* (T19, T738, T181, respectively). Peter Mathews recognized that, when combined, these elements contain the verbal root, *muk*, found on pages 533–534 of the Cordemex, which in Spanish can mean *enterrar*, to bury or to inter (Mathews 1977). The form we have here, *mukah*, is pas-

sive, and should be read "was buried." This meaning also makes sense in the context of the Lintel 3 text, because this action is something done to Ruler 4 three days after his death.

The process just outlined has led to the finding of hundreds of words in the dictionaries that make sense in the contexts in which they are found. Epigraphers working today are adding many new words almost daily to the list of deciphered collocations. Rich sources for new readings can be found in recent notebooks from the Maya Meetings at Austin, Texas (Schele 1990c, 1991d, 1992c; Schele and Grube 1994a, b, 1995a, b; Schele and Mathews 1993; and Schele and Looper 1996a, b); in *Classic Maya Place Names*, by D. Stuart and Houston (1994); in Houston's *Hieroglyphs and History at Dos Pilas* (1993); and in the two supplements to the first edition of this volume (Harris 1993, 1994). Table 3:2 contains a sampling of syllable combinations from which Maya words have been derived. Many of these will be encountered in later chapters of this volume.

NOTES

1. For summaries of the development of the concept of phoneticism in Maya hieroglyphic writing, and of the writing system in general, see Kelley (1962b, 1976) and Coe (1992). For excellent treatments of the history of decipherment, see Coe (1992) and G. Stuart (1992).
2. The Principle of Synharmony is by no means universal. It holds for many cases, such as the spellings of *pas* and *bakab* just given, and the spellings of *tzul* and *kutz* discussed later (Fig. 3:5). However, many spellings don't follow it; an example is shown in Figure 3:6b.
3. The word *collocation* is a handy term for referring to a complex made up of two or more signs, either affixes and/or main signs.
4. As noted above, a spelling for *kutz* (turkey) from the syllables *ku* and *tzu* had been proposed by de Rosny in the last century.
5. Further examples are given in Knorosov's articles (1958a, b) and Kelley's book, *Deciphering the Maya Script* (1976).
6. Many researchers have contributed (and are currently contributing) to this effort. In addition to Knorozov and Kelley, more recent contributors include Linda Schele, Floyd Lounsbury, Victoria Bricker, Nikolai Grube, Barbara MacLeod, Peter Mathews, David Stuart, and Stephen Houston.
7. Because of the orthography used in the Cordemex, the entry is actually spelled *tsuts*.

TABLE 3:2 *Phonetic Collocations and Maya Word Equivalents*

Bakab
ba-ka-ba
A title

Pakal
pa-ka-la
Shield

Nawah
na-wa-ha
To be adorned

Tok'
to-k'a
Flint

Tal
ta-li
To arrive

Yak'aw
ya-k'a-wa
He gave it

Yilah
yi-la-hi
He saw it

Yitah
yi-ta-hi
His sibling, companion

Yal
ya-la
Her child

Ah Nab
ah-na-be
He of water

Pas
pa-sa
To open

Ch'akah
ch'a-ka-ha
He/it was axed

Ch'ahom
ch'a-ho-ma
Dripper (title)

Yitz'in
yi-tz'i-na
His younger brother

Pitzla
pi-tzi-la
Ballplayer

U Tz'apaw
u tz'a-pa-wa
He erected

Mak
ma-ka
To close, cover

Yalah
ha-la-ah
He hurled, said

Matawil
ma-ta-wi-li
A cosmological place

Mukah
mu-ka-ah
He was buried

K'ay
k'a-yi
To die,
be extinguished

U Bak
u ba-ki
His bone,
prisoner

Ut
u-ti
To happen

U Pat
u pa-ti
His/its back

TABLE 3:2 *cont'd.*

Nuk
nu-ku
Large

Lakam
la-ka-ma
Large

Yichnal
yi-chi-NAL
Accompanied by

U Natal
u na-ta-la
The first
(arrival)

Ti Xukpi
ti xu-ku-pi
As a bird

Witz Mo
wi-tzi mo-o
Mountain macaw

Yatan
ya-ta-na
His wife

Ch'at
ch'a-ti
Dwarf

Tok
to-ko
Cloud

U Lak
u la-ka
His plate

Lom
lo-mu
Staff

Lah
la-ha
To end

4

K N O W N   M A Y A   G L Y P H S :   T H E   V O C A B U L A R Y

When learning any new language, one has to cope with the grammar and the vocabulary. In this chapter, we will examine some of the glyphs whose semantic values are known, i.e., the vocabulary; we will get to grammar later. Some of the glyphs we will see are logograms; in some cases, the Maya word represented by the logogram is known, but in others only the meaning is recognized. Other entries are phonetic spellings of Maya words. Only those phonetic combinations whose meanings are known are included—there are many collocations that obviously spell words not found in the dictionaries and whose contexts do not allow the assignment of unambiguous meanings.

The known glyphs are grouped by category: verbs, relationship glyphs, titles, toponyms, Emblem Glyphs, and so on. In Chapter 2 you have already met several groups of glyphs whose meanings are known, e.g., numbers, time units, day signs, and month signs. From the very nature of the inscriptional texts, most of the vocabulary we will encounter is related to events in the lives of the elite.

All the examples below are taken from texts, and in many cases only one example is given for each word. It should be recognized, however, that there is often considerable variation in the depiction of any particular glyph—the scribes, or their masters, were individualistic!

The decipherments reported in this chapter have been made by many scholars. The major modern contributors are Floyd Lounsbury, Linda Schele, David Stuart, Stephen Houston, Nikolai Grube, Peter Mathews, and Barbara MacLeod. It would have been virtually impossible to cite the contributor for every reading presented. Instead, some of the more important contributions and their authors are cited as the chapter progresses. We hope that none of the major players or major contributions have been neglected.

VERBS

The meanings of many verbal glyphs are now known, but in addition, many other glyphs are known to be verbs by their positions in clauses, and/or by the affixes they have. A great number of verbs of known and unknown meaning have been tabulated in *Maya Glyphs: The Verbs*, by Linda Schele (1982). Many newly recognized verbs and new readings for previously recognized verbs can be found in the notebooks and transcripts for the annual Maya hieroglyphic workshops at the University of Texas at Austin by Linda Schele and coworkers (e.g., Schele and Looper 1996a,b; Schele and Grube 1995a,b; 1994a,b; and the notebooks for earlier years), and in the supplements to the first edition of this work (Harris 1993, 1994). Verbal morphology is discussed in *Maya Glyphs: The Verbs* (Schele 1982), in the Texas Workshop Notebooks by Linda Schele and coworkers just referred to, in "Cholan and Yucatecan Verb Morphology and Glyphic Verbal Affixes in the Inscriptions" (1984) and *An Epigrapher's Annotated Index to Cholan and Yucatecan Verb Morphology* (1987), both by Barbara MacLeod, and in Victoria Bricker's *A Grammar of Mayan Hieroglyphs* (1986). In order to deal with verbs and their morphology, we need to examine some grammatical concepts. Grammar will be dealt with more extensively in Chapter 5.

Inflection refers to the case, tense, aspect, number, mood, and voice of a verb. Inflection may involve a modification in the form of a verb, but it does not change the verb's basic meaning. Several forms of verbal inflection have been identified in the Maya writing system, and they usually involve affixes attached to the verbal root.

Derivation involves changing the meaning of a verb to something else. Some examples in English are: force vs. enforce; latch vs. unlatch; make vs. remake. Derivational devices are also known in Maya writing.

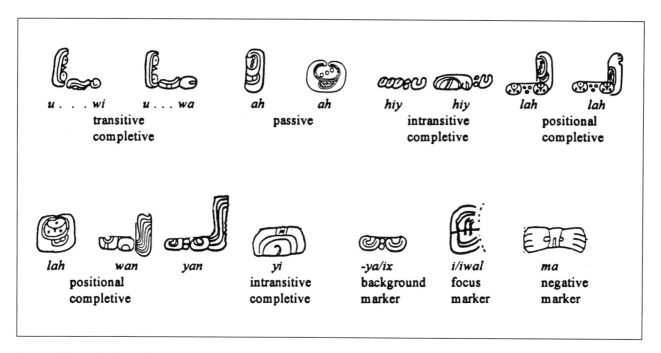

Figure 4:1   Verbal affixes.

Aspect is a term used to indicate whether an action is beginning (incomplete aspect), is in progress (also incomplete aspect), or has ended (completive aspect).[1] Aspect can also be indicated in Maya texts, and is more important in modern Maya languages than is tense.

Transitive verbs are verbs that take objects, while *intransitive verbs* do not.

Active verbs indicate something done by the subject, while with *passive verbs*, the action is done to the subject.

Positional verbs denote the taking of a position, e.g., in Maya, "seating" is a positional verb.

Verbs consist of a verbal root, most often a main sign, usually with attached affixes. Verbal morphology in the Maya writing system is indicated by these verbal affixes or by auxiliary verbs. Some verbal affixes have been identified; these are generally small signs, most of which are also known to have specific phonetic values (Fig. 3:8). It is not always clear, however, whether these affixes are functioning simply as phonetic elements, or as inflectional or derivational devices for the verbal root. This can present problems in the assignment of morphological function. Some of the verbal affixes and their functions so far recognized are listed in Figure 4:1.

Before looking at examples of the use of these affixes, we must consider one of the most frequently occurring affixes, the third person pronoun. Since hieroglyphic texts are primarily narratives about the exploits of rulers and other elite persons in Maya society, the individual sentences are most fre-

quently third person statements, and when a pronoun is used in these statements, it is the third person pronoun: he, she, it, his, hers, its, they, them, their, etc.[2] All of these third person pronouns in Cholan and Yucatec are rendered as *u*. Landa gave us a symbol for *u* (Fig. 4:2a), and an allograph was evident in the codices (Fig. 4:2b). A similar sign, designated T1 by Thompson, occurs in the inscribed texts, and by the process of substitution, as discussed in the chapter on phonetics, many other symbols have been found to be contextually equivalent to T1, and are thus also *u*. A sampling of these is listed in Figure 4:3. In most of the cases we will encounter, the pronoun *u* occurs as a prefix to a transitive verb, or to a noun when the noun is possessed. For example, the transitive verb *ch'amaw* and the possessed noun *tok' pakal* both have prefixed *u*'s (Fig. 4:4a,b). When the word to which the pronoun is attached

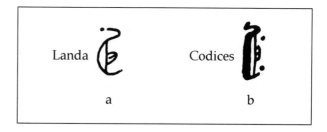

Figure 4:2   U signs given by Landa and found in the Maya Codices.

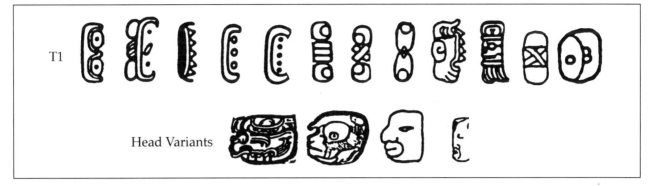

Figure 4:3   U *allographs.*

begins with a vowel, then the third person pronoun *u* changes to *y*. Thus, when the verb *ak'aw* has a third person pronoun prefixed to it, it isn't written as *u ak'aw*, but instead as *yak'aw* (Fig. 4:4c). Similarly,

when the noun, *otot*, has a third person possessive pronoun, it isn't written as *u otot*, but as *yotot* (Fig. 4:4d). Table 4:1 contains examples of verbs with some of the affixes shown in Figure 4:1.

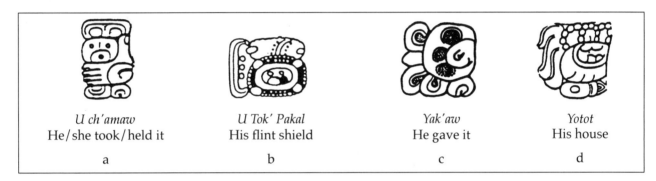

U ch'amaw He/she took/held it	*U Tok' Pakal* His flint shield	*Yak'aw* He gave it	*Yotot* His house
a	b	c	d

Figure 4:4   *Verbs and possessed nouns prefixed with the third-person pronouns* u *and* y.

   Two of the affixes shown in Figure 4:1 can be used to indicate the relative times and importance of two or more events. These are T126, *ya* or *ix*, usually subfixed to the backgrounded and earlier event, and T679, *iwal* or *i*, most often prefixed to indicate the

later or the focus event.[3] The example in Figure 4:5 from the text of the Temple of the Cross at Palenque shows how these markers are used.
·   In English, the sentence reads: "It was two k'ins, 11 winals, 7 tuns, 1 k'atun and two bak'tuns

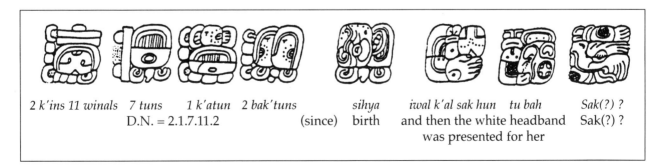

| *2 k'ins 11 winals* | *7 tuns*
D.N. = | *1 k'atun*
2.1.7.11.2 | *2 bak'tuns* | *sihya*
(since) birth | *iwal k'al sak hun*
and then the white headband
was presented for her | *tu bah* | *Sak(?) ?*
Sak(?) ? |

Figure 4:5   *A sentence from the text of the Temple of the Cross Tablet from Palenque showing the use of T126 and T679.*

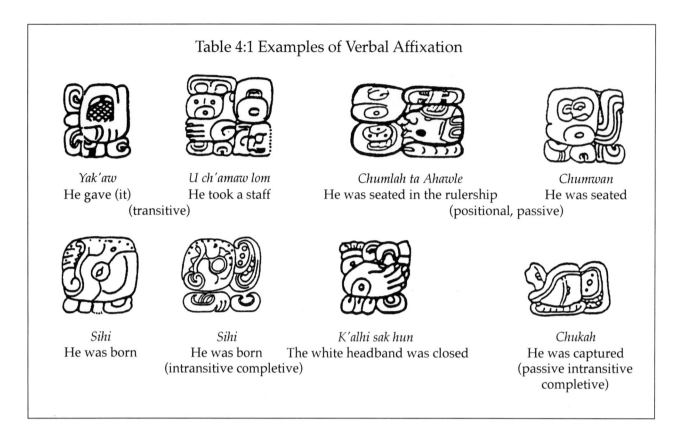

Table 4:1 Examples of Verbal Affixation

Yak'aw
He gave (it)
(transitive)

U ch'amaw lom
He took a staff

Chumlah ta Ahawle
He was seated in the rulership
(positional, passive)

Chumwan
He was seated

Sihi
He was born

Sihi
He was born
(intransitive completive)

K'alhi sak hun
The white headband was closed

Chukah
He was captured
(passive intransitive
completive)

since the birth and then the white headband was closed for her, Sak(?) ?." Note that the earlier event, *sihya*, "birth," has the T126 subfix, indicating it as the background event (Fig. 4:6a). Note also that at least two of the items in the Distance Number, the tun and bak'tun signs, are also subfixed with the T126 background marker, indicating that time is being counted from the backgrounded event. The later event, *k'al sak hun tu bah*, the closing of the white headband (i.e., the accession), has the T679 focus marker indicating that it is the later and focus event of the sen-

tence (Fig. 4:6b). Sometimes T679 is infixed within the verbal main sign as shown in Figure 4:7. T679, prefixed or infixed, is also sometimes used alone to highlight a verb indicating that it is the important event in a text.

Figure 4:7   The scattering verb with an infixed T679 (Tikal Stela 21).

All the affixes that we have considered so far are inflectional, i.e., they do not change the basic meaning of the verb. The *ma* prefix is of the derivational type; it changes (in fact it reverses) the meaning of the attached verb. Figure 4:8 illustrates the use of the *ma* prefix to change the meaning of the verb root *il* from "to see" or "witness" to the negative.

There follows a tabulation and discussion of many of the verbs whose meanings are now known. These examples have been taken primarily from inscriptional texts, and are shown intact, with affixes

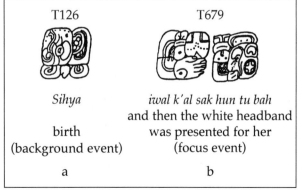

T126 | T679

Sihya
birth
(background event)
a

iwal k'al sak hun tu bah
and then the white headband was presented for her
(focus event)
b

Figure 4:6   The background and focus events from the text in Figure 4:5.

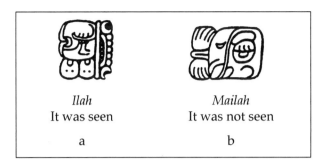

Ilah
It was seen

a

Mailah
It was not seen

b

Figure 4:8   *The use of the* ma *prefix to change the meaning of the verb* ilah.

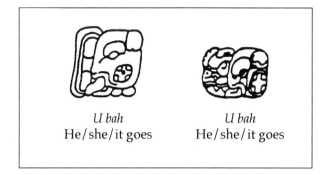

U bah
He/she/it goes

U bah
He/she/it goes

Figure 4:9   *The T757 verb,* u bah.

still in place. In most cases, Maya words have been determined or proposed for the verb. Some of the glyphs are logographs, but others are composed of phonetic elements that lead to the reading shown. In still other cases, the given phonetic value for the word does not appear obvious from the collocation as written; rather it has been derived from other occurrences of the word (not shown) that have critical phonetic determinatives. No doubt some of the word equivalencies will be changed in the future.

Some General Verbs.

A common verb, often used as an auxiliary verb, is based on T757 (Fig. 4:9). Combined with the

pronoun *u*, the reading is *u bah*, which reads in English, "he/she/it goes." It is often used in a special type of verbal structure called a "*ti* construction," which we will consider later. It is also found in some of the child-of-parent expressions we will examine later, and it is used as a device to introduce name phrases. Several of the allographs of *u* can be used in this verb; two of them are shown in Figure 4:9. Another very important group of verbs used to place events with respect to relative time is based on the verbal root, *ut*, "to happen." (Fig. 4:10a). Several of the forms so far recognized are shown in Figure 4:10. An event that has taken place before another event, may be preceded by *uti(x)*, which can be read as "it had happened" (Fig. 4:10b,c). Here again several allographs of u may be used, two of which are shown. There has been much

Ut
To happen

a

Uti(x)
It had happened /
it happened at

b

Uti(x)
It had happened /
it happened at

c

Uhti
It happened at

d

Iwal/i ut
And then it happened

e

Iwal/i ut
And then it happened

f

Utom
And then it will happen

g

Utom
And then it will happen

h

Figure 4:10   *Verbs based on the root* ut.

discussion about the pronunciation of the sign represented by (b) and (c) in Figure 4:10. Depending upon the phonetic value assigned to the T126 affix, either *ya* or *ix*, the sign is pronounced *uti* or *utix*. In any event, it refers to an action or a date that precedes another action or date. When *uti(x)* precedes locatives in toponymic phrases, it is translated "it happened at." Another form of *ut*, also used in toponymic phrases, and sometimes called the "Chuwen Count" glyph, is rendered *uhti*, "it happened at," and is found especially in Early Classic texts (Fig. 4:10d).

The form of the *ut* verb, which may precede the later of two dates or events, contains the elements *iwal/i*, *ut* and *ti*, forming *iwal/i ut* (Fig. 4:10e,f), translated as "and then it happened." *Uti(x)* and *iwal/i ut* are often used in tandem in complex clauses where both an earlier or backgrounded event and a later, featured event are presented. Such complex clauses often begin with a Distance Number; we will see examples in the chapter on grammar (Chapter 5).

The last form of the *ut* verb to be considered precedes an event or date that has not yet taken place at the current point in the narrative. It is usually formed of the elements *u*, *to*, and *ma*, to give a reading *utom*, which means "and then it will happen" (Fig. 4:10g,h). *Utom* often precedes a Period Ending date, which follows one or more earlier events.

The final verb to be considered in this section is the widely used u kahi expression (Fig. 4:11). For an excellent summary of the history leading to the current understanding of *u kahi*, see Schele and

Grube (1994a,b). The *u kahi* expression is usually translated into English as "he caused it to be done," or "he caused it," but it is sometimes rendered simply as "by." The line of text from Caracol Stela 3 shown in Figure 4:12 shows how the *u kahi* expression works. These two clauses pertain to a war made on Naranjo by the ruler of Caracol. The first clause states that something was done to a person from Naranjo. The second clause begins with *u kahi* and tells who caused it to be done. *U kahi* expressions have been useful in establishing relative site hierarchies. For example, an accession of a ruler of a dominated site may be stated to have been carried out *u kahi* the ruler of a dominating site. Such expressions have allowed the detection of alliance and domination networks and the changes therein among Classic Maya sites (Schele and Grube, 1994a,b, 1995a,b).

U kahi   U kahi   U kahi
He caused it to be done

Figure 4:11   U kahi *expressions.*

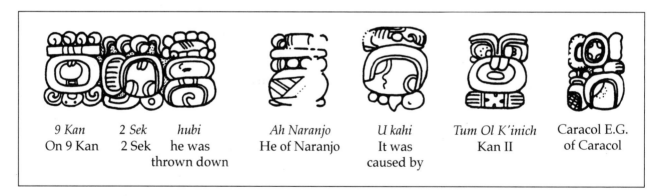

9 Kan / On 9 Kan   *2 Sek* / 2 Sek   *hubi* / he was thrown down   *Ah Naranjo* / He of Naranjo   *U kahi* / It was caused by   *Tum Ol K'inich* / Kan II   Caracol E.G. of Caracol

Figure 4:12   *An* u kahi *expression from Caracol Stela 3 (Beetz and Satterthwaite 1981, fig. 4).*

Birth

The most frequently occurring birth expression is the so-called upended frog glyph (Fig. 4:13a,b). It is a logograph, probably representing the Yucatec word *sih*, which can mean "birth." In the example shown in Figure 4:13a, the verbal subfixes *hi* + *ya* indicate a completive past tense verb, i.e., "he

was born." When T181, *ha*, is also present in addition to a form of *hi* as in Figure 4:13b, the T181 is probably not a verbal affix indicating a passive statement, but is instead a phonetic complement (*ha*) supporting the final *h* on the word *sih*. The collocation in Figure 4:13c looks like the birth verb; however, it is an example in which the upended frog is not a logograph, but is instead a phonetic element, *hu*, which with the *li* suffix, spells *hul*, a verb root meaning "to arrive." The verbs "birth" and "arrive" of course have overlapping meaning, and in some of the places where the *hul* verb is used, it actually does refer to birth. The forms in Figure 4:13d,e are also known to stand for birth, but it is not yet certain what the entire Maya reading is. Each begins with the pronoun *u* (he/she), and the final part is *kab* (earth), either as a logograph as in Figure 4:13d, or spelled out phonetically as in Figure 4:13e. The uncertain part is the hand. It has been suggested that in this context it reads *pan*, giving a reading of *u pan kab*, meaning "he touched the earth" (Lounsbury, 1989a). In any case, from the contexts in which these glyph complexes occur, they are obviously metaphors for birth, and can be glossed "he/she was born."

Sihi	*Sihi*	*Huli*	*U ? kab*	*U ? kab*
a	b	c	d	e

Figure 4:13   *Birth and related expressions.*

Heir Designation and Other Preaccession Events

The Palenque texts contain many references to events that rulers-to-be performed or had done to them before they came to rule, and some of these were no doubt heir designation events. There are also a few references at other sites to pre-accession events. A sampling of these events is discussed below.[4]

The "deerhoof" event (Fig. 4:14a) is probably an heir designation event, although the Maya reading is still obscure. The decipherment of the flat hand verb, which occurs in several contexts, has been a problem, and over the years several readings have been proposed. *K'al* is the reading currently accepted. The distribution of the deerhoof glyph is very limited, and no reading has yet been determined for it. The deerhoof event was undergone by young boys who may later become rulers, e.g., K'an Hok' Chitam II (at age 12) and Akul Ah Nab III (at age 13). Interestingly, Hun Nal Ye (GI'), an important creator god in the Palenque cosmology texts (see Chapter 8), also underwent a deerhoof event when he was eight years old. Its significance in that context is also unclear.

In several presumed heir designation events, the expression includes words based on *och* (to enter), *och te* (to enter the tree), or *och tele(l)* (to enter the treeship). These expressions seem to be metaphors for entering into a special status, probably as heir-designate in the ruling lineage. For example, in Figure 4:14b, *och* is used as a verb, "to enter," and what was entered was a "Sprout Tree House," a metaphor for the ruling dynasty founder's lineage. In Figure 4:14c, the *och te* root is now a noun and is used with the flat hand holding a mirror. The sense of this whole expression is that the young Kan Balam "was placed in Entering-the-treeship," i.e., he entered

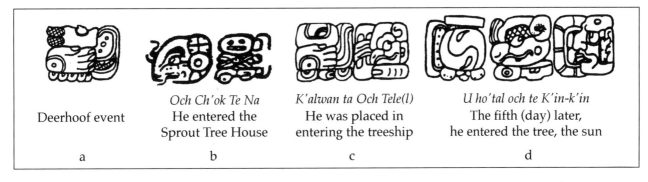

Deerhoof event	*Och Ch'ok Te Na* He entered the Sprout Tree House	*K'alwan ta Och Tele(l)* He was placed in entering the treeship	*U ho'tal och te K'in-k'in* The fifth (day) later, he entered the tree, the sun
a	b	c	d

Figure 4:14   *Preaccession events at Palenque.*

the ruling dynasty lineage. Apparently this event for Kan Balam lasted at least five days, because the text goes on to say that "five days later, he entered the Tree, the Sun" (Fig. 4:14d).

Another expression using the *och te* metaphor is shown in Figure 4:15a, which literally says, "he went as entering the treeship, the First (*ba*) Sprout," which probably means he entered the ruling lineage as the first or primary heir-designate. Another way of expressing attaining the status as First Sprout involves the *chum* seating verb (which we will discuss later) as shown in Figure 4:15b, which in English says, "He was seated in the First Sproutship."

Still another mode of expressing the presumed heir-designation of Kan-Balam II is suggestive of temple rituals. For example, in Figure 4:16a, a logograph for a temple is used in an expression which seems to say, "He was temple-introduced as Tree-enterer." This event was followed over a year later by another event represented by the *hubiy* verb, which can mean "to come down" (probably from the temple) into the "Enterer-treeship," i.e., the ruling dynasty lineage (Fig. 4:16b), or as the "Sprout Partition Person" (Fig. 4:16c). This last

U bah ta Och Tele(l) Ba Ch'ok
He went as entering the Treeship, the First Sprout

a

Chumwan ta Ba   Ch'oklel
He was seated in the First Sproutship

b

Figure 4:15   Preaccession expressions incorporating the terms ch'ok or ch'oklel.

Lem Ch'ulna ta Och Te
He was Temple-introduced as Tree-enterer

a

Hubiy ta Och Tele(l)
He came down in Enterer-treeship

b

Hubiy tikil Ch'ok tzuk
He came down as the Sprout Partition Person

c

Figure 4:16   Preaccession events that are presumably temple-related.

expression may imply some sort of political post involving the partitions of the kingdom. We will encounter the verb *hubiy* later in war contexts where it means to bring down or throw down in a military sense.

It's known from many contexts that bloodletting was an important part of a ruler's ritual life, so it is no surprise that there are statements that suggest rulers-to-be also underwent bloodletting rituals. On Caracol Stela 3, K'an II underwent a "first harvesting" when he was 5 years old, 25 years before his accession (Fig. 4:17a). This was done under the auspices (*u kahi*) of his father, and was no doubt an indicator of his destiny to rule. A similar event was ascribed to the ruler portrayed on the Hauberg Stela

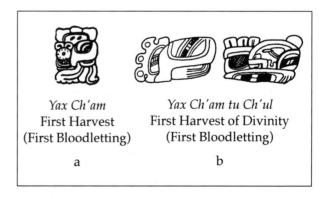

Yax Ch'am
First Harvest
(First Bloodletting)

a

Yax Ch'am tu Ch'ul
First Harvest of Divinity
(First Bloodletting)

b

Figure 4:17   First bloodlettings recorded on **a.** Caracol Stela 3 and **b.** the Hauberg Stela.

52 days before his accession, but since it was so close to the accession, it probably was a ritual associated with that event (Fig. 4:17b).

Finally, there are other pre-accession events written in the texts whose connection with accession is not certain. For example, as recorded on Stela 19 and other monuments at Yaxchilan, Shield Jaguar I of Yaxchilan captured his most heralded captive, *Ah Nik*, from an unknown site named *Man,* about 6 winals before his accession (Fig. 4:18). Perhaps this act was a requirement for Shield Jaguar's assumption of office, or maybe a prestigious sacrificial victim was required for the accession ritual itself. At Piedras Negras a *nawah* event, which was probably marriage, was done by (or to) Lady K'atun Ahaw in concert with Ruler 3-to-be just days before Ruler 3's predecessor, Ruler 2, died (Fig. 4:19). Whether this marriage(?) was a requirement for Ruler 3's accession is not known.

Lady K'atun Ahaw was from the site of *Man,* the home site of the prisoner *Ah Nik,* taken by Shield Jaguar of Yaxchilan about six years previously. These two events allow some insight into power politics of the time; thus the ruler of Yaxchilan captured an elite

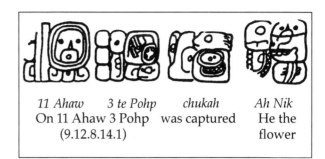

11 Ahaw	3 te Pohp	chukah	Ah Nik
On 11 Ahaw 3 Pohp		was captured	He the
(9.12.8.14.1)			flower

Figure 4:18   *The capture of* Ah Nik *as recorded on Yaxchilan Stela 19.*

person from *Man* a few years before a soon to-be ruler of Piedras Negras married an elite woman from the same site. This suggests that in the time frame of these events, Piedras Negras and Yaxchilan were probably on opposite sides of a conflict along the Usumacinta River. For an excellent analysis of this and other political relationships revealed in Classic Maya texts, see Schele and Grube (1994a,b, 1995a,b).

1 Kib 14 K'ank'in	nawah	Na K'atun Ahaw	Na Man Ahaw	ichnal	K'inich Yokibnal
(9.12.14.10.16)	was	Lady K'atun Ahaw	Lady Man Ahaw	accompanied	Ruler 3
	adorned			by	of Piedras Negras

Figure 4:19   *Presumed marriage of Lady K'atun Ahaw from Man to Ruler 3 of Piedras Negras as recorded on Piedras Negras Stela 3.*

Accession

Considering the importance of accession in the life of Maya polities, it is not surprising that the act was represented in a variety of ways in monumental inscriptions. One early form, found on the Yaxchilan lintels recording the accessions of early rulers, is almost pictographic in nature; the main sign appears to be a squatting or sitting lower body and legs (Fig. 4:20a). It is superfixed with an Ahaw symbol, and even though the Maya word(s) for the legged portion isn't known, the reading of the entire collocation must have included *Ahaw*. It is read in English as "he was seated as Ahaw." Later and somewhat similar sym-

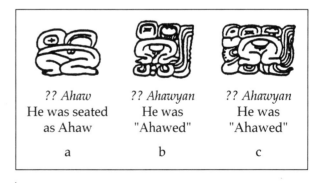

?? Ahaw	?? Ahawyan	?? Ahawyan
He was seated	He was	He was
as Ahaw	"Ahawed"	"Ahawed"
a	b	c

Figure 4:20   *Accession glyphs featuring representations of the lower body.*

bols have been described as "bottom-up" views of someone in the act of sitting (Fig. 4:20b,c). These two examples have the affix *yan(i)*, which is indicative of a positional verb, but also signifies a noun which has been converted into a verb. A possible reading for these forms is *ahawyan*, or "he was ahawed."

Another early form of the accession verb also apparently had pictographic origins. On a re-used Olmec jade, now in the Dumbarton Oaks collection, was inscribed a figure of a seated Maya lord with an accompanying inscription (Fig. 4:21). The two-glyph verb starts with a symbol that clearly resembles the torso and leg of the seated figure in the inscribed scene. It is followed by an early form of the Ahaw glyph (Fig. 4:22a). The phrase thus says

Figure 4:21   Reused Olmec Jade with an Early Mayan inscription in the Dumbarton Oaks Collection (drawn by Linda Schele).

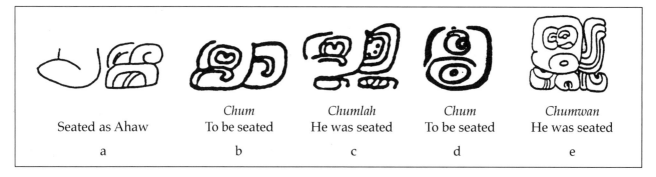

Seated as Ahaw	*Chum* To be seated	*Chumlah* He was seated	*Chum* To be seated	*Chumwan* He was seated
a	b	c	d	e

Figure 4:22   Accession glyphs based on the word chum.

"He was seated as Ahaw," which is exactly what the inscribed scene shows. Unfortunately, the inscribed text contains no date, but it probably dates to the very late Pre-Classic or Early Classic Period. A somewhat later piece, the Lieden Plaque, which has a Long Count date of 8.14.3.1.12, also has the same seating verb, still rather representively rendered. (Fig. 4:22b,c). These examples are obviously forerunners of the seating expression which is now known to be a logograph for the Maya word *chum*, which means "to be seated" (Fig. 4:22d). Usually the Late Classic

version of the word has the postfix *wan(i)*, characteristic of a positional verb as shown in Figure 4:22e, but it may also have as postfix *lah(a)*, another positional verb indicator. The logogram for *chum* often has an infixed phonetic complement *mu* indicating that the root ends in *m*, as in the examples in Figure 4:22d,e. Usually *chumwan* or *chumlah* is followed by the office into which the protagonist was seated. Some examples for "seating as Ahaw" are shown in Figure 4:23. In these examples, the *Ahaw* is terminated by *le*, or *lel(e)*. In Cholan, the *lel* suffix can change a real noun

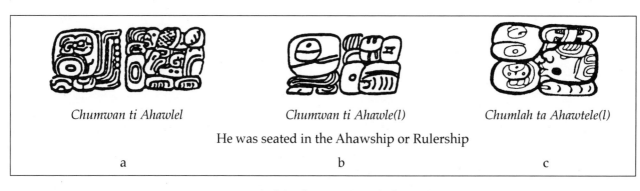

Chumwan ti Ahawlel	*Chumwan ti Ahawle(l)*	*Chumlah ta Ahawtele(l)*
	He was seated in the Ahawship or Rulership	
a	b	c

Figure 4:23   Accession expressions comprised of the chum *verb and* Ahawlel.

into an abstract one, so that when the *-lel* or *-le* suffix is attached to Ahaw, it changes the reading from Ahaw, lord or ruler, to Ahawship, lordship or rulership.

The *chum* expression can be used in a variety of other ways; for example, in Figure 4:24a, the phrase involves an important piece of clothing used in the accession ritual—the headband that a ruler put on (more about headbands later). In Figure 4:24b, the phrase involves seating on a jaguar throne, also an important symbol of rulership. The example in Figure 4:24c reminds us that this same *chum* verb was used in calendrics to indicate the beginning or the seating of a new month (Chapter 2).

The presentation of a special headband to the acceding ruler, or its closing on his head, was a highly important part of the accession ritual, and we have just encountered the "seated with headband" expression (Fig. 4:24a). There is another series of headband expressions for accession which use the "flathand" verb *k'al*, and these are used especially frequently at Palenque. A feature of these expres-

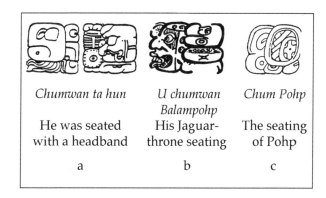

Chumwan ta hun	*U chumwan Balampohp*	*Chum Pohp*
He was seated with a headband	His Jaguar-throne seating	The seating of Pohp
a	b	c

Figure 4:24   *Seating expressions involving* chum.

sions is the multiple ways in which the word for headband, *hun*, is represented.[5] In some cases it is spelled out phonetically, using the upended frog as the syllable *hu*, as in Figure 4:25a. In other cases it is represented by a logograph, e.g., a tied knot, the

U k'al hun	*K'al sak hun tu bah*	*K'al sak hun tu bah*	*Iwal k'al sak hun tu bah*
He closed the headband	The white headband was closed for him	The white headband was closed for him	And then the white headband was closed for him
a	b	c	d

Figure 4:25   *Accession expressions employing the flat hand verb and a headband.*

God K head, or the dotted winik glyph (Fig. 4:25b–d). The headband is often described as a "white headband" (*sak hun*), as in Figure 4:25b–d. Most of the headband accession expressions are followed by *tu bah*, which means "for him/her," suggesting that the headband was put on the ruler by a second party in the accession ritual. Presentations of headbands are pictured in accession scenes on several carved monuments. Another group of accession expressions is based upon the so-called "toothache" glyph, which was the first recognized accession term (Fig. 4:26). This was from the brilliant work of Tatiana Prouskouriakoff (1960, 1961a). The essential element of these expressions is a verticle band topped by a tied knot. This figure is a logogram for the word *hok'*, which can mean "to tie", or "to exit." Both meanings

have relevance for accession: to tie can refer to the tying on of the headband, and to exit can refer to the coming out of a temple by a new ruler after his accession. The expression may appear alone, as in Figure 4:26a, associated with Ahaw as in Figure 4:26b, or with "Ahawship" terms we have seen with other kinds of accession expressions (Fig. 4:26c,d).

The last accession expression to be considered is based upon a title that we will encounter later, which simply reads Ahaw, or Ahawte, meaning Ahaw (Fig. 4:26e). There follows a series of verbs dealing with rituals that rulers and other elite persons engaged in during their lives and into their deaths. Although many of these words can be "read," the exact nature and the details of the event in many cases aren't known.

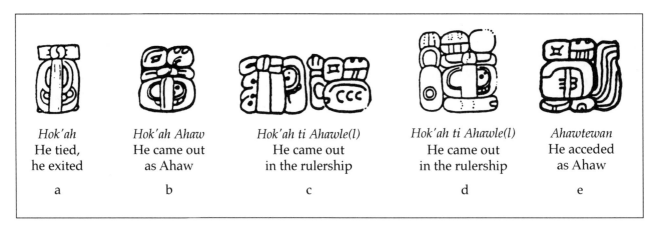

Hok'ah He tied, he exited	*Hok'ah Ahaw* He came out as Ahaw	*Hok'ah ti Ahawle(l)* He came out in the rulership	*Hok'ah ti Ahawle(l)* He came out in the rulership	*Ahawtewan* He acceded as Ahaw
a	b	c	d	e

Figure 4:26   Accession expressions based on Hok' *and* Ahaw.

Bloodletting, Scattering, Conjuring (Manifesting)

Over the years, several glyphs have been proposed as symbols for ritualistic bloodletting, a most important activity in the ritual lives of rulers. Appropriate Maya words have been found for some of these collocations. The main sign (T712) of the forms in Figure 4:27 is apparently a representation of an obsidian bloodletter, and it has been read as *ch'am*, which means "to harvest," or *ch'ab*, meaning "to sacrifice" (Fig. 4:27a). Whichever word it represents, the metaphorical meaning in the context of ritual activity in the inscriptional texts seems to be "to let blood." Two additional examples of this verb, which were affixed with *yax*, were given in the discussion of preaccession events. The meaning in those cases was "first harvesting/sacrificing," or "first bloodletting" (Fig. 4:27b). In Figure 4:27c is shown an example where the verb is used with the auxiliary, *u bah*, in a *ti* construction (Chapter 5). We

will see a similar expression using the T712 bloodletter as main sign when we discuss parentage statements.

The down-pointing scattering hand (T710) has presented problems in decipherment. Alone it is known to represent the syllable *ye* (Fig. 4:28a). There are many cases in which the hand is scattering something droplike, and this very image suggests that the verb is transitive (Fig. 4:28b,c). The object of the verb is what is being scattered, and in most cases there is an affixed pronoun *u* as the subject of the verb. The nature of the material being scattered has engendered much debate over the years. Variously it has been been proposed to be drops of water, drops of blood, seeds, or incense (copal). The argument is not yet completely settled—perhaps it is not always the same substance, but varies with the ritual being performed. Several proposals have been put forward for the Maya word(s) representing the hand that is scattering something. Currently the reading *chok*, a word

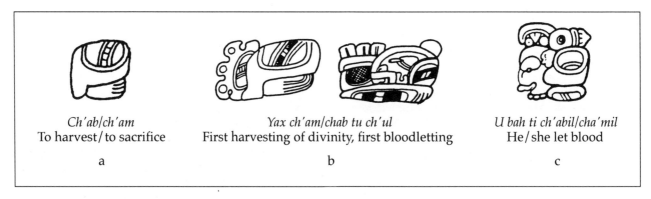

Ch'ab/ch'am To harvest/to sacrifice	*Yax ch'am/chab tu ch'ul* First harvesting of divinity, first bloodletting	*U bah ti ch'abil/cha'mil* He/she let blood
a	b	c

Figure 4:27   Bloodletting expressions based on T712.

Ye T710	*Chok* To scatter (drops)	*U chok ch'a(h)* He scattered drops	*U chok ch'a(h)* He scattered drops	*U chok ch'a(h)* He scattered drops
a	b	c	d	e

Figure 4:28   Scattering expressions.

which can mean "scattering" or "sprinkling," is accepted by some of the leading epigraphers, and that is the value used here. There are cases in which *ch'a*, which can mean drops, follows the hand as in Figure 4:28d, and in these cases it seems that drops are indeed indicated. The reading in this case would be *chok ch'a(h)*. Another rarely occurring expression which seems fully equivalent to the hand scattering event is shown in Figure 4:28e. This expression probably also reads *chok ch'a(h)*. Scattering rituals seem to occur especially on the dates of Period Endings. For several years the "fish-in-hand" glyph (Fig. 4:29a) was thought to represent a bloodletting expression, but it is now known that the root is *tzak*, which means "to manifest," or "to conjure up." It is usually followed by the name of the

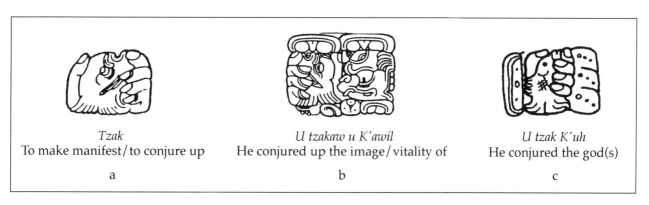

Tzak To make manifest / to conjure up	*U tzakaw u K'awil* He conjured up the image / vitality of	*U tzak K'uh* He conjured the god(s)
a	b	c

Figure 4:29   The "fish-in-hand" verb.

thing which is conjured up, for example a vision serpent, or a *way*, and then the name of the person doing the conjuring. Thus it is also one of the rare transitive verbs in the Maya inscriptional texts. In Figure 4:29b the head that follows the fish-in-hand represents *K'awil*, which is the name of a god associated with lineages, and a word for image, sustenance or vitality. In Figure 4:29c, the fish-in-hand is followed simply by *k'uh*, a word for god or divinity. It was usually the ruler who did these conjuring events—the ruler was the principal shaman in his domain.

To Receive/Display, To Dance, To Be Dressed, To Be Adorned, To Marry, His Wife, To Make a Contract

A collocation that at one time was thought to be an accession verb has as its main sign a left- facing open hand (T670) (Fig. 4:30a). This hand is now known to represent the word *ch'am*, which means "to receive," "to grasp," or "to display." It often appears with an *Ahaw* face in the hand as in Figure 4:30b. What is displayed or grasped may be shown in the hand as in Figure 4:30c, or it may appear to the right

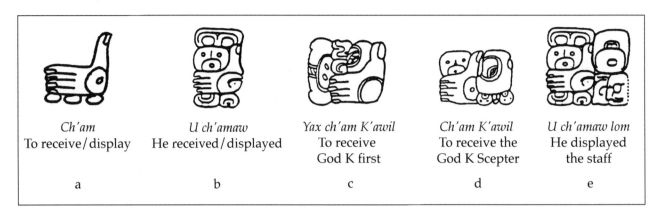

Ch'am	U ch'amaw	Yax ch'am K'awil	Ch'am K'awil	U ch'amaw lom
To receive/display	He received/displayed	To receive God K first	To receive the God K Scepter	He displayed the staff
a	b	c	d	e

Figure 4:30   *Verbs based on ch'am (T670), to grasp, receive, or display.*

(Fig. 4:30d,e). The object associated with the hand is sometimes a God K symbol (Fig. 4:28c,d), and God K's connection with rulership explains the early association of the hand plus God K with accession. But it is now known that *ch'am* rituals can occur on occasions other than accession.

A relatively recent change has also occurred in the decipherment of a verb whose main sign is represented by T516 (Fig. 4:31a,b). A few years ago it was thought to represent another general verb similar in function to the T757 verb, *u bah*. Research by Nikolai Grube (1992) has subsequently shown that T516 can be a logograph for the word *ak'ot*, which is a verbal root meaning "to dance" (Fig. 4:31c,d). T516 is often affixed with a T103 sign, *ta*, to reinforce the *t* in *ak'ot* (Fig. 4:31c-e). Some monuments have texts containing the *ak'ot* verb associated with carved scenes showing a person with raised foot suggestive of dancing. The glyph following the verb, introduced by the preposition *ti*, designates the kind of dance or the object used in the

dance. For example, in Figure 4:31d, the *ak'ot* verb is followed by a collocation reading *ti xukpi*. *Xukpi* is a kind of bird, and indeed the scene acconmpanying the text shows two personages holding bird crested-staffs in their hands (Yaxchilan Lintel 3). In Figure 4:31e, the dance was done with some kind of macaw figure.

Nawah (Fig. 4:32a) is a verb that means "to be adorned," or "to be dressed." It is used in a variety of circumstances, for example, prisoners may undergo *nawah* before they are sacrificed. It is also used in contexts where a marriage or betrothal, or preparations for these events, seem appropriate. *Tupah* (Fig. 4:32b), a rarely occurring verb in the inscriptions, has a related meaning, and seems to be used in situations where ritual dressing is indicated. *Yatan* (Fig. 4:32c), also a rarely occurring glyph, can be a verb meaning "he/she was married," or a possessed noun meaning "his wife." Possibly related to betrothal or marriage is *makah* (Fig. 4:32d), which can mean "to make a contract."

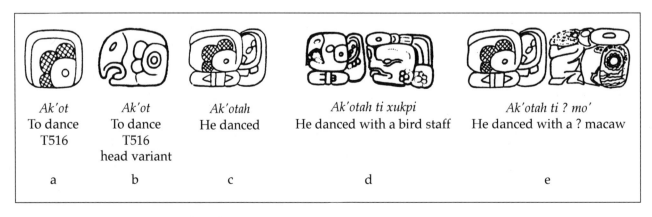

Ak'ot	Ak'ot	Ak'otah	Ak'otah ti xukpi	Ak'otah ti ? mo'
To dance T516	To dance T516 head variant	He danced	He danced with a bird staff	He danced with a ? macaw
a	b	c	d	e

Figure 4:31   *The dance verb, ak'ot (T516).*

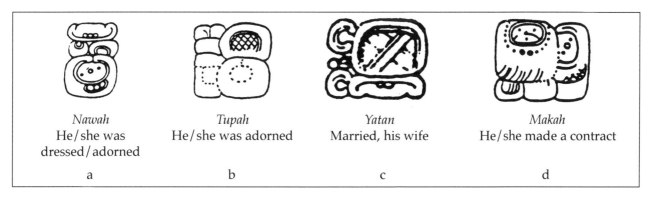

Nawah
He/she was
dressed/adorned

a

Tupah
He/she was adorned

b

Yatan
Married, his wife

c

Makah
He/she made a contract

d

Figure 4:32   Glyphs meaning to be dressed, to be adorned, to be married, his wife, and to make a contract.

Anniversary Events and Period Endings

One of the most common categories of events recorded in the inscriptional texts is the nota-tion of anniversaries of important events in the lives of elite persons, and Period Endings (Chapter 2). A common verb used in these expressions is a right-facing hand with a jewel or bauble hanging at the end of the fingers. The verb often has a *yi* verbal suffix,

Homi
It was completed

a

Homiah holhun K'atun
Was completed 15 k'atuns

b

Homi u hun K'atun ta Ahawlel
Was completed the first k'atun of rulership

c

Homi
It was completed

d

Homiah u hotun ta Ahawle
Was completed the fifth tun of Ahawship

e

Tzutzah
It expired,
it was finished

f

K'al tun
The tun was closed,
the stone was set

g

U k'al tun
He closed the tun,
he set the stone

h

U k'al yax tun
He closed the first tun

i

Figure 4:33   Anniversary and period-ending expressions.

and it has been proposed that the word represented is either *homi* or *tzutz*, which means "was completed" or "was ended" (Fig. 4:33a). Figure 4:33b is an example of the use of this verb in Period Endings—here the completion 15 k'atuns. An anniversary event, the completion of a first k'atun of rulership, is noted in Figure 4:33c. A rarer verb whose main sign is an upside down bat head, usually with a *yi* affix, also probably represents the word *homi* (Fig. 4:33d), and is used to indicate anniversaries as in Figure 4:33e, where five tuns of rulership is recorded.

Tzutzah (Fig. 4:33f), based on the verbal root *tzutz*, meaning "to finish" or "to expire," is also used to note the end of periods of time. Another important completion expression is composed of the flat hand verb, *k'al*, holding a *tun* sign with a *ni* phonetic complement (Fig. 4:33g–i). Since *tun* can refer to the Maya 360-day year, this expression has usually been translated as "closing of the tun." But *tun* can also mean "stone," and there are some contexts where "setting of the stone" seems a more likely reading.

Tz'ap To set up/erect	*U tz'apaw tun* He set up the stone	819-Day Count Verb It was set up	*Och k'ak'* Fire entered	*Och k'ak'* Fire entered
a	b	c	d	e

Figure 4:34   *Verbs meaning to erect or to set up and to dedicate.*

The Setting Up of Monuments and Dedication Events

The Maya scribe possessed an arsenal of expressions for the variety of rituals used by the Classic Maya elite in the dedications of structures, parts of structures, plazas, stelae, altars, and other monuments (Schele 1990b). Several of these have been deciphered in recent years. One of the first to be understood is an expression for the erection/dedication of stelae, whose root is *tz'ap* (Fig. 4:34a,b) which literally means "to plant" or "to stick in the ground." It is one of the relatively few transitive verbs encountered in the inscriptional texts, so following the verb is usually the name of the object erected, and then the name of the person responsible for erecting it. (We will see a complete clause illustrating *tz'ap* as a transitive verb in Chapter 5, Fig. 5:23.) The date accompanying the *tz'ap* statement is usually the dedicatory date of the monument. The "819-day count" verb (Chapter 2) appears in contexts where it is behaving like the *tz'ap* verbal root, and must also mean "to set up" or "to put in place," although a Maya word equivalent has not yet been determined (Fig.4:34c). A verb used for the dedication of buildings consists of the *och/ok* verb (rattlesnake tail segments), sometimes

with a chi phonetic complement, prefixed to a symbol for fire (Fig.4:34d,e). It is read as *och k'ak'*, meaning "fire entered," and this reading suggests that vessels containing burning materials (such as incense) were carried into a building being dedicated.

The "T79" dedication verbs constitute a modest group of dedication expressions featuring the T79 affix. These are associated with the dedication of buildings, plazas, and monuments (Fig. 4:35a-d). David Stuart has recently suggested that the T79 affix stands for the word *pat*, meaning "to form" or "to make," but other epigraphers see it as one of the signs in the *k'a/k'al* group. A variety of components can follow the T79, and some of them resemble houses.

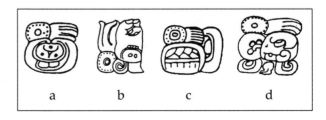

| a | b | c | d |

Figure 4:35   *Dedication expressions based on T79.*

? Nah House dedication	*Hoy/Huy* To prepare / to make sacred	*Hoy/Huy* To prepare / to make sacred	*Hoy Wite Nah* To make sacred the Wite House
a	b	c	d

Figure 4:36   Miscellaneous dedication verbs.

A collocation comprised of symbols resembling a bowl with a plate (*lak*) as lid and a *k'in* sign on the bowl body constitutes another dedication expression (Fig. 4:36a). This arrangement is probably simulating a lip-to-lip cache, and the statements using this glyph are presumably indicating the deposition of such caches as part of building dedication rituals. No satisfactory Maya word has yet been determined for these expressions. The God N verb (Fig. 4:36b,c), which is a common feature of the Primary Standard Sequence found on Classic Maya ceramics (MacLeod 1990), also appears as a dedicatory verb in inscriptional texts. It has been read as *hoy* or *huy*, which can mean "to prepare" or "to make sacred," although not all epigraphers accept this reading. As in the ceramic texts, the God N verb has a substitute, which is a step-shaped glyph, also possibly reading *hoy* or *huy* (Fig.4:36d).

Dedication verbs are often followed by glyphs designating the kind of object dedicated, the name of the object, a name closure phrase, and the owner of the object, not necessarily in that order. An example employing a fire dedication verb is shown in Figure 4:37.

Och k'ak' Fire entered (dedication)	*Ox- ? na* name of structure	*U ch'ul k'aba* is its divine name	*yotot* it is the house of	*Hoy(?) Ch'ul Na* Precious Companion Lady	*Na Sak Chanyan* Lady White Snake(?)

Figure 4:37   Dedicatory clause with a fire dedication verb (Yaxchilan Lintel 56).

War and Related Events

The old image of the Classic Maya as peaceful people concerned primarily with ritual and calendrics has been shattered in recent years in part because of the developments in decipherment which show that inscriptional texts often tell of wars, conquests, prisoners, sacrifices, and the like. One of the early recognized glyphs sometimes associated with war is the so-called Venus sign, also called the "star" glyph. The full Venus glyph occurs in the texts accompanying the Venus tables in the Dresden Codex (Fig. 4:38a), and it also occurs in the inscriptional texts, for example on Altar 21 of Caracol, but it is rare (Fig. 4:38b). More common in the inscriptional texts are three types of Venus glyphs: the star-over-earth, star-over-shell, and the star plus site glyph (Fig. 4:38c–e). The dates associated with these inscriptional Venus glyphs are often dates of war events and/or dates of significant positions of the planet Venus, such as first appearance as evening star, or maximum elongation as evening star. In those cases where toponyms for specific sites are mentioned, as in Figure 4:38e, war was no doubt made on or at that site. Further discussion of the astronomical and the war implications of "star" glyphs is given in Chapter 7, "Glyphs and

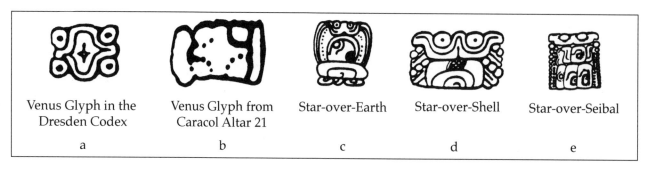

Venus Glyph in the Dresden Codex	Venus Glyph from Caracol Altar 21	Star-over-Earth	Star-over-Shell	Star-over-Seibal
a	b	c	d	e

Figure 4:38   Venus glyphs from the Dresden Codex and inscriptional texts.

Astronomy." It is not yet certain what Maya word is represented by the Venus/star glyph, although some scholars have proposed *ek'*, a word for "star."

Chukah (Fig. 4:39a,b) is a relatively common verb meaning "was captured." It is a passive verb, and is followed by the name of the person captured as in Figure 4:39c. The agent who does the capturing is usually named in a statement immediately following, which may be an *u kahi* statement, meaning "he caused it to be done" (see earlier discussion under General Verbs), or an *u bak* statement (Fig.

4:39d,e; Fig. 4:40a). *U bak* means "his bone," "his captive," or "he is the captive of," and it serves to connect the names of the captive and captor (Fig. 4:40a). Although titles will be dealt with later in this chapter, one type of title will be considered here because it is related to captives and contains the term *bak*, bone/captive. This is the "count of captives" title that was described by David Stuart (1985a). These titles occur in the name/title strings of rulers and other elite persons, and take the form, *ah* - number - *bak* (Fig. 4:40b–d). They are usually rendered in English as

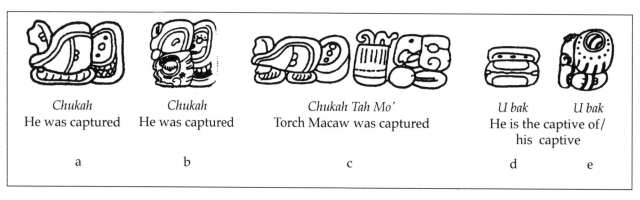

Chukah He was captured	*Chukah* He was captured	*Chukah Tah Mo'* Torch Macaw was captured	*U bak* *U bak* He is the captive of/ his captive
a	b	c	d e

Figure 4:39   Capture and captive expressions.

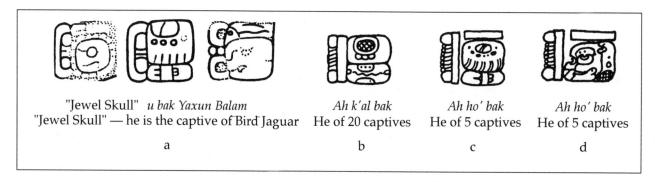

"Jewel Skull" *u bak Yaxun Balam* "Jewel Skull" — he is the captive of Bird Jaguar	*Ah k'al bak* He of 20 captives	*Ah ho' bak* He of 5 captives	*Ah ho' bak* He of 5 captives
a	b	c	d

Figure 4:40   Prisoner expressions employing the term *bak*.

"He of X captives." Another group of captive-related expressions contains the term *u chan*, which means "his captor," or "his guardian," followed by the name of the captive (Fig. 4:41). Recent studies of these expressions suggest that the relationship of captor and captive may have had a protector quality to it, i.e., once a captive was taken, the captor acted as his guardian prior to the captive's probable demise as a sacrificial victim.

In recent analyses of Classic Maya warfare by Linda Schele and Nikolai Grube, the verb *hubi* received a lot of attention (Schele and Grube 1994a,b). We have encountered this verb before in pre-accession rites, where it was used to describe the "bringing down" or "coming down" from a temple/pyramid of an heir designate. In war contexts it is used in a destructive sense and means "to throw down" or "to tear down" (Fig. 4:42a). It is usually composed of three elements, *hu*, *bu*, and *yi*—the arguments for the readings of these elements are reviewed in detail in Schele and Grube (ibid.). When used as a war verb, *hubi* is usually followed by the name of the thing or person thrown down, e.g., *u tok' pakal* (his flint shield), a metaphor for a war banner (Fig. 4:42b). Apparently an objective in battle was

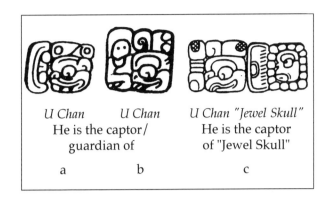

Figure 4:41   U chan *expressions.*

the throwing down and capturing of an enemy's *tok' pakal*. The name of a person or place may also follow *hubi*, suggesting that buildings or walls of cities were destroyed in battle, and that elite persons could be "thrown down" and captured or killed (Fig. 4:42c,d). From its use and contexts the verb is intransitive and passive.

Lok' and *xan*, recently deciphered by Nikolai

Figure 4:42   Hubi *expressions meaning to tear down or to throw down.*

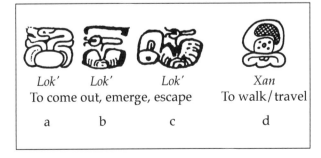

Figure 4:43   *The verbs,* lok', *to escape, and* xan, *to walk.*

Grube, are verbs also associated with war related events (Schele and Grube 1994a,b). The logograph for the intransitive verb *lok'* consists of a snake emerging from a split shell (Fig. 4:43a–c). Although a snake or part of a snake sometimes represents the word *chan*, and a shell can represent the syllable *yi*, here in combination they constitute a logograph for *lok'*, which means "to come out," "to emerge," or "to escape." The word appears both in the inscriptional texts (Fig. 4:43a) and in the codices (Fig. 4:43b,c), and it was occurrences in the Dresden Codex which had a prefix *lo* that provided an important clue to the word represented (Fig. 4:43c). The verb sometimes

Ch'ak To be axed / destroyed	*Ch'akah* He was axed / destroyed	*Iwal ch'akah Yomop* Then Yomop was axed / destroyed	*Ch'akah* It was axed / destroyed	*Ch'ak* The Axer (a title)
a	b	c	d	e

Figure 4:44   Expressions using the ch'ak *verb.*

follows a star-war event against a place, and in these cases it appears that as a result of the war, someone emerged or escaped. Several of the occurrences in the inscriptions are found in Dos Pilas texts. *Xan* is a rarely occurring verb meaning "to travel" or "to walk," and it is also related to war events. It is represented by a logograph consisting of an *ek'* sign infixed with the sign for the syllable *bi* (Fig. 4:43d). The example shown has a *ni* sign as phonetic complement. There are occurrences in texts on ceramics which also have a prefixed *xa* sign as a phonetic complement. The occurrence of these two phonetic complements is strong evidence that the reading is indeed *xan*. Like *lok'*, *xan* can occur in texts following a star-war event, and it presumably represents the departure of a ruler as a result of the war.

Finally, there is the verb *ch'ak*, deciphered by Jorge Orejel (1990) and Nikolai Grube, which means "to be decapitated" or "to be destroyed." In its logographic form, it is rather pictographic, since the main element is an axe (Fig. 4:44a). Usually the axe has a *ka* sign as a phonetic complement. The verb appears both in the inscriptional texts (Fig. 4:44a, c-e) and in the codices (Fig. 4:44b). The name of the person or place axed or destroyed usually follows the verb as in Figure 4:44c. In at least one case, the verb is spelled out phonetically (Fig. 4:44d) in a context that suggests that the center of Palenque (and its buildings ?) was torn down. *Ch'ak* can also appear as a title where it probably means "The Axer" or " The Destroyer" (Fig. 4:44e).

Death and Burial

The Maya scribe had almost as many expressions for declaring the deaths of elite persons as he had for their accessions. One of the most common of these is the so-called "winged-shell-Ahaw-Ik'" phrase (Fig. 4:45a), which is now

known to read something like, "died his white maize flower," as a metaphor for death. It is composed of two elements; *k'ay* or *u k'ay*, a verb meaning "to die," or "to be ended," and a grouping containing *u sak niknal* (his white maize flower). The latter element may be a metaphor for soul or spirit. Another metaphorical expression, first studied in the text on the sarcophagus lid of the tomb of the great Pakal of Palenque, contains the elements *och bih*, which literally means "he entered the road" (Fig. 4:45b,c). The road is no doubt the road to Xibalba (the underworld), and entering this road is a metaphor for death. In these examples, the *och* is represented by rattlesnake tail segments as we saw in dedication expressions also utilizing the verb *och*. In a more recently recognized form of *och bih*, the *och* is represented by a hand holding an atlatl (Fig. 4:45d). Another expression utilizing the hand/atlatl form of *och*, combines *och* with *ha'* (water), and this means literally "he entered the water," presumably referring to the primordial sea (Fig. 4:45e). This also is a metaphor for death. Other death expressions include glyphs that represent skulls and read *kimi* (*chami* in Chol) meaning "he died" (Fig. 4:45f,g), and *u bah ti waynal*, "he goes to a sleeping place," or "he became a nagual" (Fig. 4:45h).

The last death expression to be considered is another metaphor, this time involving the accession headband. This death statement (Fig. 4:46) says "the white headband was opened"—thus the headband was presumably removed from a ruler's head when he died, and that action served as a symbol for the ruler's death.

In contrast to the array of death expressions, only two are so far known for burial, and these are relatively rare. The more common verbal root, *muk*, was deciphered by Peter Mathews (1977). It is usually formed by the combination of *mu* and *ka* signs, and it means "to be buried" or "to be interred." The collocation usually seen is the completive, intransi-

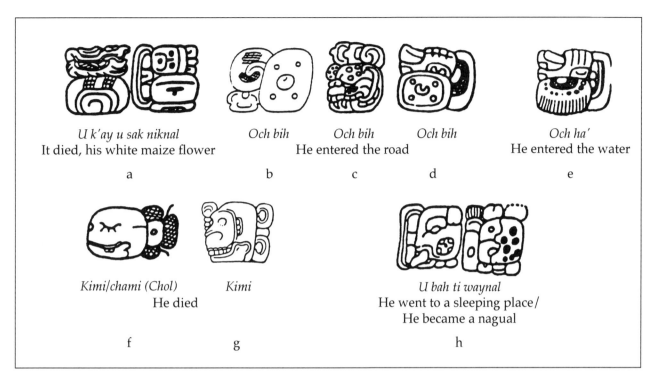

Figure 4:45 Expressions for death.

tive, passive form *mukah*, equivalent to "he was buried" or "he was interred" (Fig. 4:47a,b). Sometimes *mukah* is followed by a toponym, which names the place of burial. For example, in Figure 4:47c, the burial place of Ruler 3 of Piedras Negras is said to be *Ho Hanab Witz*, "Five Flower Mountain," possibly the name of one of the pyramids at the site. Related to the verb is the noun *muknal*, which is based upon the same root, and means "burial place" (Fig. 4:47d). Another recently recognized verb meaning "to bury" or "to cover" is based on the root *but'*, and it is transitive in the form so far observed (Fig. 4:47e).

Hamali u sak hun
His white headband was opened

Figure 4:46 Opening the headband as a metaphor for the death of a ruler.

Figure 4:47 Words pertaining to burial.

Sculpturing

Finally, there is a large number of examples of short statements written on stone monuments that begin with the enigmatic "lu-bat" glyph (Fig. 4:48a,b) (Stuart 1986). As indicated by the nickname, two of the primary components of the collocation are a bat head and a *lu* sign, usually infixed within the bat head (Fig. 4:48a), but sometimes it occurs as an affix (Fig. 4:48b). There is also a *yu* (T61) prefix. The collocation is followed by names/titles of the presumed sculptor of the monument on which it is found. From the elements present, a logical reading of the complete glyph would be *yuxul*, but it may be more complicated than that. In

any event, the contexts imply a reading, "he is the sculptor," or "his sculpture." Piedras Negras Stela 14 has several examples of these statements, implying that several artists worked on the carving of this monument. One of these is shown in Figure 4:48c.

Most of the verbs discussed above pertain primarily to important activities in the lives of the Classic Maya rulers and other elite. In recent years many other verbs have been deciphered that deal with more prosaic actions, e.g., to open, to close, to arrive, to say, to see, etc. Table 4:2 contains a listing of many of these verbs. Additional examples will be found in supplements to the first edition of this volume (Harris 1993, 1994).

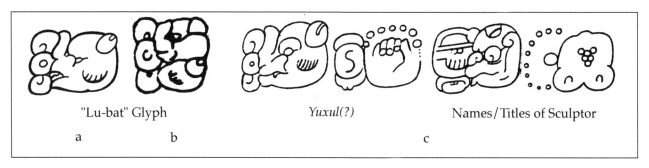

"Lu-bat" Glyph   *Yuxul(?)*   Names/Titles of Sculptor

a   b   c

Figure 4:48   The "lu-bat" glyph in sculptors' signatures.

RELATIONSHIP GLYPHS.

In a landmark paper on the decipherment of codex hieroglyphic texts published in 1955, Yuri Knorozov proposed a reading for a collocation in the Dresden Codex (Fig. 4:49) that implied a husband-wife relationship (Knorozov 1955, p. 124, table III, entry 18). Although his Maya word equivalency for the collocation was incorrect, this was the first relationship expression discovered in the Maya corpus. In 1977 Chris Jones pointed out a consistent pattern of glyphs in Tikal texts preceding the names of the presumed parents of Tikal Rulers A, B, & C, implying that these introductory glyphs designated child-parent relationships of some sort (Jones 1977). For example, in the Lintel 3 text from Temple I at Tikal, the sequences shown in Figure 4:50 follow the name of Ruler A, and they name his mother and father. The sequences begin with introductory glyphs, but at the time decipherment had not progressed sufficiently far for Maya words to be assigned. They turned out to be parentage designators. Later, Linda Schele and Peter Mathews found additional parentage expressions in the inscriptions of many other sites, and further introductory glyphs were recognized (1983).

Together these reports were the first recognitions of a very important series of collocations, the relationship glyphs. Subsequently, additional examples of relationship designators have been recognized, and currently about 15 are fairly well understood. The recognition of these expressions has allowed the establishment of familial relationships within the ruling families of particular sites. In some cases relationship glyphs point to connections between families of different sites, suggesting political ties between them. There follows a discussion of some of the relationships so far discovered and their Maya word equivalents if known.

Figure 4:49   A collocation reading yatan, *"his wife" (Dresden Codex, p. 19).*

Table 4:2. Miscellaneous Verbs

Huly
(hu-li-ya)
To arrive

U Hul
(u-hu-lu)
He arrived

Hulah
(hu-li-ah)
To have come

Tal
(ta-ll)
To arrive

Takah
(ta-ki-ah)
To have come

Hamali
(ha-ma-li-yi)
It was opened

U K'al
(u-k'a-li)
He closed

Tzutzah
(tzu-tza-ah)
It was closed

Tzutzah
(tzu-tza-ah)
It was closed

Mak
(ma-ka)
To close

Pas
(pa-sa)
To open

Mak Pas
(ma-ka-pa-sa)
Closed & opened

Yak'wa
(ya-k'a-wa)
He gave it

Yak'wa
(ya-k'v-wa)
He gave it

Mitzil
(mi-tzi-li)
To invoke,
to appear

Kuchtah
(kuch-ta-ah)
It was carried

Och

To enter

Ahal
(ah-ha-li)
To create,
to defeat

Petihi
(pet-hi-ya)
To turn,
to rotate

Yatah
(ya-ta-hi)
To be
companioned

Yalah
(ya-la-ah)
He said,
he hurled

Hal

To say, to
make manifest

Yilah
(yi-il-ah)
He saw, he
witnessed

Susah
(su-sa-ah)
It was cut up,
it was rasped

Lah
(la-ah)
To end,
to finish

Introductory glyph | Ruler A's Mother's names and titles

Introductory glyph | Ruler A's Father's names and titles

Figure 4:50   Parentage statements from Temple I Lintel 3 from Tikal.

Parentage

Parentage expressions are the most widely used and probably the most important relationship expressions so far recognized. When parentage is given in texts, generally both mother and father are given, although sometimes only one, usually the father, is recorded. When both are given, the mother is most often named first. The typical pattern begins with the names/titles of the child, followed by a child-of-mother glyph, the names/titles of the mother, a child-of-father glyph, and finally the names/titles of the father. The text of Yaxchilan Hieroglyphic Stairway 3, Step IV-tread records the parentage of Shield Jaguar I of Yaxchilan, and is a typical example (Fig.

4:51). Several expressions designating parentage are now known in the inscriptions. We have already encountered some in the examples above. In Figure 4:52a–f are several examples of child-of-mother expressions. A common one is based on the verb root *tan*, meaning to be cherished. In the parentage glyph, the root is prefixed with a form of *u*, and *hun* (one), which together with the *tan*, reads *u hun tan*, he/she is the cherished one (Fig. 4:52a). Another rather common form is *yal*, which translates "her child" (Fig. 4:52b), and this is apparently also the reading of several other collocations that feature a main sign consisting of the T670 hand holding one of several figures (Fig. 4:52c–f). Finally, in the mother category, is a collocation consisting of a bat head

Itzam Balam
Shield Jaguar

yal
child of mother

Na Pakal
Lady Pakal

Na Na Yaxchilan Ahaw
Great Lady, Yaxchilan Lord

U nikil
child of father

Kan K'atun Ahaw
Four K'atun Lord

Ah Wak Tun
He of Six Stones

Yaxun Balam
Bird Jaguar

Ch'ul Yaxchilan Ahaw
Divine Yaxchilan Lord

Kalomte
Kalomte

Figure 4:51   Parentage of Shield Jaguar I from the Yaxchilan Hieroglyphic Stairway 3, Step IV Text.

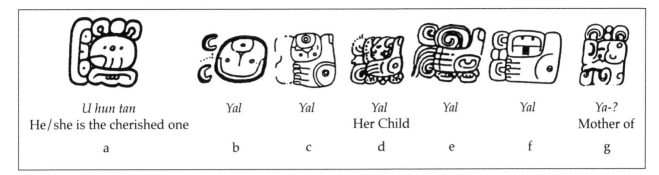

U hun tan	Yal	Yal	Yal	Yal	Yal	Ya-?
He/she is the cherished one			Her Child			Mother of
a	b	c	d	e	f	g

Figure 4:52   Child-of-mother expressions.

with emanations from the mouth and prefixed with *ya* (Fig. 4:52g). The Maya reading for this grouping has not yet been established, but by context it must mean mother of.

The most common expression performing the child-of-father function is based upon an Ahaw face, which is a logograph for the word *nik/nich*, meaning "flower." *Nik* is prefixed with a form of *u*, and usually there is a *li* suffix (Fig. 4:53a,b). Altogether this reads *u nikil*, which literally means "he is the flower of." Often the Ahaw face has emanations from the top, probably smoke, and this glyph used to be called "decorated Ahaw" (Fig. 4:53b). Another important relationship glyph used for "child-of-father" is based on the T712 verb, which means "to harvest" (Fig. 4:53c,d). Recall that T712 apparently represents an obsidian bloodletter, and its use in a parentage expression probably implies blood lineage. In the parentage relationship, T712 is usually preceded by *u bah*, or sometimes *u lot*, and these expressions can be translated as "he goes as the harvest of," or "he is received(?) as the harvest of," metaphors for "he is the child of." David Stuart has identified another child-of-father designator, the *yunen* glyph (Fig. 4:53e), which is relatively rare (Stuart 1985c).

As just discussed, the T712-derived designations are usually employed as child-of-father expressions as we saw in the Tikal Temple I Lintel 3 example above, but they are sometimes used to designate child-of-mother as well. The text on Yaxchilan Stela 7 contains such an expression for designating the mother of Shield Jaguar II (Fig. 4:54).

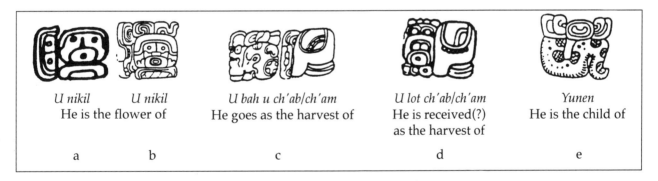

U nikil	U nikil	U bah u ch'ab/ch'am	U lot ch'ab/ch'am	Yunen
He is the flower of		He goes as the harvest of	He is received(?) as the harvest of	He is the child of
a	b	c	d	e

Figure 4:53   Child-of-father expressions.

U bah ch'am	Names/titles	Na Chak Kimi	Na Sahal
He goes as the harvest of		Lady Great Skull	Lady Sahal

Figure 4:54   Child-of-mother expression for Shield Jaguar II from the Yaxchilan Stela 7 Text.

Other Familial Relationships

The meanings of the parentage expressions we've just examined were initially identified primarily by their positions in texts, because they occur between the name of a person and the names of other persons presumed to be parents. Most of these terms were recognized over ten years ago. More recently, another level of familial relationships has been recognized based largely on the phonetic readings of glyphs also occurring in likely positions for relationship glyphs (Fig. 4:55). Major contributors to the decipherment of these examples have been David Stuart (1989b), Linda Schele, and Barbara MacLeod. *Yitah* was originally proposed to mean "sibling" in the extended family sense, but it is now gen-

erally thought to mean "companion" (Fig. 4:55a). *Itz'i* or *itz'in* is a term for "younger brother," shown in the possessed form in Figure 4:55b. The *i* in *itz'i* is represented in the examples shown in Figure 4:55c,e,h by T679 (also read as *iwal* in some contexts). In Figure 4:55d, the *i* is represented by a graphic sign comprised of a vulture plucking out the eye of a jaguar. *Suku* means "older brother" (Fig. 4:55f), and *yichan* is a rarely occurring term meaning "mother's brother" (Fig. 4:55i). All these terms can be used with one another or in concert with other titles to form complex designators as in Figure 4:55e,g,h. Finally, there is the term for wife, *yatan*, which as mentioned above, was recognized many years ago by Knorozov as a relationship glyph in the Dresden Codex. It has also been found in inscriptional texts (Fig. 4:55j).

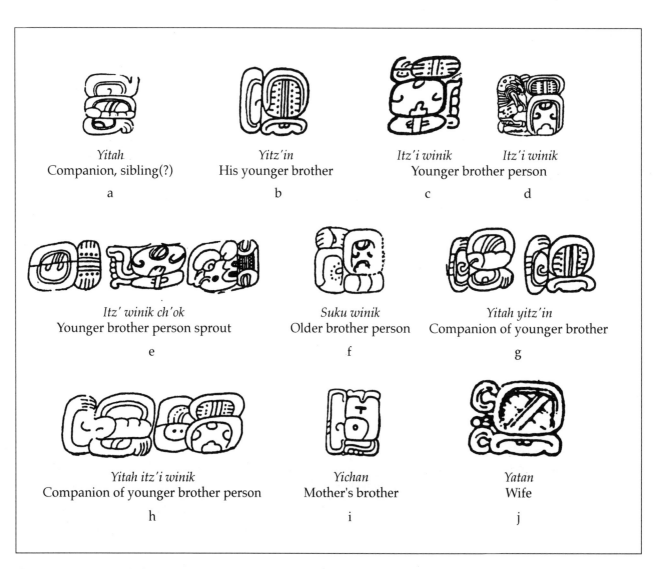

Yitah
Companion, sibling(?)
a

Yitz'in
His younger brother
b

Itz'i winik
Younger brother person
c

Itz'i winik
Younger brother person
d

Itz' winik ch'ok
Younger brother person sprout
e

Suku winik
Older brother person
f

Yitah yitz'in
Companion of younger brother
g

Yitah itz'i winik
Companion of younger brother person
h

Yichan
Mother's brother
i

Yatan
Wife
j

Figure 4:55   *Familial expressions.*

TITLES

One of the largest categories of glyphs in the inscriptions comprises names and titles for rulers and members of the ruling families. Of this group, titles constitute a major portion, and several categories of titles are discussed below. Some titles can be held by both men and women; when carried by women, they are often preceded by *na* (meaning woman or lady), but not always. Although Maya words for many titles have been determined, the exact significance of some of them remains obscure. The relatively long string of names/titles for Bird Jaguar IV shown in Fig-ure 4:56 is typical. As in many examples, this one begins with the name of the person, *Yaxun Balam*, or Bird Jaguar. We have seen the first two titles before in the discussion of war events: *U K'al Bak*, "He of 20 Captives," and *U Chan Ah Uk*, "He is the Captor/Guardian of *Ah Uk*." Then follows the title, *Ox K'atun Ahaw*, "The Three K'atun Ruler." The next two glyphs are the two Yaxchilan Emblem Glyphs, and the string ends with *Bakab*, a title frequently carried by rulers, and one that is often the final item in a name/title string. The last four titles in this example will be discussed further below. Parentage data, if given, usually follows the names and titles.

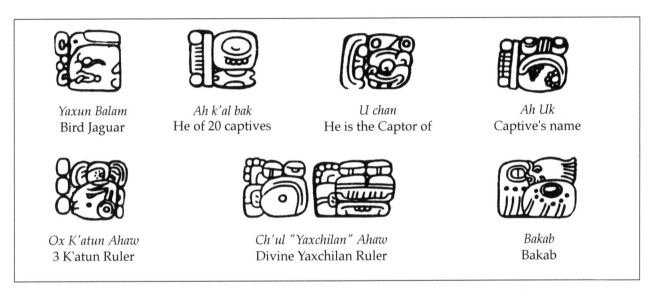

| *Yaxun Balam* Bird Jaguar | *Ah k'al bak* He of 20 captives | *U chan* He is the Captor of | *Ah Uk* Captive's name |

| *Ox K'atun Ahaw* 3 K'atun Ruler | *Ch'ul "Yaxchilan" Ahaw* Divine Yaxchilan Ruler | *Bakab* Bakab |

Figure 4:56   Names and titles for Bird Jaguar IV of Yaxchilan from the text on Yaxchilan Lintel 2.

One of the most important titles is *Ahaw*, which means "Ruler" or "Lord." It is carried by rulers at most sites, by other members of the ruling family, and in some cases by heads of non-ruling elite families. Some of the most frequently occurring *Ahaw* titles are logographs. For example, in Figure 4:57a, the figure is a representation of a young lord's profile; he is wearing a headband, one of the symbols of royal status, and he has an *Ahaw* figure on his fore-head. Another common logograph for *Ahaw* comprises a vulture head with an *Ahaw* face or a Jester God figure on the forehead (Fig. 4:57b,c). These also usually wear the *Ahaw* headband. Such logographs often have phonetic complements, which give hints

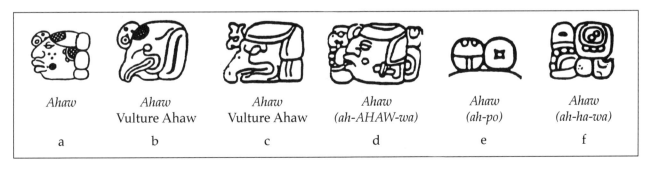

| *Ahaw* | *Ahaw* Vulture Ahaw | *Ahaw* Vulture Ahaw | *Ahaw* (ah-AHAW-wa) | *Ahaw* (ah-po) | *Ahaw* (ah-ha-wa) |
| a | b | c | d | e | f |

Figure 4:57   Glyphs representing Ahaw.

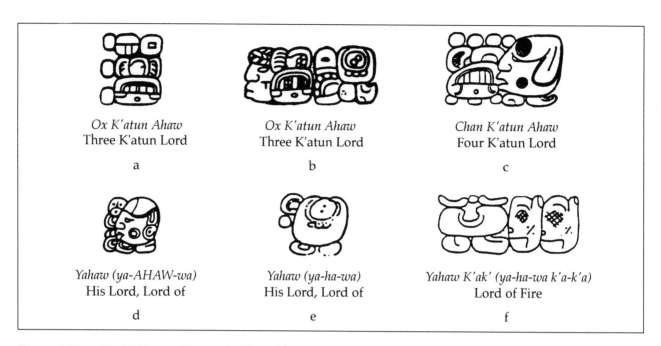

Ox K'atun Ahaw
Three K'atun Lord

a

Ox K'atun Ahaw
Three K'atun Lord

b

Chan K'atun Ahaw
Four K'atun Lord

c

Yahaw (ya-AHAW-wa)
His Lord, Lord of

d

Yahaw (ya-ha-wa)
His Lord, Lord of

e

Yahaw K'ak' (ya-ha-wa k'a-k'a)
Lord of Fire

f

Figure 4:58   *The X K'atun Ahaw and Yahaw titles.*

as to how the word begins or ends. For example in Figure 4:57d, the young lord's head has an *ah* prefix telling us that the word for which the logograph stands begins with *ah*, and a *wa* suffix indicating it ends in *w*. These complements reinforce the conclusion that the word intended is *Ahaw*. Another symbol (or pair of symbols) representing *Ahaw* is the "ben ich" compound (T168), which contains the syllables *ah* and *po* and literally reads "He of the Mat" (Figure 4:57e). *Ahaw* may also be spelled out phonetically as in Figure 4:57f.

As we saw above in the title string for *Yaxun Balam* (Fig. 4:56), the *Ahaw* title sometimes has connected with it an *X K'atun* element that usually refers to the age of the title holder (Fig. 4:58a–c). For example, a 3 *K'atun Ahaw* title suggests that the holder was in his third k'atun of life, between 40 and 60 tuns of age. In some cases, we see an appropriate change in the k'atun designator in the inscriptions of a ruler as he ages.

A very important variation on the *Ahaw* title is *Yahaw* (Fig. 4:58d,e). In this title *Ahaw* is prefixed with the third person pronoun *y*, which gives the reading, "His *Ahaw*/Lord" or "*Ahaw*/Lord of." This title is carried by someone who is an Ahaw, but who is subordinate to or possessed by a higher ranking person, for example, an Ahaw of another site. The *Yahaw* title occurs in an individual's name/title string, and is immediately followed by the name or names/titles of the overlord. For example, on Arroyo de Piedra Stela 2, the Ahaw of Tamarandito is called the Yahaw (a subordinate lord) of the Ahaw of Dos Pilas (Fig. 4:59). The understanding of the *Yahaw* title has been important in sorting out political relations of dominance and subordination among Classic Maya sites. Its occurrence in Classic texts has been extensively analyzed by Linda Schele, Nikolai Grube, and Simon Martin (Schele and Grube 1994a,b, 1995a,b; Martin and Grube 1995). As we will see, other possessed titles occur, also suggesting superior/subordi-

Chak-be-? Ak
Name

Ch'ul Tamarandito Ahaw
Divine Tamarandito Lord

Yahaw
The Ahaw of

Itza K'awil
Name

Ch'ul Mutul Ahaw
Divine Dos Pilas Lord

Figure 4:59   *Text from Arroyo de Piedra Stela 2 stating the subordinate status of a Tamarandito lord to a Dos Pilas lord.*

nate relationships. There are also occurrences of the Yahaw title, however, that do not imply the dominance of one individual over another. For example, at Chichen Itza the title *Yahaw K'ak'*, "Lord of Fire'" is an important one (Fig. 4:58f).

Yahawte is a similar title which can be held by Ahaws and other elite personages (Fig. 4:60a,b). It has been translated as "Lord of the Tree", but it can also be equivalent to the term *Ahaw*. In some cases it appears to be a title implying subordination to another Ahaw, in which case it is prefixed with *u*—his/her. In other contexts it appears to be simply a title. The Ahaw portion can be represented with the same variety of symbols as the Ahaw title itself. *Ch'ahom*, meaning "The Dripper," or "One Who Scatters Drops." is a common title for rulers and other elite personages (Fig. 4:60c–e). It can be elaborated, e.g., by an *X K'atun* phrase (Fig. 4:60e).

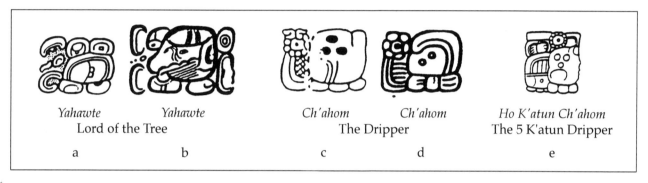

Yahawte	*Yahawte*	*Ch'ahom*	*Ch'ahom*	*Ho K'atun Ch'ahom*
Lord of the Tree		The Dripper		The 5 K'atun Dripper
a	b	c	d	e

Figure 4:60   The Yahawte and Ch'ahom titles.

Figure 4:61 illustrates another relatively common title for rulers and other elite persons. The early rulers of Tikal labled themselves with this title rather than *Ahaw*. The title occurs in two forms— one comprising a head and a hand holding an axe combined with a *te* sign as suffix (Fig. 4:61a), and the other usually having as the main element combined *Kawak* and *te* signs, topped by *ma* (Fig. 4:61b). Over the years, epigraphers have given several names to this title, including *Macuch*, *Batab*, *Chakte*, and most recently *Kalomte*. A possibly definitive example of the title is found on Stela 19 from Copan (Fig. 4:61c) containing the phonetic elements *ka*, *lo*, *ma*, and *te*, and this occurrence supports the conclusion by several epigraphers that *Kalomte* is indeed the correct reading (Stuart, Grube, and Schele, 1989, Copan Note 58). In most of the recent literature, however, *Chakte* is the term used. The meaning of the title is not yet certain; in some versions it seems to be a war title. It can be elaborated, e.g., with directional indicators, usually west, and X *K'atun* phrases, and it can also be carried by elite women (Fig. 4:61c–f).

Other titles carried by rulers include the very common *Bakab* title (Fig. 4:62a–c), possibly meaning "The Stood-up One;" *Pitzil* (Fig. 4:62d), "The Ballplayer;" *Chan K'awil* (Fig. 4:62e), the "Sky God K" title; *K'inich* (Fig. 4:62f–i), "Sun-eyed;" and *K'in Ahaw* (Fig. 4:62j), "Sun Lord." The titles shown in Figure 4:62f–h were previously read as *Mak'inah*, meaning "Ruler," but the consensus among most epigraphers now seems to be that they are all read as *K'inich*, as

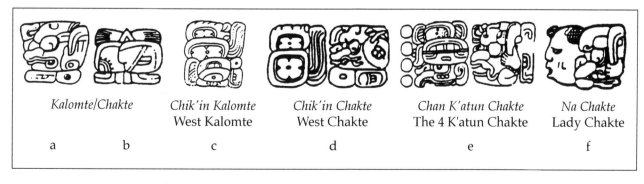

Kalomte/Chakte		*Chik'in Kalomte*	*Chik'in Chakte*	*Chan K'atun Chakte*	*Na Chakte*
		West Kalomte	West Chakte	The 4 K'atun Chakte	Lady Chakte
a	b	c	d	e	f

Figure 4:61   The Kalomte/Chakte title.

Figure 4:62   The Bakab, Pitzil, Chan K'awil, K'inich and K'in Ahaw titles.

is the sign shown in Figure 4:62j. Some of these titles are also carried by women, especially the *Bakab* title (Fig. 4:62c).

Numbered successor titles have helped establish the sequence of rulers at several sites. These phrases give information about the positions of rulers in the dynastic sequence counted from a ruling lineage founder (Schele 1992a). Numbered successor statements usually contain the "hel" glyph (T573 or T676), which is a verbal root, *tz'ak,*

meaning "to change" or "to succeed," and they sometimes name the lineage founder. The structure of succession phrases differs from site to site and even within the texts of one site. In Figure 4:63 are shown two examples of numbered sucession phrases, one for Ruler B of Tikal (Stela 5), who was the 27th successor of a founder named *Yax Moch Xok*; and for one of the Bird Jaguars at Yaxchilan (Lintel 37), who was the eighth successor of a founder unnamed in this text.

Figure 4:63   Numbered succession expressions.

The last major group of titles carried by rulers to be considered are Emblem Glyphs. In the 1950's, Heinrich Berlin recognized a series of hieroglyphs that were site specific (Berlin 1958). He was not sure whether these glyphs represented sites, and/or polities, and/or lineages, but it was clear to him that they had something to do with the specific sites in whose inscriptions they occurred. He thus designated them by a general term, "Emblem Glyph," often abbreviated E.G. In retrospect, Berlin's paper was a landmark one, because it was the earliest serious glyphic research to imply that inscriptions may contain historical material. Important subsequent work on Emblem Glyphs has been carried out by Joyce Marcus (1976a) and Peter Mathews (1991).

Typically an Emblem Glyph consists of three elements (Fig. 4:64a). The first is the "water group" affix on the top or left edge of the main sign composed of a row of droplets signifying blood, topped by a small sign, usually a *k'an* sign, a shell sign, or an upside-down *Ahaw*, the composite standing for *k'ul* (*ch'ul* in Cholan), and read as "divine" or "holy." The water group may also include or consist solely of a God C head—the "complete" blood element—which in this context also reads *k'ul* or *ch'ul* (Figure 4:64b). The second element is a superfixed sign for *Ahaw* or lord, usually the *ah po* sign (T168), and the third element is a main sign that is currently believed to designate the site or polity (i.e., a toponym). There is often a phonetic complement, *wa*, subfixed to the main sign to reenforce the final *w* of *Ahaw*. Typically, the reading order of the three main elements is *K'ul*, site designator, and *Ahaw*; there is clear evidence in a few cases that *Ahaw* is to be read last in these collocations. Figure 4:64a shows the elements as they occur in a typical form of the Tikal Emblem Glyph, and it reads in English, "The Divine Tikal Ahaw." So far over 40 Emblem Glyphs have been recognized, and many of these are listed in Table 4:3. As the table shows, some sites have two or more Emblem Glyphs. Yaxchilan is unique in that both forms of its Emblem Glyph are usually given together. Dos Pilas and Aguateca, which are relatively close, have the same Emblem Glyph, and decipherment of texts from these sites suggests that they were part of the same polity, at least for a time. The Dos Pilas/Aguateca Emblem Glyph is essentially identical to that of distant Tikal; apparently at one time there was a political or lineage connection between Tikal and these sites. In several cases, changes in the Emblem Glyph of a site are noted over time.

Emblem Glyphs are found primarily in the name strings of rulers and other elite personages. They are really titles. They, or the site-specific portions, are sometimes found associated with the Venus/war glyph, indicating the place at which or on

Figure 4:64   Emblem glyphs: **a.** *main components of the Tikal E.G.;* **b.** *Seibal E.G. with God C.*

which war was made. The site-specific portion may also be found in toponymic phrases, often introduced by *uti*, indicating the place where an event occurred. Since Emblem Glyphs are thought by some scholars to be polity-specific, to represent areas over which sites had political control, they have been used to construct maps of presumed polities in the Maya lowlands. The principal researchers in this regard are Joyce Marcus (1976a), and especially Peter Mathews (Mathews 1990, 1991, Mathews and Willey 1991). Using Emblem Glyphs, it has been possible to map probable changes in polity areas and distributions over time. These efforts, coupled with decipherments of pertinent texts, have provided insight into the nature of interactions between sites.

The Maya word readings of the main signs of several Emblem Glyphs are now known. For example, recent analysis of the main sign of Copan's Emblem Glyph, which is composed of a bat, reading *xu*, combined with the syllables *ku* and *pi*, suggested the reading *xukpi*, the name of a bird in Central America (Fig. 4:65a) (Looper 1991d). Also recently, the main sign of Tikal's Emblem Glyph was determined to be *Mutul*, and of course that of Yaxha has been known for a long time to read *Yaxha*, meaning "Great-," "Green-," or "First Water" (Fig. 4:65b,c). It is also tempting to assume that the main sign of the Seibal Emblem Glyph, which consists of three tun signs (Fig. 4:65d), was pronounced *Ox Tun*, possibly a reminder of the three stones set at creation (Chapter 8). The elements of the main sign of Ucanal's Emblem Glyph clearly read *K'an Witz Nal*, or "Yellow Mountain Place" (Fig. 4:65e). The Piedras Negras main sign, *yokib*, is a word for valley, and it possibly refers to the gorge-like aspect of the Usumacinta River as it approaches the vicinity of Piedras Negras (Fig. 4:65f). Perusal of Table 4:3 reveals several other Emblem Glyphs whose main signs are composed of readable elements.

Related to Emblem Glyphs are "titles of origin," a group named and discussed by David Stuart and Stephen Houston (1994). These titles usually

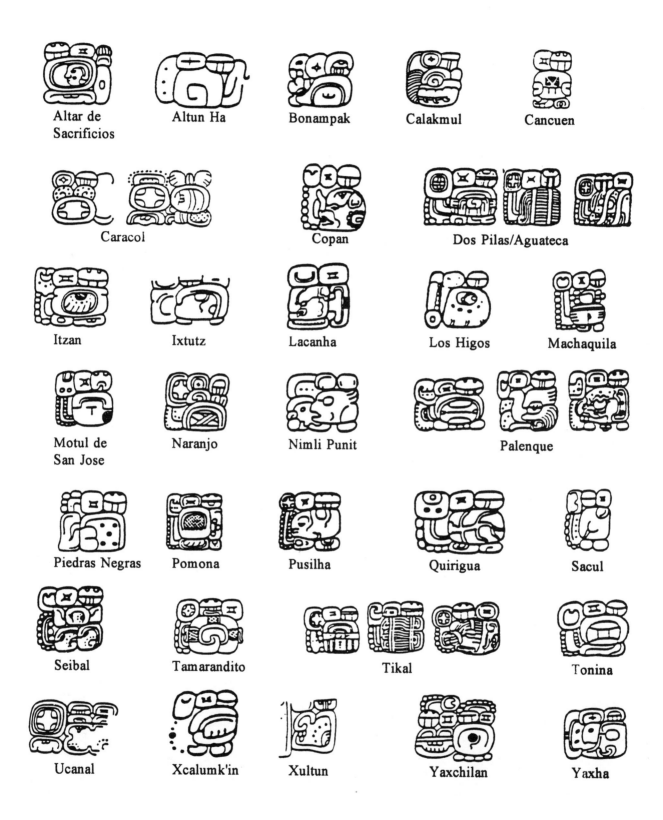

Altar de
Sacrificios

Altun Ha

Bonampak

Calakmul

Cancuen

Caracol

Copan

Dos Pilas/Aguateca

Itzan

Ixtutz

Lacanha

Los Higos

Machaquila

Motul de
San Jose

Naranjo

Nimli Punit

Palenque

Piedras Negras

Pomona

Pusilha

Quirigua

Sacul

Seibal

Tamarandito

Tikal

Tonina

Ucanal

Xcalumk'in

Xultun

Yaxchilan

Yaxha

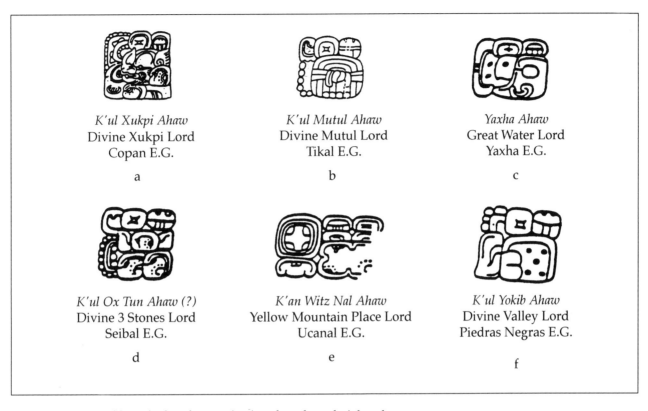

K'ul Xukpi Ahaw
Divine Xukpi Lord
Copan E.G.

a

K'ul Mutul Ahaw
Divine Mutul Lord
Tikal E.G.

b

Yaxha Ahaw
Great Water Lord
Yaxha E.G.

c

K'ul Ox Tun Ahaw (?)
Divine 3 Stones Lord
Seibal E.G.

d

K'an Witz Nal Ahaw
Yellow Mountain Place Lord
Ucanal E.G.

e

K'ul Yokib Ahaw
Divine Valley Lord
Piedras Negras E.G.

f

Figure 4:65   Emblem glyphs whose main signs have been deciphered.

follow the name of a person, and they state the name of the place from which the person comes. They are usually composed of the agentive pronoun, *ah*, followed by a glyph or glyphs naming the place. In English they are generally rendered, "He/she of - name of a place." One example has already been encountered in the discussion of the *hubi* war verb, where we had the statement, "He of Naranjo was thrown down" (Fig. 4:42c). Figure 4:66 contains several examples of these titles.

There are now known several titles held by individuals who were below the ruler in the Maya socio/political hierarchy. For example, *Ch'ok* was a special title that could be held by heir apparents (Fig. 4:67a). Literally it means "sprout" or "youth," and it was usually discarded by a ruler upon his accession. It can appear in a variety of expressions (Fig. 4:67b–d).

At some sites that were subordinate to larger, more important sites, the title of the ruler was

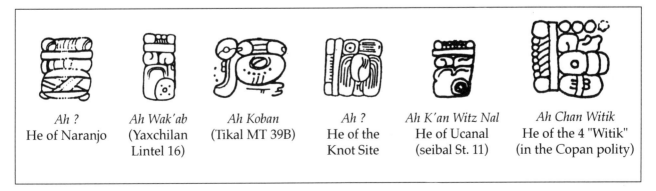

Ah ?
He of Naranjo

Ah Wak'ab
(Yaxchilan
Lintel 16)

Ah Koban
(Tikal MT 39B)

Ah ?
He of the
Knot Site

Ah K'an Witz Nal
He of Ucanal
(seibal St. 11)

Ah Chan Witik
He of the 4 "Witik"
(in the Copan polity)

Figure 4:66   Place of origin titles.

Ch'ok	Ba Ch'ok	Ch'ok Winik	Ta Ba Ch'oklel
Sprout, Youth	First Sprout	Sprout Man, Youth	In the first "Sproutship"
a	b	c	d

Figure 4:67   The Ch'ok title.

Sahal (Fig. 4:68a,b). Thus far, there is no generally agreed upon translation for *Sahal*. The *Sahal* title can be elaborated in the same manner as the *Ahaw* title, and it can be held by women (Fig. 4:68c,d). According to the texts of some subordinate sites, sahals derived their positions and authority from specific rulers of a dominant site. For example, the texts of El Cayo record a series of Sahals, much like a sequence of Ahaws at a dominant site, who acknowledge their subordination to rulers of Piedras Negras. The specific dominance of a partic-ular ruler over a *sahal* may be indicated by the *sahal* title being possessed, as we saw earlier for *Ahaw* titles. In these cases the affixed third person possessive pronoun is *u*, instead of *y* as it was with *Ahaw* (Fig. 4:68e).

Another subordinate title that has recently been discussed by Linda Schele and Nikolai Grube is the *Ah K'u Hun* title, meaning "He of the Sacred Books" (Fig. 4:69a) (Schele and Grube, 1995a,b). Often the title does not contain all the elements shown in Figure 4:69a, but is conflated to *Ah*

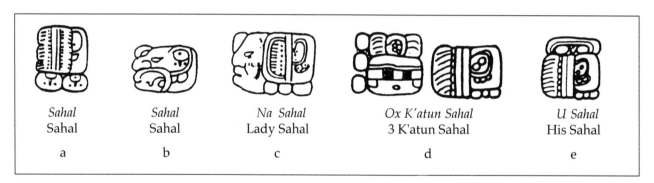

Sahal	Sahal	Na Sahal	Ox K'atun Sahal	U Sahal
Sahal	Sahal	Lady Sahal	3 K'atun Sahal	His Sahal
a	b	c	d	e

Figure 4:68   Sahal titles.

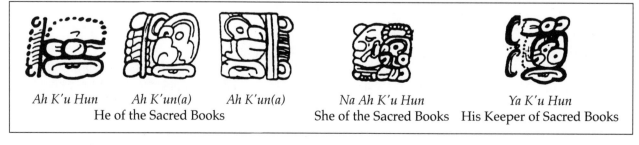

Ah K'u Hun	Ah K'un(a)	Ah K'un(a)	Na Ah K'u Hun	Ya K'u Hun
He of the Sacred Books			She of the Sacred Books	His Keeper of Sacred Books

Figure 4:69   The Ah K'u Hun Title—He/She of the Sacred Books.

Ah Sul	*Ah Nab*	*Ya Nab*	*Hoy(?) Ch'ul Na*	*Hoy(?) Ch'ul Na*
He the Administrator(?)	He of Water	His/He of Water	Companion	Divine Lady
a	b	c	d	e

Figure 4:70   The Ah Sul, Ah Nab, and Hoy(?) Ch'ul Na titles.

K'un(a) (Fig. 4:69b,c). The title's elements consist of an *ah*, usually T12, a God C main sign or an equivalent for *k'u* or *ch'u*, and then, if it's not a conflated form, a sign or phonetic combination representing *hun*. *Hun* is a word for book or codex, in addition to paper or headband as we saw earlier under accession expressions, and sometimes *hun* is represented by T60 as in Figure 4:69a. This title can also be carried by women (Fig. 4:69d), and it sometimes occurs in the possessed form, *Ya K'u Hun* (Fig. 4:69e). Another interpretation of the conflated form, *Ah K'u Na* or *Ah K'ul Na*, emphasises the *Na* as a word for house, and has been read "He of the Holy House."

    Ah Sul is also a subordinate title (Figure 4:70a). Its meaning isn't clear, but it probably designates an administrator of some sort. Another title sometimes carried by rulers is *Ah Nab*, "He of Water;" this title also occurs in the possessed form, *Ya Nab*, "His He of Water" (Fig. 4:70b,c). Some elite women carry a title, all of whose elements are not completely understood. It usually consists of: (1) an upside-down vessel containing a *k'in* sign, which

may read *hoy*, meaning companion/wife; (2) a row of blood drops reading *k'ul* or *ch'ul* as in Emblem Glyphs; and (3) a woman's profile head, *na* (Fig. 4:70d,e). A possible reading for this title is "Companion Divine Lady."

    Several titles that indicate artists are known. For example, *Ah Tz'ib* is a title designating painters and writers. It reads "He the Scribe" (Fig. 4:71a). When possessed, it reads *Ya Tz'ib*, "He is the Scribe of" (Fig. 4:71b). *Itz'at* is a title meaning "sage" or "artist," and it may be carried not only by mortals, but by deities as well (Fig. 4:71c–e). For example, the Paddlers are referred to as *Itz'at* for their role in creating the universe. This title can be elaborated, for example as shown in Figure 4:71d, e. A title for sculptors related to the previously discussed "lu-bat" glyph is shown in Figure 4:71f,g. There is still uncertainty about the Maya reading of this title, although the phonetic elements present suggest the reading shown.

    The inscriptions contain many more titles than are mentioned in this survey. Some additional examples are tabulated in Table 4:4.

Ah Tz'ib	*Ya Tz'ib*	*Itz'at*	*Ba Itz'at*	*Ch'ul Itz'at*	*Ah Uxul(?)*	*Ba Uxul(?)*
He the Scribe	He is the Scribe of	Artist/Sage	First Artist/Sage	Holy Sage	He the Sculptor	First Sculptor
a	b	c	d	e	f	g

Figure 4:71   Artist's titles.

Table 4:4 Titles

Sak Ahaw Te
White Tree
Lord

Yax Ch'ul Ahaw Te
1st Holy Tree Lord

Ch'ul Ahaw Ahaw
Divine Lord of Lords

Ox Witz Ahaw
3 Mountain Lord

Mo Witz Ahaw
Macaw Mt. Lord

Witik Ahaw
Lord of Witik

K'uy Nik Ahaw
Bird Flower Lord

Ek' Xukpi Ahaw
Black Copan Lord

Tukun Ahaw
Dove Lord

Tok Tan Ahaw
Cloud Center
Lord

Ch'ul To(k) Tan Ahaw
Holy Cloud Center
Lord

Koxop Ahaw
"Koxop" Lord
(Koxop = a bird)

Yahaw K'ak'
Lord of Fire

Yahaw K'ak'
Lord of Fire

Ch'ul ? Ahaw
Divine Mannikin
Lord

Ek' Waynal Ahaw
Black Hole
Place Lord

Ba Ahaw
1st Lord

U Luk' Ba Itz'at
His 1st Artist
of Clay

Ba Al
1st Born

Ah Chan Kun
He of the
Sky Seat

Tok Tan Winik
Cloud Center
Person

Ah Ho Ch'ul Na
He of 5 temples

Ah Payal
He the
Leader

Hemnal
Valley
Lady

Ch'akwal Bate
Decapitator
Warrior

Yoxuk'in(?)
An Elite
Title

Chan ? na
Sky God
Title

Chan Yoat
Sky Penis
Title

TOPYNYMS

At the Penn Maya Weekend in April 1987, Stephen Houston presented a paper in which he announced the recognition of several place names in the inscriptions, especially the names of polities (Houston 1992b). Since then many additional names of polities, places within polities, and geographical features have been recognized. An analytical summary of this important work has recently been published by David Stuart and Stephen Houston (1994).

Toponymic expressions occur in a variety of forms and are usually found in or after a clause relating an event. They may occur after the event glyph or at the very end of the clause, and they tell where the event has taken place. They often take the form of an additional clause introduced by the *uti* or *uhti* form of the verb *ut* read in these contexts as, "it happened at." The *uti* form of this verb usually has as its main sign one of the allographs of *u*, affixed by *ti* and *ya*. The verb is then followed by the name of a place. Figure 4:72 contains a clause from the mythological portion of the text from Quirigua Stela C in which a toponymic phrase beginning with *uti* follows a setting-up event. These clauses are part of the creation text on Quirigua Stela C which we will consider in detail

in Chapter 8. This part of the text tells us that the "Paddlers," two important Maya deities that we will meet later, set up a stone—one of the three stones that were put in place at creation—and that it happened at House Five Sky, a mythological place associated with the Paddlers. Figure 4:73a illustrates another toponymic clause also using *uti*, but this time with a different *u* allograph than was used in the Quirigua Stela C text. The location indicated is *Tok Tan,* Cloud Center, a place associated with Palenque. This expression is translated simply as, "It happened at Cloud Center." The example in Figure 4:73b from the Tikal Stela 31 text, uses the *uhti* form of the verb that has a *Chuwen* skull as main sign to supply the *uh* part of the verb, affixed with *ti* and *ya*. The place named, *Wi Te Na*, may be the name of the Tikal structure where the associated event took place. The *uhti* form appears primarily in Early Classic texts, and there are several examples in the text on Tikal Stela 31. You will note that the English translation of all of these expressions requires that we supply a preposition—at, in, etc.—yet no preposition appears in the glyph sequence.

Some toponyms are signaled by the presence of special indicators, for example, the combination of a sky glyph, *chan* (T561), and an "impinged

| *U Tz'apaw* They set up | *Tun* the stone | The Paddlers | *Uti* It happened at | *Na Ho' Chan* House Five Sky | *Ix Tz'am(?) Tun* Jaguar Throne Stone |

Figure 4:72   A dedication statement with a toponymic clause beginning with uti *(Quirigua Stela C).*

| *Uti* It happened at | *Tok Tan* Cloud Center | *Uhti* It happened at | *Wi Te Na* Wi Te Na |
| a | | b | |

Figure 4:73   Toponymic phrases from Palenque and Tikal.

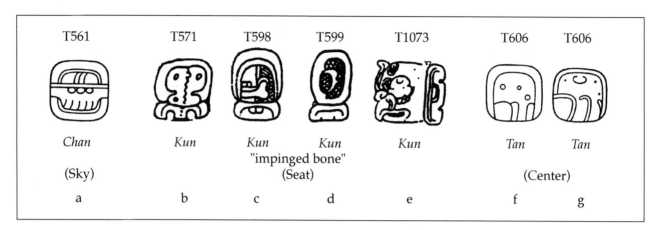

Figure 4:74   Glyph elements used in toponymic statements.

bone" glyph, *kun* (Fig. 4:74a–e). The "impinged bone," like the *chan* glyph, usually has a *na* phonetic complement. This indicator often appears in toponymic clauses that are introduced by *uti* or *uhti*. Several forms of the "impinged bone" glyph are used in these expressions, e.g., T571, T598, T599, and a head variant with a trifoil element over the eye, T1073 (Fig. 4:74b–e). Usually the indicator occurs after the

place name as in Figure 4:75a, where the expression says, "It happened at *Lakam Ha'*," a place name for Palenque, or in Figure 4:75b, which says, "It happened at ??," probably a place in Tikal. This indicator sometimes occurs after directional glyphs, for example, in 819 Day Count expressions as shown in Figure 4:75c. On occasion, the "impinged bone" glyph may appear as the sole place indicating element.

Uti Lakam Ha'
It happened at Great Water
a

Uhti   ??
It happened at a place in Tikal
b

Lak'in
East
c

Figure 4:75   Toponymic expressions using chan and "impinged-bone" glyphs.

Another place indicator is the T606 + "impinged bone" combination, but it does not occur as frequently as the *chan* glyph + "impinged bone." It usually occurs before a place name (Fig. 4:76a,b) and like the "impinged bone" glyph, T606 may sometimes be used alone as in Figure 4:76c. It also often has a *na* phonetic complement. There has been some ambiguity in understanding the function of both the "impinged bone" and the T606 indicators, because logographic values are known for these glyphs. The Maya reading for the "impinged bone" is *kun*, a word for "seat," and for T606, the Maya word is *tan*, meaning "center." Thus the *chan* + "impinged bone" combination has sometimes been translated as "sky seat," a meaning which can make sense in

some of the contexts in which it is found. Similarly, T606 + "impinged bone" has sometimes been read as "center seat," also a meaning that makes sense in some contexts.

Another common place indicator that is usually part of a place name glyph as a superfix is T86 (Fig. 4:77a), a logograph for the Maya word *nal*, one meaning of which is "place." Examples using this device are shown in Figure 4:77b–e. There is evidence that *nal* is read last in these collocations even though it appears at the top of the place name.

There are also toponyms that have no special indicator except the position they have in the clause. They usually follow a verb, and they tell where the action indicated by the verb was carried out. For

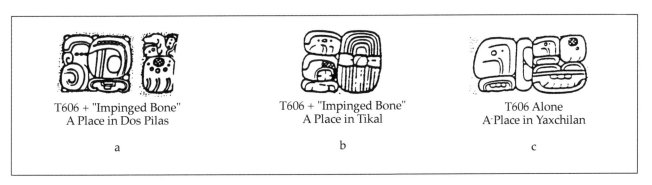

T606 + "Impinged Bone"
A Place in Dos Pilas

a

T606 + "Impinged Bone"
A Place in Tikal

b

T606 Alone
A Place in Yaxchilan

c

Figure 4:76   Toponymic expressions using T606.

example, after a Venus-war verb, or even within the same collocation, the name of the polity on which or at which war was made is sometimes given (Fig. 4:78a). Similarly, after the verb for "burial," the place of burial may be given (Fig. 4:78b).

Finally, as mentioned previously, the main signs of Emblem Glyphs can be viewed as toponyms because they probably represent a name or designation for a polity. In some cases, it has been determined that other signs, which differ from the Emblem Glyph main sign, are also toponyms for a site or places within the site. Some of these are shown in Table 4:5. This table also contains additional toponyms, including some mythological place names.

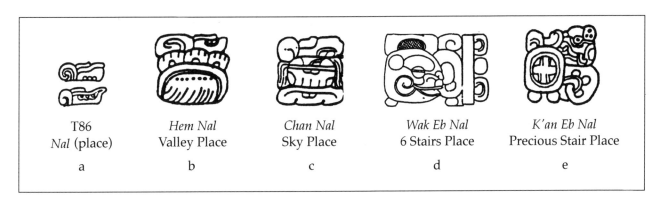

T86
Nal (place)

a

Hem Nal
Valley Place

b

Chan Nal
Sky Place

c

Wak Eb Nal
6 Stairs Place

d

K'an Eb Nal
Precious Stair Place

e

Figure 4:77   Toponymic expressions using nal, place.

?-yi Yaxha
War on Yaxha

a

Mukah Ho Hanab Witz
He was buried at
Five Flower Mountain

b

Figure 4:78   Toponymic phrases without a special indicator.

NAMES OF THINGS

For many years, the names for numerous "things," e.g., *tun* for "stone," *pakal* for "shield," and *k'in* for "day," have been known. We have already encountered the names of several other things in the calendrics and phonetics chapters. In recent years many additional terms for objects have been recognized, in part from the study of dedication statements and from name-tagging notations. The contributions of Linda Schele and David Stuart working at Copan have been important, especially with regard to objects identified from dedication statements (Schele 1990b). As with other categories of glyphs we've examined so far,

Table 4:5 Place Names

Ka Nal
Fish Place

Tukun Witz
Dove Mountain

Wak Kabnal
Six Earth Place

Ich'ak Tun
Jaguar Paw Stone

Tan Kun Mutul
Tikal Center Seat

Mutul Nal
Tikal Place

Yemal K'uk' Lakam Witz
Descending Quetzal
Great Mountain

Sa(k) Ha' Witznal
Clear Water
Mountain Place

Nab
Water, Sea

Nab Tunich
Watery Stone

K'ak' Nab
Firey Water
Place

Sak Ha'
White Lake

K'in Ha' Nal
Day Water Place

Lakam Ha'
Great Water

Yompi

Tan Kun Ox Witz Ha'
(Center Seat) 3 Hill
Water

A Waxaktun
Place Name

? Ha'
A Dos Pilas
Place Name

Maxam
A Naranjo
Place Name

Ox Witik
A Copan
Place Name

Mo Witz
A Copan
Place Name

Names of Some Mythological Places

Ek' Way Nal
Black Hole
Place

Matawil
A Cosmological
Place

Ho Nik Nal
Five Flower
Place

Yax Ox Tun Nal
1st 3 Stone
Place

Wak Ek' Nab Nal
Six Black Water
Place

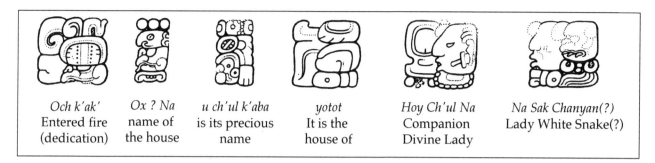

Och k'ak'	*Ox ? Na*	*u ch'ul k'aba*	*yotot*	*Hoy Ch'ul Na*	*Na Sak Chanyan(?)*
Entered fire (dedication)	name of the house	is its precious name	It is the house of	Companion Divine Lady	Lady White Snake(?)

Figure 4:79   House dedication statement from Yaxchilan Lintel 56.

some of the names are logographs, while others are clearly phonetic spellings. Some of the identified objects were also given proper names by the Maya, e.g., *Sak Nuk Nah* ("White Great House"), is House E in the Palace complex at Palenque, and *K'an Tun* ("Yellow/Precious Stone") is the name given to the Tablet of 96 Glyphs, also from Palenque. Such proper names are sometimes followed by *u k'aba* ("is its name"), or *u ch'ul k'aba* ("is its holy name"), phrases frequently used as name closure expressions. For example, in the text on Lintel 56 from Yaxchilan, a fire dedication verb is followed by the name of the structure dedicated, a name closure phrase (*u ch'ul k'aba*), and then another statement telling us whose structure it was (Fig. 4:79). Names of objects is a very fast growing area of decipherment, and each year several new ones are reported. Table 4:6 contains some of the terms so far recognized. In a few cases both a logograph and a phonetic spelling for a term are given. Also included are a few examples of proper names.

DEITIES

In 1904, Paul Schellhas published the results of his analysis of the Maya deities in the codices (Schellhas 1904). He designated each deity with a letter, labeling them God A, God B, etc., up to God S, and identified glyphs in the codices that corresponded to each one. Over the intervening years, some revising of his series has been done, and up to date information can be found in *The Major Gods of Ancient Yucatan*, by Karl Taube (1992), and *The Gods of Ancient Mexico and the Maya*, by Mary Miller and Karl Taube (1993). So far only some of the Schellhas deities have been correlated with deities mentioned in texts on carved monuments. For a comprehensive discussion of the Maya concept of deity, a recent paper by Stephen Houston and David Stuart (1996) is recommended.

Most inscriptional texts are primarily about events in the lives of rulers and other elite persons,

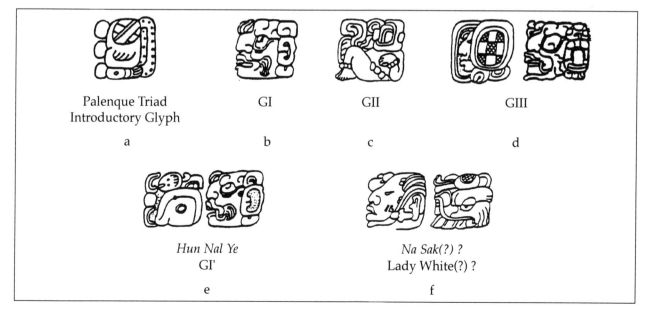

Palenque Triad Introductory Glyph

a

GI

b

GII

c

GIII

d

Hun Nal Ye
GI'

e

Na Sak(?) ?
Lady White(?) ?

f

Figure 4:80   Palenque dieties.

Table 4:6 Names of Things

 Otot House

 Yotot His house

 Na House

 K'al Hun Na Accession House

 Sak Nuk Na White Great House

 Tun Stone

 *U Lakam Tun* His LargeStone

 Wak Ahaw Tun 6 *Ahaw* Stone (Stela)

 K'an Tun Yellow Stone

 Pakal Shield

 Pakal Shield

 Pibnah Underground house

 Lom Staff

 Makom Calabash tree

 Ix Tzam(?) Jaguar Throne

 *K'inich Tzam(?) Tun* Sun-eyed Throne Stone

 Kohaw Helmet

 U-Pakab His lintel

 Hun Headband, book

 Hunal Headband

 Ek' Hun Black headband

 K'obah Image, statue

 Tok' Flint

 Tok' Flint

 Eb Stair

 Yeb(al) His stair

 Tah Torch

 U Sak Lak Tun His stone incensario

 *U-Lak* His plate

 Yowal Its portal, crack

 Ki Heart

 Hub Shell

 Ch'ah Drops of resin

 U-Pasil The doorway of

and the deities are dealt with rather sketchily. The exceptions are some of the Palenque texts, which relate the births of three major gods, GI, GII, and GIII (The Palenque Triad) and their parents, GI' (*Hun Nal Ye*) and Lady Sak(?) ? (Fig. 4:80). The father, GI' (Fig. 4:80e), is involved in important cosmological events related in the texts of the Palenque Cross Group (Chapter 8). There are numerous references to these deities in the Palenque texts and also some references to them in texts from other sites. They are sometimes noted as protagonists of events, or said to accompany a ruler as he performs an important ritual.

Among the Schellhas deities mentioned in the inscriptions are God A', one of the death gods (Fig. 4:81a); God D, or *Itzamna* (Fig. 4:81b), who in Postclassic times in the Yucatan was the principal deity; God K, or *K'awil* (Fig. 4:81c), equivalent to Palenque's GII and associated with royal lineages; and God N (Fig. 4:81d,e), the "Old God," who appears as a name/title, e.g., at Piedras Negras, and frequently as a verb in dedication statements. The symbol for God C appears very frequently, and is read *ch'ul* or *k'ul*, which has the adjectival meaning "holy" or "divine", or the nominal meaning "deity" (Fig. 4:82a). Other Schellhas deities appear as head variants of numbers, e.g., God A, the Death God (Fig. 4:82b), represents the number 10, and God E, the Maize God (Fig. 4:82c), represents the number 8. Other dieties represented in inscrip-

God A' Death God	God D *Itzamna*	God K *K'awil*	God N Name/title	God N Verbal
a	b	c	d	e

Figure 4:81   Maya deities represented in the inscriptions.

tional texts include *Hunahaw* (Fig. 4:82d), one of the Hero Twins, and a Sky God (Fig. 4:83a), which occurs as a title, for example, for Bird Jaguar IV of Yaxchilan. The "Sky God" is often accompanied by a pair of glyphs including *te kuy* and an upside-down vessel with affixed deer antlers, but so far the meaning of this whole grouping is unclear (Fig. 4:83b). Two very important gods mentioned in the inscriptions are the Paddlers, so designated from their initial recognition as canoe paddlers pictured on carved bones from Tikal. The Jaguar Paddler usually has jaguar spots on his

cheeks (Fig. 4:83c), and the Stingray Paddler has a stingray spine through the septum of his nose (Fig. 4:83d). The Paddlers appear in several contexts including as protagonists in creation events. As David Stuart and others have shown, the Paddler pair can be represented in a variety of ways glyphically and iconographically; for example, they are sometimes represented in texts by *ak'bal* and *k'in* signs (Fig. 4:83e).

Deities sometimes appear as the protagonists of events, as in the Palenque texts, or as companions to rulers carrying out important events; fre-

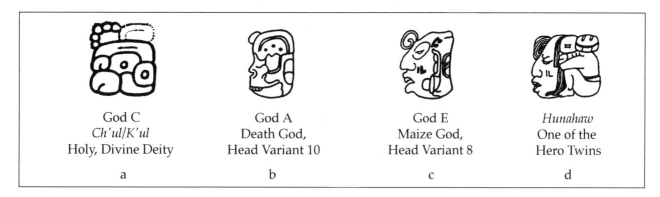

God C *Ch'ul/K'ul* Holy, Divine Deity	God A Death God, Head Variant 10	God E Maize God, Head Variant 8	*Hunahaw* One of the Hero Twins
a	b	c	d

Figure 4:82   Maya deities represented in the inscriptions.

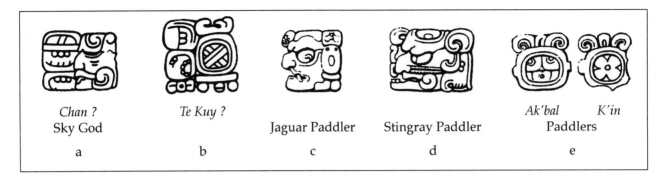

Chan ?	Te Kuy ?			Ak'bal	K'in
Sky God		Jaguar Paddler	Stingray Paddler	Paddlers	
a	b	c	d	e	

Figure 4:83   *Maya deities represented in the inscriptions.*

quently they are found in the names/titles strings of rulers and other elite persons. Other gods also appear in the texts, e.g., *Chak*, the god associated with rain, sacrifice, and warfare, and there are many other glyphs in the texts which presumably represent deities, but which are not yet clearly understood.

Further discussions of Maya deities that appear in the inscriptional texts as well as in iconography can be found in *The Blood of Kings*, by Linda Schele and Mary Miller (1986), A *Forest of Kings*, by Linda Schele and David Friedel (1990), and in Linda Schele's and Nikolai Grube's *Notebook for the XVIIth Maya Hieroglyphic Workshop at Texas* (1994a).

MISCELLANEOUS GLYPHS

Finally, there follows a series of miscellaneous glyphs that do not fit into any of the previous categories, for example directional and color glyphs (Fig. 4:84). These two sometimes occur together in Maya texts, for example in the chapter on calendrics, it was noted that the 819-day cycle is divided into quadrants, each usually associated with a direction and a color. These glyphs, however, especially the directional ones, occur in other contexts as well (Fig. 4:84a–d). As we saw in the discussion of titles, a directional glyph, usually west (Fig. 4:84b), can form part of a title occuring in the name/title strings of elite

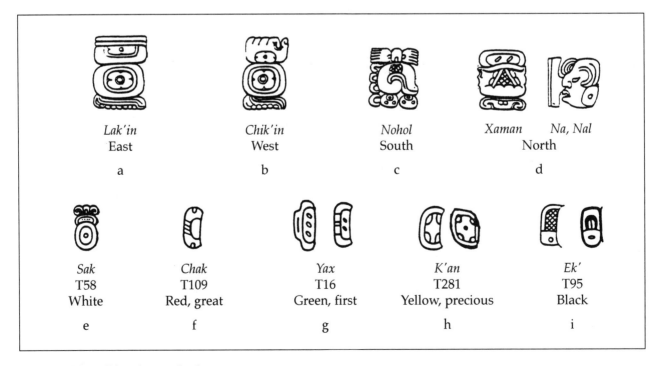

Lak'in	Chik'in	Nohol	Xaman	Na, Nal
East	West	South	North	
a	b	c	d	

Sak	Chak	Yax	K'an	Ek'
T58	T109	T16	T281	T95
White	Red, great	Green, first	Yellow, precious	Black
e	f	g	h	i

Figure 4:84   *Directions and colors.*

persons. An unusual occurence of the directional glyphs is found in the main text of Copan Stela A, where all four of them are given together. The color glyphs usually appear as affixes, and some of them occur as components of month signs; some color glyphs have other adjectival meanings (Figure 4:84e–i).

The inscriptional texts also contain male and female articles (agentives), which we have already seen in several contexts (Figure 4:85a–c).

Several signs have been determined to mean "first" (Schele 1990a). For example, *ba* (T757 and T501) can mean "first" as a component of titles, such as *Ba Ahaw* and *Ba Sahal* (Fig. 4:85d,e). *Ba* is probably indicating "first" in the sense of the highest ranking among a group of equally titled persons. Two other elements, *yax* and *na*, can also mean "first" (Fig. 4:85f,g).

NOTES

1. Further discussion of aspect is found in Chapter 5.
2. There is further discussion of pronoun use in Maya languages and hieroglyphic texts in Chapter 5.
3. There has been much discussion about the phonetic value of T126. Most epigraphers now believe that it represents the syllable *ya*, but there is evidence that in some cases at least, *ix* may be the correct reading. Possibly the sign can represent either sound depending upon the context.
4. In this discussion several glyphs will be encountered that belong to categories that will be treated in more detail in later sections of this chapter.
5. As we will see later in this chapter in the discussion of titles, *hun,* represented by the knot, can also mean "book" or "codex," in addition to headband, or the bark paper from which headbands can be made. Its meaning is determined by the context.

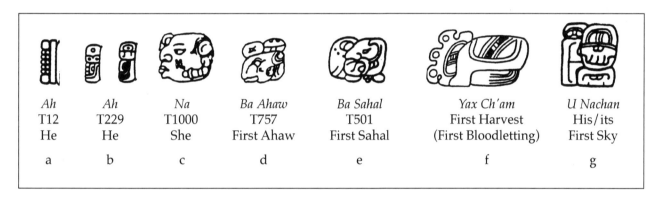

Ah	*Ah*	*Na*	*Ba Ahaw*	*Ba Sahal*	*Yax Ch'am*	*U Nachan*
T12	T229	T1000	T757	T501	First Harvest	His/its
He	He	She	First Ahaw	First Sahal	(First Bloodletting)	First Sky
a	b	c	d	e	f	g

Figure 4:85   Male and female articles and "first" indicators.

5

THE NATURE OF HIEROGLYPHIC TEXTS: THE GRAMMAR

For many years the grammar of Mayan hieroglyphic texts was poorly understood. Significant progress began to be made when it was finally realized that the language of the hieroglyphs was closely related to the languages spoken today by millions of Mayan people. For detailed treatments of the current understanding of the grammar of hieroglyphic texts the reader is directed to *A Grammar of Mayan Hieroglyphs*, by Victoria Bricker (1986), *Maya Glyphs: The Verbs*, by Linda Schele (1982), *An Epigrapher's Annotated Index to Cholan and Yucatecan Verb Morphology*, by Barbara MacLeod (1987), and recent *Notebooks for the Maya Hieroglyphic Workshops at Texas*, by Linda Schele (for example, 1992c).

SYNTAX

As mentioned previously, this volume deals primarily with texts inscribed on stone monuments, texts written mainly to record the events in the public lives of rulers, or to legitimize their right to reign; they are a special kind of history. The codex texts, as so far known, do not contain such material. The study of the codex texts, however, has been very important in leading to an understanding of the basic syntax of Maya texts in general.

The monumental texts are written primarily in simple independent clauses, where each sentence has its own verb. Most clauses contain a temporal element, either a Long Count date, a Calendar Round date, or a Distance Number. In simple English sentences, the position of temporal elements can be variable, for example, both (a) and (b) are good English:

(a) On the 12th of April, 1997, Eloise attended the fifteenth Maya Weekend.

(b) Eloise attended the fifteenth Maya Weekend on the 12th of April, 1997.

The position of the temporal indicator in such a sentence may be dictated by an intended subtle difference in emphasis. The positions of the other elements in simple English sentences are less variable; any syntactical order other than subject- verb- object (S-V-O), seems stilted (or maybe poetic!) or blatantly incorrect. The syntax of the above simple English sentences can be represented as:

(a) T-S-V-O   (T = a temporal element)

or

(b) S-V-O-T

Most clauses in Maya inscriptions have the syntactical order:

T-V-O-S

In contrast to English sentences, the position of the temporal element is rather invariable; it most generally comes first. Applying this Maya word order to the simple English sentence above would give:

On the 12th of April, 1997, attended the fifteenth Maya Weekend Eloise.

There are exceptions to the T-V-O-S word order in Maya texts. There are also many Maya clauses which lack one or more of the T, V, O, and S elements; for example, objects are quite rare in Maya inscriptions. Other elements such as toponymic phrases sometimes occur, in addition to the T, V, O, and S elements. We will see examples of some of these features later when we consider the analysis of specific texts.

We will now consider how the codices were used to establish the V-O-S word order in Maya texts. (Codex texts usually contain no temporal element directly in the text itself.) The usefulness of the codex texts for this purpose lies in the pairing of texts with pictures. Assuming a connection between texts and associated scenes, subjects, objects, and verbal elements can be identified in the texts by studying the scenes. First we willl see how verb-initial word order can be established. On pages 5 and 6 of the Dresden Codex, each of the three panels shown in Figure 5:1a,b features a different god, and each god seems to be doing the same thing, that is, drilling a grasping hand-like object iwth a stick. In the texts above each of the three figures, the first two glyphs are the same, and since the pictured actions are identical, it seems likely that these glyphs represent the verbal function. The last two glyphs in the three texts are different, and since the three gods depicted are different, these glyphs are logically the name glyphs of the gods. This analysis suggests that the first glyphs in each text constitute the verb and the third and fourth are the subject. The order is verb, subject:

V-S

Thus, without knowing the semantic values of any of the individual glyphs, we have been able to postulate a verb-initial word order for these texts. Application of this kind of analysis to many codex texts gives the same result.

Additional confirmation for the initial position of the verb comes from texts in which the verb is actually of a pictographic nature. For example, on page 68 of the Dresden Codex, the first scene shows two gods sitting back-to-back (Fig. 5:1c). The first glyph in the associated text is composed of two figures seated back-to-back, i.e., it depicts the condition or position of the two deities shown, and it thus most likely is performing the verbal function.

Examples that show a presumed V-O-S relationship appear on page 13 of the Dresden Codex (Fig. 5:1d). Here three gods are shown holding the same object, a *wa* sign which, in these contexts, may stand for the word *bread*. In each text, the first glyph (the verb) is the same since the gods are doing the same thing. The second glyphs are also identical, and each is a *wa* sign, the same as the object being held. Thus the object of each verb's action is the same, and the object clearly follows the verb in syntactical position. Again the third and fourth glyphs represent the names of the gods portrayed. Thus, the word order in these texts seems to be verb, object, subject.

Another example illustrating this word order involves a scene in which one god is obviously doing something to another god. For example, on page 67a, Panel 3, of the Dresden Codex, God B is the larger figure portrayed, and he is acting upon a smaller figure, God K (Fig. 5:1e). In the associated text, the glyph for God K is the second glyph in the text and it immediately follows the verb. The glyph for God B occurs later in the text. Thus in this text, where

two gods are mentioned, the order of their glyphs in the text is object (God K, the recipient of the action by God B) followed by the subject, God B, as it should be in our V-O-S scheme.

From these and many other examples in the codices, the usual syntactical order of elements in hieroglyphic texts is clearly established as verb-object-subject:

V-O-S

It is reassuring that in modern Maya languages, many sentences exhibit this same syntax.

In the inscribed texts, the order is generally the same, but as mentioned above, there is usually an added temporal element almost always at the beginning:

T-V-O-S

In codex scenes, Maya gods are usually portrayed as the actors, i.e., the subjects. Determination of the syntactical position of the subject in codex texts has been based on the early work of Schellhas (1904), who, as mentioned in Chapter 4, made an extensive study of the figures in the scenes and the glyphs in the associated texts. In this work, which established the well-known God A, God B, God C, and so on, series, Schellhas found a tight correlation: in the scenes depicting a particular god, the same glyphs were always present, and these were usually the final glyphs in the associated texts. Because the gods were almost always the actors, the terminal glyphs had to be the grammatical subjects. As we have seen in the Dresden Codex pages we've far examined, the glyphs that seem to be naming the actor are at the ends of the texts.

SIMPLE CLAUSES

The codex texts we've just examined are examples of "simple" clauses: they make single statements with one verb, one actor (or subject), and often an object (or patient). The inscriptions also contain many examples of simple clauses, which in addition to elements we saw in the codex texts, usually also contain a temporal element. However, they rarely contain objects. A simple clause from Yaxchilan Stela 12 is shown in Figures 5:2 and 5:3. In this example the clause begins with a Calendar Round, 6 *Imix* 12 *Yaxk'in*; it continues with a two-glyph verbal phrase, which is one of the death verbal expressions, and it ends with names and titles of the subject, *Itzam Balam* (Shield Jaguar), the person who died on 6 *Imix* 12 *Yaxk'in*. In English this clause can be paraphrased as, "On 6 Imix 12 Yaxk'in died The Dripper, The 5 K'atun Ruler, Shield Jaguar, Captor of He the Flower."

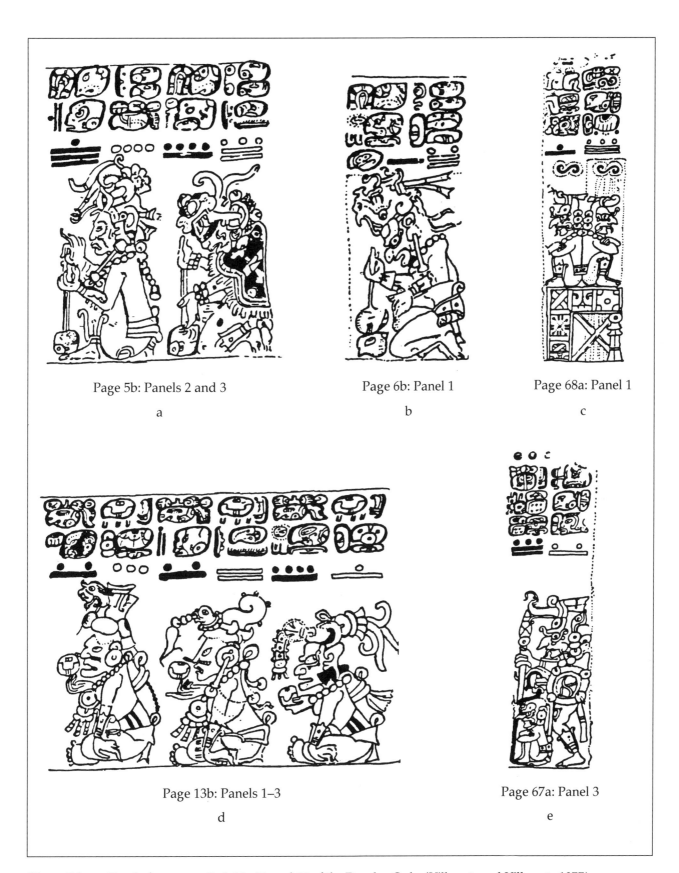

Page 5b: Panels 2 and 3

a

Page 6b: Panel 1

b

Page 68a: Panel 1

c

Page 13b: Panels 1–3

d

Page 67a: Panel 3

e

Figure 5:1. *Panels from pages 5, 6, 13, 67, and 68 of the Dresden Code. (Villacorta and Villacorta 1977).*

Figure 5:2.   A Text from Yaxchilan Stela 12 (Drawn by Linda Schele).

Inscriptional clauses can be even simpler than this. In the Yaxchilan Lintel 15 text (Fig. 5:4), Columns C and D, is a clause that begins with the T757 general verb, followed by the name of one of the figures shown in the scene (Fig. 5:5). This clause has no temporal indicator, and it reads: "She goes as (i.e., her name is) Companion Precious Lady, Lady 6 Tun, Lady Ahaw of Motul de San Jose, Lady Bakab." Such clauses are frequently used to name figures in scenes on monu-

ments, and they are usually positioned near the person named. Another example appears on Tikal Altar 8 (Fig. 5:6), where a short text again starts with the T757 general verb, and then names and titles of the bound prisoner shown on the altar are given (Fig. 5:7). In some cases, the group of labeling glyphs contains no verb, but just the name/titles of the person are given. Often the name glyphs of prisoners are written on the body or the clothing.

6 Imix	12 Yaxk'in	u k'ay it ended	u nikil his flower	Ch'ahom Dripper	Ho K'atun Ahaw 5 K'atun Ruler	Itzam Balam Shield Jaguar	U Chan Captor of	Ah Nik He the Flower
Temporal		Verb				Subject		

Figure 5:3.   Clause from the text on Yaxchilan Stela 12.

Figure 5:4.   Yaxchilan Lintel 15 (Drawn by Ian Graham).

Simple clauses making a single historical statement can have much more elaborate temporal indicators than we've just seen. For example, in the initial clause of Piedras Negras Stela 3 (Fig. 5:8), the date is given both as a Long Count and a Calendar Round (Fig. 5:9). In addition the ruling Lord of the Night and lunar data are provided. In English, this text can be rendered as, "Nine bak'tuns, 12 k'atuns, 2 tuns, 0 winals, and 16 k'ins (after the current era began) on the day 5 Kib [when the seventh Lord of the Night reigned, the lunation was twenty-seven days old, the second lunation (in the current cycle of six) had been completed, X was the lunation's name, and it was a 29-day lunation] 14 Yaxk'in, was born Lady K'atun Ahaw, Lady Man Ahaw." This has been called a "simple" clause because on the surface it seems to have a single verb. Some of the glyphs that constitute the lunar and Lord of the Night information, however, probably also comprise small clauses, each with its own verb. We have oversimplified matters by including all of these glyphs in the temporal category. More will be said about this in Example 2 of Chapter 9.

A further elaboration of single statement clauses is sometimes encountered, especially in the inscriptions from Palenque, Copan, and

U bahil She goes as	Hoy (?) Ch'ul Na Companion Precious Lady	Na Wak Tun Lady 6 Tun	Na Motul de San Jose Ahaw Lady Motul de San Jose Ahaw	Na Lady	Bakab Bakab

Figure 5:5.   Clause From the text on Yaxchilan Lintel 15.

Figure 5:6.   *Tikal Altar 8 (Drawn by William C. Coe).*

Quirigua, where head numerals or full-figured glyphs may be used in Long Counts. Figures 5:10 and 5:11 are examples of each from Quirigua. The same kind of calendrical information is given in these examples; it is just more elaborately packaged.

U bah
He goes as   Names/titles of the prisoner

Figure 5:7.   *Text on Tikal Altar 8.*

CLAUSES CONNECTED BY DISTANCE NUMBERS

Many inscriptions contain more than one clause, and often each clause involves an event occurring on a different date. In these cases a Long Count date may be given for the initial clause, and the dates of the subsequent clauses are often connected by Distance Numbers. In rare cases, each clause starts with its own independent calendrical statement. The Piedras Negras Stela 3 text, whose first clause we just looked at, is a multiclause text with Distance Numbers (Figs. 5:8 and 5:9). The second clause begins with a Distance Number of 12 tuns, 10 winals, and 0 k'ins, which counts ahead from the date of the previous clause to the date of the event of the second clause. The analysis of this clause is shown in Figure 5:10. In English the clause reads, "It was 12 tuns, 10 winals and 0 k'ins (from the

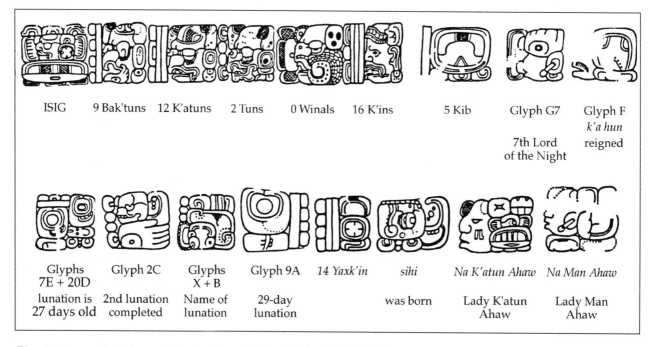

Figure 5:9.   *First clause of the text from Piedras Negras Stela 3, back.*

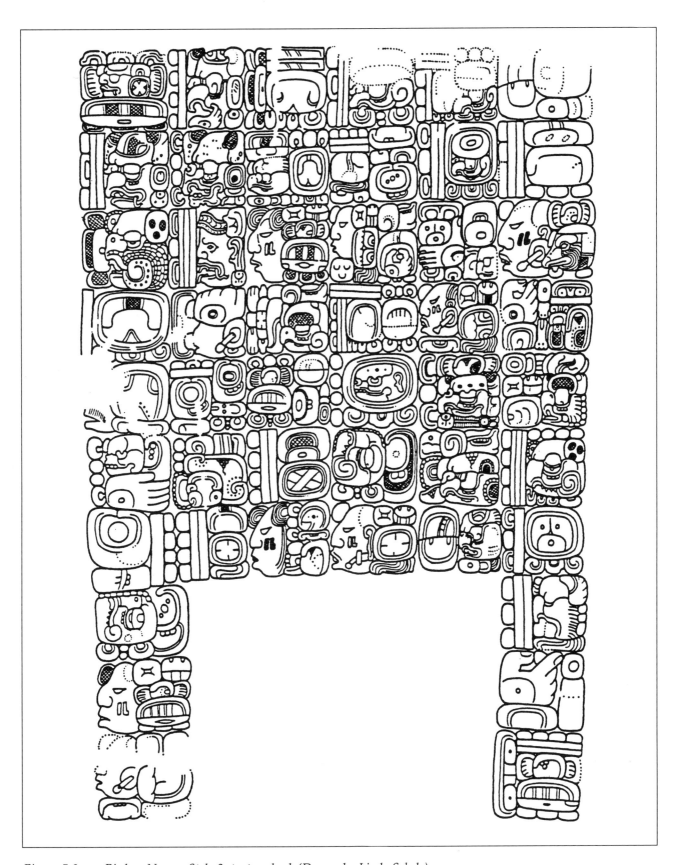

Figure 5:8.   *Piedras Negras Stela 3, text on back (Drawn by Linda Schele).*

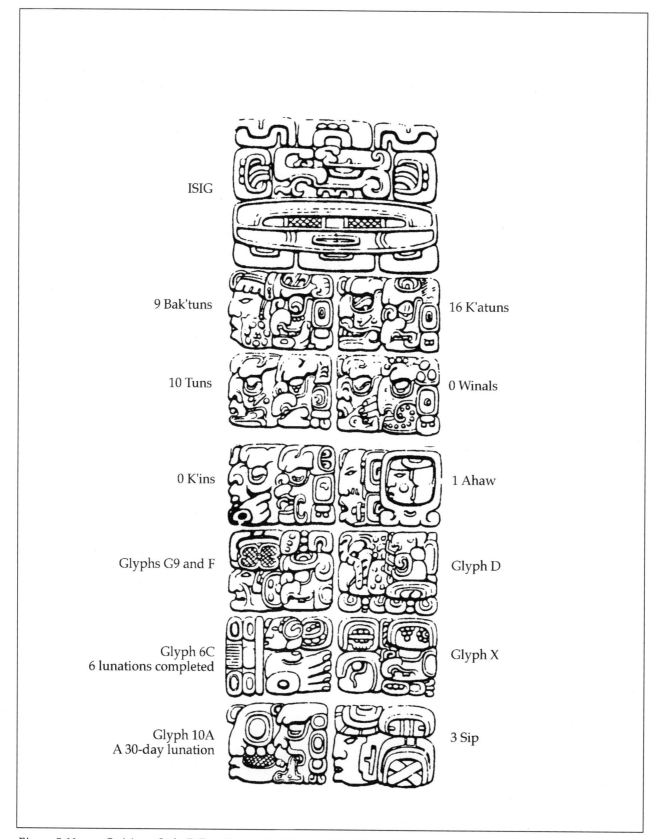

ISIG

9 Bak'tuns   16 K'atuns

10 Tuns   0 Winals

0 K'ins   1 Ahaw

Glyphs G9 and F   Glyph D

Glyph 6C
6 lunations completed   Glyph X

Glyph 10A
A 30-day lunation   3 Sip

Figure 5:11.   Quirigua Stela F, East Face, Initial Series (Maudslay 1889).

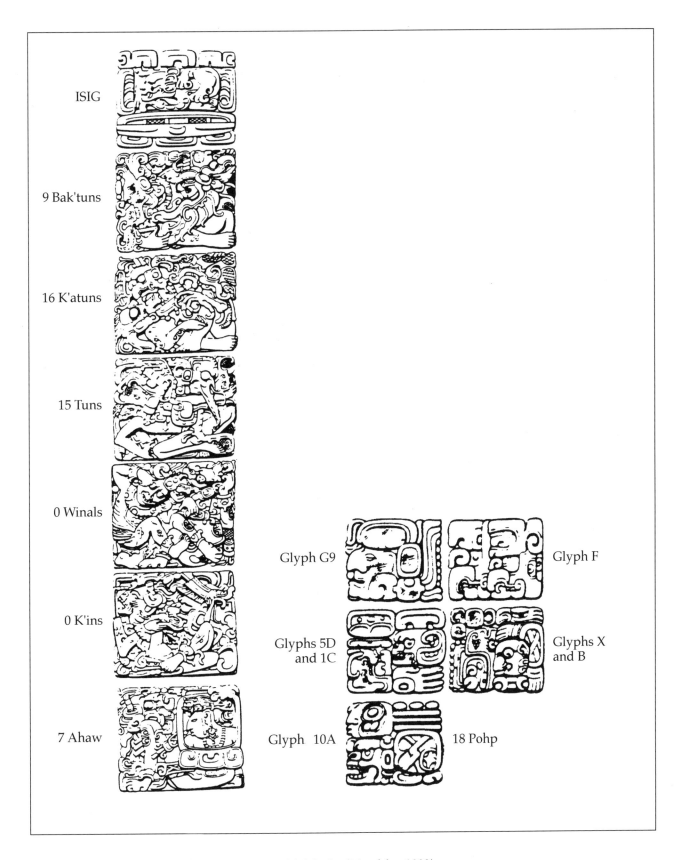

ISIG

9 Bak'tuns

16 K'atuns

15 Tuns

0 Winals

Glyph G9   Glyph F

0 K'ins

Glyphs 5D   Glyphs X
and 1C   and B

7 Ahaw   Glyph 10A   18 Pohp

Figure 5:12.   Quirigua Stela D, East Face, Initial Series (Maudslay 1889).

| D.N. = 12.10.0 | *iwal ut* and then happened | *1 Kib 14 Yaxk'in* | *nawah* was adorned | *Na K'atun Ahaw* Lady K'atun Ahaw | *Na Man Ahaw* Lady Man Ahaw | *ichnal* accompanied by | *K'inich Yokibnal* Ruler 3 |

Figure 5:10.   The second clause from the text on the back of Piedras Negras Stela 3.

birth of Lady K'atun Ahaw) and then happened the day 1 Kib 14 Yaxk'in when a *nahwah* event was carried out by Lady K'atun Ahaw, Lady Man Ahaw, accompanied by Ruler 3." As was mentioned in Chapter 3, *nawah* can mean "to be dressed" or "adorned," and here it probably indicates a betrothal or marriage, or preparation for one of these events.

Note that in this clause we counted the time indicated by the Distance Number in the forward direction. As you learned in Chapter 2, we were signaled to

do this by the *iwal ut* between the Distance Number and the Calendar Round. Often there is such an indicator which tells which direction we must count, but sometimes there is not. In those cases, unless there is some other reason for knowing which direction to count, it must be determined by trial and error.

Distance Numbers are also used to connect two events occurring on different dates but given in a single statement (Fig. 5:13), as illustrated in an example from Piedras Negras Stela 36 (Fig. 5:14). In

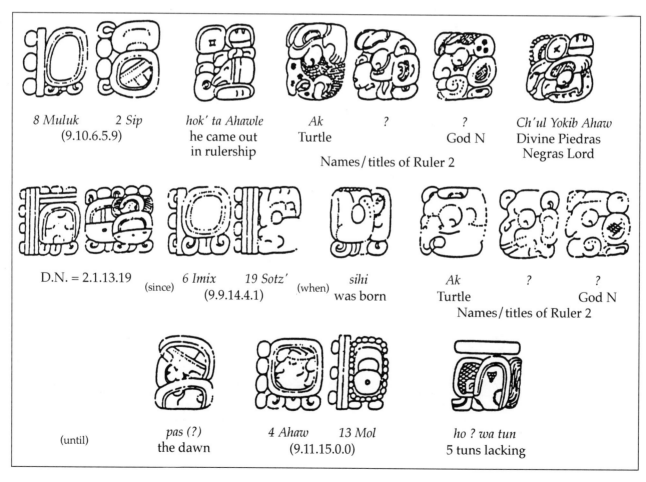

| *8 Muluk   2 Sip* (9.10.6.5.9) | *hok' ta Ahawle* he came out in rulership | *Ak* Turtle | ? | ? God N | *Ch'ul Yokib Ahaw* Divine Piedras Negras Lord |

Names/titles of Ruler 2

| D.N. = 2.1.13.19 (since) | *6 Imix   19 Sotz'* (9.9.14.4.1) (when) | *sihi* was born | *Ak* Turtle | ? | ? God N |

Names/titles of Ruler 2

| (until) | *pas (?)* the dawn | *4 Ahaw   13 Mol* (9.11.15.0.0) | *ho ? wa tun* 5 tuns lacking |

Figure 5:13.   Partial text from Piedras Negras Stela 36.

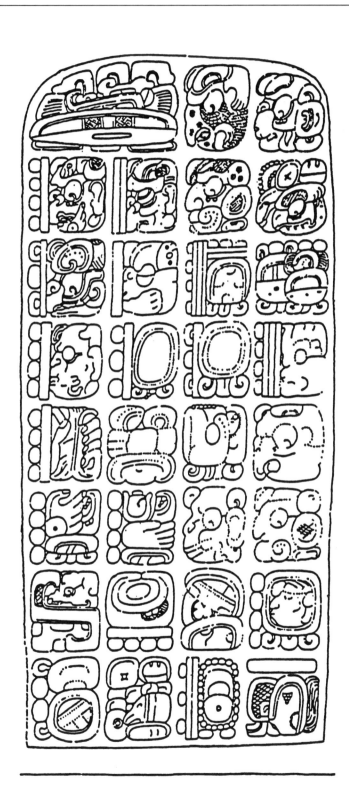

Figure 5:14.   Piedras Negras Stela 36 (Drawn by John Montgomery).

this case the text begins with the accession of Ruler 2.[1] It continues with a new clause introduced by a Distance Number connecting two different events not yet mentioned in the text. Neither of these latter events is connected chronologically to the first event in the text. The abbreviated first clause reads: "On 8 Muluk 2 Sip he came out in rulership [i.e., he acceded], Turtle, ? God N [title], Divine Piedras Negras Ahaw." The second clause reads: "It was two k'atuns, one tun, 13 winals, and 19 k'ins since 6 Imix 19 Sotz' when was born Ruler 2, until the dawn of 4 Ahaw 13 Mol when was ended 15 tuns [i.e., 5 tuns lacking of a complete k'atun]." In the second clause, there is no *iwal ut* to tell us that the Distance Number counted forward in time. However, the T126 subfixes on elements of the Distance Number and on the birth verb indicate that the birth is the earlier event, and thus the Distance Number must count *forward* to the 4 Ahaw 13 Mol Period Ending.

In many cases, Distance Numbers are preceded by a Distance Number Introductory Glyph (DNIG):

Distance Number Introductory Glyph (DNIG)

U tz'akah
It changed

The main sign is usually the "hel" glyph (T573), a logograph for the verbal root *tza'k*, meaning "to change." The second clause in the Yaxchilan Stela 12 text (Fig. 5:3), whose first clause we looked at above, begins with a Distance Number Introductory Glyph.

DELETIONS

Scribes often used special devices to tighten up texts, thereby eliminating redundant information. This was done in such a way, however, that there was no ambiguity in the meaning intended. We have already seen one example of such a device: in the first two clauses of Piedras Negras Stela 3, which we looked at above, there was an omission of information in the second clause (Figs. 5:9 and 5:10). A somewhat abbreviated translation of the first clause is: "On . . . 5 Kib . . . 14 Yaxk'in was born Lady K'atun Ahaw, Lady Man Ahaw." If the scribe had wished to include in the second clause all of the possible elements needed to refer back to the first clause, it could

have read: "Twelve tuns and 10 winals later [after 5 Kib 14 Yaxk'in when happened the birth of Lady K'atun Ahaw, Lady Man Ahaw] happened the day 1 Kib 14 K'ank'in when a nawah event was carried out etc." Glyphs representing the bracketed words were not written because they represented information that had already been given in the first clause, and it was not necessary to give the information again. No ambiguity resulted from the omission.

Although there were some deletions in the example from Piedras Negras Stela 3 we've just looked at, the protagonist was named in each clause even though it was the same person. Further shortening could have been achieved by deleting her name in one of the two clauses. We do this frequently in English when we link events occurring on different dates, but with the same protagonist. For example:

On the 12th of July, 1932, John Smith was born. Eight years and two months later, on the 15th of September, 1940, he became a Boy Scout.

The Maya did the same. For example, in the Temple of the Sun text from Palenque (Fig. 5:15), beginning at P6 there are three clauses that mention three different events on three different dates involving the famous Kan Balam, but his name is given only once. We pick up the text at P6-Q6 with the Calendar Round, 9 Ak'bal 6 Xul (Fig. 5:16). In the analysis in Figure 5:16, the deletions of Kan Balam's name are indicated in brackets. In English, the text reads: "On 9 Ak'bal 6 Xul he [Kan Balam] took office [i.e., became heir designate]. Five days later, he entered the tree, the sun [i.e., obtained some other title or status], Sun-eyed Kan Balam, the 'Boney Nahual,' accompanied by GI [one of the Palenque Triad]. It was six tuns, two winals, and 18 k'ins since 2 Kimi 19 Sotz' when he was born [Kan Balam] and then he entered the tree [became heir designate] [Kan Balam]."

Maya texts also contain a great number of examples in which two or more actions are performed on a single date by one individual, and the protagonist's name is given only once. For example, on severely fragmented Aguateca Stela 5 (Fig. 5:17), the Calendar Round of the second clause appears at C1-D1, and it is followed by two verbs before the names and titles of the protagonist are given (Fig. 5:18). It was not necessary to give the name of the protagonist after each verb because it is clear that the same actor carried out both of the actions. This part of the text can be read as: "On 8 Ahaw 8 Wo 13 K'atuns were completed, he scattered drops, he danced with a *hotob*(?), ??, with a mannikin, Etz'nab Sky God K, captor of ??, the 4 K'atun Ahaw, Divine Aguateca Ruler."

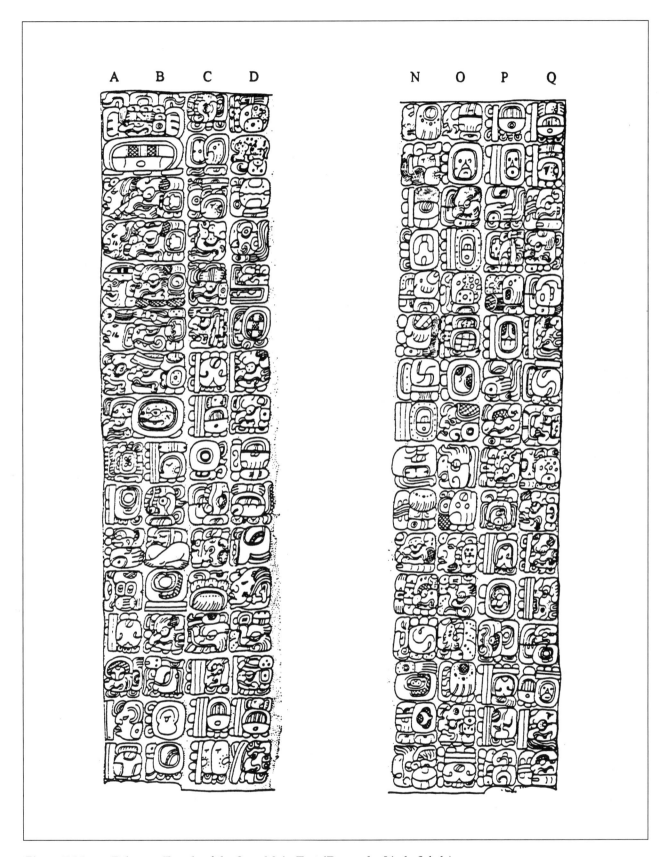

Figure 5:15.   *Palenque Temple of the Sun, Main Text (Drawn by Linda Schele).*

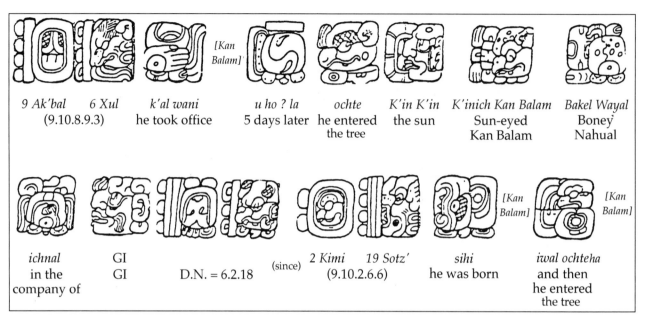

Figure 5:16.   Part of the text from the Temple of the Sun Tablet at Palenque.

COUPLET STRUCTURES

One of the characteristics of modern Maya speech is the delivery of important information in couplet form, i.e., stating an event twice or even more often with each statement done in a some- what different manner or with different ancillary information. The inscriptional texts contain many examples of couplets; they are used to emphasize important events in the lives of rulers. Palenque texts are especially rich in couplet structures. For example, in the text of the Palace Tablet (Fig. 5:20),

Figure 5:18.   Clause from text on Aguateca Stela 5.

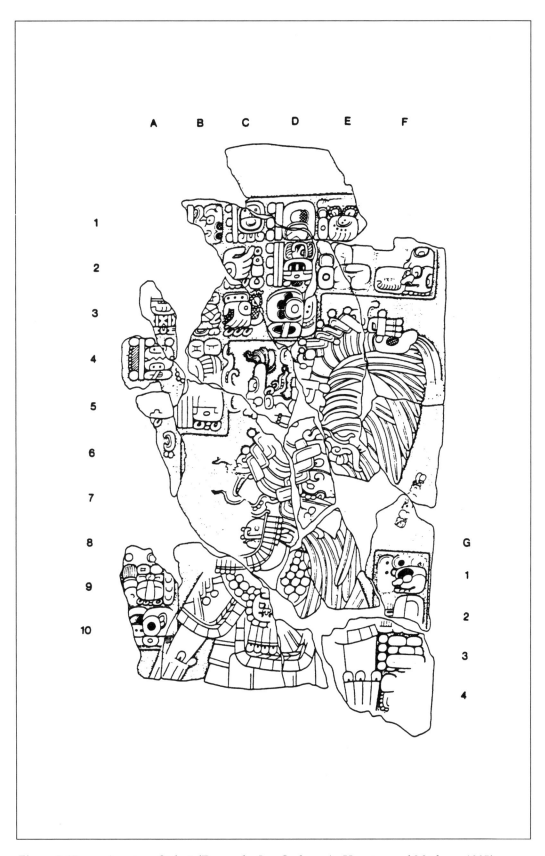

Figure 5:17.   *Aguateca Stela 5 (Drawn by Ian Graham, in Houston and Mathews 1985).*

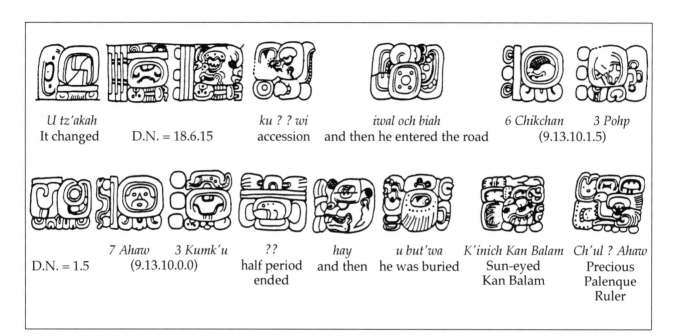

| U tz'akah | D.N. = 18.6.15 | ku ? ? wi | iwal och biah | 6 Chikchan | 3 Pohp |
| It changed | | accession | and then he entered the road | (9.13.10.1.5) | |

| D.N. = 1.5 | 7 Ahaw   3 Kumk'u | ?? | hay | u but'wa | K'inich Kan Balam | Ch'ul ? Ahaw |
| | (9.13.10.0.0) | half period ended | and then | he was buried | Sun-eyed Kan Balam | Precious Palenque Ruler |

Figure 5:19.   A couplet from the text of the Palace Tablet from Palenque.

the death of Kan Balam is presented in couplet fashion beginning at L15 (Fig. 5:19). In English the text reads: "It was 18 tuns, 6 winals, and 15 k'ins since his accession, and then he entered the road [i.e., he died] on 6 Chikchan 3 Pohp. It was 1 winal and 5 k'ins since 7 Ahaw 3 Kumk'u, the half period ended, and then he was covered [buried], Sun-eyed Kan Balam, Divine Palenque Ruler." In the first half of the couplet, Kan Balam's death is related to the date of his accession; in the second half, an associated event, his burial, is related to a half-period ending. Note that different information is given in the two components of the couplet, and that the subject is given only in the second clause.

The text on Tikal Stela 22 (Fig. 5:22) contains an example of a lengthy couplet that also illustrates deletion (Fig. 5:21). The first element of the couplet reads in English: "On 13 Ahaw 18 Kumk'u, the seventeenth k'atun (9.17.0.0.0), the tun was completed by Flower Mountain, Kan Boar, the Divine Tikal Ruler, the twenty-ninth successor of Yax Moch Xok (the founder). He is the son of ?? Kan K'awil, the Sun-eyed Man, the Divine Tikal Ruler, the 4 K'atun Chakte." The second element reads: "It was 2 tuns, 1 winal and 16 k'ins since 11 Kan 12 K'ayab (9.16.17.16.4) when he was seated as Chakte, and then he scattered drops [i.e., on 9.17.0.0.0]." The first part of the couplet is rather elaborate; in addition to announcing a Period Ending (9.17.0.0.0), and that Kan Boar "ended the tun,"

it also gives as additional information Kan Boar's succession number counted from the dynasty founder, and his father's name. The second part connects the Period Ending via a Distance Number to the date of Kan Boar's accession, and it elaborates on his ending of the tun given in the first part by adding that he also scattered drops (probably blood). Thus both elements of the couplet relate the same event—the ending of the tun by Kan Boar at the end of the seventeenth K'atun—but each element gives different information. There are deleted items in the second part of the couplet; for the two verbs given, the seating and the scattering verbs, no protagonist is stated, but it is clear that it must be Kan Boar. Additional examples of couplets are found in many other texts, for example, in the texts from the Temple of the Cross and the Temple of the Foliated Cross, both from Palenque, and Lintel 3 of Temple I from Tikal.

Another type of relationship between statements, though not strictly a couplet, comprises the linkage of two similar events, one done by a current ruler, and the other by a previous ruler or even a deity, usually from a time long before the time of the current ruler. The motive for such statements was probably the enhancement of prestige or the legitimization of rulership for the current ruler by connecting his event with an event of an illustrious predecessor/ancestor. An example of this kind of coupling occurs in the text on the west

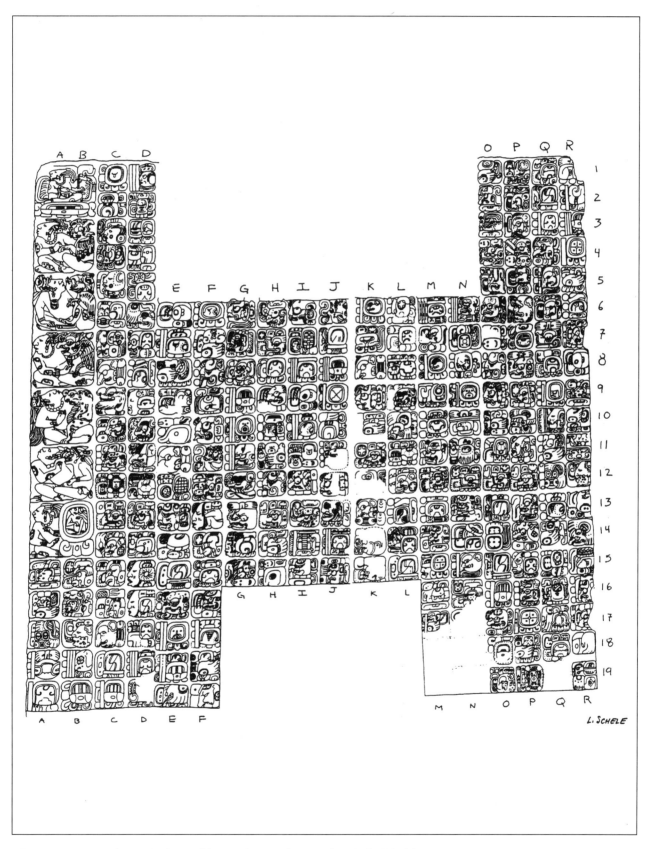

Figure 5:20. *Palenque Palace Tablet, Main Text (Drawn by Linda Schele).*

First Element of the Couplet

13 Ahaw   18 Kumk'u
(9.17.0.0.0)

u wuklahun k'atun
the 17th k'atun

k al tun
he closed
the tun

Nik Witz
Flower
Mountain

Kan Boar
Ruler C

Ch'ul Mutul Ahaw
Divine Tikal Lord

Yax Moch Xok
founder's name

U bolon k'al
29th

tz'ak
successor

??

U Nik
His Flower

Kan K'awil
Sky God K (Ruler B)

K'inich Winik
Sun-eyed Man

Ch'ul Mutul Ahaw
Divine Tikal Ruler

Kan K'atun
4 K'atun

Chakte
Chakte

Second Element of the Couplet

D.N. = 2.1.16

11 K'an   12 K'ayab
(9.16.17.16.4)

chumlah
he was seated

ti Chakte
as Chakte

iwal chok ch'ah
and then he
scattered drops

Figure 5:21.   Couplet from the Tikal Stela 22 Text.

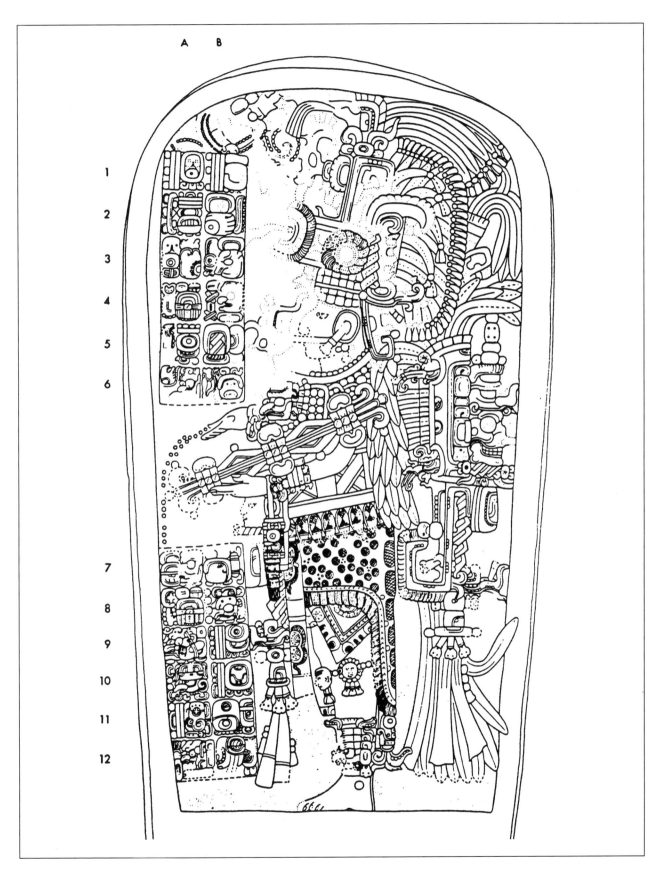

Figure 5:22. *Tikal Stela 22 (Drawn by William R. Coe).*

side of Stela C from Quirigua (Figs. 5:23 and 5:24). The first clause begins with a Calendar Round 6 Ahaw 13 Yaxk'in (9.1.0.0.0) (in the complete text the Long Count is also given), which is followed by the verb "he erected," and then the object erected, probably a stela. Next is the protagonist, Tutum Yol K'inich, who was apparently an early ruler of Quirigua, possibly the royal lineage founder. There follows a toponymic clause beginning with "it happened at," and the name of the place where the event took place. The second clause begins with a Distance Number of 17.5.0.0 (it should be 16.5.0.0) connecting the first clause Period Ending with what is probably the dedication date of Stela C, also a Period Ending date, 6 Ahaw 13 K'ayab (9.17.5.0.0). The rest of the clause records a scattering of drops by K'ak' Tiliw (Two Legged Sky) on the occasion of the dedication of and probably the erection of Stela C. This part of the Stela C text relates the Period Ending scattering by K'ak' Tiliw in current time to a Period Ending stela erection carried out 325 tuns previously by an early and presumably prestigious ancestor.

There are several other examples in the inscriptions of this prestige establishing coupling, for example, in the Temple of the Sun text at Palenque and in the text of Lintel 21 at Yaxchilan.

Ti CONSTRUCTIONS

Over a decade ago Linda Schele and coworkers recognized a special verbal structure in the inscriptions which consists of an auxiliary verb coupled to a verbal noun prefixed with *ti* (T59); these were named "*ti* constructions," and are used in modern spoken Maya (Josserand, Schele, and Hopkins 1985). In the texts the auxiliary verb is usually the T757 rodent head glyph (*ba*), prefixed with *u*, and it has a rather general meaning: he goes, he does, etc. This element is a constant in *ti* constructions. It is the verbal noun prefixed with *ti* that adds the specific semantic value to the expression; it tells what is done. These verbal nouns are glyphs that can appear in other contexts in verbal positions with verbal affixing, but in *ti* constructions

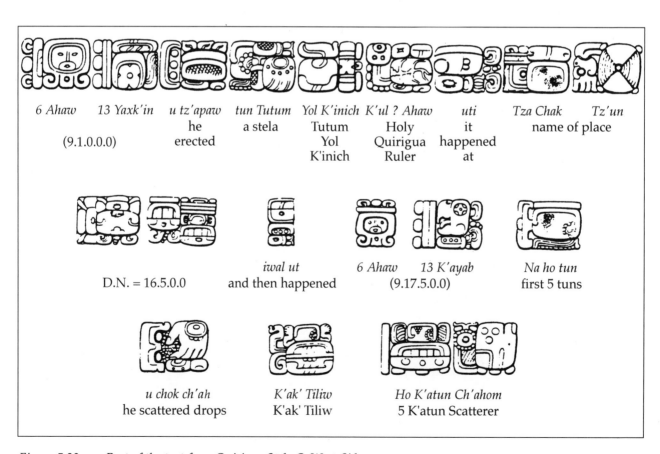

6 Ahaw	13 Yaxk'in	u tz'apaw	tun Tutum	Yol K'inich	K'ul ? Ahaw	uti	Tza Chak	Tz'un
		he	a stela	Tutum	Holy	it	name of place	
(9.1.0.0.0)		erected		Yol K'inich	Quirigua Ruler	happened at		

D.N. = 16.5.0.0	iwal ut	6 Ahaw	13 K'ayab	Na ho tun
	and then happened	(9.17.5.0.0)		first 5 tuns

u chok ch'ah	K'ak' Tiliw	Ho K'atun Ch'ahom
he scattered drops	K'ak' Tiliw	5 K'atun Scatterer

Figure 5:23.   Part of the text from Quirigua Stela C, West Side.

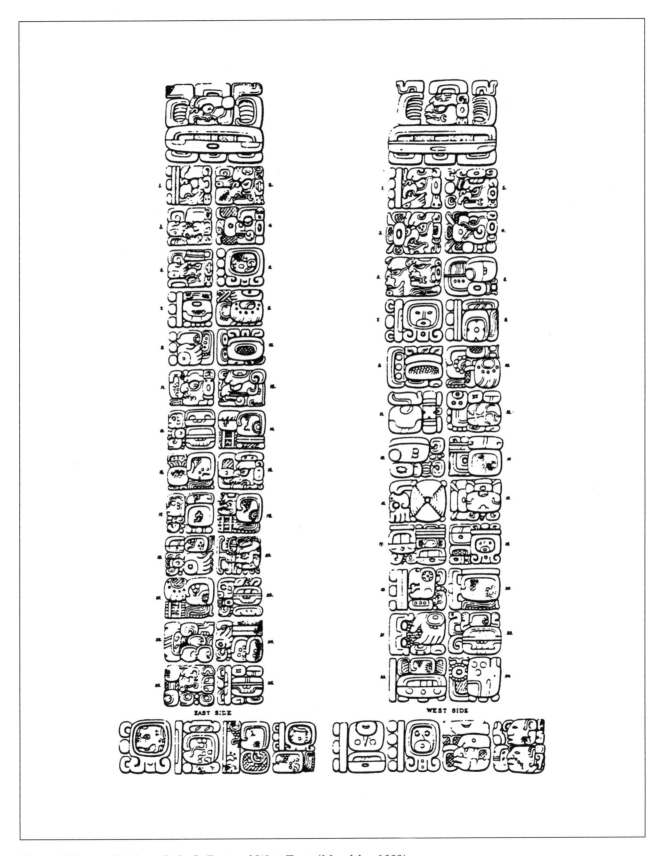

Figure 5:24.   *Quirigua Stela C, East and West Texts (Maudslay 1889).*

they do not carry the usual verbal indicators. *Ti* constructions are especially frequent in Yaxchilan texts, but they are also found at Piedras Negras, Naranjo, Copan, Bonampak, and other sites. The text on the back of Stela 1 from Piedras Negras contains a typical example (Figs. 5:25 and 5:26). The pertinent clause begins with a Distance Number and a Calendar Round date, which are followed by the T757 general verb prefixed with *u* (Fig. 5:25). The next glyph is the verbal noun, prefixed with *ti*, and although its meaning isn't precisely known, an anniversary celebration is implied. The date is the one-k'atun anniversary of the accession of Ruler 3 of Piedras Negras, but the protagonist of the event isn't Ruler 3—it is Lady K'atun Ahaw, who was probably Ruler 3's wife. In English this clause reads: "It was 1 k'atun, 2 winals, and 5 k'ins [since a previous event] until 5 Imix 19 Sak when happened an anniversary event carried out by Lady K'atun Ahaw."

The text of Yaxchilan Lintel 42 (Figs. 5:27 and 5:28) contains a *ti* construction which is part of a complex verbal structure. After the date, 12 Ahaw 8 Yaxk'in, comes the *ti* construction starting with *u bah*, followed by *ti* and the "Ahaw-in-hand glyph." In this case, "Ahaw-in-hand" probably means, "to take/hold the God K Scepter," which is what the protagonist is doing in the scene on Lintel 42. The second part of the verbal complex is comprised of *ak'ot*, the dance verb, and *ti-?*, which describes the nature of the dance or the object used in the dance. The final glyph apparently starts the name string of the protagonist, Yaxun Balam, or Bird Jaguar IV. An abbreviated translation of the passage in English is: "On 12 Ahaw 8 Yaxk'in the God K scepter was displayed, and a dance with ? was performed by Bird Jaguar IV." Recall from Chapter 4 that the overall form of the dance expression is similar to the form of a *ti* construction in that the dance verb, *ak'ot*, is followed by a collocation beginning with *ti*.

Ti constructions are members of a large group of verbal constructions consisting of a verb followed by a prepositional phrase often beginning with *ti*. We will see additional examples in the chapter on structural analysis.

PRONOUNS AND ERGATIVITY

The grammar we've learned so far in order to cope with Maya inscriptions has been fairly straight-forward. Other than some differences in syntax, the forms we've encountered are understandable in the same framework we use to understand English or the Romance languages. Maya languages, however, have a feature linguists term "ergativity," which English-speakers may indeed find "foreign." A characteristic of ergative languages, and the one that we should at least be aware of, concerns sets of pronouns and their uses.

The Maya languages we are dealing with have two sets of pronouns: Set A, the Ergative set, and Set B, the Absolutive set. Set A pronouns are used as the subjects of transitive verbs (i.e., verbs that have objects) and as the possessors of nouns. (It is consistent to have this pair of functions performed by the same pronouns, because in a sense the possessor of a noun *is* a subject, i.e., he/she/it who possesses.) If English were an ergative language, the same pronoun would be used in the following two sentences:

He carries apples.   (subject of the transitive verb *carries*)

His apples are here. (possessor of the noun *apples*)

Set B pronouns are used as subjects of intransitive verbs (i.e., verbs without objects) and objects of transitive verbs. Again, if English were ergative, the same pronoun would be used in the following two cases:

He runs fast.   (subject of the intransitive verb *runs*)

Mary loves *him*. (object of the transitive verb *loves*)

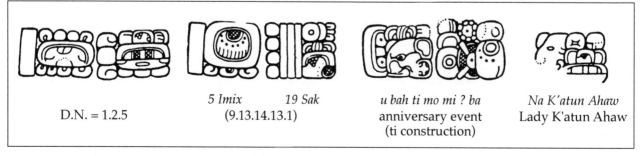

| D.N. = 1.2.5 | 5 Imix   19 Sak (9.13.14.13.1) | u bah ti mo mi ? ba anniversary event (ti construction) | Na K'atun Ahaw Lady K'atun Ahaw |

Figure 5:25.   *Ti construction in the text of Stela 1 of Piedras Negras.*

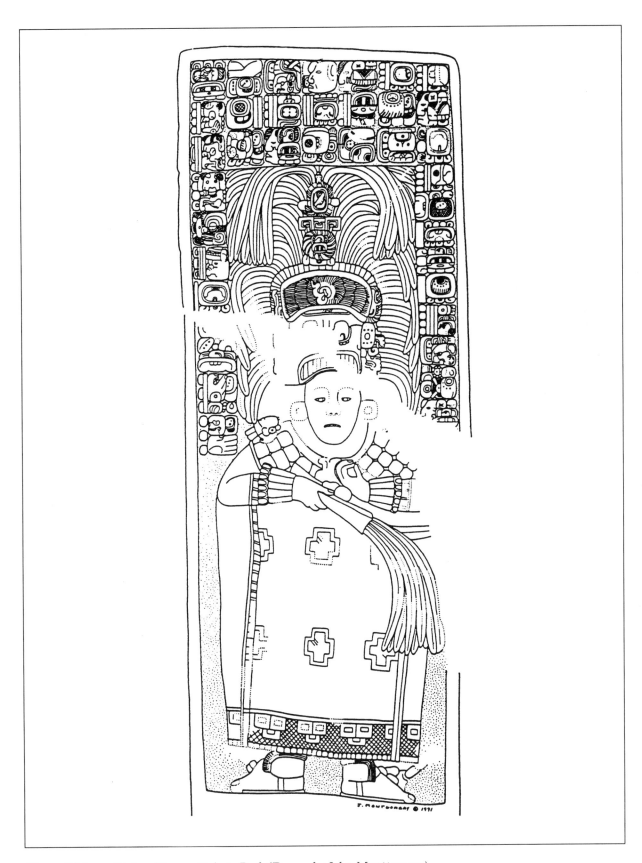

Figure 5:26.   *Piedras Negras Stela 1, Back (Drawn by John Montgomery).*

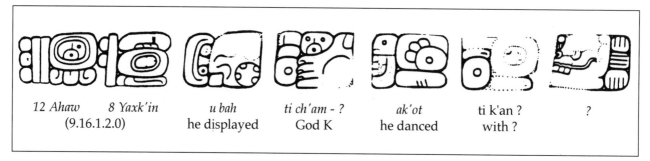

| 12 Ahaw
(9.16.1.2.0) | 8 Yaxk'in | u bah
he displayed | ti ch'am - ?
God K | ak'ot
he danced | ti k'an ?
with ? | ? |

Figure 5:27.   Ti construction as part of a verbal complex in the text of Yaxchilan Lintel 42.

We might expect that this situation could lead to major complications in the understanding of the inscriptions, but there are two mitigating factors that help to keep things simple. The first is that the clauses in the inscriptions are for the most part in the third person singular; they relate things that a person did, for example:

Ruler A (he) acceded.

Lady K'atun Ahaw (she) did a *nawah* event.

His First K'atun

So if a pronoun is used, it would be expected to correspond to an English third person singular pronoun (he, him, his, she, her, hers, etc).

The second simplifying factor is that the third person pronouns of Set B, the Absolutive set, are not voiced or written in Cholan and Yucatec, and thus we would not expect to find them in the hieroglyphic writing system. So what we are left with are the third person pronouns that serve as the subjects of transitive verbs or the possessors of nouns, i.e., the third person pronouns of Set A. In Yucatec and Cholan, this pronoun is *u*. Landa gave us a symbol for *u* (Fig. 5:29), and a similar sign (T1) occurs in the codices in places expected for such a pronoun, for example, as a prefix to a noun that is possessed. A similar sign, also designated T1 by Thompson, was found similarly affixed to nouns in the inscriptions, and by application of the substitution process discussed in Chapter 3, many other glyphic elements were found to be contextually equivalent to T1, and are thus also *u*. Some of these are shown in Figure 5:30.

We have already encountered clauses that use the pronoun *u* as the subject of a transitive verb (Set A). For example, in the text from Aguateca Stela 5 (Fig. 5:18), the scattering verbal expression, *u chok ch'ah*, is such a case (Fig. 5:31a). Even though a separate glyph block isn't devoted to an object, there is an object, represented both by the

dots emanating from the scattering hand and the *ch'a* postfix, a word for drops. One of the allographs of *u* is prefixed to the hand. The text line from Quirigua Stela C (Fig. 5:23) contains another example, where immediately after 6 Ahaw 13 Yaxk'in is the verb *tz'apaw*, which means "he erected it" or "he set it up" (Fig. 5:31b). This verb is transitive and the next glyph tells what was set up. Appropriately the verb is affixed with *u* (he). Because in these two cases a transitive verb is involved, and the pronoun represents the subject of the verb, the appropriate pronoun is from Set A, and it should be voiced, as it indeed is. We have also encountered some examples of intransitive verbs, which would take a Set B pronoun as subject, and as expected, no pronoun is seen since it should be unvoiced. For example, in the Aguateca Stela 5 text we saw that the dance verb *ak'ot* has no pronoun (Fig. 5:31c). Similarly, the seating verb *chumlah*, in the Tikal Stela 22 text (Fig. 5:21), also has no pronoun (Fig. 5:31d).

There are many examples of the use of the pronoun *u* as a possessor of nouns (the Set A pronoun) in "nametagging" statements found especially on portable objects. For example, one of the carved bones from the tomb of Ruler A of Tikal (Burial 116) contains an inscription starting with *u bak*, which literally means "his bone" (Fig. 5:32). The text, shown in Figure 5:33, reads: "His bone, *Ha Saw* (Ruler A), Title, Holy Tikal Ruler, West Chakte, His Flower (child of father) Shield Skull, Holy Tikal Ruler." The text not only announces the ownership of the bone, but also gives the owner's father's name. There is a companion incised bone (Miscellaneous Text 43) whose text starts in the same way, but ends by giving the owner's mother's name. These were obviously a pair.

Grammatically, these ownership statements begin with a "stative," i.e., an element that looks like a noun, but which is being used as a verbal element. A typical example of this kind of structure from the monumental inscriptions occurs in the

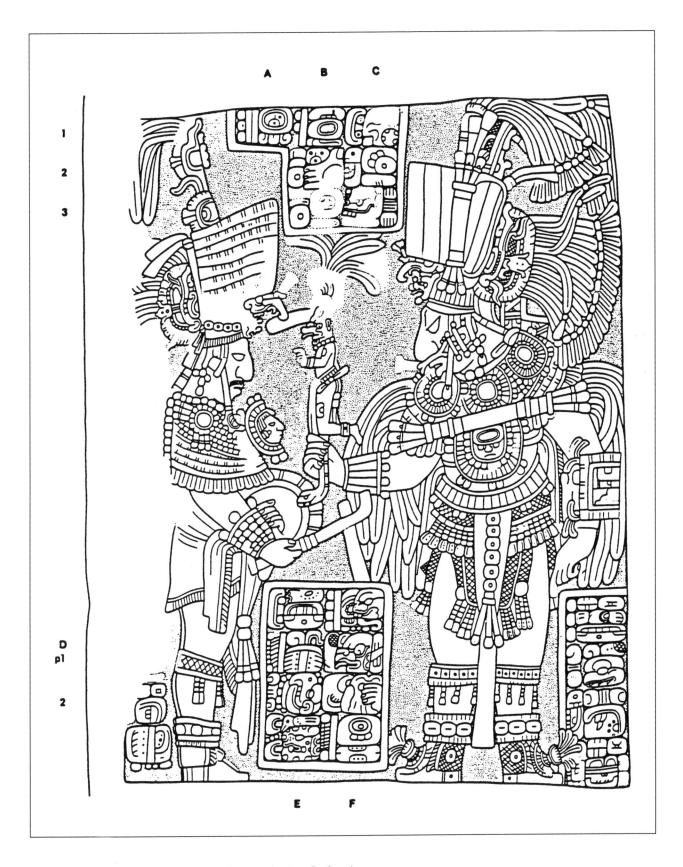

Figure 5:28.   Yaxchilan Lintel 42 (Drawn by Ian Graham).

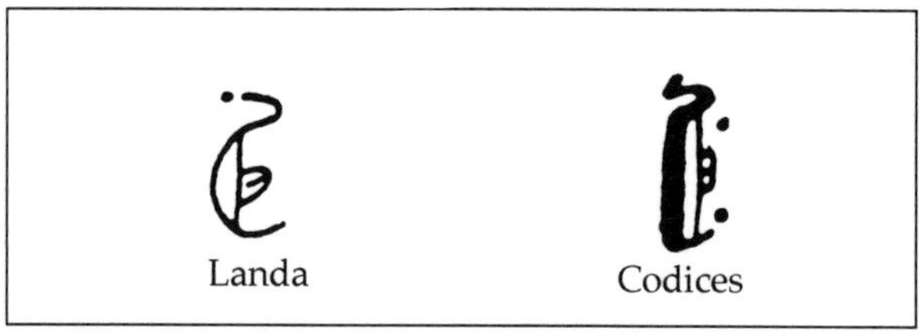

Figure 5:29. The Pronoun u from Landa and in the Codices.

Figure 5:31. Examples of pronoun use with transitive and intransitive verbs.

main text from Yaxchilan Lintel 8 (Figs. 5:34 and 5:35). This statement contains two clauses. The first one, which starts with the date, reads: "On 7 Imix 14 Sek was captured Jewel Skull."[2] The second clause starts with *u bak*, a stative element meaning "his bone" or "his captive." But *u bak* is acting as the verbal element of this second clause and it could be read as "He is the captive of." The clause then ends with the name of the captor, "Bird Jaguar, Holy Yaxchilan Ruler." This text might appear at first glance to be a single clause with one transitive verb (capture), an object (Jewel Skull), and a protagonist (Bird Jaguar). Because normal structuring in Maya languages discourages the introduction of more than one major nominal in each statement, however, it would not be good usage to have both the captive and the captor in the same clause. Thus the statement consists of two clauses. This is one reason why transitive verbs and grammatical objects are relatively rare in the texts—the presence of both subject and object would require that there be two nominals in a single statement.

It has previously been stated several times that virtually all of the statements in the inscriptional texts so far deciphered are cast in the third person because they are narratives, and the ubiquitous *u* is the third person pronoun used. However, there are a few cases now known involving another pronoun, *ni* or *in*, which in the languages we are dealing with

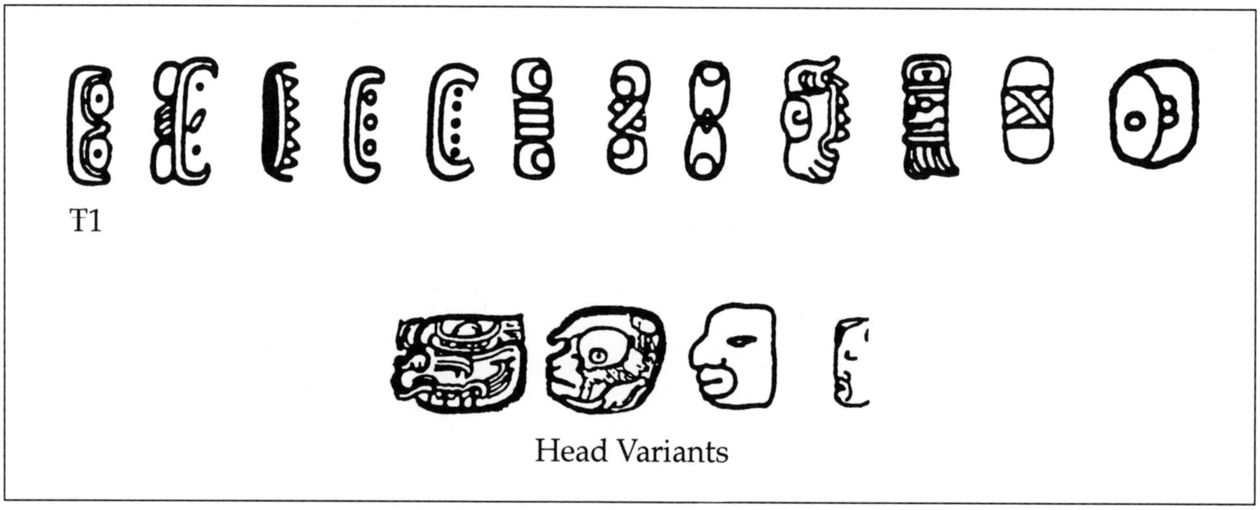

Figure 5:30. Allographs of the pronoun u.

Figure 5:32.   An incised bone from Burial 116 of Tikal (Tikal Miscellaneous Text 44, Drawn by Annemarie Seuffert).

is a *first person* pronoun, meaning *I*, *my*, or *me*. David Stuart has pointed out both verbs and nouns with T116 prefixes in a vase text (Kerr #1398, in Kerr 1989) which seem to contain first person statements made by figures in the vase's scene (Stuart 1989c). The T116 prefix apparently represents the pronoun *I* when prefixed to a verb and *my* when prefixed to a noun. One of the possible verbs, with a *ch'am* main sign affixed with *in*, is shown in Figure 5:36a. This collocation presumably reads, "I presented it" or " I held it." There is also an example in the inscriptional corpus of Copan. On Structure

10L-22 there is a text that contains a *k'atun* glyph prefixed with *in* *and *wi* (Fig. 5:36b). The *wi* probably means "one" or "first" in this context, and so the collocation is saying, "my first k'atun."

There is an additional item we must consider before we finish with grammar, and that is *aspect*. In English sentences, a major defining dimension is the time frame in which an event takes place: the present, past, or future. This parameter is the familiar *tense*. Maya clauses also express tense, as we saw above in the discussion of verbs, but a more important concern in modern spoken

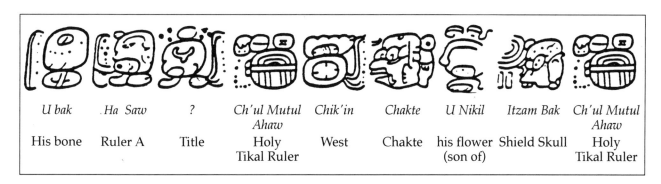

U bak	*.Ha Saw*	*?*	*Ch'ul Mutul Ahaw*	*Chik'in*	*Chakte*	*U Nikil*	*Itzam Bak*	*Ch'ul Mutul Ahaw*
His bone	Ruler A	Title	Holy Tikal Ruler	West	Chakte	his flower (son of)	Shield Skull	Holy Tikal Ruler

Figure 5:33.   Miscellaneous Text 44 from a bone found in Burial 116 at Tikal.

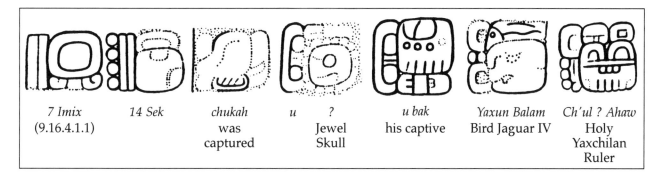

7 Imix (9.16.4.1.1)	*14 Sek*	*chukah* was captured	*u*	*?* Jewel Skull	*u bak* his captive	*Yaxun Balam* Bird Jaguar IV	*Ch'ul ? Ahaw* Holy Yaxchilan Ruler

Figure 5:34.   Part of the text from Lintel 8 of Yaxchilan.

Figure 5:35.   *Yaxchilan Lintel 8 (Drawn by Ian Graham).*

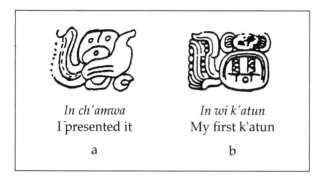

In ch'amwa   *In wi k'atun*
I presented it   My first k'atun

a   b

Figure 5:36.   Examples of collocations with first person pronouns.

Maya is *aspect.* Aspect tells whether an event is beginning, is continuing, or has finished. Linguists use such terms as "imperfective" or "incompletive" for an action that is not completed, and "perfective" or "completive" for one that is finished. In English we tend to use helping words to express aspect:

He begins to smile.   - incompletive

He continues to smile.   - incompletive

He is finished smiling.   - completive

Tense can be combined with aspect; the English examples just given are all present tense. In modern spoken Maya, aspect can be indicated by markers on pronouns and verbs, but thus far no aspect markers have definitely been identified in the inscriptional texts. So one might think that it's not necessary to be concerned with aspect at all. In addition to the possibility that markers may yet be found in the texts, however, one further condition may require attention to aspect. Analysis of modern

Cholan and Yucatec suggests that in clauses in the incompletive aspect (i.e., clauses with verbs that express an ongoing action), the pronouns of Set A are used as subject for both transitive *and intransitive* verbs; verbs in the completive aspect use the ergative pattern discussed above. This new pattern has been labeled "split ergativity." The net result is that in those cases in the inscriptions mentioned above for which the subject pronouns were from Set B (the subjects of intransitive verbs), and were thus silent and not expected to be found, we may now indeed expect to find pronouns in clauses which involve the incompletive aspect. One possible example of this split ergativity pattern is the very common verbal expression we have encountered several times, *u bah.* A currently accepted reading for this verbal expression is "he goes," which is intransitive and incompletive. The split ergativity concept would require that the voiced Set A third-person pronoun, *u,* be used, and indeed it is:

U bah

Currently, the concept of split ergativity in the inscriptional texts is controversial, and epigraphers are looking for examples that fit the split ergativity pattern.

NOTES

1. For simplicity, elements of the Initial Series and Supplementary Series have been omitted.
2. In the drawing, the numerical prefix of Imix is 10, but it must be 7.

6

THE ORIGINS OF CLASSIC MAYA
HIEROGLYPHIC WRITING

Now that we have seen how the Maya writing system works, and have been introduced to a substantial body of vocabulary, we will survey what is known about the early developments that led to Maya writing. Mesoamerica was the only area in the New World to develop writing systems, and several of them were in use at the time of the Conquest. Only two, Maya writing and a pre-proto Zoquean hieroglyphic system represented on the recently discovered La Mojarra Stela 1 (Veracruz), became essentially full-blown writing systems. Mesoamerican writing had its beginning sometime in the Preclassic period, probably in the early part of the first millennium B.C., but the earliest known monuments are from the middle of that millennium. A Zapotec writing system from the Oaxaca area is the earliest known to reach a moderate degree of sophistication, but its later development languished. Much of the later writing, except Mayan and pre-proto Zoquean, was pictorial in nature, with symbols for places and persons. Mixtec and Aztec writing are the best known of these, and they are two of the systems in use when the Spanish arrived.

Tracing the developments that led to Classic Maya hieroglyphic writing is a difficult task because the evidence, especially for the early stages, is so very sketchy (Coe 1976; Marcus 1976b, 1992c; Justeson 1986; Justeson et al. 1985b). We can document the path that led to a text like the inscription on the back of Piedras Negras Stela 1 (Fig. 6:1 and see Fig. 5.26), a text representing the epitome of the writing system as it flourished in the southern Maya lowlands in the sixth to eighth centuries A.D. As we have seen, a typical inscriptional text is composed of one or more clauses, and the elements used to form the glyphs in the clauses can fully represent spoken Maya. Used together they can generate all the needed grammatical elements: verbs, nouns, adjectives, prepositions, temporal

elements, etc. Also as we have seen, the syntactical order in texts generally follows a sequence common in modern spoken Maya: temporal element, verb, object (if any), and subject (T-V-O-S).

We will consider the first clause of the text on the back of Piedras Negras Stela 1 (Fig. 6:2) in detail, and look for the introduction of the components we find there in our survey of early inscriptions. This first clause has an Initial Series date beginning with an Initial Series Introductory Glyph (ISIG). The ISIG is composed of several significant elements. The main sign is a *tun* sign, and above it is a symbol representing the Patron of the Month in which the Long Count date falls, in this case Yaxk'in. The patron is flanked by two *ka* signs, and surmounted by a T125 affix. After the ISIG comes a Long Count date consisting of numerical coefficients and time unit signs—bak'tun, k'atun, tun, winal, and k'in—then a day sign with coefficient. There follows a Supplementary Series composed of Glyphs G and F, telling which Lord of the Night reigned, and Glyphs E–A, giving lunar information about the date. The entire text is followed by a month sign with coefficient. The clause continues with a verb indicating the action (birth), and is completed by giving the names and titles of the protagonist. This first clause is relatively long because of the elaborate temporal element. The remaining clauses are of similar form, except they have much simpler temporal elements. (This text is structurally analyzed in Chapter 9.) Ideally, in tracing the development of Maya writing, we should be able to document the introduction of each one of the features we have noted in the first clause of the Piedras Negras Stela 1 text, and as we will see, much of this is possible.

It is still not clear just where in Mesoamerica writing had its beginning. Some scholars favor the central Mexican area around Oaxaca, and oth-

2nd Clause

3rd Clause

1st Clause

4th Clause

Figure 6:1. Piedras Negras: Stela 1, back. (Drawn by John Montgomery)

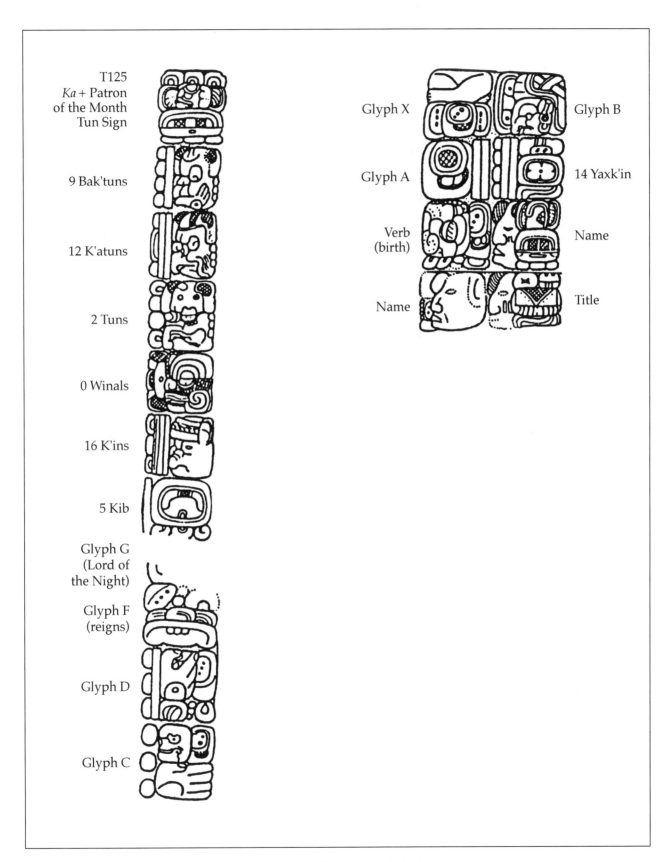

Figure 6:2. *First clause of the text on the back of Piedras Negras Stela 1.*

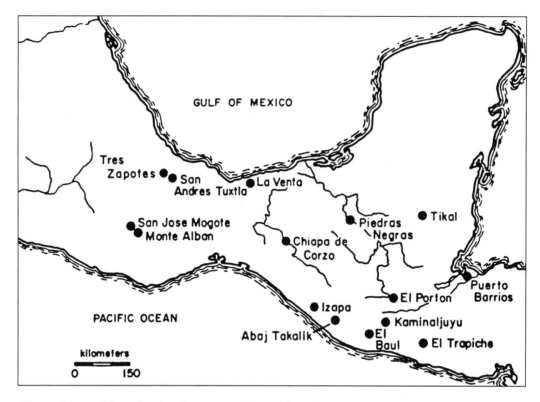

Figure 6:3.   Map showing important sites with early Mesoamerican texts (From Marcus 1976b).

ers support an Olmec origin in Veracruz and surrounding regions (Fig. 6:3). Early steps in the development of writing no doubt involved the extraction of units from iconographic compositions and the use of them to convey a semantic message. An example of this process in progress is the unprovenanced Humboldt Celt, estimated to date to about 900 B.C. (Fig. 6:4). This celt, attributed to the Olmec, contains an interesting configuration of designs, for example, the folded arms, the presenting hand, headdress elements, combs, staffs or scepters, a "pawnshop" symbol, a central *K'an* cross, and at least two elements that are similar to Maya *u* signs. Most of these elements are familiar in later compositions that we know are indeed writing. The Humboldt Celt has been seen as an early attempt to arrange separate iconographic elements in a form conveying a semantic message, but it's not really writing. Because of its early date, however, the celt is cited as evidence by those who propose an ultimate Olmec origin for all of Mesoamerican writing. Prior to the development of writing itself, bar/dot numerals were probably in use for counting for a long time over much of Mesoamerica, and no doubt the 260-day calendar was also widely in use.

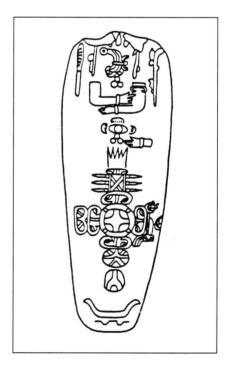

Figure 6:4.   Humboldt Celt (From Coe 1976).

Perhaps the earliest example of monumental art containing a hieroglyph, possibly a 260-day calendar notation, comes from a cave at Oxtotitlan in Guerrero (Grove 1970). In one of the Olmecoid style painted murals, dated at 900–700 B.C., is a possible day sign with a dot numeral coefficient (Fig. 6:5). The earliest known carved stone monuments that have hieroglyphs come from two areas, and from approximately the same time—a century or so after the Oxtotitlan murals. One of these, La Venta Monument 13 (Fig. 6:6), is from the Olmec heartland (Drucker 1952). In addition to a walking figure, the monument has a column of glyphs in front of the figure and a glyph shaped like a foot at the back. The last glyph in the column looks like a bird's head, suggesting that the column may constitute the names/titles of the figure. The foot, which in later Maya writing can mean road or way, could be a verb indicating travel. Thus the glyphs on this very early monument may constitute a simple clause containing a verb and a protagonist. The archaeology at La Venta places this monument at about 600 B.C.

Another monument of approximately equal age comes from a village site in the Oaxacan valley, San Jose Mogote, a forerunner to Zapotec Monte Alban, which archaeology places in the Rosario phase of the Oaxacan sequence. The monument, San Jose Mogote Monument 3 (Fig. 6:7), dated at about 600 B.C., shows a slain figure, possibly a captive, with two glyphs under his legs which have been read as "1 Earthquake," either a day name and number, or the calendar name of the slain figure (Flannery and Marcus 1983). While these two monuments contain little of what we see in the fully developed Maya writing system as exemplified by Piedras Negras Stela 1, their relative sophistication suggests that there must have been earlier examples of writing, which have not survived or been discovered.

The famous Danzante monuments of Building L at Monte Alban, dated to about 500–400 B.C. (a century or two after the San Jose Mogote Rosario Phase), display figures similar to the mutilated figure on San Jose Mogote Monument 3. Twenty or so of these also contain glyphic passages, for example, Danzante 55 (Fig. 6:8), which has a text of at least eight glyphs (Marcus 1983). Contemporaneous with these are two important monuments, Monte Alban Stelae 12 and 13 (Fig. 6:9), which go together, and in contrast to the Danzante monuments and San Jose Mogote Monument 3, consist of text only (Caso 1928). Here we now see some of the key characteristic elements of Classic Maya texts: two columns, bar dot numerals, main signs with affixes, day signs, "hand" glyphs which are probably verbs, and human and jaguar heads, at least one of which

Figure 6:5.   Oxtotitlan Painting 3 (From Grove 1970).

Figure 6:6.   La Venta Monument 13 (Drawn by Jane Mariouw; from Marcus 1976b).

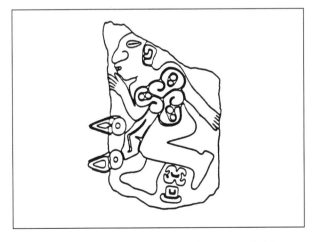

Figure 6:7.   San Jose Mogote Monument 3 (Drawn by Mark Orsen; from Marcus 1976b).

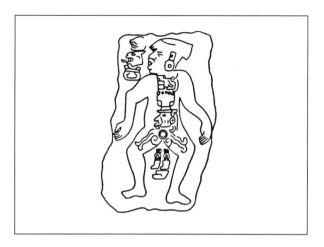

Figure 6:8.   Monte Alban Danzante 55 (Drawn by Mark Orsen).

Figure 6:9.   Monte Alban Stelae 12 and 13.(Drawn by Jane Mariouw; from Marcus 1976b).

may be naming a protagonist. This text, and other contemporaneous texts from Monte Alban, are the earliest known examples of a relatively advanced writing system. However, these are *not* Maya texts—they are Zapotec.

Another monument probably coeval with the ones we've been considering comes from the Middle Preclassic levels of El Porton, a site in the highland Salama Valley of Guatemala. El Porton Monument 1 (Fig. 6:10) is a stela which once had a central carved scene, now almost completely eroded, flanked by at least one column containing some very Maya-looking glyphs including numerals (Sharer and Sedat 1973). The surviving text contains no readable date, but the archaeology suggests that the monument was erected about 400 B.C., possibly making it the

earliest known example of Maya writing. As mentioned, El Porton is a highland site and, as we shall see, later examples of early Maya writing have also been found in the highlands.

The earliest monuments so far known containing Long Count dates come from Chiapa de Corzo in Chiapas and Tres Zapotes in Veracruz. Chiapa de Corzo Stela 2 (Fig. 6:11) is a fragment of a monument possessing some of the coefficients of a Long Count date and a day sign with a numerical coefficient (Lowe 1962). The date has been reconstructed as 7.16.3.2.13 (36 B.C.). The Long Count has no period signs as on Piedras Negras Stela 1, but there is part of a day sign that does not look Mayan. Tres Zapotes Stela C (Fig. 6:12) also has a Long Count date given in coefficients only

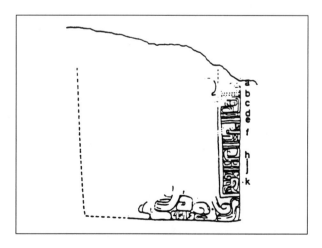

Figure 6:10.   El Porton Monument 1 (From Sharer and Sedat 1973).

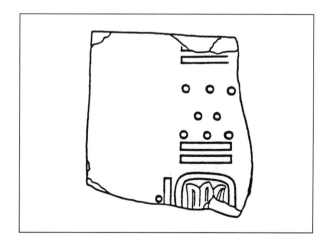

Figure 6:11.   Chiapa de Corzo Stela 2 (From Coe 1976).

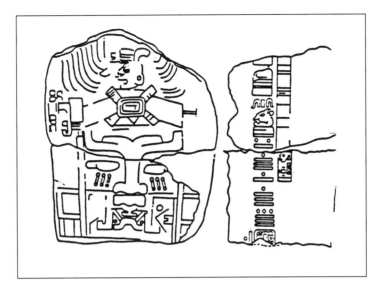

Figure 6:12. Tres Zapotes Stela C (From Coe 1976).

(7.16.6.16.18, 32 B.C.), and for the first time we see a Long Count introduced by an ISIG (Stirling 1940). This ISIG has the T125 superfix, a month patron (Wo), but no *tun* main sign. There are two columns of glyphs here, but in contrast to most later Maya texts, they are read separately, and there are text glyphs *above* the ISIG. Over all, neither the inscription nor the scene on the other side looks "Mayan."

It has been proposed by some scholars that these two monuments with the earliest Long Count dates were made by people who spoke a language ancestral to the Mixe Zoquean group of languages. Since these monuments were found in or near the area earlier occupied by the Olmec, it has also been suggested that the Olmec were in fact Mixe Zoquean speakers. If these monuments represent a Mixe Zoquean language, they may be early precursors of the other full-blown Mesoamerican writing system which has just recently been recognized. La Mojarra Stela 1 (Fig. 6:13), discovered in 1986 in the Veracruz region of Mexico, contains in addition to Long Count dates of 8.5.3.3.5 (A.D. 143) and 8.5.16.9.7 (A.D. 156), a very lengthy non-Maya hieroglyphic text which contains some signs also found in the Maya script (Winfield Capitaine 1988). The text surrounds a beautifully carved image of a standing ruler with an elaborate headdress and a complicated image above his head—a very Maya-like theme. The Tuxtla Statuette (Fig. 6:14) from San Andres Tuxtla, also in Veracruz, contains a shorter text in the same script with a date of 8.6.2.4.17 (A.D. 162) (Covarrubias 1946; Coe 1976). In these texts Long Count dates are given as bar/dot numerals. Each text is read in sin-

Figure 6:13. La Mojarra Stela 1 (Drawn by George Stuart).

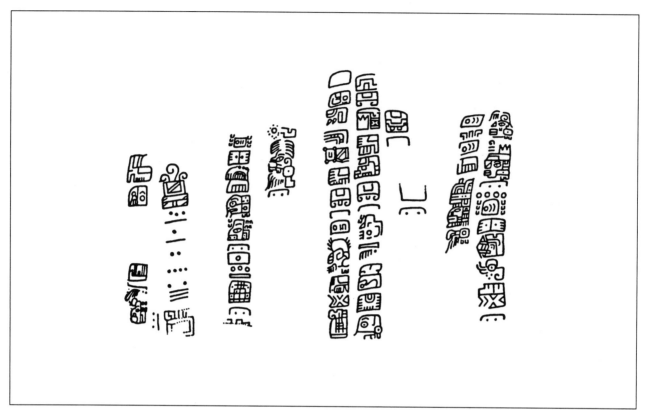

Figure 6:14.   Text from Tuxtla Statuette (From Coe 1976).

gle columns like Chiapa de Corzo Stela 2 and Tres Zapotes Stela C, and each has an ISIG like Tres Zapotes Stela C. These texts, along with a few other short ones in the same script, have recently been partially deciphered by J. S. Justeson and T. Kaufman (1993), who claim that they represent a pre-proto Zoquean language. Although this writing system is not Mayan, it obviously developed along side the Maya system, and there was clearly mutual interaction and borrowing.

To return to the sequence that led to Maya writing, we next consider two monuments dating to the seventh bak'tun from the Pacific slope sites of Abaj Takalik and El Baul in Guatemala. This is part of the Southern Maya area, where some of the earliest examples of Maya writing have been found. Abaj Takalik Stela 2 (Fig. 6:15) has a Long Count date beginning with 7 b'aktuns and 16 k'atuns—the rest of the date is lost—i.e., about 40 B.C. (Coe 1957). The largely eroded text consists of a single column of glyphs with a Long Count given as numbers only, introduced by an ISIG which is topped with T125, and which has the *tun* sign as main sign. This is the earliest known example of an ISIG with a *tun* sign. The surrounding scene contains two elab-

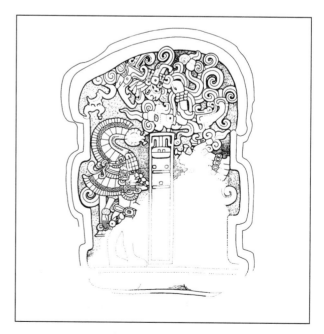

Figure 6:15.   Abaj Takalik Stela 2 (Drawn by James Porter under direction of Larry H. Benson, courtesy of John Graham).

Figure 6:16.   El Baul Stela 1 (Drawn by Linda Schele.

Figure 6:17.   Abaj Takalik Stela 5 (Drawn by James Porter under direction of Larry H. Benson, courtesy of John Graham).

orately dressed standing figures with a floating god/spirit in the clouds above them—a familiar scene on some Classic Mayan monuments. El Baul Stela 1 (Fig. 6:16) has a Long Count of 7.19.15.7.12 (A.D. 37) given simply as numbers without an ISIG, and a second double coulmn of glyphs (Coe 1957). In an unusual arrangement, the day sign and number, 12 Eb, *precedes* the Initial Series numerals. The accompanying scene consists of a single standing figure, holding a staff(?) with a floating figure above.

A somewhat later monument, Abaj Takalik Stela 5 (Fig. 6:17), contains two columns of glyphs,

each with an Initial Series date of numbers only (8.3.2.10.5, A.D. 103, and 8.4.5.17.11, A.D. 126) beginning with an ISIG topped by T125, and each date is followed by several other glyphs. There are standing figures on each side of the glyph columns, with floating figures above. These examples on the Pacific coastal plain suggest a connection with, or extension of, centers like Kaminaljuyu in the southern Maya highlands. There are no known monuments with absolute dates from this period at Kaminaljuyu, but the presumably contemporaneous exquisitely carved Stela 10 (Fig. 6:18) contains

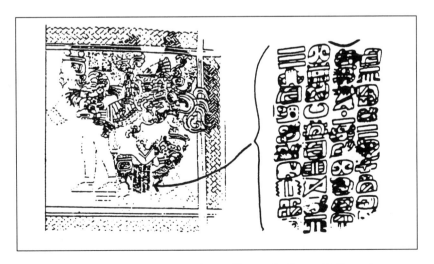

Figure 6:18.   Kaminaljuyu Stela 10 (Drawn by James B. Porter).

iconography and a text which seem to be Mayan (Coe 1976: fig. 10). Taken together, these examples from the southern Mayan area demonstrate that an extensive writing system was in operation in the southern highlands and on the Pacific slope near the end of the Preclassic.

What was going on in the Maya lowlands at this time? At the entrance to Loltun Cave in the Yucatan there is an early relief comprising a standing figure with several glyphs above, including a day sign with a coefficient of three (Fig 6:19; Grube and Schele 1996). The Jester God iconography on the headdress and the hand-carried weapons suggest that this is a ruler garbed for war. The glyphs have been interpreted as a Period Ending statement, possibly in the Late Preclassic at around A.D. 100, which would make this the earliest known dated monument from the Maya lowlands.

Other early indications that the Maya elite were beginning to use hieroglyphic writing as a means of proclaiming and solidifying their right to rule are seen at southern lowland Late Preclassic sites like Cerros in Belize. Structure 5C-2nd at Cerros is adorned with carved masks (Fig. 6:20) which contain easily identified single glyphs as part of the compositions: *yax* (great or blue), *k'in* (day or sun), and a knot which could be representing *hun*, a word for the headband that Maya rulers put on at their accessions (Freidel 1979). Unfortunately, there are no dates in these compositions, but the archaeology suggests that they are from about 50 B.C.

Probably within a hundred years or so after the Cerros masks, there are examples of texts, unfortunately also undated, which demonstrate the existence of well-developed texts in the Maya lowlands. For example, the Dumbarton Oaks jade (Fig. 6:21), a reused Olmec piece apparently from Quintana Roo, has a relatively lengthy text (Coe 1966).

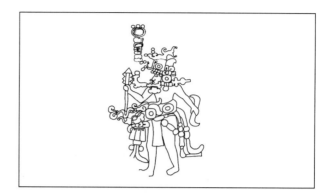

Figure 6:19.   Loltun Cave Relief (Drawn by Linda Schele).

Several of the glyphs can be read, and they describe the seating of a ruler who is named in the text. Accompanying the text is a drawing of a "seated" ruler, and his name glyph appears at his shoulder. A really monumental early text was carved on a cliff face at San Diego in the southern Peten of Guatemala (Fig. 6:22) (Schele and Mathews 1993:2). There is no Long Count, but oddly there is an ISIG with a *tun* sign and a T125. There is also a day sign and coefficient, elements of a Supplementary Series, but unfortunately the month glyph with its coefficient positioned above the ISIG, is eroded. Several of the glyphs in this composition can be read, including a bloodletting verb, and a probable toponym, *Yaxha*. The accompanying scene is composed of a standing ruler with a possible companion spirit figure (*way*) over his head. These and a few other undated short texts apparently belong to about the first century A.D., the Late Preclassic.

yax   k'in   hun

Figure 6:20.   Cerros Str. 5C-2nd (Drawn by Linda Schele).

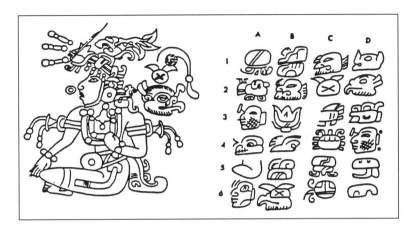

Figure 6:21. *Dumbarton Oaks Panel (Drawn by Linda Schele).*

The next group of inscriptions to be considered are dated, and they bring us into the early Classic. An elegant example is the unprovenanced Hauberg Stela, which lacks a Long Count, but has both day and month signs with coefficients, forming a Calendar Round date (Fig. 6:23). Recent research suggests a Long Count date of 8.7.17.14.4 (A.D. 197) (Schele, Mathews and Lounsbury 1990a). The text is relatively elaborate, beginning with an ISIG complete with *tun* sign, T125, and Patron of the Month, elements of a Supplementary Series, two event glyphs—a "first" bloodletting and an accession—and then the name of the protagonist. The accompanying scene shows the ruler whose events are described in the text. He is holding a double-headed serpent bar loaded with cosmological imagery. Although small in size, the Hauberg Stela is the earliest dated stela known from the lowlands.

The next monument in our sequence, Tikal Stela 29 (Fig. 6:24), is dated at 8.12.14.8.15, a.d. 292, and is the earliest securely dated monument from the Maya lowlands from a known archaeological context (Shook 1960; Jones and Satterthwaite 1982). The Long Count date is introduced by an ISIG complete with *tun* sign, Patron of the Month and T125, and for the first time both bar/dot numerical coefficients *and* the cycle symbols for bak'tun,

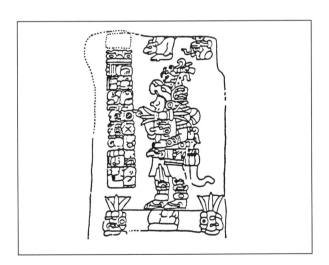

Figure 6:22. *San Diego Cliff Carving (Drawn by Ian Graham).*

Figure 6:23. *Hauberg Stela (Drawn by Linda Schele).*

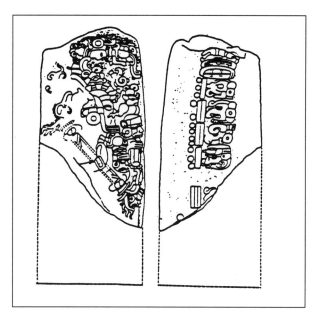

Figure 6:24.   Tikal Stela 29 (Drawn by William Coe).

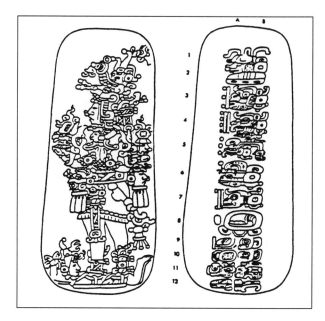

Figure 6:25.   Leiden Plaque (Drawn by Linda Schele).

k'atun tun, and so on, are used. That is essentially all that is preserved of the inscription. The scene on the other side shows a ruler holding a double-headed serpent bar, with a floating god or ancestor over his head—a scene typical of many Classic monuments.

The final inscription to be considered is that on the Leiden Plaque (Fig. 6:25), a relatively small object found near Puerto Barrios in the vicinity of the mouth of the Motagua River (Morley and Morley 1938). The text on this piece contains an Initial Series date of 8.14.3.1.12, a.d. 320. As on Tikal Stela 29, the ISIG has the three characteristic elements we have noted, and the date has both numerals and time unit symbols. In addition it has Glyph G of the Supplementary Series, both day and month signs with coefficients, glyphs representing a verb and protagonist, and glyphs

arranged in double columns—essentially all the elements we see in the text on the back of Piedras Negras Stela 1, our model for a full-blown Classic Maya text.

This brief survey outlines some of the steps that led to Maya hieroglyphic writing as seen at its height in the Late Classic. Essentially all the items discussed were carved on stone surfaces; early writing on perishable materials just hasn't survived. From the earliest known examples, it seems that writing on stone, coupled with iconography, is primarily about the acts of rulers and other elite personages, and it's clear that the purpose of these compositions was the enhancement of the ruling elite's prestige and its right to rule. In early times, writing may also have been used for mundane purposes, but the evidence for it hasn't survived.

7

GLYPHS AND ASTRONOMY

It has been known for a long time that the ancient Maya were intensely concerned with the positions and motions of certain astronomical objects. The early Spanish chroniclers tell of the identifications made by the Maya of Venus and other planets with some of their deities. In the codices there are extensive calendrical tables, the "Venus Tables," which deal with features of the synodic cycle of Venus, and tables which have been linked to the movements of Mars. Another group, the "Eclipse Tables," contains patterns of calendrical intervals which were used to predict the potential occurrences of both lunar and solar eclipses. The Venus and eclipse features of the codices were recognized many years ago.[1]

In the monumental inscriptions attention to the day-by-day motions of the moon is evidenced by the lunar glyphs, often given with Long Count dates. These were discussed in Chapter 2, and have also been generally understood for a long time.

In the last twenty years or so, new evidence for interest by the Maya in the positions of astronomical objects has emerged from increased understanding of the inscriptional texts. The planet Venus has been especially prominent in this work, although concern with Jupiter and Saturn has also been recognized. Three types of phenomena will be discussed as representative of this area of research.

VENUS EVENTS

From investigations begun primarily by Lounsbury (1982) and Closs (1979b, 1981), it is now known that several events in Maya texts indicated by "Venus" glyphs (Fig. 4:38), i.e., star-over-shell, star-over-earth, and star-over-site glyphs, were timed to coincide with specific positions of the planet Venus with respect to the sun. Other events, for example, accessions, were also found to occur on dates of sig-

nificant Venus positions. The potentially significant positions of Venus are the maximum elongations as morning or evening star, and the first and last appearances as morning or evening star.

A few definitions are in order:

Evening Star refers to a planet observed in the western sky after sunset.

Morning Star refers to a planet that rises in the east before sunrise.

Celestial Longitude is the angular distance in degrees from the sun of the projection on the ecliptic of the position of an object in the sky measured from the position of the sun at the vernal equinox (about March 21 in the Gregorian Calendar). Longitudes are measured in the easterly direction from the vernal equinox position, and are thus always positive (+). The sun's motion is always to the east through the sky with respect to the starry background. Its longitude is 0 degrees at the vernal equinox position, and it increases about 1 degree per day until it reaches 360 degrees (a complete solar year) when it reverts again to 0 degrees.

Ecliptic is the projection upon the sky of the plane of the earth's revolution about the sun. The ecliptic is the same as the apparent path of the sun through the sky each year.

Celestial Latitude is the angular position in degrees of a celestial object in the sky above or below the ecliptic. Latitude is positive (+) for objects above the ecliptic, and negative (-) for objects below the ecliptic. Since the planes of the orbits of the visible planets around the sun are very close to the plane of the earth's orbit, the apparent paths of the planets preceding or following the sun are very close to that of the sun; thus latitudes are very small, and for our purposes negligible.

Altitude is the angular distance of a celestial object from the horizon. Altitudes are not related to the starry background or the position of the sun in the sky.

Elongation is the difference in degrees between the celestial longitude of an astronomical object and the celestial longitude of the sun. It is thus the angular distance from the sun of the projection of an object on the ecliptic. Elongation is obtained by subtracting the longitude of the sun from the longitude of the object:

Elongation of X = Longitude of X - Longitude of the Sun

Elongations can be either positive (+) or negative (-). Objects that are east of the sun, for example, following it in the evening/night sky after sunset, have positive (+) elongations, while objects that are west of the sun, for example, preceding it before it rises in the east, have negative (-) elongations. In the following discussions involving Venus and other planets, elongations and longitudes are the quantities that are the most useful. To learn how to determine longitudes and elongations the reader should consult Appendix K, which shows how to determine the longitude and elongation of Venus on specific dates.

We will now consider the case of Venus specifically (Figure 7:1). From an observational point of view, when Venus is east of the sun, as an evening star, its elongation by convention is positive (+). Conversely, when Venus is a morning star, it is west of the sun, and its elongation is negative (-).

Figure 7:1 helps to visualize the changes in the position of Venus with respect to the sun as viewed from the earth as it makes a complete cycle in its motion in the sky. Both Venus and the earth are revolving about the sun in the same direction, but since we are interested only in the movement of Venus relative to the earth and the sun, the diagram assumes that only Venus is moving. Let's start when Venus is at 1, the point at which it is exactly between the earth and the sun (inferior conjunction), and is hidden from our view by the sun's brightness. As Venus moves out of the sun's disc (counterclockwise in our diagram), it first becomes visible as a morning star when it is about 5–7 degrees from the sun in the early morning sky at 2. This initial appearance is termed "first appearance as morning star" or "heliacal rising." To us here on earth, it appears to continue to move away from the sun until it reaches 3, whereupon it reverses its movement and begins to approach the sun. Position 3 is called the "maximum elongation as morning star," its farthest extension from the sun in the late night-early morning sky as seen from the earth. Its elongation, or its angular distance from the sun at this point, is about 45–47 degrees. As the apparent motion of Venus continues, it reaches 4, after which it disappears in the sun's brightness. Position 4 is called "last appearance as morning star." As at first appearance, Venus is about 5–7 degrees from the sun at this point. It remains hidden from our view behind the sun for about fifty days, during which it goes through superior conjunction, 5, when it is directly opposite the earth behind the sun. It emerges on the other side of the sun, making a "first appearance as evening star," 6, when it is 5–7 degrees above the sun in the early night sky. Its apparent distance from the sun increases until 7 is reached, the "maximum elongation as evening star," when it is about 45–47 degrees behind the sun in the night sky. As it swings back toward the sun on suc-

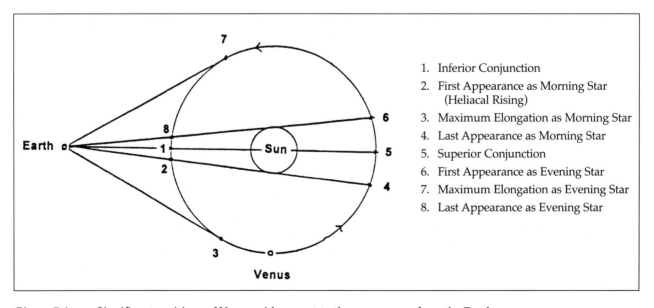

1. Inferior Conjunction
2. First Appearance as Morning Star (Heliacal Rising)
3. Maximum Elongation as Morning Star
4. Last Appearance as Morning Star
5. Superior Conjunction
6. First Appearance as Evening Star
7. Maximum Elongation as Evening Star
8. Last Appearance as Evening Star

Figure 7:1.   Significant positions of Venus with respect to the sun as seen from the Earth.

cessive nights, it eventually reaches 8, the "last appearance as evening star," and disappears from our view in the brightness of the sun's disc, ready to repeat the cycle. Each cycle, known as the synodic cycle of Venus, takes an average of about 584 days, or somewhat over a year and a half.

Now that we've defined the positions of Venus of potential significance to the Maya, let's look at some examples in the inscriptional texts. We will be dealing both with events that carry the "Venus" glyph, and events that occur when Venus is at a significant position in the sky. Because these two do not always coincide, we need to consider three categories of events: A—events carrying the "Venus" glyph and whose dates find Venus in one of its significant positions; B—events indicated by a "Venus" event glyph but on whose dates Venus wasn't at a significant position; and C—events which do not carry a "Venus" glyph, but on whose dates Venus was at one of its significant positions. Table 7:1 contains a sampling of events in these three categories.

The entries in the A portion of Table 7:1 have both a Venus glyph and a significant position of Venus. It has been proposed that Venus glyphs suggest a war activity, and in some examples this certainly seems to be the case. Thus in entries (1), (2), and (4) of Table 7:1A, toponyms for sites are mentioned, no doubt naming the site on which war was made or where it was carried out. The example in entry (4) comes from Aguateca Stela 2 (Figs. 7:2, 7:3), and involves a war event carried out on Seibal by the ruler of Dos Pilas. There is a pair of clauses, the first of which is the war event ("star-over-shell") on/at Seibal, and this is followed on the next day by an ax event. This part of the text reads in English: "On 8 *K'an* 17 *Muwan*, a war event was carried out at/on Seibal. One day later, on 9 *Chikchan* 18 *Muwan*, the writing of the formed image was axed (i.e., broken up)." On the first date of the text, 8 *K'an* 17 *Muwan*, the elongation of Venus was +7.13 degrees, which means it was just visible after sunset in the western sky, i.e., essentially at first appearance as evening star. The scene on Aguateca Stela 2 shows Ruler 3 of Dos Pilas appropriately garbed in *Tlaloc*-style war gear, and carrying a spear and *Tlaloc* shield. He is standing over a bound prisoner, probably one taken in the war on Seibal described in the text. This is an excellent example illustrating how text and iconography go hand in hand.

Not all the events that carry Venus glyphs in Table 7:1A are war events, for example, entry (5). Perhaps in such cases the Venus glyph is indicating a Venus ritual or is noting the special position that Venus occupied in the sky on that day.

The events in the B section of Table 7:1 also have Venus glyphs, but the dates do not correspond to special positions of Venus, at least as we currently understand them. However, some of these events

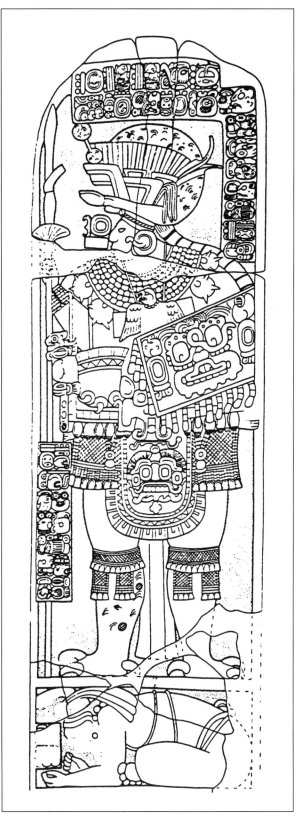

Figure 7:2.   Aguateca Stela 2 (Drawn by Ian Graham, in Houston and Mathews 1985).

TABLE 7:1 VENUS EVENTS IN MAYA DESCRIPTIONS

	Long Count Calendar Round Julian Date	Event	Protagonist	Venus Data Elongation (°)	Text
A. EVENTS WITH BOTH VENUS EVENT GLYPH AND SIGNIFICANT VENUS POSITION					
1	9.9.18.16.3 7 Ak'bal 16 Muwan Dec. 24, 631	Star-over-Shell (Naranjo)	Ruler V of Caracol	+5.13 first appearance as evening star	Caracol Stela 3
2	9.10.3.2.12 2 Eb 5 Wayeb March 1, 636	Star-over-Shell (Naranjo)	Ruler V of Caracol	-45.66 about 1° past max. elong. as morning star	Naranjo HS
3	9.12.0.0.0 10 Ahaw 8 Yaxk'in June 28, 672	Star-over-Shell	??	+45.60 max. elong. as evening star	Palenque TI (middle)
4	9.15.4.6.4 8 K'an 17 Muwan Nov. 29, 735	Star-over-Shell (Seibal)	Ruler 3 of Dos Pilas	+7.13 first appearance as evening star	Aguateca Stela 2
5	9.15.15.12.16 5 Kib 9 Pohp Feb. 11, 747	Star-over-??	Chak Ek' Yax Pas of Copan	+7.00 first appearance as evening star	Copan Temple 11
6	9.17.10.6.1 3 Imix 4 Sotz' March 29, 781	Star-over-Shell	Ruler 7 of Piedras Negras	+45.01 max. elong. as evening star	Piedras Negras Throne 1
B. EVENTS WITH VENUS EVENT GLYPH BUT NO SIGNIFICANT VENUS POSITION					
7	9.10.11.9.6 13 Kimi 14 Sek June 1, 644	Star-over-Earth	Balam Ahaw	-27.45	Tortuguero Stela 6
8	9.15.12.2.2 11 Ik' 15 Ch'en July 28, 743	Star-over-Shell (Yaxha)	Ruler B of Tikal	-23.67	Tikal Temple IV, Lintel 3
9	9.15.12.11.13 7 Ben 1 Pohp Feb. 4, 744	Star-over-??	Ruler B of Tikal	+23.44	Tikal Temple IV, Lintel 2
10	9.16.4.1.1 7 Imix 14 Sek May 5, 755	Star-over-Shell	Bird Jaguar IV	+28.32	Yaxchilan Lintel 41
C. EVENTS WITHOUT VENUS EVENT GLYPH BUT WITH SIGNIFICANT VENUS POSITION					
11	9.4.16.13.3 4 Ak'bal 16 Pohp April 13, 531	Accession	Ruler II of Caracol	+5.96 first appearance as evening star	Caracol Stela 15
12	9.11.0.0.0 12 Ahaw 8 Keh Oct. 11, 652	Unknown Verb + Venus Skull	??	+7.83 first appearance as evening star	Palenque TI (middle)
13	9.14.0.0.0 6 Ahaw 13 Muwan Dec. 1, 711	Period Ending	Ruler A of Tikal	+5.75 first appearance as evening star	Tikal Stela 16
14	9.15.9.3.14 3 Ix 2 Keh Sept. 13, 740	Capture	??	+7.52 first appearance as evening star	Bonampak Lintel 3
15	9.17.10.9.4 1 K'an 7 Yaxk'in May 31, 781	Accession	Ruler 7 of Piedras Negras	-7.15 first appearance as morning star	Piedras Negras Throne 1

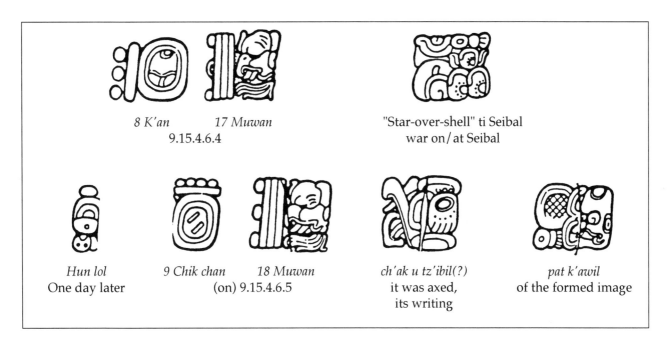

Figure 7:3. *Text from Aguateca Stela 2.*

clearly correspond to war events, for example, entry (8), which includes a toponym. Perhaps choosing the date for a war event without a significant Venus position was a matter of practical necessity.[2]

The third category of events in Table 7:1, those without "Venus" glyphs but carried out on dates with Venus in significant positions, is probably the largest category. As the small sampling in Table 7:1C shows, a variety of events is in this category. All the examples of this sample are first appearances of Venus as either morning or evening star, but Venus can be in other positions as well. The accessions in Table 7:1C on dates with Venus in significant positions are an interesting group, and they suggest that in setting dates for important events in the lives of rulers, Venus positions were probably considered. Accessions at significant Venus positions are not frequent, however, so when a coincidence does occur, there must be some question as to whether the date was intentionally chosen because of the position of Venus. The context has to be considered in each case: the iconography on the monument, and the other date/events in the text. In entry (15) of Table 7:1C, the date of the accession of Piedras Negras Ruler 7 follows the date of a Venus event that had occurred on a significant position of Venus just sixty-three days earlier (Table 7:1A, entry 6). It thus seems highly likely that the Piedras Negras Maya were following Venus positions in this time period, and that they chose to set the accession on the date of a significant Venus position.

In summary, there is not a 1:1 correlation of Venus event glyphs with either war-related events or significant positions of Venus, nor is there a 1:1 correlation of dates of war-related events with significant positions of Venus. However, there seem to be enough correlations to confirm that many of the coincidences we see are not accidental.

There have been several studies, mostly unpublished, in which the positions of Venus and the other visible planets have been determined for all of the dates recorded at a particular site, or associated with particular rulers, in the search for significant patterns. One published example is a study by Linda Schele and coworkers of the dates for four rulers of Copan: Smoke Imix God K, 18 Rabbit, Smoke Monkey, and Yax Pas—Rulers 12, 13, 14, and 16 in the Copan dynastic sequence (Copan Notes 99-101: Schele and Fash 1991; Schele and Larios 1991; Schele 191). The results are tabulated in Table 7:2.

Perusal of the table clearly suggests an intentional timing of important events in the ritual lives of these rulers with significant positions of Venus.[3] This correlation is heralded by two events recorded on Altar Q by Yax Pas and attributed to the dynasty founder, Yax K'uk' Mo', about 350 years before Yax Pas's time. The first of these events is probably the accession of Yax K'uk' Mo', and it falls on a date when Venus was nearing a maximum elongation as morning star. The second event, an "arrival" three days later, occurs *exactly* on the day of the maximum elongation. It's not certain that these are the actual dates for the Yax K'uk'

		TABLE 7:2 VENUS EVENTS NOTED AT COPAN			
		(Adapted from data given in Copan Notes 99-101}			
	Long Count Calendar Round Julian Date	Event	Protagonist	Venus Data Elongation (°)	Text
1	8.19.10.10.17 5 Kaban 15 Yaxk'in Sept. 5, 426	Took God K Scepter	Yax K'uk' Mo' (recorded by Yax Pas)	-46.20 near max.elong. as morning star and max. alt.	Altar Q
2	8.19.10.11.0 8 Ahaw 18 Yaxk'in Sept. 8, 426	Arrival	Yax K'uk' Mo' (recorded by Yax Pas)	-46.22 max. elong.as morning star	Altar Q
3	9.0.18.0.0 1 Ahaw 3 Mol Sept. 6, 453	Retrospective event	Noted by 18 Rabbit	-10.09 just past first appearance as morning star	Stela J
4	9.3.8.1.19 9 Kawak 17 Muwan Jan. 26, 503	Dedication	Ku Ix (noted by 18 Rabbit)	+46.23 12 days past max. elong. as evening star and near max. alt.	HS
5	9.9.14.17.5 6 Chikchan 18 K'ayab Feb. 5, 628	Accession	Smoke Imix God K	-46.18 10 days before max. elong.as morning star	Stela 2
6	9.10.19.5.10 9 Ok 3 Kumk'u Feb. 4, 652	Event(?)	Smoke Imix God K	-46.57 4 days before max. elong. as morning star	Stela 3
7	9.10.19.15.0 4 Ahaw 8 Ch'en Aug. 12, 652	Event(?)	Smoke Imix God K	-7.92 near last appearance as morn. star; close to sun's zenith passage	Stela 19
8	9.11.0.0.0 12 Ahaw 8 Keh Oct. 11, 652	Period Ending	Smoke Imix God K	+7.83 just past first appearance as evening star	Stelae 2,3,10, 13,16, 19, 23, C
9	9.12.0.0.0 10 Ahaw 8 Yaxk'in June 28, 672	Period Ending	Recorded by 18 Rabbit	+45.60 max. elong. as evening star	Ball Court West
10	9.13.3.5.11 3 Chuwen 4 Yaxk'in June 19, 695	Burial of Smoke Imix God K	Recorded by 18 Rabbit	-36.20 Summer solstice	HS
11	9.13.18.17.9 12 Muluk 7 Muwan Nov. 25, 710	Dedication of a phase of Str. 10L-26	18 Rabbit	+46.79 11 days past max. elong. as evening star and near max. altitude	HS
12	9.14.0.0.0 6 Ahaw 13 Muwan Dec. 1, 711	Period Ending	18 Rabbit	+5.75 first appearance as evening star	Stelae 16, C
13	9.15.0.0.0 4 Ahaw 13 Yax Aug. 18, 731	Period Ending	18 Rabbit	+46.30 6 days before max. elong. as evening star	Stela C
14	9.15.6.8.13 10 Ben 16 K'ayab Jan. 6, 738	Dedication of Ball Court III	18 Rabbit	+46.43 10 days before max. elong. as evening star	Ball Court III text
15	9.15.6.16.5 6 Chikchan 3 Yaxk'in June 7, 738	Accession	Smoke Monkey	-45.67 max. elong. as morning star.	HS
16	9.15.15.0.0 9 Ahaw 18 Xul May 31, 746	Dedication of Str. 22A	Smoke Monkey	-45.59 5 days before max. elong. as morning star	Str. 22A

	Long Count Calendar Round Julian Date	Event	Protagonist	Venus Data Elongation (°)	Text
	TABLE 7:2 CONT'D				
17	9.15.15.12.16 5 Kib 9 Pohp Feb. 11, 747	Venus Event	Chak Ek' (Yax Pas)	+7.00 near first appearance as evening star	Temple 11, east door
18	9.17.0.0.16 3 Kib 9 Pohp Feb. 5, 771	Event(?)	Yax Pas	+7.34 near first appearance as evening star	Temple 11, west door
19	9.17.12.5.17 4 Kaban 10 Sip March 15, 783	1 K'atun as ruler	Yax Pas	-46.35 1 day past max. elong. as morning star	Stela 8

Mo' events—the Maya were certainly capable of ret-rosetting events to coincide with significant positions of Venus.

Of particular interest for the tabulated events of the four rulers is the alternating pattern evident in the data. Thus the dates of Smoke Imix God K are primarily on days when Venus was in a significant position as *morning star*, as were the dates of the dynastic founder, Yax K'uk' Mo'. The next ruler, 18 Rabbit, reversed the trend set by his predecessor, and linked some of his events to Venus-as-*evening-star* episodes. In a couple of cases where dates of events recorded by 18 Rabbit did not fall on significant Venus positions (these are not in Table 7:2), the monument carrying the date/event had prominent Venus iconog-raphy, and thus a connection with Venus was still being proclaimed. Also for both Smoke Imix God K and 18 Rabbit, several Period Ending dates fortu-itously fell on dates with significant Venus positions: 9.11.0.0.0, 9.12.0.0.0, 9.14.0.0.0, and 9.15.0.0.0. Another reversal occurs in the events of Smoke Mon-key who set his accession and an important structure dedication to coincide with maximum elongations of Venus as *morning star*. The final reversal is by Yax Pas, who set two events to coincide with first appear-ances of Venus as *evening star*. His one k'atun anniversary as ruler fell on a maximum elongation of Venus as morning star, no doubt also seen to be of importance, because it was he who recorded early important events in the ritual life of the dynasty founder that were also set on dates when Venus was at or near a maximum elongation as morning star. Such connec-tions via Venus positions of an event in a ruler's life with an event of a revered predecessor were probably seen to be of great importance. Another example of this connection phenomenon is the dedication by 18 Rabbit of an important phase of Structure 10L-26 on a maximum elongation by Venus as evening star and the dedication by Ku Ix (the fourth ruler) of an early building on a date with the same Venus position but

over two hundred years earlier. All these Venus phe-nomena we have been considering are connected to one another by cycles of varied time periods as set forth in the Venus tables in the Dresden Codex, and no doubt such tables were used by Mayan rulers to make connections of their events to events of dynastic ancestors via Venus phenomena.

KAN BALAM AND THE PLANET JUPITER

Searching for correlations between astro-nomical events and events in the life of the illustrious Palenque ruler Kan Balam, Floyd Lounsbury found that several events occurred a short time after sec-ond stationary positions of the planet Jupiter (Louns-bury 1989c). In order to understand the significance of this correlation, we must first examine the details of the "retrograde motion" of planets.

To the viewer on earth, the retrograde phe-nomenon is an apparent reversal in the motion of a planet as it moves ever eastward through the sky in reference to the starry background. In contrast to the elongation of Venus that we have just discussed, where we were interested in the position of Venus with respect to the sun (which also constantly moves in an eastward direction with respect to the fixed stars), here the reference is the fixed stars them-selves. Hence it is the longitude that we are inter-ested in when looking for retrograde motion, and not elongation.

Retrograde motion is easily observed with the visible superior planets—those that are farther from the sun than the earth: Mars, Jupiter, and Sat-urn. The phenomenon is caused by the earth actu-ally catching up with and passing the planet as they both revolve around the sun in the same direction. What one sees from the earth is illustrated in Figure 7:4. Remember, our reference is the stellar back-ground. We begin at the right side of the diagram with

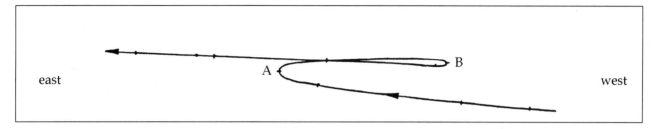

Figure 7:4.   Retrograde motion of a superior planet.

the planet moving on successive nights along the line in an easterly direction among the fixed stars (to the left in the diagram). When the planet reaches point A, it appears to halt its eastward motion, and after a short hesitation, it starts to move in a westward direction. That first halting, point A, is called the "first stationary position." The motion after A, now in a westerly direction, is called "retrograde motion." Eventually the planet again comes to a halt at point B in the diagram, and then resumes its normal eastward motion. Point B is called the "second stationary position." It is this position in the retrograde episodes of the planet Jupiter that seems to have been important in the timing of several events associated with

Kan Balam of Palenque. The retrograde motion phenomenon occurs rather frequently. In the case of Jupiter, it happens about every thirteen months, and each retrograde episode lasts about four months.[4]

Table 7:3 lists the events associated with Kan Balam that closely followed second stationary positions of Jupiter. The table includes two events from other sites which also closely followed Jupiter's second stationary positions. None of the dates in the table corresponds exactly to a second stationary position; it appears that the Maya waited until movement from the point could be clearly detected. The coincidences in the Kan Balam—related events are striking, and although there were other ceremonial

		TABLE 7:3. POSITIONS OF JUPITER WITH RESPECT TO THE PRECEDING SECOND STATIONARY POSITION			
	Long Count Julian Date	Event	Position of Jupiter after 2nd Stat. Position (°)[5]	Days after 2nd Stat. Position	Text
		KAN BALAM OF PALENQUE			
1	9.10.8.9.3 June 14, 641	Heir Designation	1.15	28	Temple of the Cross
2	9.12.11.12.10 Jan. 7, 684	Accession	0.37	15	Temple of the Cross
3	9.12.18.5.16 July 20, 690	2 Kib 14 Mol Event	0.34	15	Temple of the Sun
4	9.13.10.8.16 July 17, 702	12th Anniv. of 2 Kib 14 Mol	0.08	8	Temple of Inscriptions
5	9.13.13.15.0 Nov. 2, 705	"Apotheosis" Event	0.26	12	Temple XIV
		SHIELD JAGUAR OF YAXCHILAN			
6	9.12.9.8.1 Oct. 20, 681	Accession	0.17	10	Lintel 25
		RULER 4 OF PIEDRAS NEGRAS			
7	9.14.18.3.13 Nov. 9, 729	Accession	0.14	9	Altar 2

events associated with the life and reign of Kan Balam that weren't related to second stationary positions of Jupiter, the pattern of coincidences could not have been accidental. The table also contains two accession dates from other sites, one from Yaxchilan and one from Piedras Negras, which also occur just after second stationary positions of Jupiter. These may also have been intentionally set to correspond with departures from second stationary positions; however, in these cases there is no pattern of several coincidences in the events associated with these rulers which would confirm intentional settings.

JUPITER-SATURN CONJUNCTIONS

About every twenty years, we on earth observe Jupiter and Saturn undergoing a long-term conjunction that lasts for several months. The Maya were obviously watching these encounters, and apparently set some of their events to coincide with them, or with special features of them. Details of such an encounter are best visualized by examining a plot of the longitudes of the two planets during one of these episodes.

Figure 7:5 is a graph of the longitudes of Jupiter, Saturn and Mars during the conjunction which occurred in A.D. 689–690. The plot starts when the planets are about 10 degrees apart in the middle of October, 689. At this point, both are slowly moving eastward (toward the top of the plot). By the middle of February, 690, they have come very close to one another, but their paths do not actually cross. This point of near encounter also closely corresponds to a halt in their eastward progressions, at their first stationary positions.[6] The planets begin to move apart again as they retrograde to the west, and they reach a maximum separation during the episode around the middle of July, 690, when they each come to

standstills again (second stationary positions) on different days. Their motions are reversed, they resume their eastward journeys, and approach each other again with their paths actually crossing in the middle of September. The planets once again begin to diverge, reaching a separation of about 10 degrees by the middle of December. They are now on their long journeys to widely separated parts of the sky for the next nineteen years or so.

The conjunction just described is rather typical, but in some cases other striking features are evident. For example, in the A.D. 709–710 conjunction, the next one after the 689–690 example, the paths of the two planets actually cross early in the conjunction, and then near the second stationary positions, they linger for well over a month at virtually the same longitude providing a spectacular view of long-term intimacy. In other cases, after a crossing of the paths early in the episode, two more occur near the second stationary positions, resulting in three path crossings altogether.

The Maya probably saw great significance in these rare Jupiter-Saturn conjunctions. The planets can be very bright during these events, and that brilliance, coupled with the weavings in and out of the planets' paths through the sky, must have seemed especially portentous. During the conjunction just analyzed, the famous 2 Kib 14 Mol event celebrated by Kan Balam of Palenque took place. This was the first of a series of events carried out over a period of several days that seem to have been of great importance, although the exact nature of some of them is not completely understood. They are recorded in the inscriptions of the Cross Group temples at Palenque. Floyd Lounsbury was the first to point out that the date of the 2 Kib 14 Mol event occurred just after Jupiter and Saturn were at second stationary positions, or more precisely when the first detectable movements from these positions would have been

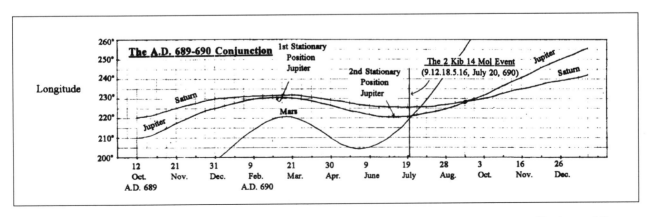

Figure 7:5. *A plot of the longitudes of Jupiter, Saturn, and Mars for the* A.D. *689–690 conjunction of Jupiter and Saturn.*

observable (Schele 1987:129–130). We have already seen that other events in the life (and afterlife) of Kan Balam were set to correspond to the movement of Jupiter from second stationary positions, and this one must have had added significance because of the concurrent conjunction of Jupiter and Saturn. Even further significance probably resulted from the close approach of Mars on the very day of the 2 Kib 14 Mol event (Fig. 7:5).

During the next two long term Jupiter-Saturn conjunctions in A.D. 709–710 and A.D. 729–730, events of significance took place at Yaxchilan in the reign of the great Shield Jaguar. In the A.D. 709–710 episode, after an early crossing of the paths of the two planets, but before the first stationary positions, bloodlettings and a building dedication were carried out by Shield Jaguar and Lady Xoc, presumably his wife. These events took place on 9.13.17.15.12, and were noted on Yaxchilan Lintel 24. During the next conjunction in A.D. 729–730, several events took place at Yaxchilan, still under the reign of Shield Jaguar, on the exact one k'atun anniversary of the events held during the previous conjunction. In this case, Jupiter and Saturn were just about to start retrograde motion, having been at first stationary positions. The events that were carried out on the day 9.14.17.15.12, included a capture and a bloodletting, both by Shield Jaguar. These are chronicled on Stela 18 of Yaxchilan (Harris 1990b).

It is not certain that the just-recounted events at Yaxchilan occurring during the A.D. 709–710 and the A.D. 729–730 conjunctions were really timed to coincide with these long-term Jupiter-Saturn conjunctions. They did not occur at particularly striking features of the conjunctions, and, as has been pointed out, the conjunctions last a relatively long time, so some events are bound to have occurred during them.

The three topics discussed above represent just some of the findings that have accrued which connect important recorded events in Maya history with planetary phenomena. In addition, other events have been found to coincide with conjunctions of two

or more planets. Also, some events in the reigns of the late period kings of Tikal seem to coincide with significant positions of the planet Mercury (Harris 1989c). No doubt through further study of known texts, and those yet to be discovered, many other events in Maya history will be found to occur on dates when significant planetary events took place. In addition to planetary considerations, increasing attention is being paid to the possible significance of the positions of individual stars and constellations, the occurrences of eclipses, and the appearance of comets on the dates of important Maya events. The crucial question which must be asked in each case is: Did the Maya intentionally set the date to coincide with the astronomical event? In the examples discussed above, it seems highly likely that they did because of the patterns evident. Without such patterns, coincidences must be questioned. For a statistical survey of the coincidences of planetary phenomena with events recorded on Maya monuments, see Aveni and Hotaling (1994).

The above discussions have been about cases involving astronomical phenomena connected with events recorded in Maya inscriptions. There is another whole area that comprises associations of astronomical phenomena with Maya iconography. Although it is not a purpose of this chapter to discuss broadly such associations, some were hinted at above when reference was made to Venus/ Tlaloc–style war gear worn by the ruler depicted on Aguateca Stela 2, and we will look at one specific case involving a motif in the Bonampak murals.

On the north wall of Room 2 of Structure 1 at Bonampak is a linear arrangement of four cartouches situated above part of the main scene (Fig. 7:6). All these cartouches, in addition to the figures they feature, contain several Venus or star signs clearly suggesting astronomical implications. The left cartouche pictures a pair of copulating peccaries, and the one on the right contains a turtle with three Venus signs on its back. The middle car-

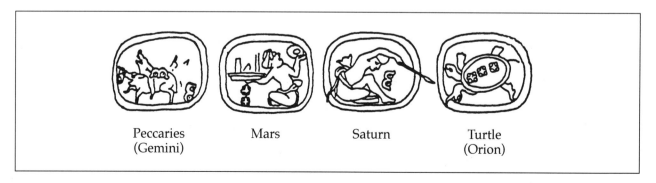

Peccaries   Mars   Saturn   Turtle
(Gemini)   (Orion)

Figure 7:6.   *Cartouches on the North Wall of Room 2 in Structure 1 of Bonampak (drawn by Linda Schele).*

touches feature posed anthropomorphic figures. Speculations over Maya associations of peccaries and turtles with astronomical constellations have been summarized by Floyd Lounsbury and Mary Ellen Miller, who suggest that Orion was certainly involved, although specific associations were not made (Miller 1986:48–50).

In developing ideas about the Maya view of creation as portrayed in the heavens (see Chapter 8), Linda Schele and coworkers have concluded that the turtle represents stars corresponding to part of our constellation Orion, including the three belt stars, and the peccaries are represented by the constellation Gemini (Schele 1992c; Freidel, Schele and Parker 1993). According to this proposal, the three Venus signs on the back of the turtle represent the belt stars of Orion. The two figures in between the two animal cartouches are similar to figures that have been observed to represent planets in other contexts. When Linda Schele examined the sky on the date given in this Bonampak mural (August 2, 792—Julian), she found that two planets, Mars and Saturn, are located between Orion and Gemini. She concluded that the two center cartouches must represent the planets Mars and Saturn, and that these four cartouches are an iconographic representation of an important part of the sky as it appeared on the date associated with the murals. Thus the Bonampak Maya were pictorially representing an important part of the heavens as

they appeared on that date. As we will see in the chapter on Glyphs and Cosmology (Chapter 8), the ancient Maya apparently projected on this part of the sky much of the symbolism connected with their concept of creation.

NOTES

1. For recent discussions of astronomy in Mayan codices, the reader is referred to *The Sky in Mayan Literature*, edited by A.F. Aveni (1992b), and several papers by Victoria Bricker (1988a,c) and Victoria and Harvey Bricker (1983, 1986b, 1989).
2. The above discussion refers to two groups of war-related events with Venus glyphs, some of which occur on dates when Venus is in a significant position, and some when Venus is not. There is another category of dates/events, not recorded in Table 7:1, which are war related, but neither carry a Venus glyph nor find Venus in a significant position.
3. It must be emphasized that for some of these rulers there are many other events known which do not fall on dates of significant Venus positions.
4. Appendix L contains a method for determining whether a date occurs during an episode of retrograde motion.
5. These values were obtained by use of a computer program called Ka'an, developed by Jorge Orejel of the University of Texas at Austin. The values were calculated for the specific longitude and latitude of each site.
6. During these long term conjunctions, Jupiter and Saturn each go through a retrograde motion episode. In the plot of Fig. 7:5, the prevailing eastward motion of the planets is upward, to ever increasing longitude. (In Fig. 7:4, ever increasing longitude is to the left.).

8

GLYPHS AND COSMOLOGY

One of the most exciting developments in the study of Maya hieroglyphs to come along in recent years is the detailed decipherment of several texts which have been known for a long time, but which now are known to deal with the ancient Maya view of the creation of the universe. This chapter will deal primarily with readings of several key texts and the ideas these readings reveal. Its primary purpose is to show how the decipherment of these texts has led to penetration into the world of cosmological thought of the ancient Maya. This development is due primarily to the insight of Linda Schele and several of her coworkers, including David Freidel, Barbara MacLeod, and several of Linda Schele's graduate students at the University of Texas.

The decipherments of specific key glyphs have resulted from the research of several investigators; in addition to Linda Schele, who has been central in all of this work, Barbara MacLeod, David Stuart, Nikolai Grube, Werner Nahm, and Stephen Houston have made major contributions. Much of the information contained in this chapter was presented by Linda Schele at the 1992 Maya Hieroglyphic Workshop at Austin, Texas. For further understanding of the ancient Maya creation story, the reader is referred to *Maya Cosmos: Three Thousand years on the Shaman's Path* (Freidel, Schele and Parker 1993) and to Linda Schele's *Workbook for the XVIth Maya Hieroglyphic Workshop at Texas* (Schele 1992c, d).[1]

The first texts to be considered are the main inscriptions from the Cross Group at Palenque: the Temple of the Cross, the Temple of the Sun, and the Temple of the Foliated Cross. These three texts are constructed in similar fashion; the first part of each deals with mythological material, and the second part with history. They are from the time of the famous Kan Balam, so their historical focus is on events leading up to and including his reign.

An important part of the mythological portions of these texts recounts the births of the Palenque Triad (GI, GII, and GIII) and their parents, who are key deities at Palenque (Berlin 1963). These birth events have been fairly well understood for almost two decades. Intertwined with the births are specific events involving creation, and it's the nature of these era-beginning events that has been obscure until the recent decipherments. The chronology of the mythological portions of the texts posed considerable difficulty in early studies, but keen analyses, principally by Floyd Lounsbury, have straightened out the chronological problems (Lounsbury 1976, 1980).

We will begin with the main text of the Temple of the Cross Tablet (Fig. 8:1). The mythological portion of this text relates the births of the parents of the Palenque Triad, who are called Hun Nal Ye Tzuk (GI') the father, and Na Sak(?) ("Lady Beastie") the mother,[2] and the birth of one of the Triad, GI. The mythological portions of the texts of the Temple of the Sun and the Temple of the Foliated Cross relate the births of GIII and GII, respectively, and the Temple of the Sun text also reiterates some of the events connected with creation.

All three texts begin with a lengthy temporal statement comprising an Initial Series date, a Supplementary Series, and an 819 Date Count expression (Chapter 2), but in the following analyses these lengthy temporal statements are omitted, and just the Long Counts and Calendar Rounds are given.

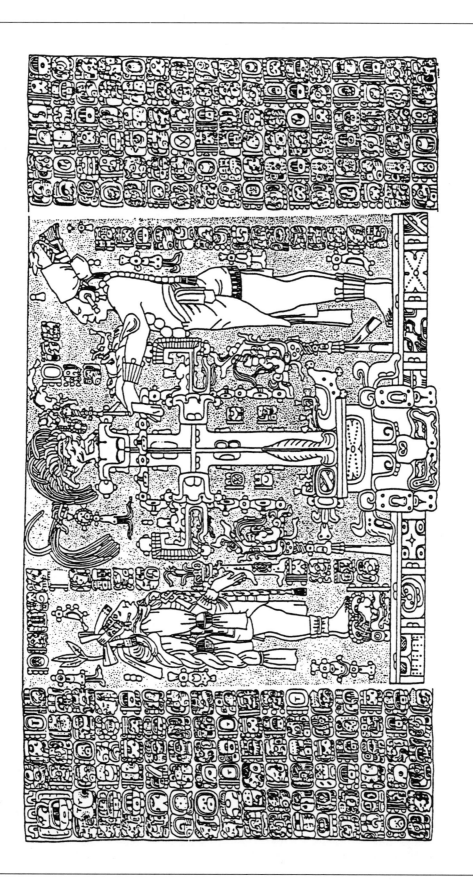

Figure 8:1.   Palenque: Temple of the Cross Tablet (Drawn by Linda Schele).

Palenque: Temple of the Cross (mythological portion)

The beginning date (12.19.13.4.0) corresponds to an event that took place in the era previous to the current era. We pick up the text with the birth verb following that date (Fig. 8:2).

English Translation

Twelve bak'tuns, 19 k'atuns, 13 tuns, and 4 winals (after the previous era began), on 8 Ahaw 18 Sek was born Lady Sak(?). It was 8 tuns and 5 winals since the birth (on 12.19.11.13.0) (of GI', not Lady Sak(?) and then a "deer hoof" event was carried out(for/by him) on 4 Ahaw 8 Kumk'u (13.0.0.0.0). Thirteen bak'tuns were completed. It was 1 tun, 9 winals and 2 k'ins since the image was made visible (on 13.0.0.0.0) at the Closed Sky, the First Three Stone Place, and then Hun Nal Ye Tzuk (GI') entered the sky. On 13 Ik' 20 Mol (0 Ch'en) (0.0.1.9.2) he (Hun Nal Ye Tzuk, GI') prepared/dedicated the Raised-up Sky Place, Eight House Partition is its holy name, it is the House of the North. It was 1 bak'tun, 18 k'atuns, 3 tuns, and 12 winals since Raised-up Sky Heart was set in motion by Hun Nal Ye Tzuk (GI') and then he (GI, one of the Palenque Triad) arrived at Matawil (a mythological place). On 9 Ik' 15 Keh (1.18.5.3.2), he (GI) touched the earth (i.e., he was born) at Matawil. He (GI) is the child of (literally he goes as the harvest of) Sak(?), Ox Ya Ch'okle Lady. It was 2 bak'tuns, 1 k'atun, 7 tuns, 11 winals, and 2 k'ins since her birth and then the white headband was closed for her (i.e., she acceded to rulership) Sak(?) on 9 Ik' 0 Sak (2.0.0.10.2) (Table 8:1).

Comments

The text starts with the birth of Lady Sak(?) on 12.19.13.4.0 of the previous era, and then it links the birth of Hun Nal Ye Tzuk (GI') to a "Deer Hoof" event carried out for/by him on the day beginning the present era, 4 Ahaw 8 Kumk'u (13.0.0.0.0). Lady Sak(?) and Hun Nal Ye are presumably equivalent to the first creator goddess and god mentioned in the Popol Vuh (the First Mother and First Father). Hun Nal Ye is also equivalent to an important deity in Maya thought and iconography, the Maize God. The nature of the "Deer Hoof" event is not yet understood. In form, the event glyph is similar to one that appears to be an heir designation event for future Palenque rulers. We are not given the actual date of the birth of GI' in this passage—it must be calculated from the date given for the "Deer Hoof" event and the Distance Number, 8.5.0. Like the birth date of Lady Sak(?), the birth of GI' also occurs in the previous era; it's about a year and a half before Lady Sak(?)'s. GI' is not actually mentioned in the birth-deer hoof clause, but he is the protagonist of the next clause, so it is clear that he is the protagonist of the birth-deer hoof clause as well.

This next clause is very important—it records the appearance of an image at Closed Sky (the sky is still dark), at First Three Stone Place. First Three Stone Place is extremely important in the creation story, and as we will see, it is mentioned in several other texts. Later, on 0.0.1.9.2, Hun Nal Ye Tzuk (GI') "entered the sky," and he "prepared/ dedicated the Raised-up Sky," which we are told is in the north. The "Raised-up Sky," which GI' prepared, is named the "Eight-House Partition," and this probably refers to the establishment of the

TABLE 8:1
Chronology/Events: Text of Temple of the Cross from Palenque

Long Count	Julian Date	Calendar Round	Event
12.19.11.13.0	June 16, 3122 B.C.	1 Ahaw 8 Muwan	Birth of GI'
12.19.13.4.0	December 7, 3121 B.C.	8 Ahaw 18 Sek\4	Birth of Lady Sak (?) ?
13.0.0.0.0	August 13, 3114 B.C.	Ahaw 8 Kumk'u	Image made visible at Closed Sky, the first Three Stone Place, Deer Hoof Event for/by GI'
0.0.1.9.2	February 5, 3112 B.C.	13 Ik' 0 Ch'en	GI' entered the sky GI' prepared/dedicated the Raised-up Sky Place GI' set in motion Raised-up Sky Heart
1.18.5.3.2	October 21, 2360 B.C.	9 Ik' 15 Keh	Birth of GI
2.0.0.10.2	September 7, 2325 B.C.	9 Ik' 0 Sak	A White Headband was closed for Sak (?) ?

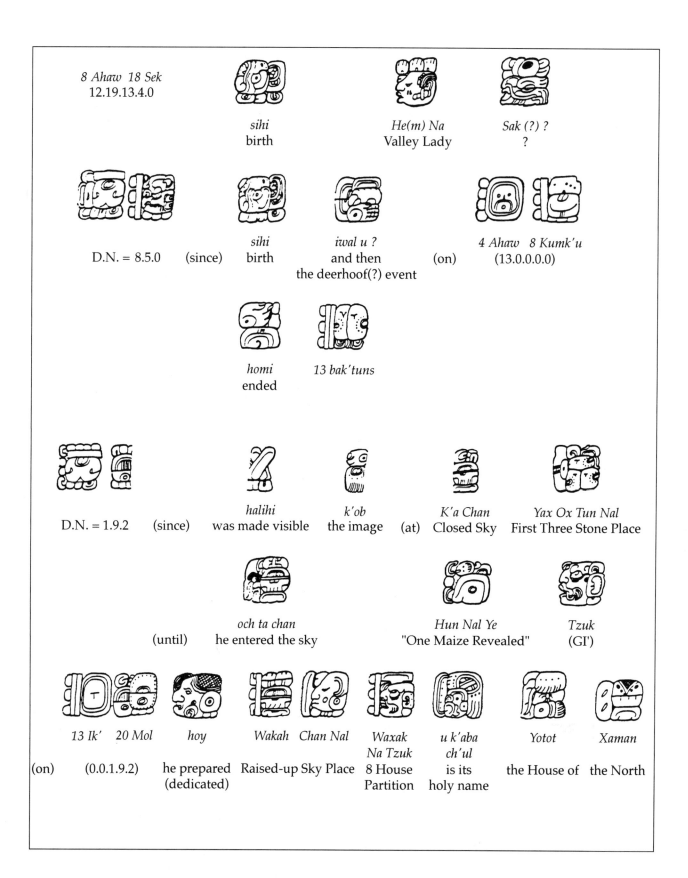

Figure 8:2   Palenque Temple of the Cross tablet (mythological portion).

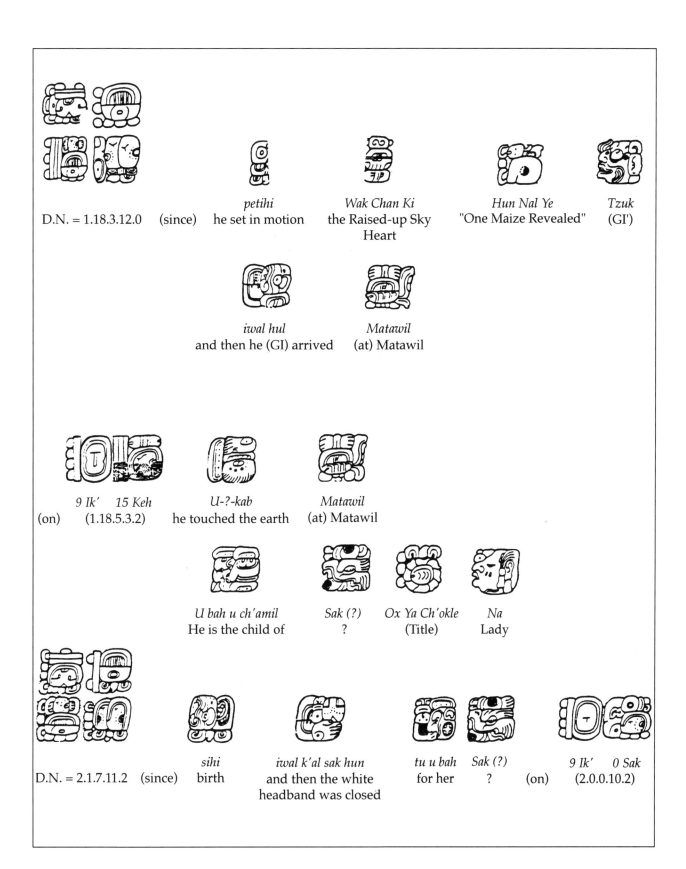

Figure 8:2 cont'd.   Palenque Temple of the Cross tablet (mythological portion).

geometry of the universe, analogous to the eight directional coordinates found on the walls of a tomb at Rio Azul. We have a contrast here: on 13.0.0.0.0 the sky was referred to as "Closed Sky," indicating that it was dark, and then on 0.0.1.9.2 of the current era, it was raised up, probably a metaphor for becoming illuminated. We then learn that on this same date, GI' "set in motion" the Raised-up Sky Heart: he set the sky/universe in motion around the celestial north pole (the Sky Heart). The text then continues with the arrival (birth) of GI (one of the Palenque Triad) at the mythological place, Matawil, on 9 Ik' 15 Keh (1.18.5.3.2), and it tells us that GI is the child of Lady Sak(?). The final statement in the text links the birth of Lady Sak(?) with the closing of a headband for her on 9 Ik' 0 Sak (2.0.0.10.2).

PALENQUE: TEMPLE OF THE SUN (MYTHOLOGICAL PORTION)

Unlike the mythological portion of the Temple of the Cross inscription, the Temple of the Sun text begins with a date in the current era, after 13.0.0.0.0, 4 Ahaw 8 Kumk'u (Fig. 8:3). The text continues with the birth verb (Fig. 8:4).

English Translation

One bak'tun, 18 k'atuns, 5 tuns, 3 winals, and 6 k'ins (after the current era began) on 13 Kimi

19 Keh was born GIII (one of the Palenque Triad). It was 1 bak'tun 18 k'atuns, 5 tuns, 3 winals, and 6 k'ins since the Raised-up Sky Heart was set in motion (by GI'), and then he (GIII) arrived (was born) at Matawil. He (GIII) is the child of the Valley Lady Sak(?)?, the Holy Palenque Lord. It was 9 bak'tuns, 12 k'atuns, 18 tuns, 5 winals, and 16 k'ins since was made visible (by GI') the image at Closed Sky, the First Three Stone Place on 4 Ahaw 8 Kumk'u (13.0.0.0.0), and then happened 2 Kib 14 Mol (9.12.18.5.16) (Table 8:2).

Comments

The new item we learn of in this text is the birth of GIII on 1.18.5.3.6 of the current era. (Several of the names/titles for GIII are poorly understood.) There are also references to two of the creation events we have encountered in the Temple of the Cross text: the making visible of an image at Closed Sky at the First Three Stone Place and the setting in motion of Raised-up Sky Heart. According to this text, both of these happened on 13.0.0.0.0, 4 Ahaw 8 Kumk'u. There is a discrepancy with the Temple of the Cross text, in that the chronology of that text as currently understood puts the setting in motion of Raised-up Sky Heart at 0.0.1.9.2. The mythological portion of the Temple of the Sun text ends by connecting, via a very large Distance Number, the making-visible event with the 2 Kib 14 Mol event in the reign of Kan Balam.

TABLE 8:2			
Chronology / Events: Text of Temple of the Sun from Palenque			
Long Count	Julian Date	Calendar Round	Event
13.0.0.0.0	August 13, 3114 B.C.	4 Ahaw 8 Kumk'u	Image made visible at First Three Stone Place, Raised-up Sky Heart set in motion
1.18.5.3.6	October 25, 2360 B.C.	13 Kimi 19 Keh	Birth of GIII Arrival of GIII at Matawil
9.12.18.5.16	July 23, A.D. 690	2 Kib 14 Mol	Event during reign of Kan Balam

PALENQUE: TEMPLE OF THE FOLIATED CROSS (MYTHOLOGICAL PORTION)

As in the text of the Temple of the Sun, the Initial Series of the Temple of the Foliated Cross text corresponds to an event that took place in the current era, after 13.0.0.0.0, 4 Ahaw 8 Kumk'u (Fig. 8:5). The text continues with the birth verb (Fig. 8:6).

English Translation

One bak'tun, 18 k'atuns, 5 tuns, and 4 winals after the beginning of the current era on 1 Ahaw 13 Mak, GII (one of the Palenque Triad), the third one, was born. It was 1 k'atun, 14 tuns, 14 winals, and 0 k'ins since GII arrived (was born), and then happened the completion of 2 bak'tuns. On 2 Ahaw 3 Wayeb (2.0.0.0.0), the gods were conjured up by the Valley Place Lady Sak(?), the Holy Matawil Ruler. It

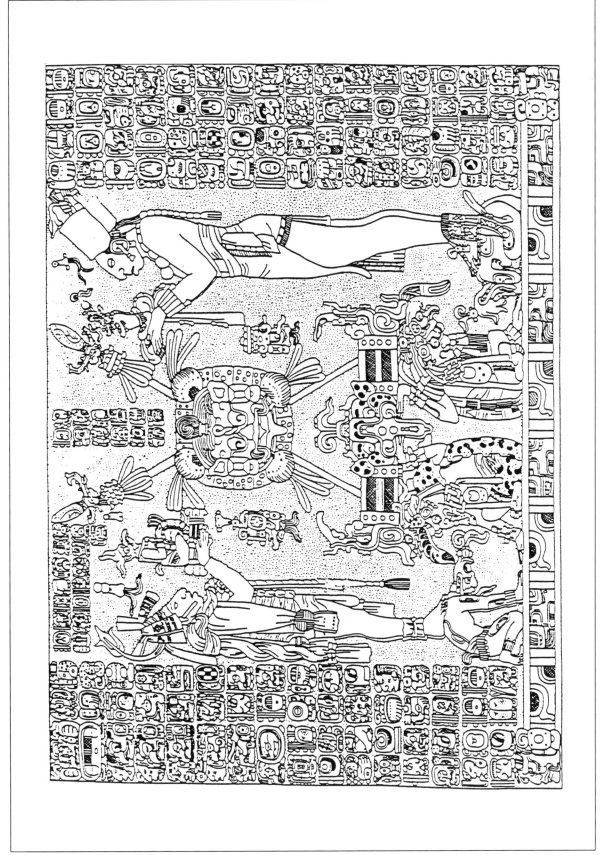

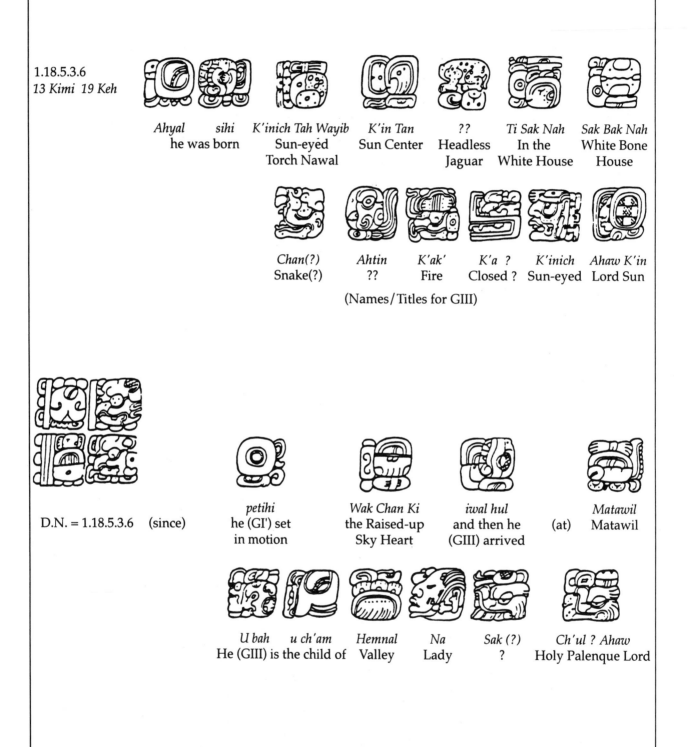

Figure 8:4   Mythological portion of the Temple of the Sun text from Palenque.

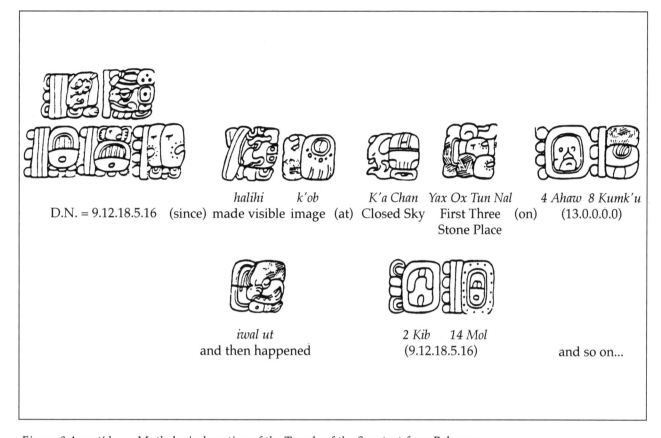

D.N. = 9.12.18.5.16   (since) made visible image (at) Closed Sky   First Three (on)   (13.0.0.0.0)
                       halihi   *k'ob*   *Yax Ox Tun Nal*   *4 Ahaw 8 Kumk'u*
                                                          Stone Place

iwal ut   *2 Kib   14 Mol*
and then happened   (9.12.18.5.16)   and so on...

Figure 8:4 cont'd.   *Mythological portion of the Temple of the Sun text from Palenque.*

happened at First True Mountain White Flower Born, the First Tree Precious (the mythological place where the conjuring up took place) (Table 8:3).

Comments

This text tells us only of the birth of GII and of a conjuring up of gods by Lady Sak(?) on the Period Ending 2.0.0.0.0. It does not mention details of the creation like those found in the Temple of the Cross and Temple of the Sun texts.

The analyses of these three texts have provided a framework for understanding the ancient Maya concept of creation. Several events and places mentioned—for example, the image made to appear at creation and the First Three Stone Place—not recounted in detail are clarified in other texts. The births of the Palenque Triad and their parents are given prominence as are important events brought about by a key player, the father of the Palenque Triad—GI', Hun Nal Ye (One Maize Revealed—the Maize God). He frequently appears

TABLE 8:3 Chronology/Events: Text of Temple of the Foliated Cross from Palenque			
Long Count	Julian Date	Calendar Round	Event
1.18.5.4.0	November 8, 2360 B.C.	1 Ahaw 13 Mak	Brith of GII
2.0.0.0.0	February 17, 2325 B.C.	2 Ahaw 3 Wayeb	Period Ending Lady Sak (?) ? conjured up gods at a mythological place

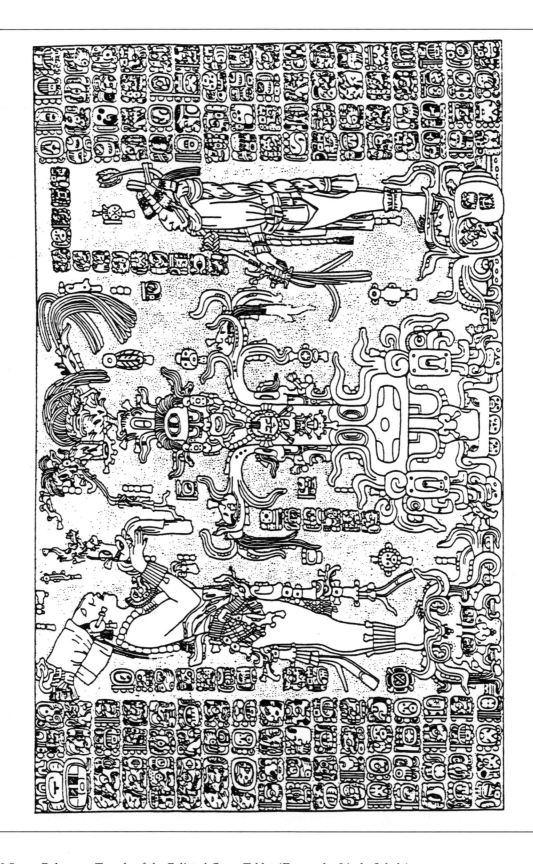

Figure 8:5.   Palenque: Temple of the Foliated Cross Tablet (Drawn by Linda Schele).

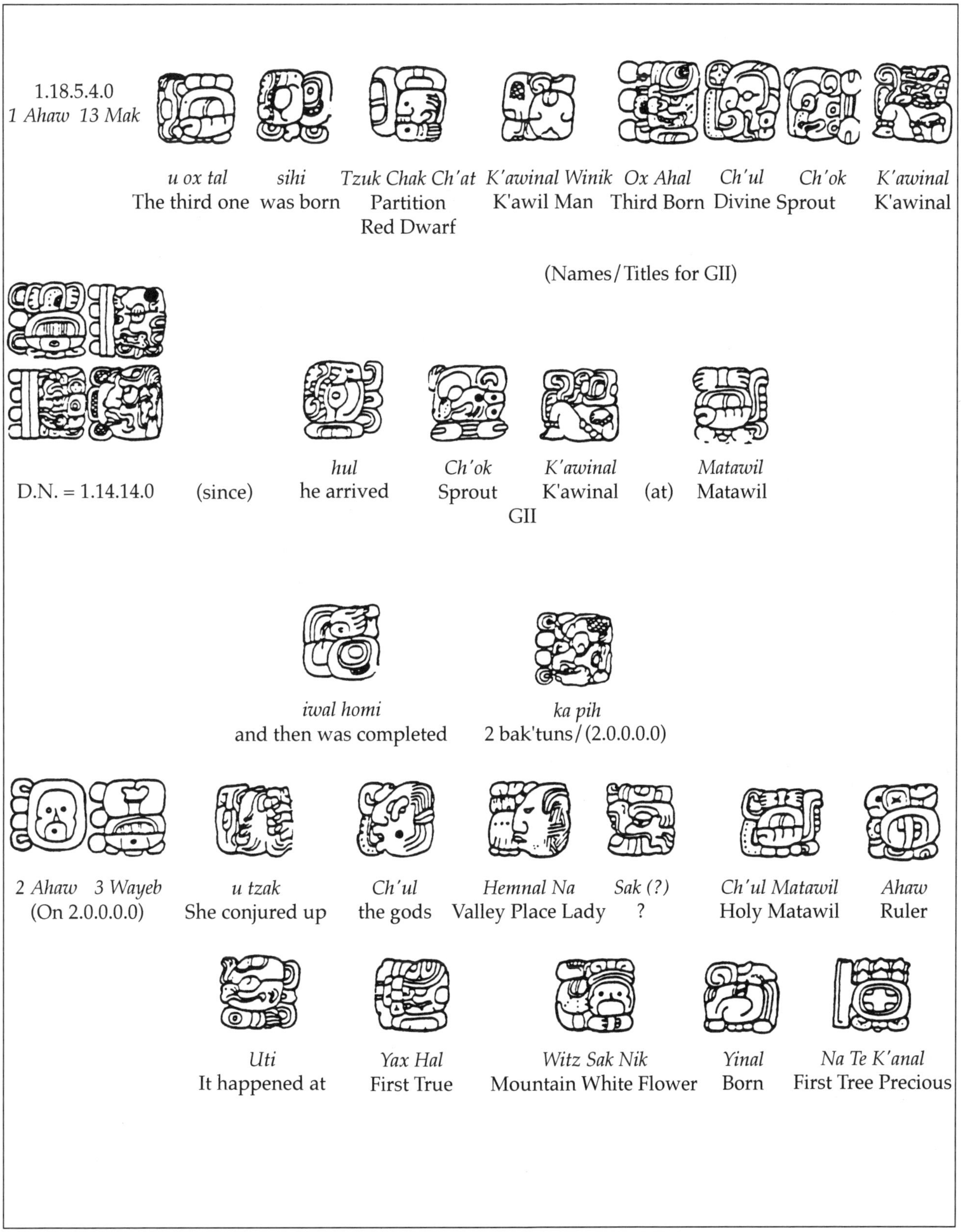

1.18.5.4.0 *1 Ahaw 13 Mak*							
u ox tal The third one	*sihi* was born	*Tzuk Chak Ch'at* Partition Red Dwarf	*K'awinal Winik* K'awil Man	*Ox Ahal* Third Born	*Ch'ul* Divine	*Ch'ok* Sprout	*K'awinal* K'awinal

(Names/Titles for GII)

D.N. = 1.14.14.0	(since)	*hul* he arrived	*Ch'ok* Sprout GII	*K'awinal* K'awinal	(at)	*Matawil* Matawil

	iwal homi and then was completed	*ka pih* 2 bak'tuns/(2.0.0.0.0)

2 Ahaw 3 Wayeb (On 2.0.0.0.0)	*u tzak* She conjured up	*Ch'ul* the gods	*Hemnal Na* Valley Place Lady	*Sak (?)* ?	*Ch'ul Matawil* Holy Matawil	*Ahaw* Ruler
	Uti It happened at	*Yax Hal* First True	*Witz Sak Nik* Mountain White Flower	*Yinal* Born	*Na Te K'anal* First Tree Precious	

Figure 8:6   Palenque Temple of the Foliated Cross (mythological portion).

Figure 8:7.   Partial text from an unprovenanced panel.
(Mayer 1991: pl. 96) (Drawn by Linda Schele).

Figure 8:9.   Madrid Codex, page LXXI (Villacorta
and Villacorta 1976).

elsewhere in both texts and iconography, but the other Palenque deities encountered in the Cross Group texts are infrequently mentioned in other texts as far as is currently known. Additional deities, however, appear as important players in other texts dealing with creation. We will now consider some of these texts.

In the Cross Group creation story, we are told that an image was made to appear on 13.0.0.0.0, 4 Ahaw 8 Kumk'u, but no details were given about the image. As Linda Schele has pointed out, on a panel recorded in a photograph in

Karl Herbert Mayer's 1991 volume on unprovenanced Maya monuments, there is a 4 Ahaw 8 Kumk'u passage which says that the image appearing was of a turtle (Figs. 8:7 and 8:8; Schele 1992c:122–123; Mayer 1991: pl. 96).

The association of a turtle with creation makes sense, especially when we look at page LXXI of the Madrid Codex, which shows a turtle with three stones on its back (recall the "First Three Stone Place" mentioned in the Temple of the Cross text) suspended by cords from sun glyphs (Fig. 8:9). Another iconographic connection between a

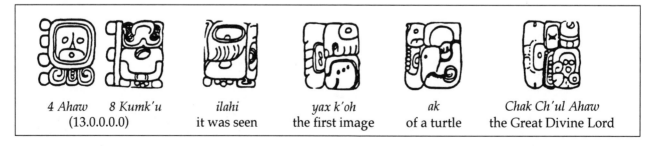

4 Ahaw 8 Kumk'u	ilahi	yax k'oh	ak	Chak Ch'ul Ahaw
(13.0.0.0.0)	it was seen	the first image	of a turtle	the Great Divine Lord

Figure 8:8   Text from unprovenanced panel describing the appearance of the image of a turtle.

Figure 8:10.   *Ceramic plate (drawn by Linda Schele).*

turtle and creation is the scene on a polychrome plate showing the Corn God (GI' or Hun Nal Ye) emerging from a split turtle shell (Fig. 8:10). In this scene Hun Nal Ye is flanked by the Hero Twins, who are witnessing his rebirth as recounted in the Popol Vuh. Thus a turtle represents an important element in the creation complex, and it's not surprising that it is the image of a turtle that is made to appear by GI' on creation day.

STELA C FROM QUIRIGUA (MYTHOLOGICAL PORTION)

The next text to be discussed tells us much about the "First Three Stone Place" and about other gods who were instrumental in establishing creation. This is Stela C from Quirigua, which, like the Cross Group texts, is divided into mythological (east side) and historical (west side) parts (Fig. 8:11). Only one date is given in the mythological section—4 Ahaw 8 Kumk'u (13.0.0.0.0). The first event recorded for that date is the appearance of an image, as in the Palenque Temple of the Cross text (Fig 8:12).

English Translation

It was the day of creation (13.0.0.0.0), 4 Ahaw 8 Kumk'u, when appeared the image. Three stones were set. The Jaguar Paddler and the Stingray Paddler set up a stone. It happened at House Five Sky, the Jaguar Throne Stone. Black House First(?) set up a stone. It happened at Earth Place(?), the Snake Throne Stone. And then it happened that Itzamhi placed a stone, the Sea Throne Stone. It happened at Closed Sky, First Three Stone Place. Thirteen Cycles (bak'tuns) were completed. The Raised-up Sky Lord (i.e., Hun Nal Ye) caused it to be done.

Comments

The text begins by telling us that the image appeared on 13.0.0.0.0, 4 Ahaw 8 Kumk'u, and that three stones were set. We had learned of the appearance of an image and of the "First Three Stone Place" in the Temple of the Cross text. How-ever, the First Three Stones were given only as a location in that text. Here we find out that the three stones were set up by separate deities. The first one

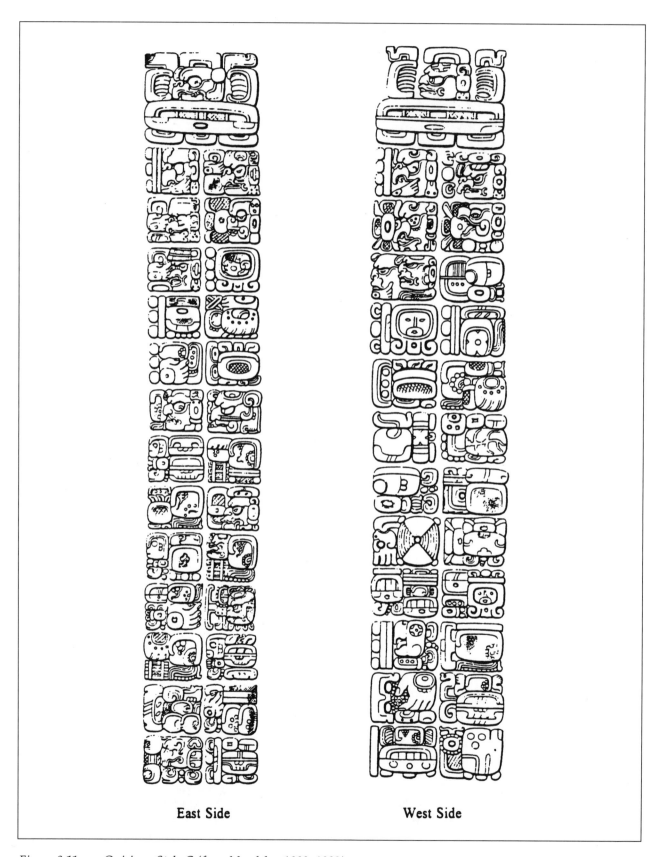

East Side   **West Side**

Figure 8:11.   *Quirigua Stela C (from Maudslay 1889–1902).*

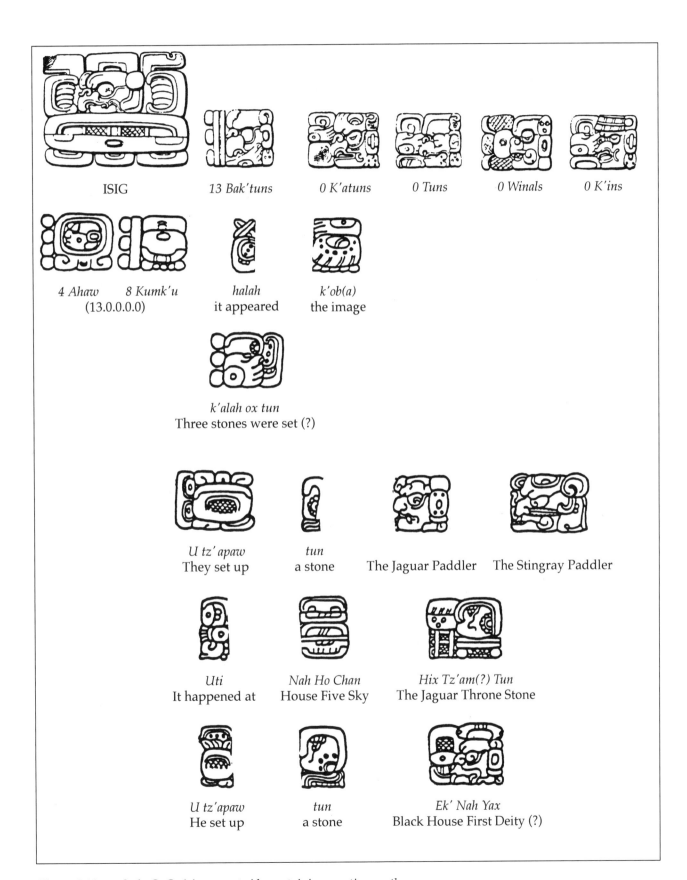

ISIG   13 Bak'tuns   0 K'atuns   0 Tuns   0 Winals   0 K'ins

4 Ahaw   8 Kumk'u
(13.0.0.0.0)

halah
it appeared

k'ob(a)
the image

k'alah ox tun
Three stones were set (?)

U tz'apaw
They set up

tun
a stone

The Jaguar Paddler

The Stingray Paddler

Uti
It happened at

Nah Ho Chan
House Five Sky

Hix Tz'am(?) Tun
The Jaguar Throne Stone

U tz'apaw
He set up

tun
a stone

Ek' Nah Yax
Black House First Deity (?)

Figure 8:12   Stela C, Quirigua, east side containing creation myth.

<table>
<tr><td>*Uti*
It happened at</td><td>*Kab ?*
Earth Place(?)</td><td>*Chan Tz'am(?) Tun*
The Snake Throne Stone</td><td></td></tr>
<tr><td>*Iwal ut*
And then happened</td><td>*k'al tun*
he set the stone</td><td>*Na Itzamhi*
Itzamna</td><td>*Nab Tz'am(?) Tun*
The Sea Throne Stone</td></tr>
<tr><td>*Uti*
It happened at</td><td>*K'a Chan*
Closed Sky</td><td>*Yax Ox Tun Nal*
First Three Stone Place</td><td></td></tr>
</table>

Homi
Ended

oxlahun pih
13 Bak'tuns / (13.0.0.0.0)

U kahi
He caused it to be done

Wak Chan Ahaw
Raised-up Sky Lord (Hun Nal Ye, GI')

Figure 8:12 cont'd.   Stela C, Quirigua, east side containing creation myth.

was set up by the Paddlers, that pair of gods shown paddling the canoe on the Tikal bones (see Chapter 4). The name of the stone was the Jaguar Throne Stone and the setting happened at Na Ho Chan, a cosmological place associated with the Paddlers. We will shortly see another text which connects this place with the Paddlers on creation day. The glyph for Jaguar Throne Stone contains a logograph for throne under the *Hix* sign for "jaguar." So far there is no firm evidence that *tz'am* is the word for throne intended here—it's just conjecture at this point. The next stone, the Snake Throne Stone, was set up by a deity, Ek' Na Yax - ?, who isn't known from other texts, so all we know about him is a partial name and that he set one of the three stones at creation. This stone setting happened at Earth Place. The final stone was placed by *Itzamhi*, which is the Classic name for *Itzamna*, one of the major gods of the Post-classic Maya. This stone was named the Sea Throne Stone, and the setting was done at Closed Sky, the First Three Stone Place. Each of the stones that was set is associated with one of the three domains of the universe: sky (*chan*), earth (*kab*), and water (*nab/ha*). After we learn these details concerning the setting of the three stones, the text repeats that all of this was done at the end of 13 bak'tuns (13.0.0.0.0), and that it was caused by Raised-up Sky Lord. Raised-up Sky Lord is obviously Hun Nal Ye (the Maize God, GI'), since it was he, as we are told in the Temple of the Cross text, who raised up the sky as one of the important events in the creation complex. Thus he is given credit for overseeing the events related in the mythological portion of the Stela C text.

To round out the story so far revealed in the glyphs and to solidify a couple of the connections we've seen, we will look at three more texts. The first is on a panel from Tila shown as a photograph and a drawing in Mayer's 1991 volume on unprovenanced Mayan monuments (Figs. 8:13 and 8:14; Mayer 1991: pls. 206, 224, and 225).

The text says that on creation day, 4 Ahaw 8 Kumk'u, Jaguar Paddler and Stingray Paddler "were companioned." It's not wholly clear what this means,

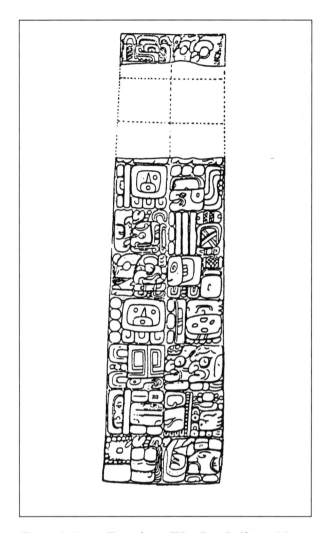

Figure 8:13.   Text from Tila Panel (from Mayer 1991:pl. 225).

4 Ahaw 8 Kumk'u
(13.0.0.0.0)

yatah
were companioned

Jaguar Paddler
Stingray Paddler

Nah Ho Chan Ahaw
The House Five Sky Lords

Figure 8:14.   A portion of the Tila text (drawn by Linda Schele; 1992c:124)

but they did something together—we know from Quirigua Stela C that together they set one of the three stones on creation day. In the Tila text, the Paddlers are associated with Na Ho Chan; in fact they are designated as the Ahaws of that cosmological place. Recall that we learned in the Quirigua Stela C text that the stone set by the Paddlers was located at Na Ho Chan.

VASE OF THE SEVEN GODS

The next text we will look at is from the Vase of the Seven Gods (Coe 1973) (Fig. 8:15). This vase shows an aged god (God N) seated on a Jaguar Throne of stone, one of the thrones mentioned in the Quirigua Stela C text, smoking a cigar and attended by six gods, who are named in the accompanying text. The date given at the beginning is creation day, 4 Ahaw 8 Kumk'u, 13.0.0.0.0, and the six gods shown are involved in creation in some manner (Fig. 8:16).

English Translation

On 4 Ahaw 8 Kumk'u, Black its Center was put in order by the God of the Sky Place, the God of the Earth Place, the God of Nine Enter Tree, the Divine Three Born Together, the God of Ha Te Chi, and the Divine Jaguar Paddler, Tzuk.

Comments

This text tells us that "Black its Center" was put in order on Creation day. "Black its Center" may be referring to the celestial north pole, around which the universe appears to turn in the view of one located in the northern hemisphere. Recall that in the Temple of the Cross text it was in the "the House of the North" that Hun Nal Ye carried out some of the creation events. The celestial north pole was dark on the creation date, since at that time the star we see at the North Pole, Polaris, was not in that position; in fact no star was. We can recognize at least one of the deities referred to among those credited in this text with setting the Universe in order: the Jaguar Paddler. Possibly The Divine Three Born Together is referring to the Palenque Triad. It's not clear why the text begins with the name of one of the gods, Tzuk. One explanation is that the artist ran out of room when painting the other six names, and out of necessity stuck the last name at the beginning. The name, however, seems to have been treated specially, because the glyph is larger, and it doesn't have the same format as the other names. Perhaps the glyph is naming the seated GI', since he has Tzuk in his name in the Temple of the Cross text. To whomever Tzuk refers, it seems that

the Old God, God N, is orchestrating the scene on the pot. Incidentally, it's no doubt significant that the background of the Vase of the Seven Gods is black because the date of the scene shown there is 13.0.0.0.0, when the sky was "closed," or dark.

PIEDRAS NEGRAS ALTAR 1

The last text we will consider, Altar 1 from Piedras Negras, gives us a somewhat different slant to the creation story. This inscription is severely eroded, but it obviously contains cosmological material. The section reproduced below (drawn by John Montgomery), begins with the end of the ninth bak'-tun, not of the current era, but of the previous one (Fig. 8:17).

English Translation

It changed. On 8 Ahaw 18 Pax, 9 bak'tuns were completed (9.0.0.0.0). ?? ?? the Divine Piedras Negras Lord witnessed it. It happened at ?? ??, the Divine ? Tun Seat. It was 4 bak'tuns until 4 Ahaw 8 Kumk'u when 13 bak'tuns were completed (13.0.0.0.0). The Paddlers(?) and ?? made the image visible. It happened at Closed Stone(?), the First Three Stone Place. ?? the Divine Piedras Negras Lord witnessed it.

Comments

This part of the Altar 1 text starts with a glyph that is probably a head variant form of the so-called Distance Number Introductory Glyph, except here it is used to announce a time change without a Distance Number. The main signs of the day and month symbols are eroded, but coefficients of 8 and 18 are evident. The "completed 9 bak'tuns" statement tells us that the Calendar ·Round must correspond to a Long Count date of 9.0.0.0.0. It cannot be the ending of the ninth bak'tun in the current era, because the Calendar Round of that date is 8 Ahaw 13 Keh. The Calendar Round for 9.0.0.0.0 of the previous era is 8 Ahaw 18 Pax, and since these numerical coefficients match those in the inscription, 8 Ahaw 18 Pax must be the date intended here. Interestingly, this Period Ending is said to have been witnessed by a putative ruler from Piedras Negras, obviously an impossibility! The text goes on to say that it was four bak'tuns until 4 something 8 something, when were completed 13 bak'tuns. Even though both day and month signs are eroded, this date obviously refers to 4 Ahaw 8 Kumk'u, 13.0.0.0.0, the creation day. On that day, as we have seen several times, an image was made visible. In this case it is probably the Paddlers who are

Vase of the Seven Gods (drawn by Diana Peck).

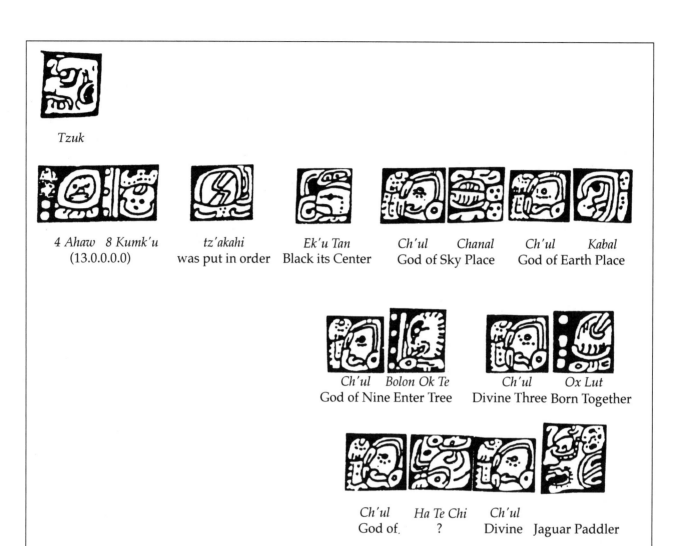

Figure 8:16.   *Text inset from Vase of the Seven Gods.*

credited with making the image visible, but in the Cross Group texts, Hun Nal Ye did it. This isn't really a problem because these texts have shown us that creation was a "group effort" with several deities taking part. The event happened at Closed Stone(?), the First Three Stone Place, a slight variation on the place name as we've seen it before. In the final statement a ruler of Piedras Negras witnessed this important creation event, an additional aspect we didn't see in the other versions. However, this impossible event makes an important point. In many Maya texts there are claims by rulers aimed at establishing connections between themselves and prestigious ancestors or deities via the performance of acts identical to acts done by an ancestor or deity, or by claiming that they were accompanied by a deity in the per-

formance of an important ritual. Here, it seems that the ruler of Piedras Negras, who was ruling when Altar 1 was carved, was attempting to establish prestige for the ruling lineage by claiming that a distant ancestral ruler witnessed an important creation event. Since the name glyphs of the ruler witnessing these events are illegible, it could be that they represent the ruler himself.

THE MAYA DEPICTION OF CREATION

From the readings of the texts discussed above, we can construct a picture of the concept of creation held by the ancient Maya. This picture consists of a series of events that occurred on or near 4

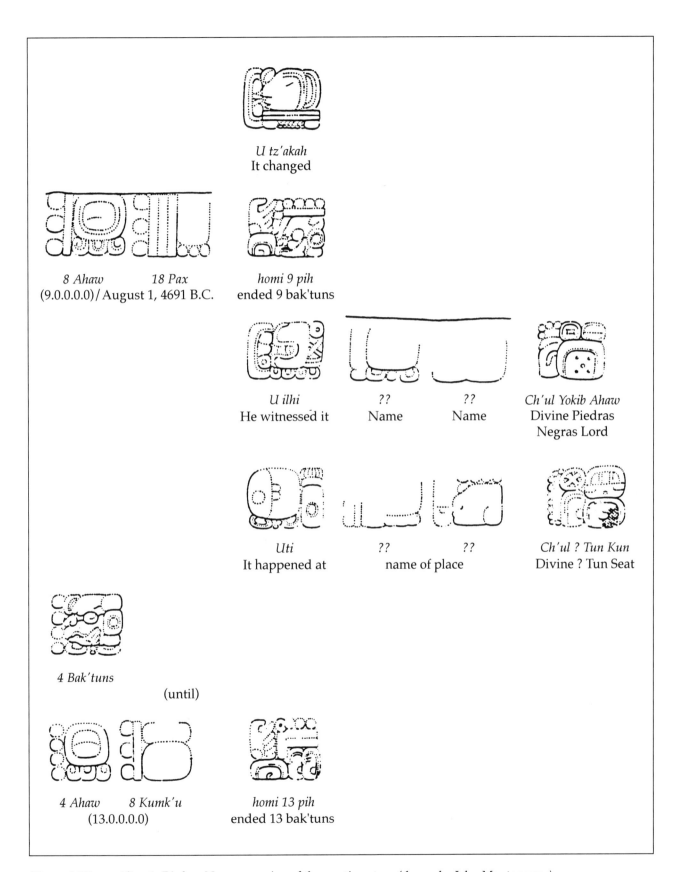

U tz'akah
It changed

8 Ahaw   18 Pax
(9.0.0.0.0) / August 1, 4691 B.C.

homi 9 pih
ended 9 bak'tuns

U ilhi
He witnessed it

??   ??
Name   Name

Ch'ul Yokib Ahaw
Divine Piedras
Negras Lord

Uti
It happened at

??   ??
name of place

Ch'ul ? Tun Kun
Divine ? Tun Seat

4 Bak'tuns

(until)

4 Ahaw   8 Kumk'u
(13.0.0.0.0)

homi 13 pih
ended 13 bak'tuns

Figure 8:17.   Altar 1, Piedras Negras, version of the creation story (drawn by John Montgomery).

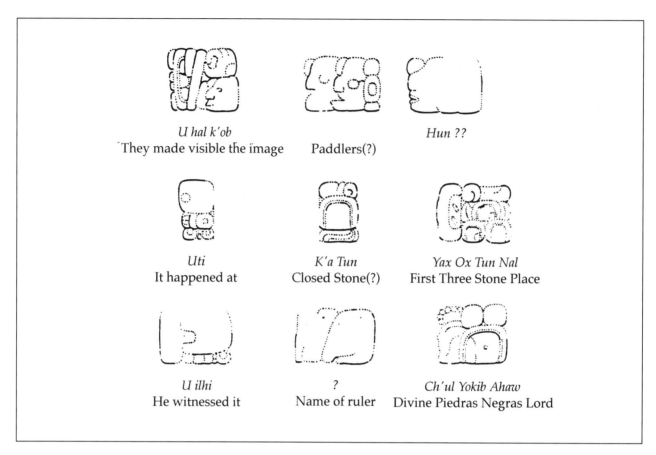

U hal k'ob
They made visible the image   Paddlers(?)   *Hun ??*

Uti
It happened at   *K'a Tun*
Closed Stone(?)   *Yax Ox Tun Nal*
First Three Stone Place

U ilhi
He witnessed it   ?
Name of ruler   *Ch'ul Yokib Ahaw*
Divine Piedras Negras Lord

Figure 8:17.   Altar 1, Piedras Negras, version of the creation story (drawn by John Montgomery).

Ahaw 8 Kumk'u, 13.0.0.0.0, creation day. Prior to the creation events themselves, the births of Hun Nal Ye and Lady Sak(?) on dates before the creation date are recorded in the Palenque texts. In the texts, Lady Sak(?) does not have much to do with creation (in contrast to her counterpart in the Popol Vuh account of creation), but Hun Nal Ye, also called Lord of Raised-up Sky, is a key player. First, on creation day he made visible an image of a turtle or a turtle carapace at the First Three Stone Place while the sky was still called Closed Sky (the universe was still dark). More than a year later, he entered the sky, he prepared, or set in order, the Raised-up Sky Place (he raised up the axis of the sky in the north and it became illuminated), he established a house of eight partitions in the north (he established the coordinates of the universe), and then set the universe in motion around the north celestial pole. Thus Hun Nal Ye is responsible for setting up the framework of the entire universe. In the Palenque texts we also learn of the births of GI, GII, and GIII (the children of Lady Sak(?) and Hun Nal Ye), but they do not contribute further to the creation story, although they are important Palenque deities (the Palenque Triad). The other

major creation event we learn of in these texts is the "setting of three stones" on the first day of creation while the sky was still "closed" (dark). Several gods, including the Paddlers, Itzamna, and another god, Ek' Na Yax ? of whom we know very little, were involved in this important event. We are told that the stones are thrones, we learn their names, the names of the places where they were set, and that each was associated with a major domain of the universe, sky, earth, and water. We also find out that the setting of the three stones was done under the auspices of Hun Nal Ye. On the Vase of the Seven Gods, we see that additional gods were responsible for "putting in order" the "Black Center" (probably the north sky). Thus creation, according to the texts, is the work of a group of gods, as it is in the Popol Vuh. Although there are some differences in the creation stories told from site to site, there was obviously a pan-Maya concept of creation.

We also learned from the Piedras Negras Altar 1 text that rulers wished to connect themselves or their dynasties with creation in some way, no doubt to establish a supernatural sanction for their right to rule. In this case the contemporary ruler maintained that a very early ruler of his site (or possibly he, himself) actually witnessed the manifesting of the image on creation day. Recent studies of the iconography of key monuments at Quirigua, show that three of the monuments set by the great K'ak' Tiliw (the captor of 18 Rabbit of Copan) represent the three stones set at creation. Thus, in a sense, K'ak' Tiliw portrays himself as setting the three important creation stones—another case of a ruler connecting himself with creation (Koontz 1995).

The cosmological information presented here has come almost entirely from texts, and it was our intention in this chapter to show how much could be learned about the ancient Maya view of creation from a study of texts alone. However, this is only part of a much more elaborate picture of Maya creation as currently understood. This augmented view has emerged by combining the material from glyphic texts with information from ethnographic studies of modern-day Maya, with accounts given in post-Conquest Maya writings, in particular the Quichean Popol Vuh, and with astronomical studies, especially of the skies as they appeared to the ancient Maya themselves. Although it is not a purpose of this chapter to present this expanded cosmological view in detail, a few tantalizing aspects will be mentioned.

It now seems certain that the ancient Maya creation sequence we've encountered in the texts was projected onto the celestial vault. We have already seen some reference to this in the terms "raised-up sky," and "heart of sky," and in the construction by Hun Nal Ye of a "partitioned house in the north," but more elaborate associations with the firmament are also implied. For example, the "closed sky" is apparently manifested as the Milky Way when it is lying low along the horizon, and the wakah chan, or "raised-up sky," may be the Milky Way raised up and arching across the sky. The transition from the lying-down Milky Way to raised-up Milky Way takes place during the night of February 5 of the solar year, the yearly anniversary of the 0.0.1.9.2 creation date, when as the texts tell us, Hun Nal Ye entered the sky and raised it up. Thus the Maya could see (and can still see) this aspect of creation played out celestially every year on the anniversary of the 4 Ahaw 8 Kumk'u creation. The raised-up sky, or the Milky Way, may also represent the world tree shown on the Palenque sarcophagus lid, the vertical member of the cross in the Temple of the Cross Tablet, and the Road to Xibalba, the path taken by the dead to the other world. The ecliptic, the annual path taken by the

sun through the heavens and on which hangs the series of constellations portrayed in the Paris Codex and on the Hauberg Stela, is probably represented iconographically by the horizontal bar of the cross of the Temple of the Cross Tablet and also by the double-headed serpent bar often held by rulers. The "Three Stones" set at creation may be represented celestially by three stars in our constellation of Orion, including one of the belt stars, which form a triangle. According to some ethnographic accounts, these three stars also represent the three hearth stones set by contemporary Maya people when they build a house. At the center of the triangle formed by the three stars is the fuzzy Orion Nebula, which, among some modern Maya, represents the fire in the hearth formed by the three stones. Other stars in Orion, including belt stars, may represent the turtle, whom we saw was an important actor at creation. Thus the three stones set at creation and the turtle whose image was made to appear at creation are logically juxtaposed in celestial imagery as they are in the creation story and in the image shown on page LXXI of the Madrid Codex (Fig. 8:9). Stars of the constellation we call Gemini, which is not far from Orion, presumably represent copulating peccaries, who are representations of the creator god and goddess producing the creatures who inhabit the universe. Thus the hot spot of creation in the celestial frieze appears to be the area of the sky comprising Orion and Gemini, which contain representations of not only the Three Stones of Creation but also the Turtle and the creator god and goddess.

The above correlations represent but a small portion of the picture of creation that has been assembled by Linda Schele and coworkers. No doubt some details of their profound scheme will be modified or totally changed, but much of the deduced structure seems on solid ground.

NOTES

1. The following discussion is based upon currently accepted readings of key texts. No doubt there will be some modifications of these readings during the next few years.

2 So far there is no universal agreement on the name of the mother of the Palenque Triad. For a summary see Bowen and Anderson 1994.

3. The English rendition of this phrase, "he set(?) the stone," implies that the verb is transitive, but it has no affixed pronoun, so it must be intransitive. The composite flat hand/tun sign must be the verb, and a more exact translation would probably be, "he stone-set(?)."

9

STRUCTURAL ANALYSIS
OF MAYA HIEROGLYPHIC TEXTS

Based upon the material presented in the previous chapters, we will now consider the structural analysis of inscribed Maya hieroglyphic texts. By this is meant the division of texts into their constituent clauses, and the separation of each clause into its grammatical elements. Even though the semantic values of all the glyphs may not be known, this analytical process is extremely helpful in revealing the overall structure of the text, its temporal framework, what is being said, and who the main actors in the text are.

The method presented here was developed by Linda Schele, and is used extensively in her Advanced Seminars in Maya Hieroglyphic Writing, held annually at the University of Texas at Austin. It begins with the cutting up of a photocopy of a drawing of the text into its constituent clauses, keeping in mind that clauses usually begin with calendrical glyphs. The glyphs of each clause are then arranged to read in horizontal rows like English sentences. Recall that the reading order of typical clauses should be T-V-O-S. Thus the clauses will usually begin with temporal elements, and these will appear at the left. Next in the horizontal arrangement will come the verb, which may consist of more than one glyph, then the object (if any), and finally, in simple clauses at least, the subject or protagonist of the clause. Other elements such as toponymic phrases may also be encountered. It is particularly useful to arrange the constituents of each horizontal row so that like grammatical elements of the several clauses will appear in vertical columns, that is, all the temporals will be in the first column, all the verbs in the next column, and so on (Fig 9:1). This arrangement permits you to see at a glance the overall structure of the text. It also affords an easy comparison of like grammatical elements, such as verbs or name phrases, and it helps in the recognition of patterns that may be present.

Five examples of varied complexity from different sites analyzed by the method just outlined are discussed below. In addition to a "spread" of the text, a glyph-by-glyph commentary is provided that includes logographic and syllabic readings for the glyphic elements present. Syllabic values are taken from the syllabary shown in Figure 3:8. Finally, an English paraphrase is given for each text. It must be kept in mind that the semantic values of many glyphs are either unknown or are not yet known with certainty, and thus the English paraphrases must be considered tentative. A year from now these paraphrasings will no doubt be somewhat different: decipherment is still unfolding!

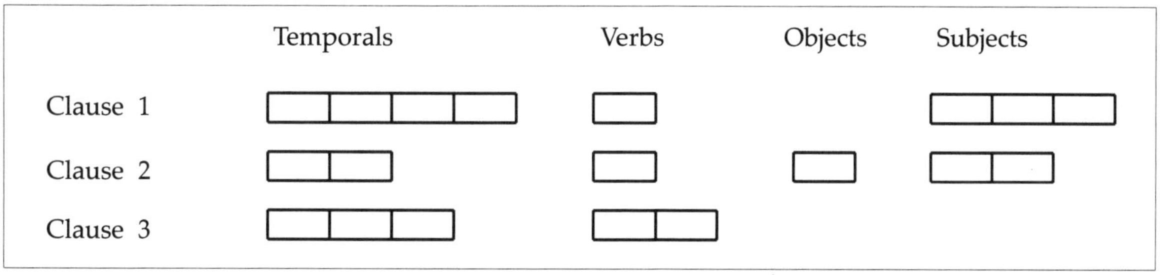

Figure 9:1.   Format for structural analysis of Maya texts developed by Linda Schele.

EXAMPLE I: TIKAL STELA 16 (Fig. 9:2).

This stela portrays Tikal's Ruler A (Ha Saw) in his war garb. The structural analysis of the text is shown in Figure 9:3. The text consists of one clause containing four kinds of elements—temporal, verbal, toponymic, and subject. As expected, it begins with a temporal element (A1-A2), in this case a Calendar Round date.

A1–A2   8 *Ahaw* 13 *Muwan* (9.14.0.0.0). Even though this temporal element does not begin with a Long Count, there is no ambiguity as to which date is intended because an absolute time anchor is contained in the upcoming verbal phrase: "was completed the fourteenth k'atun" (A3-A4). The date has to be 9.14.0.0.0 because that is the only 8 Ahaw 13 Muwan date that corresponds to the end of a fourteenth k'atun in the Classic Period.

A3–A4   *Homi u kanlahun k'atun* = "was completed the 14th k'atun." The extended hand means "completion," and it is pointing to the thing completed (i.e., the fourteenth k'atun). The *u* affix in A4 signals an ordinal numeral rather than a cardinal (i.e., fourteenth k'atun).

B1   *K'al tun* = "He ended the *tun*." In this case, the completion hand is holding the thing completed (i.e., a head variant of the tun sign). There is a *ni* affix (T116), serving as a phonetic complement for the word *tun*.

B2   *? Yax Way* = "? First Maw." This is a toponym telling where the ritual took place (Stuart and Houston 1994). The main sign (T769), has been called a "cenote" glyph, and it represents the word *way*, which in this context means hole, maw, or opening (i.e., to the underworld).

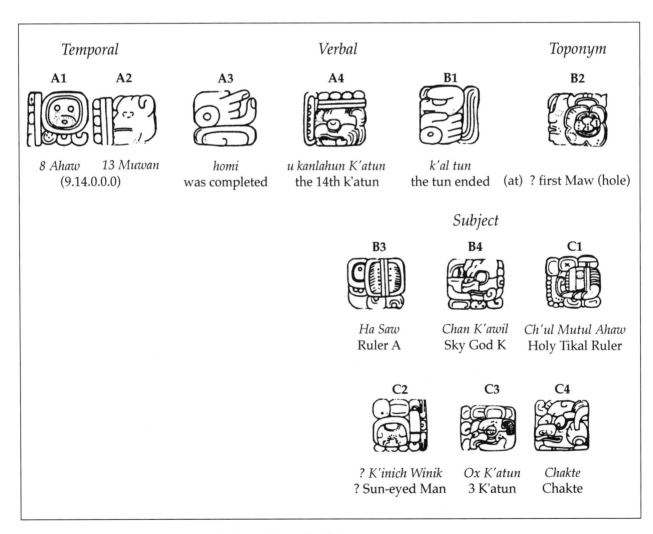

Figure 9:3.   *Structural analysis of the text from Tikal Stela 16*

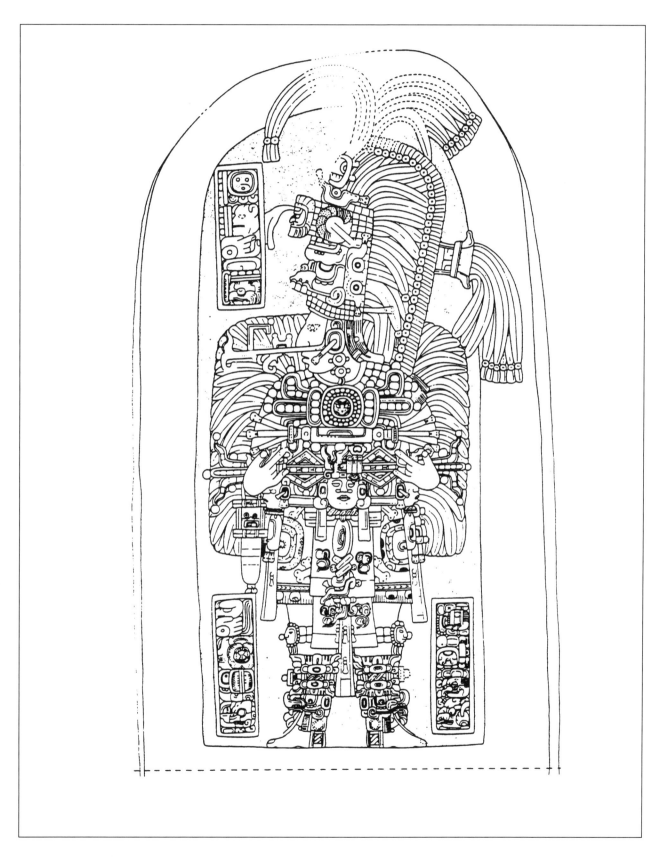

Figure 9:2.   *Tikal Stela 16 (drawn by William Coe).*

The remainder of the text (B3-C4) consists of the names and titles of the protagonist, Ruler A:

B3   *Ha Saw* = Ruler A's name. Until recently he was called *Ah Kakaw* because the main sign (T630) was thought to be a pair of *ka* signs (T25). Current opinion holds that T630 is phonetic *sa*, and with the final *wa* suffix (T131), Ruler A's name is now *Ha Saw*.

B4   *Chan K'awil* = "Sky-God K." This common title for Maya rulers gets its name from the sky glyph, *chan* (T561), prefixed to a head representation of God K. *K'awil* can also mean sustenance, spirit, image, or statue.

C1   *Ch'ul Mutul Ahaw* = "The Holy Tikal Ruler."

C2   *? K'inich Winik* = "? Sun-eyed Man." The readable elements of this title occur in many other titles.

C3–C4   *Ox K'atun Chakte* = "The 3 K'atun Chakte." The Chakte title is represented by a head and a hand holding an axe. The designation "3 K'atun" probably refers to Ruler A's age; he was in his third k'atun of life—between 40 and 60 tuns old.[1]

English Paraphrase

"On 8 Ahaw 13 Muwan, the fourteenth k'atun was completed, and the tun was ended at ? First Entrance to the Underworld, by Ruler A, Sky-God K, the Divine Tikal Ruler, the ? Sun-eyed Man, the 3 K'atun Chakte."

EXAMPLE II. YAXCHILAN STELA 11, RIVER SIDE, LOWER PANEL (Fig. 9:4)

The scene on the side of Stela 11 facing the river portrays Bird Jaguar IV and Shield Jaguar I (his father), both rulers of Yaxchilan, jointly participating in a "flapstaff" event (Fig. 9:4). An analysis of the text on the lower panel, which records the accession of Bird Jaguar IV, is given in Figure 9:5. By the analytical method outlined above, this text is a single clause text despite the large number of glyph blocks. An alternative analysis, which separates out at least two additional clauses, will be commented on below.

The text contains an uneven number of columns, so there might be some uncertainty about the reading order. Inspection shows, however, that Columns A and B must be read together, which means that Column I is to be read alone.

A1-B1   The Initial Series Introductory Glyph (ISIG) has a sky sign (*chan*) as the central element, which is the appropriate symbol for the patron of the month *Sek*.

A2–A4   The Long Count of this text is 9.16.1.0.0. The date is given with bar/dot numerals and head glyphs for the time units. An unusual feature is the *te* sign (T87) in the *tun* glyph block (A3) used here as a "numerical classifier."[2]

B4   11 *Ahaw*, the *tz'olk'in*—the first half of the Calendar Round.

C1   A conflated version of Glyphs G9 and F. The left portion is the G9 glyph, which is naming a Lord of the Night or the headband worn by the Lord of the Night. The right portion, which begins with T128, reads *k'a hun*, meaning, closed the headband. The knot, *hun*, can mean book or codex as well as headband, so there is some ambiguity as to the meaning of the phrase represented by Glyphs G and F.

C1 begins the Supplementary Series, which contains lunar information in addition to the Lord of the Night data.

D1   Glyph Y. The function of Glyph Y is not completely understood. Recently it has been proposed that it is recording a day in a seven-day cycle (Yasugi and Saito 1991).

C2   Glyph 12D: *Huli lahka* = "Twelve arrived." The current lunation is twelve days old. This glyph begins the Lunar Series proper.

D2a   Glyph 5C: *K'alah ho ?* = "Five ? ended." Five lunations in the current cycle of six are completed.

D2b   Glyph X. This is the name of the current lunation.

C3a   Glyph B: *U k'aba* = "is its name." This unit completes the lunation-naming statement begun in D2b.

C3b   Glyph 9A: *Bolonk'al* = "Twenty-nine." Glyph 9A indicates that the current lunation is a twenty-nine day lunation.

D3   8 *te Sek*. This is the *haab*, the second half of the Calendar Round. Note that here too the numerical classifier *te* is used.

These first thirteen glyph blocks, which represent a sizable portion of the text, have been devoted solely to defining the date of the upcoming event.

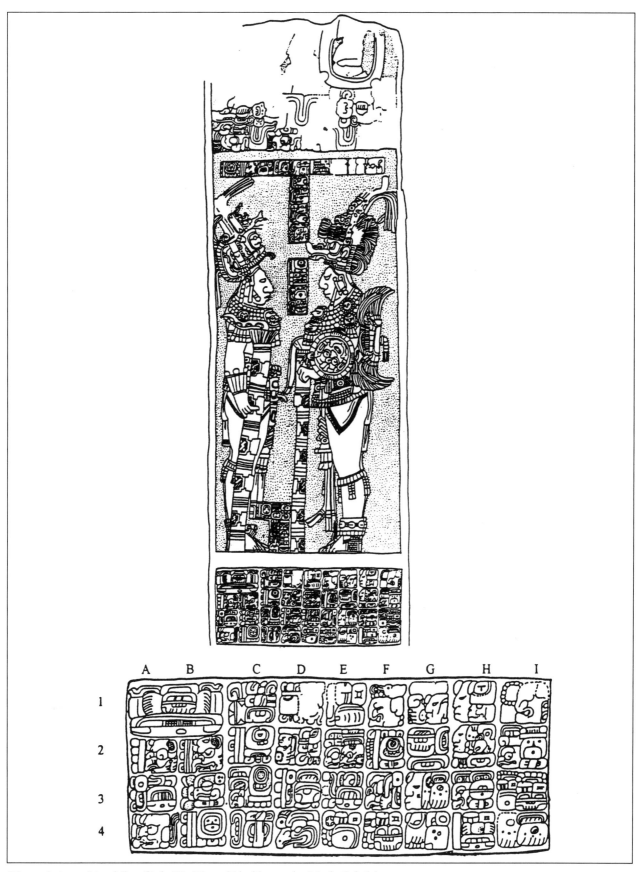

Figure 9:4.   *Yaxchilan Stela 11, River Side (drawn by Linda Schele).*

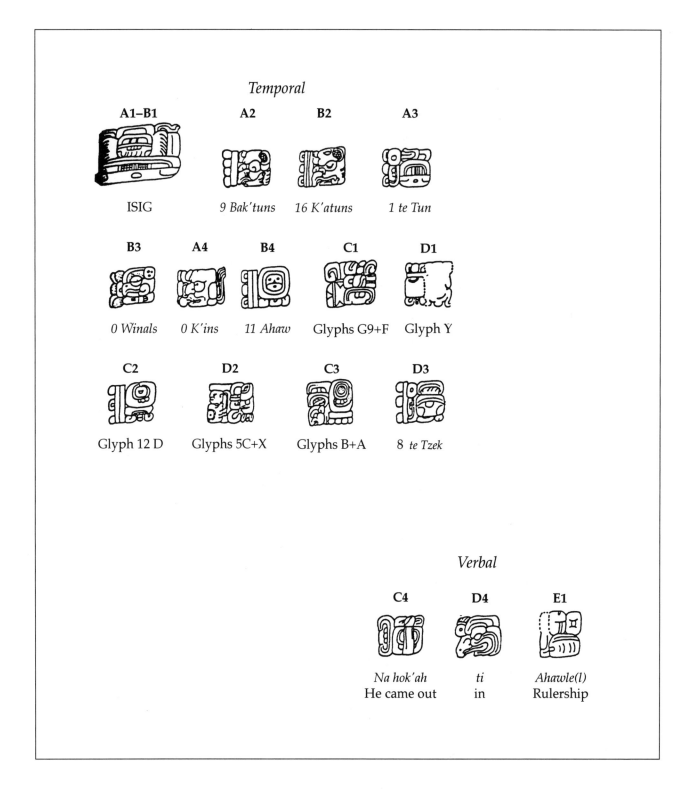

Figure 9:5. *Structural analysis of the text on Yaxchilan Stela 11, River Side, lower panel.*

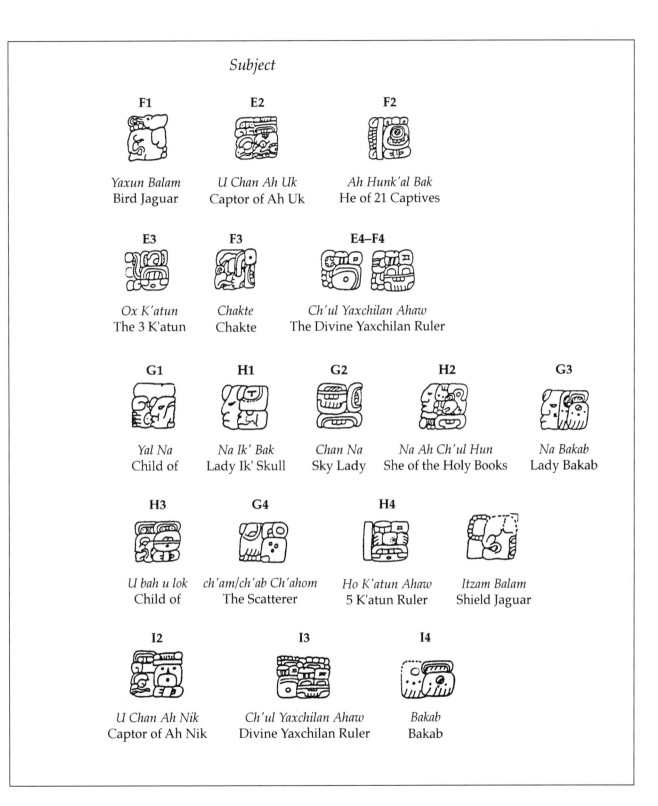

Figure 9:5 cont'd.

Although they have all been put together in the temporal category, the glyph blocks C1-C3 contain additional clauses, and we could consider separating some of them in our structural analysis. For example, the glyphs at C1 are saying something like, "The Ninth Lord of the Night put on the headband," which is a complete independent clause. Similarly, the glyph at C2 is probably also a separate clause telling us, "Twelve have arrived," or "The lunation is twelve days old," and D2a says, "Five (lunations) were completed." The combination of D2b-C3 could be saying, "X is the name of the twenty-nine-day lunation." If all of these additional clauses pertaining to the calendrical information were separated out, our structural analysis could become very complicated. Because the purpose of this structural analysis is to reveal the overall structure of the text, all of these short clauses containing calendrical information remain in the "temporal" portion of the single large clause.

C4   *Na hok'ah* = "He came out," i.e., he acceded. This is the famous "toothache" glyph (T684a). What appears to be a *na* is probably a misdrawn *ho*, which would be serving as a phonetic complement for *hok'*.

D4   *Ti*. The vulture head with a *ti* (T59) on its forehead represents the preposition *to* or *in*, as would *ti* by itself.

E1   *Ahawle(l)*. This glyph block probably begins with *ah* as a phonetic complement and features *Ahaw* (T168) and *le* (T188). The *ah* is a phonetic complement for the beginning of *Ahaw*. *Le* probably stands for the suffix *lel*, which converts Ahaw to Ahawship, or rulership. The whole verbal phrase (C4-E1) means "He acceded to the Ahawship."

The remaining nineteen glyphs (F1–I4) define the person who acceded, i.e., Bird Jaguar IV. Glyph blocks F1-F4 give his names and titles.

F1   *Yaxun Balam* (Bird Jaguar), the protagonist's name. The reason for the name assignment is obvious: the bird on top of a jaguar head. He is the fourth ruler at Yaxchilan to have this name.

E2a   *U chan* = "he is the captor of," or "he is the guardian of."

E2b   *Ah Uk* = the name of the captive.

F2   *Ah Hunk'al Bak* = "He of twenty-one Captives." Whether this title really means Bird Jaguar had taken twenty-one captives is uncertain. Twenty-one may just mean "many."

E3–F3   *Ox K'atun Chakte* = "The Three K'atun Chakte." On the date of his accession, Bird Jaguar IV was about 49 tuns old: i.e., he was in his third k'atun of life.

E4–F4   *Ch'ul Yaxchilan Ahaw* = "The Divine Yaxchilan Ruler." Yaxchilan is unusual among Classic Maya sites in having two Emblem Glyphs.

The remainder of the text presents parentage information for Bird Jaguar IV.

G1   *Yal Na* = "Child of lady," or "He is the child of lady."

The next four glyphs recite the names and titles of Bird Jaguar's mother.

H1   *Na Ik' Bak(?)* = Lady Ik' Skull, Bird Jaguar's mother's name.

G2   *Chan Na* = "Sky Lady."

H2   *Na Ah Ch'ul Hun* = "She of the Holy Books."

G3   *Na Bakab* = "Lady Bakab."

The glyphs at G1-G3 can be seen as a separate independent clause, with the glyph at G1a acting as a verb and read as "He is the child of." Thus an alternate way of structuring this part of the text would be to place the G1a block in the verbal column.

H3–G4a   *U bah u lok ch'am/ch'ab* = "He goes as the harvest of," meaning, "He is the child of." The remaining glyphs in the text are the names and titles of Bird Jaguar's father, *Itzam Balam*, more commonly referred to as "Shield Jaguar."

G4b   This may be *Ch'ahom*, "The Scatterer" title.

H4   *Ho K'atun Ahaw* = "The 5-K'atun Lord." At the time of his death, Shield Jaguar was over 90 tuns old, and thus he was in his fifth k'atun of life.

I1   *Itzam Balam* = Bird Jaguar's father's name. The affix in front of the jaguar head has been thought to represent a shield, hence the nickname "Shield Jaguar."

I2   *U Chan Ah Nik* = "Captor/guardian of He the Flower." In Shield Jaguar's texts, *Ah Nik* is his most often mentioned captive.

I3   *Ch'ul Yaxchilan Ahaw* = "The Divine Yaxchilan Ruler."

I4   *Bakab*.

Like the series of glyphs naming Bird Jaguar IV's mother, the glyph blocks H3-I4 can also be seen as an independent clause, the verb being the glyphs at H3-G4a.

English Paraphrase

"Nine bak'tuns, 16 kat'uns, 1 tun, 0 winals, and 0 k'ins after the beginning of the current era on the day 11 Ahaw [when the ninth Lord of the Night closed the headband; when the lunation was twelve days old after five lunations (in the current cycle of six) had been completed; X was the name of the twenty-nine day lunation] on the day 8 Sek acceded as Ahaw, Bird Jaguar, Captor of Ah Uk, He of 21 Captives, The 3 K'atun Chakte, The Divine Yaxchilan Ruler. He is the child of Lady Ik' Skull, Sky Lady, She of the Holy Books, Lady Bakab. He is the child of The Scatterer, The 5 K'atun Ruler, Shield Jaguar, Captor of He the Flower, Divine Yaxchilan Ruler, Bakab."

These first two examples illustrate an often encountered feature of monument texts: most of the glyphs are devoted to calendrical information and/or to information defining the protagonist. The verbs representing the major event(s) in the texts usually comprise a relatively small number of glyph blocks.

EXAMPLE III. PIEDRAS NEGRAS STELA 1, BACK (FIG. 6:1)

The text on the back of Piedras Negras Stela 1 is one of several texts from Piedras Negras that deal primarily with women. The woman featured in this text is pictured on the front of the Stela. She is shown standing, wearing an elaborate feather headdress, and holding a feather "wand" similar to the one held by the mother of the newly seated Ruler 5 shown on Piedras Negras Stela 14. Stela 1 and the other monuments that talk about women show that they were important members of the ruling elite at Piedras Negras.

The first clause of this text was briefly discussed in Chapter 6 (see Fig. 6:2). Because this inscription contains an uneven number of columns, examination of the text is required to determine the reading order. The answer is evident from inspection of the first column, which contains all the elements of the Long Count. Thus the first column is to be read in its entirety before the other columns are read in pairs in the usual manner. Figure 9:6 contains an analysis of the text. For convenience, the Initial Series is positioned across the top of the figure. A glyph-by-glyph commentary follows.

A1   An Initial Series Introductory Glyph. The head in the center of the collocation is the Patron of the Month for *Yaxk'in*.

A2–A6   The Long Count = 9.12.2.0.16. As in the Yaxchilan Lintel 11 text, the date is given by bar/dot numerals with head glyphs for the time units.

A7   5 *Kib* = the *tzolk'in*.

A8   This eroded position should contain Glyph G, which names the Lord of the Night or the appropriate headband. It should be G7. This glyph begins the Supplementary Series.

A9   Glyph F: *K'a hun* = "closed the headband." The combination of Glyphs G + F may be saying, "The seventh Lord of the Night closed the headband."

A10   Glyph 8D = *Huli waxak*, which means "Eight arrived." The current lunation is eight days old.

A11   Glyph 3C: *K'alah ox ?* = "Three ? were completed." This glyph tells us that three lunations in the current cycle of six were completed.

B1   Glyph X = the name of the lunation.

C1   Glyph B: *U k'aba ch'ok* = "is its sprout/youth name."

B2   Glyph 10A: *K'al lahun* = "thirty." The collocation tells us that the current lunation is a thirty-day lunation. With this glyph the Supplementary Series ends. Glyphs B1–B2 can e read: "X is the sprout/youth name of the thirty-day lunation."

C2   14 *Yaxk'in* = the *haab*.

B3   *Sihi* = "She was born."

C3–D1   *Na K'atun Ahaw* = "Lady K'atun Ahaw."

E1   *Na Man Ahaw* = "Lady Man Ahaw." This is a title for Lady K'atun Ahaw. Man is a site which has not yet been identified. Thus this woman, who apparently became the wife of Piedras Negras Ruler 4, is from another site. Others mentioned in the inscriptions were also from Man.

D2–E2   *Holahun (k'in) bolon winal lahka tun*. This Distance Number (12.9.15) counts from the date given in the first clause to the date of the next event.

D3   *Uti* = "it had happened." The "it" refers to the birth event.

E3   *Iwal pas(?)* = "and then the dawn."

F1–G1   9 *Chuwen* 9 *K'ank'in* (9.12.14.10.11)—the date of the next event.

F2   *Makah* = "she was covered," or "she was contracted (i.e., made a contract)." This event was preparatory to the next event, which was probably marriage.

G2   *Na Man Ahaw* = "Lady Man Ahaw." Here Lady K'atun Ahaw is referred to only by her title. The glyphs D2-G2 were shown in Figure 6:2 as comprising a single clause, but there are really two clauses as shown in this analysis.

F3   *U ho lat* = "Five days later." This is an example of the forms used for expressing small Distance Numbers.

G3–G4   1 *Kib* 14 *K'ank'in* (9.12.14.10.16)—the date of the next event.

G5   *Nawah* = "She was adorned." Here the *nawah* ritual is probably associated with marriage, specifically the marriage of Lady K'atun Ahaw to Ruler 4. The *nawah* ritual also appears in other contexts, for example, prisoners who are destined to be sacrificed may also be "adorned." No protagonist is given in this clause, but since all the other events in this text involve Lady K'atun Ahaw, it is obvious that she is the protagonist here.

G6–G7   *Ho (k'in) ka winal hun k'atun.* This Distance Number (1.0.2.5) counts forward to the next date and event. Note that there is no glyph given for tuns in this Distance Number.

G8–G9   5 *Imix* 19 *Sak* (9.13.14.13.1). This is the date of the last event in the text.

G10–G11 *U bah ti mo-mi-ba(?).* This event is expressed as a *ti* construction. It's not clear what the glyph following the *ti* means, but it must be some sort of an anniversary celebration because the date of this event is the one k'atun anniversary of the accession of Ruler 4. Interestingly the protagonist of this celebration isn't Ruler 4, but as the next glyph shows, it is his wife, Lady K'atun Ahaw.

G12   *Na K'atun Ahaw.* Although there is considerable erosion, it's clear that this glyph is Lady K'atun Ahaw's name.

English Paraphrase.

"Nine bak'tuns, 12 kat'uns, 2 tuns, 0 winals, and 16 k'ins after the beginning of the current era on the day 5 Kib [when the 7th(?) Lord of the Night closed the headband; when the current lunation was eight days old after three lunations in the current cycle of six had been completed; X was the name of the thirty-day lunation] on the day 14 Yaxk'in was born Lady K'atun Ahaw, Lady Man Ahaw. It was 12 tuns, 9

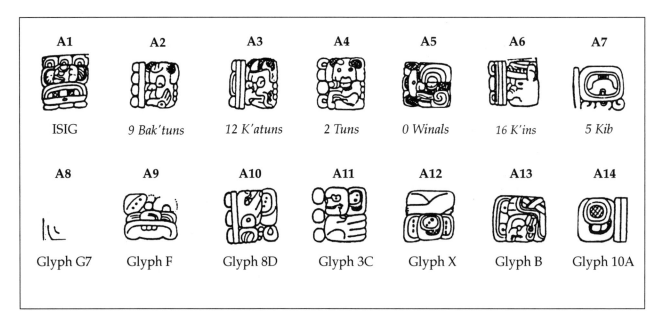

Figure 9:6.   Analysis of the text on the back of Piedras Negras Stela 1.

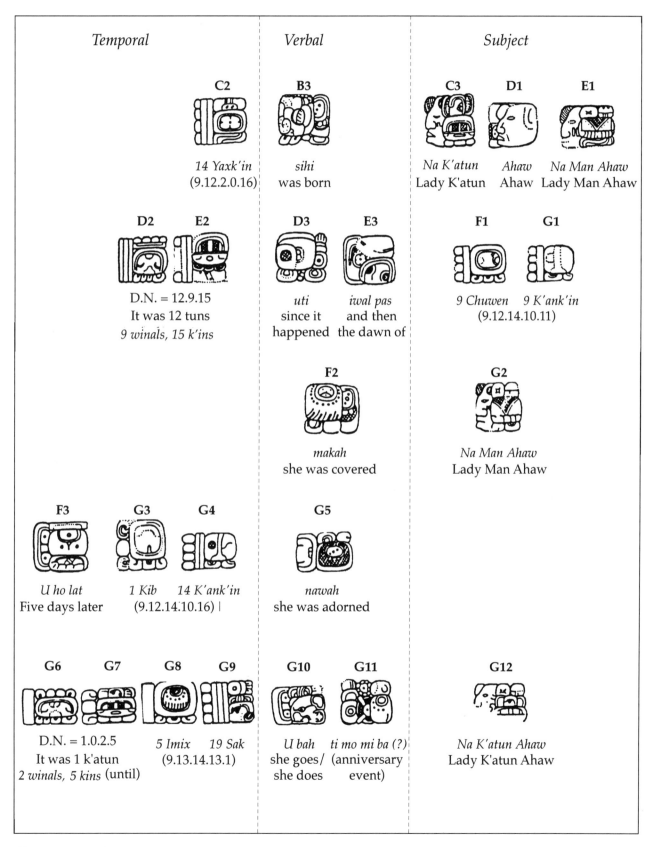

Temporal	Verbal	Subject

C2

14 Yaxk'in
(9.12.2.0.16)

B3

sihi
was born

C3 **D1** **E1**

Na K'atun *Ahaw* *Na Man Ahaw*
Lady K'atun Ahaw Lady Man Ahaw

D2 **E2**

D.N. = 12.9.15
It was 12 tuns
9 winals, 15 k'ins

D3 **E3**

uti *iwal pas*
since it and then
happened the dawn of

F1 **G1**

9 Chuwen *9 K'ank'in*
(9.12.14.10.11)

F2

makah
she was covered

G2

Na Man Ahaw
Lady Man Ahaw

F3 **G3** **G4**

U ho lat *1 Kib* *14 K'ank'in*
Five days later (9.12.14.10.16) |

G5

nawah
she was adorned

G6 **G7** **G8** **G9**

D.N. = 1.0.2.5
It was 1 k'atun
2 winals, 5 kins (until)

5 Imix *19 Sak*
(9.13.14.13.1)

G10 **G11**

U bah *ti mo mi ba* (?)
she goes/ (anniversary
she does event)

G12

Na K'atun Ahaw
Lady K'atun Ahaw

Figure 9:6 cont'd.

winals, and 15 k'ins since it (the birth) happened and then the dawn of 9 Chuwen 9 K'ank'in occurred when Lady Man Ahaw was covered (contracted). Five days later on 1 Kib 14 K'ank'in she was adorned. It was 1 k'atun, 2 winals, and 5 k'ins until 5 Imix 19 Sak when Lady K'atun Ahaw did an anniversary event."

Chronology

	9.12.02.00.16	5 Kib 14 Yaxk'in	Birth of Lady K'atun Ahaw
D.N. =	0.00.12.09.15		
	9.12.14.10.11	9 Chuwen 9 K'ank'in	Lady K'atun Ahaw was "covered."
D.N. =	0.00.00.00.05		
	9.12.14.10.16	1 Kib 14 K'ank'in	Lady K'atun Ahaw was adorned
D.N. =	0.01.00.02.05		
	9.13.14.13.01	5 Imix 19 Sak	Anniversary event by Lady K'atun Ahaw

EXAMPLE IV. AGUATECA STELA 2 (FIG. 9:7)

So far the texts we've looked at have dealt with major events in the lives of the elite which were primarily of a peaceful or non-violent nature. By contrast, other texts relate events involving war, capture, bloodletting, beheading, and sacrifice. From their inscriptions it is clear that Dos Pilas, Aguateca, Seibal, and other sites in the Petex Batun region were involved in intersite warfare over many years. Recent discoveries at Dos Pilas by Arthur Demarest and co-workers have prompted the suggestion that such warfare and the concomitant stresses on the subsistence base and social structure may have been a major factor in the collapse of Classic sites, at least those in the Petex Batun region.

The Aguateca Stela 2 text recounts an episode in this warfare and subsequent events. Although the monument is from Aguateca, it relates events associated with the ruler of Dos Pilas, who also ruled at Aguateca at this time. A text describing essentially identical events is found on Dos Pilas Stela 16 (Houston and Mathews 1985). An additional feature not seen in the previous examples is encountered in this text: all the Distance Numbers count from the initial date in the text rather than from the immediately preceding date. A structural analysis of the text is presented in Figure 9:8. A commentary follows.

A1–B1 8 *K'an* 17 *Muwan* (9.15.4.6.4). The Long Count given for this Calendar Round is secure since a date later in the text includes an anchor to absolute time.

A2a Star-over-shell. This is one of the Venus-war glyphs discussed in Chapter 4. Only about half of the Venus sign is visible because it and the shell sign are combined with the next glyph in the same glyph block. The star-over-shell glyph often suggests a Venus event of some sort. Sometimes it signifies war, especially when it is connected to a site indicator as it is here (A2b). As indicated in Chapter 7 (Table 7:1, entry 1), on the date of this event the planet Venus was at a first appearance as evening star.

A2b *Ti* + the main sign of the Seibal Emblem Glyph. This is a locative phrase telling us where the war event took place.

B2a *Hun lol* = "One day later." This is one of the several forms used for expressing small Distance Numbers. The elements usually present, in addition to the numeral, are *la* and *ta*, giving *lat*, the form used in D2a.

B2b–C1 9 *Chikchan* 18 *Muwan* (9.15.4.6.5).

D1 *Ch'ak u tz'ibil* = "Destroyed its writings." *Ch'ak*, the axe event, can mean both "to destroy" and "to decapitate." All the elements comprising *tz'ibil* are not clear in this example, but in an almost identical text on Dos Pilas Stela 16, they are.

C2 *Pat K'awil* = "the formed statue." B2a–C2 tells us that on the day after the war event at Seibal, writing, probably on a monument, was destroyed.

D2a *Wuk lat* = "Seven days later." This Distance Number, another example of the form used for small Distance Numbers, counts from the first date in the text.

D2b–E1 2 *Chuwen* 4 *Pax* (9.15.4.6.11).

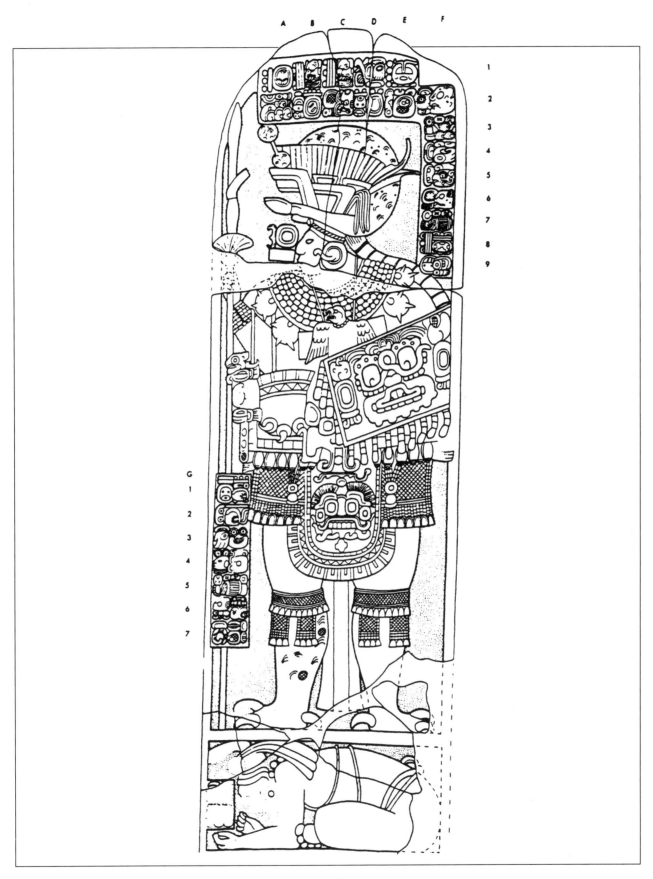

Figure 9:7.   *Aguateca Stela 2 (drawn by Ian Graham, 1967).*

E2   *Nawah* =″he was adorned,″ presumably for sacrifice.

F2   *Ich'ak Balam* = "Paw Jaguar." This is the name of the person adorned. In the text on Dos Pilas Stela 16, this victim is named logographically with a jaguar head and a jaguar paw affix. In the Aguateca Stela 2 text, the Jaguar head is clear, but the affixes are different. They are, from top to bottom, *yi* (T17), *ch'a* (T93), and *ki* (T102). Together they spell *(y)ich'ak*; in this case the scribe chose to spell out the first part of the name instead of writing it logographically.

F3   *Ch'ul Seibal Ahaw.* The Seibal Emblem Glyph. The ruler of Seibal must have been taken prisoner in the war mentioned above in A2, and then seven days later he was sacrificed.

F4   *Yichnal* = agency or "accompanied by." Two of the three expected elements for this reading are clearly evident: *yi* (T17), and the *chi* hand (T671). In the *yichnal* expression, the superfix to the hand is *nal* (T86), but it's not clear here. In the parallel Dos Pilas Stela 16 text, however, the *nal* is obvious (Fig. 9:9).

Figure 9:9.   Yichnal *from the Dos Pilas Stela 16 text.*

F5–F6   *U chan K'in Balam* = "the captor or protector of K'in Balam." This is a title belonging to the person responsible for the adorning/sacrificing.

F7   *Ch'ul Mutul Ahaw* = "Precious Dos Pilas Ruler." Thus it was the ruler of Dos Pilas who was responsible for this event and also the previous two events. This is the person designated by Houston and Mathews as Dos Pilas Ruler 3 (1985).

F8   *Waklahun (k'in) buluk winal.* This Distance Number (11.16) is counted from the first date in the text.

F9   *Iwal ut* = "and then it happened."

G1   10 *Ahaw* 8 *Ch'en* (9.15.5.0.0)—the date of the next event.

G2   *U hotun* = "the 5th tun." Here the meaning is "the end of the 5th tun." It is at this point that the chronology of the whole text is unambiguously locked into absolute time. 9.15.5.0.0 is the only 10 Ahaw 8 Ch'en date in the Classic Period which corresponds to a 5 tun ending.

G3   *U chok ch'ah* = "He scattered drops."

G4   *To-?-ni K'awil(?).* This is the name of Ruler 3 of Dos Pilas.

G5   *Ch'ul Mutul Ahaw* = "Divine Dos Pilas Ruler."

G6a   *Uti* = "It happened at."

G6b   *K'inich Witz* = "Sun-eyed Mountain."

G7a   A toponym for Tamarindito, another site in the Petex Batun. This is apparently where the scattering marking the 9.15.5.0.0 Period Ending took place.

G7b   *Chan Kun.* This is the sky-impinged bone place indicator. (See the discussion of toponyms in Chapter 4)

English Paraphrase

On 8 K'an 17 Muwan war was carried out on Seibal. One day later on 9 Chikchan 18 Muwan, writing on a statue(?) was destroyed. Seven days later on 2 *Chuwen* 4 *Pax* Paw Jaguar, the Divine Seibal Ahaw, was sacrificed under the agency of (or accompanied by) the captor of K'in Balam, the Divine Dos Pilas Ahaw (Ruler 3). Eleven winals and 16 k'ins later (after 8 K'an 17 Muwan) happened the day 10 Ahaw 8 Ch'en, the end of the 5th tun; drops were scattered by To-?-ni K'awil, the Divine Dos Pilas Ahaw (Ruler 3). It happened at Sun-eyed Mountain, Tamarindito place.

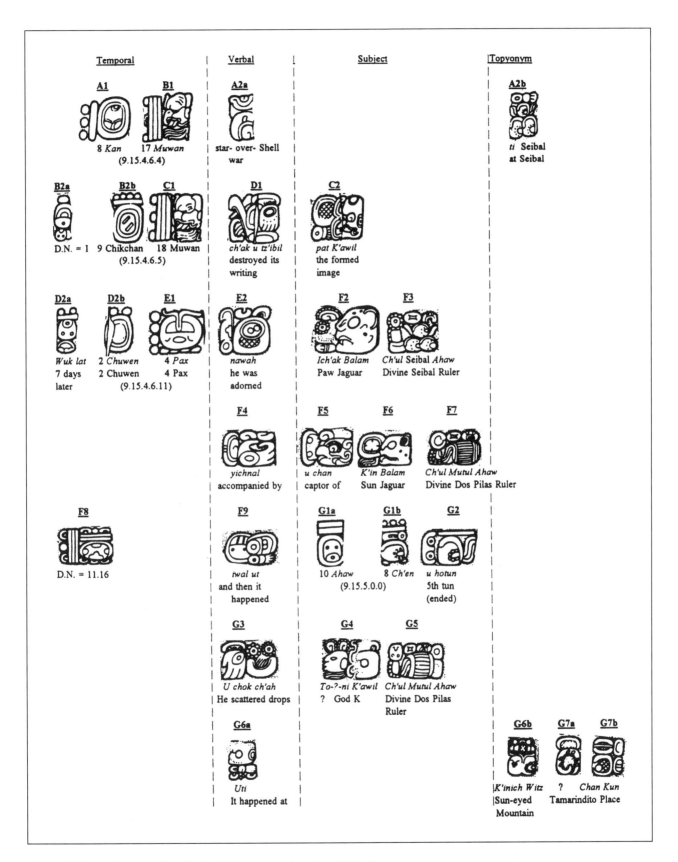

Figure 9:8.   Structural analysis of the text on Aguateca Stela 2.

Aguateca Stela 2 Chronology

	9.15.04.06.04	8 K'an 17 Muwan	War on Seibal
D.N. =	<u>0.00.00.00.01</u>		
	9.15.04.06.05	9 Chikchan 18 Muwan	Destruction event
	9.15.04.06.04		
D.N. =	<u>0.00.00.00.07</u>		
	9.15.04.06.11	2 Chuwen 4 Pax	Adorning of Paw Jaguar by Ruler 3
	9.15.04.06.04		
D.N. =	<u>0.00.00.11.16</u>		
	9.15.05.00.00	10 Ahaw 8 Ch'en	Period Ending - Ruler 3

EXAMPLE V. COPAN ALTAR Q (FIG. 9:10).

Altar Q of Copan is an extremely important monument because around its sides are arranged figures representing the 16 known rulers of Copan. Of comparable importance is an inscription on the top of the altar that relates events attributed to the first ruler, the dynasty founder, Yax K'uk' Mo'. A structural analysis of the text is given in Figure 9:11, and a commentary follows.

A1–B1 5 *Kaban* 15 *Yaxk'in* = 8.19.10.10.17. Although neither Long Count nor an anchor to a Long Count position is given in this text, there is no ambiguity because other texts (e.g., Copan Stela 63) define the approximate time for the protagonist of the event carried out on this date.

A2 *U ch'am K'awil* = "he displayed K'awil (the image or statue)."

B2 *Ch'ok Te Na* = "Sprout Tree House." This phrase probably means the house of the lineage founder. Here it may be the name of the image/statue displayed, or the name of the place where the event took place. Since *K'awil* is associated with royal lineages, this event may represent the accession of *Yax K'uk' Mo'*.

A3 *K'uk' Mo' Ahaw* = the name of the dynasty founder, the first recorded ruler. *Yax K'uk' Mo'* is the name often given to this first ruler in other texts, but here he is referred to as *K'uk' Mo' Ahaw*. Interestingly, there is reference to a *K'u Mo'* at Tikal from this same time period.

B3–A4 8 *Ahaw* 18 *Yaxk'in* = 8.19.10.11.0. On this date Venus was exactly at a maximum elongation as morning star (-46.22 degrees).

B4 *Tal* = "he arrived."

A5 *Ch'ok Te Na* = "Sprout Tree House." As indicated above, this may be a locative naming a place visited by the founder associated with his accession.

B5 *K'inich Yax K'uk' Mo'* = "Sun-eyed Yax K'uk' Mo'.

A6 *Oxlahun (k'in) wuk winal*: this Distance Number (7.13) counts from the "arrival" event to the next event. The k'in coefficient is recorded as 12, but it has to be 13.

B6 *Iwal ut* = "and then it happened."

C1–D1 5 *Ben* 11 *Muwan* = 8.19.11.0.13.

C2 *Hil* = "to put to rest" or "to terminate."

D2–D4 *Ok K'awil chik'in Chakte yit* = "foot of the image, the west Chakte, its base." The passage in C2-D4 isn't entirely clear; it is apparently referring to something done to the image whose display by Yax K'uk' Mo' was referred to in the first passage of the text.

C5–D5 *Hulih Oxwitik* = "He arrived at *Oxwitik*." *Oxwitik* is a place associated with Copan, and apparently the arrival of *Yax K'uk' Mo'* was an important event.

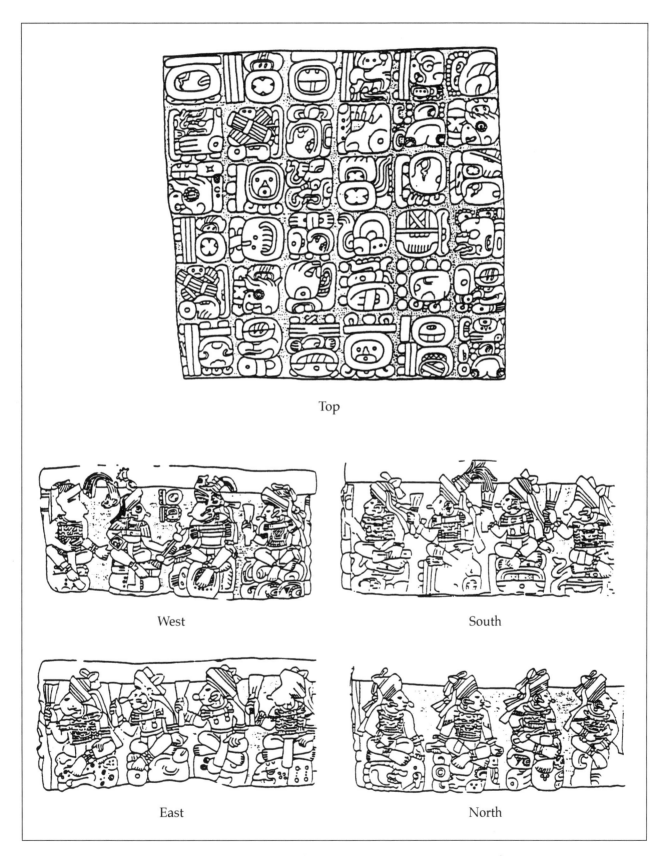

Top

West

South

East

North

Figure 9:10. *Copan Altar Q (drawn by Linda Schele).*

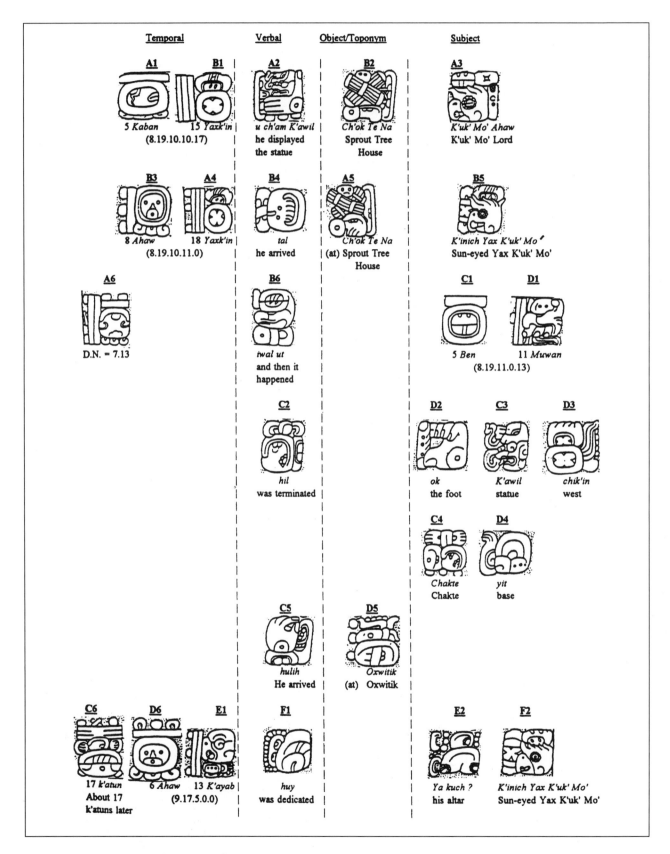

Figure 9:11.   Structural analysis of the text on Copan Altar Q.

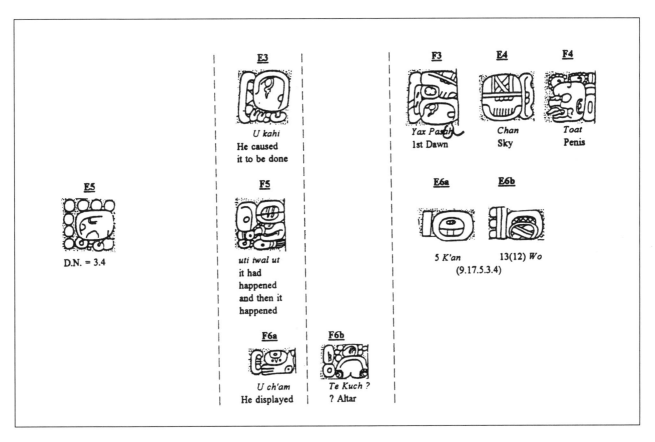

Figure 9:11.   Structural analysis of the text on Copan Altar Q.

C6   *Wuklahun k'atun* = "about 17 k'atuns later." This is an approximate Distance Number. It is announcing that a large change in time is taking place—from the time of the dynasty founder at about 9.0.0.0.0 until the time of the last ruler portrayed on Altar Q and the one responsible for the altar.

D6–E1   *6 Ahaw 13 K'ayab* = 9.17.5.0.0.

F1   *Huy* = "He dedicated, made proper." This verb substitutes for the God N verb that appears in the Primary Standard Sequence in pottery texts.

E2–F2   *Yakuch-? K'inich Yax K'uk' Mo'* = "flat altar of Sun-eyed *Yax K'uk' Mo'*." This may be referring to Altar Q.

E3   *U kahi* = "He caused it to be done."

F3–F4   *Yax Pas Chan Toat. Yax Pas* is the name of the sixteenth ruler of Copan, and *Chan Toat*, "Sky Penis," is a title he frequently carries.

E5   *Kan (k'in) ox winal*: this Distance Number

(3.4) counts from *6 Ahaw 13 K'ayab* to the next date in the text.

F5   *Uti iwal ut* = "it had happened and then it happened." This is one of those cases when both *uti* and *iwal ut* are used together to link an earlier date/event to a later one.

E6a–E6b   *5 K'an 12 Wo* = 9.17.5.3.4. 13 *Wo* is written, but it has to be 12 *Wo*.

F6a   *U ch'am* = "he displayed."

F6b   *Te kuch-?* = "the flat altar." A ritual probably involving Altar Q is involved here, but its nature isn't clear.

English Paraphrase.

On 5 Kaban 15 Yaxk'in an image (or statue) was displayed by the founder, K'uk' Mo' Lord. On 8 Ahaw 18 Yaxk'in the Sun-eyed Yax K'uk' Mo' arrived at the founder house. Seven winals and 13 k'ins later, happened the day 5 Ben 11 Muwan. The foot of the image, the West Chakte, its base, was terminated.

He (Yax K'uk' Mo') arrived at Oxwitik. About 17 k'atuns later on 6 Ahaw 13 K'ayab the Sun-eyed Yax K'uk' Mo' altar was dedicated. First Dawn, Sky Penis caused it to be done. Three winals and 4 k'ins later happened the day 5 K'an 12 Wo, when he dis- played(?) the altar.

Now that you have seen some examples of structural analysis of Maya inscriptional texts, you should try some on your own. Several of the inscrip- tions from earlier chapters in this book are good ones to try. The following list is arranged in approximate order of increasing difficulty:

Yaxchilan Lintel 42 (Fig. 5:28)
Piedras Negras Stela 3 (Fig. 5:8)
Piedras Negras Stela 36 (Fig. 5:14)
Yaxchilan Lintel 8 (Fig. 5:35)
Yaxchilan Stela 12 (Fig. 5:3)

Quirigua Stela C (Fig. 5:24)
Piedras Negras Lintel 3 (Fig. 3:15)
Palenque Temple of the Cross (Fig. 8:1)
Palenque Temple of the Sun (Fig. 8:2)
Palenque Palace Tablet (Fig. 5:20)
Have fun!

NOTES

1. There is some ambiguity here, since Ruler A's birth date isn't known. Depending upon when Stela 16 was carved, it is possible that the title refers to his tenure as ruler, although on the date in this text he was in his second k'atun as ruler. However, on the date of his successor's accession, presumably shortly after Ruler A's death, Ruler A would have been well into his third k'atun as ruler.
2. Numerical classifiers in Maya languages and Maya hiero- glyphs are discussed in Thompson's *Maya Hieroglyphic Writing* (1950:54–56).

Copan Altar Q Chronology

	8.19.10.10.17	5 Kaban 15 Yaxk'in	Image displayed by K'uk' Mo' Lord
D.N. =	0.00.00.00.03	(implied)	
	8.19.10.11.00	8 Ahaw 18 Yaxk'in	Sun-eyed Yax K'uk' Mo' arrived
D.N. =	0.00.00.07.13		
	8.19.11.00.13	5 Ben 11 Muwan	The foot of the image was terminated, Sun-eyed Yax K'uk' Mo' arrived at Oxwitik
D.N. =	~17 k'atuns		
	9.17.05.00.00	6 Ahaw 13 K'ayab	Yax K'uk' Mo' Altar dedicated by Yax Pas
D.N. =	0.00.00.03.04		
	9.17.05.03.04	5 K'an 12 Wo	Altar (Q-?) ritual by Yax Pas

APPENDIX A
MAYA NUMERICAL HEAD VARIANTS

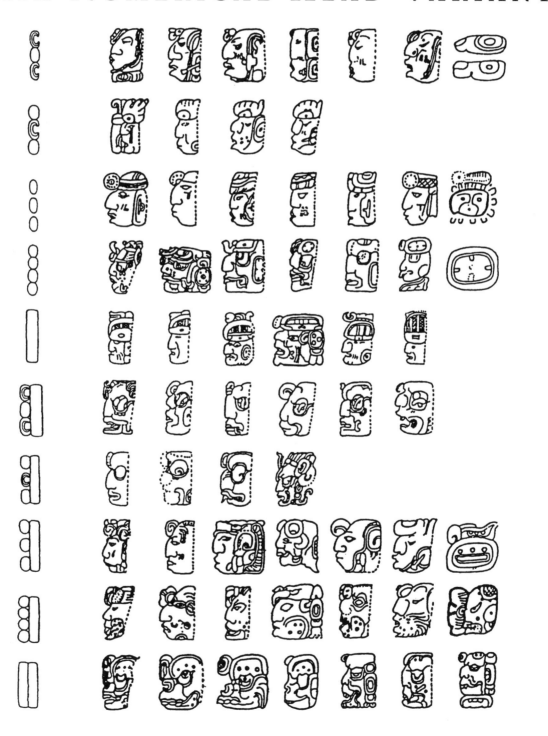

Maya Numerical Head Variants *cont'd*

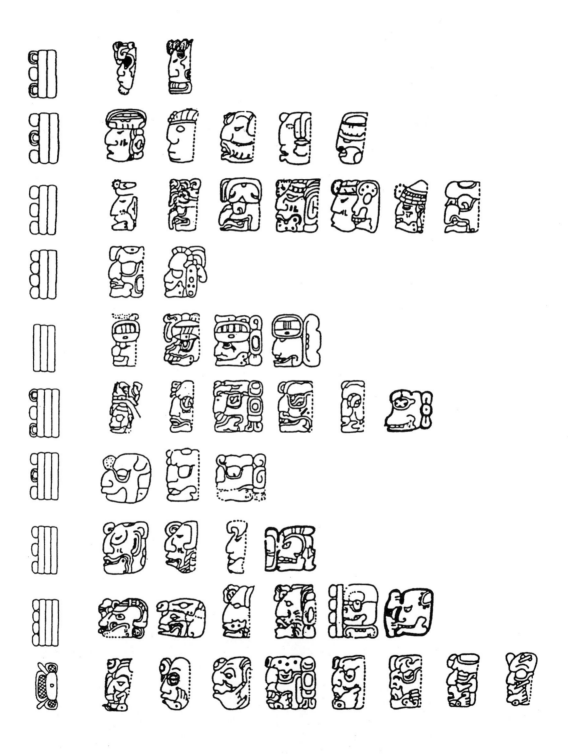

After Thompson 1971:figs. 24 and 25.

APPENDIX B

MAYA CALENDRICAL DAY NAMES

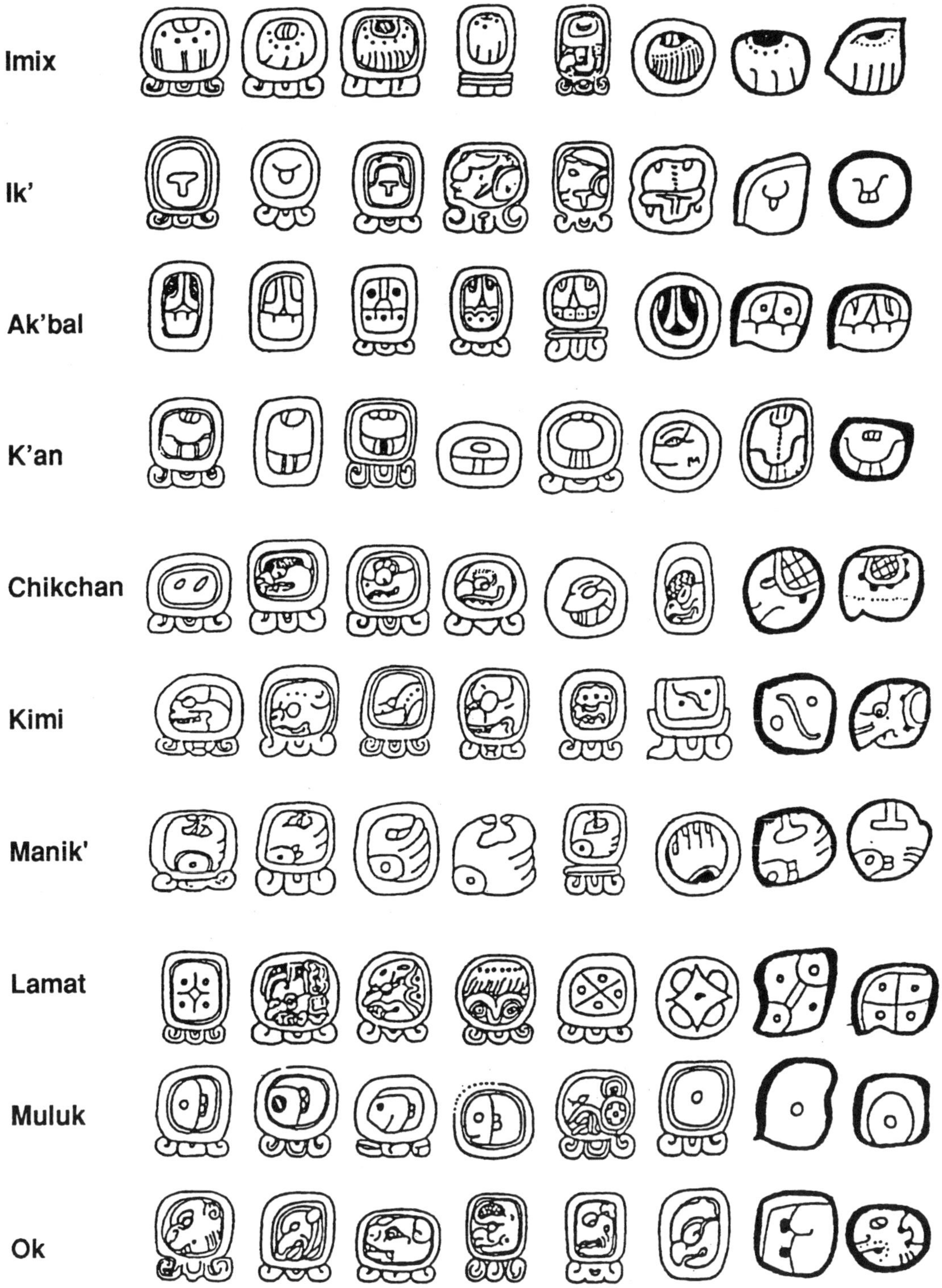

Imix

Ik'

Ak'bal

K'an

Chikchan

Kimi

Manik'

Lamat

Muluk

Ok

MAYA CALENDRICAL DAY NAMES *cont'd*

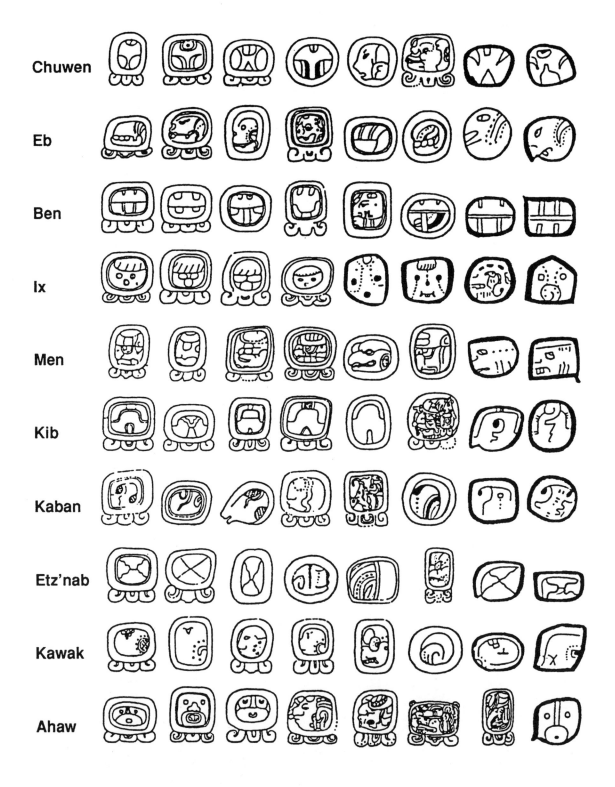

After Thompson 1971:figs. 6–11.

APPENDIX C

MAYA CALENDRICAL MONTH NAMES

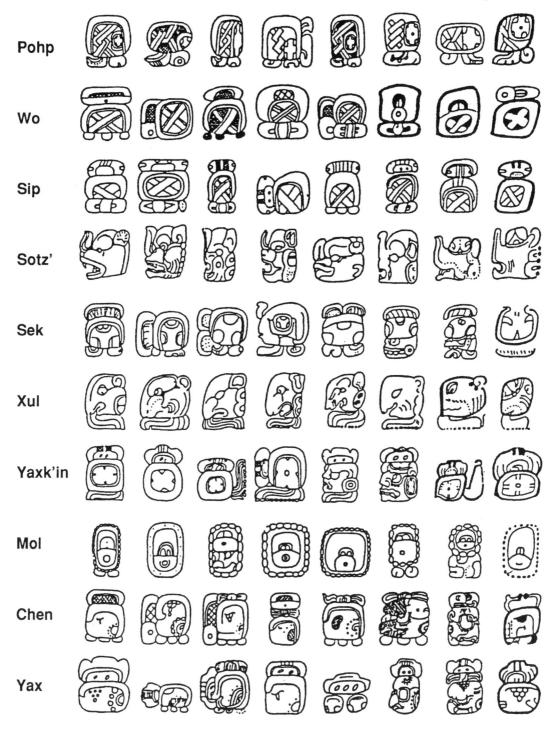

Pohp

Wo

Sip

Sotz'

Sek

Xul

Yaxk'in

Mol

Chen

Yax

MAYA CALENDRICAL MONTH NAMES *cont'd*

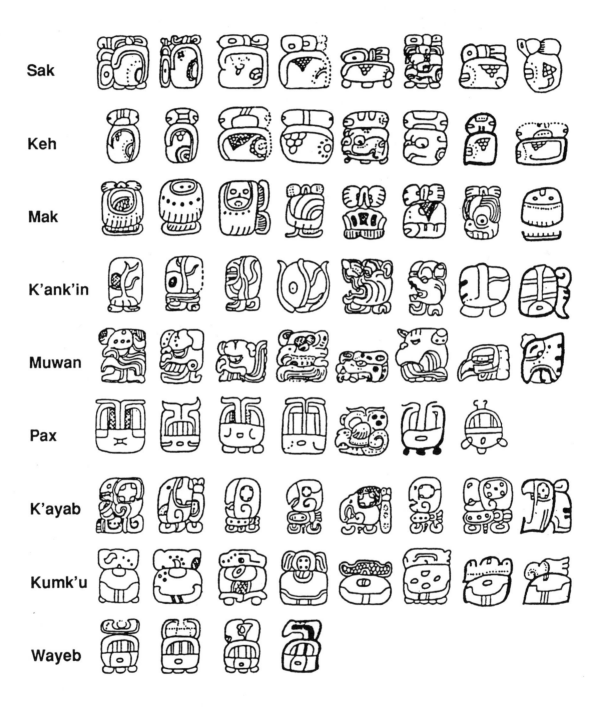

Sak

Keh

Mak

K'ank'in

Muwan

Pax

K'ayab

Kumk'u

Wayeb

After Thompson 1971:figs. 16–19.

APPENDIX D

MAYA CALENDRICAL HAAB PATRONS

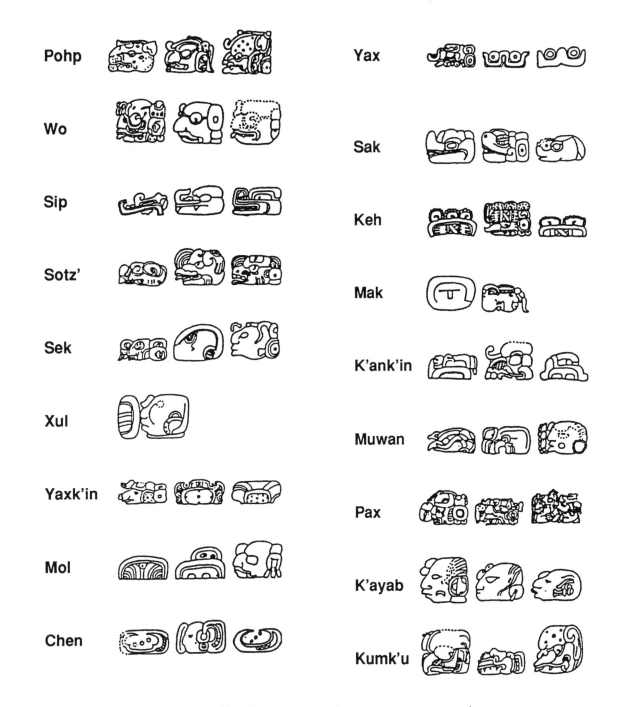

Pohp

Wo

Sip

Sotz'

Sek

Xul

Yaxk'in

Mol

Chen

Yax

Sak

Keh

Mak

K'ank'in

Muwan

Pax

K'ayab

Kumk'u

After Thompson 1971:figs. 22 and 23.

APPENDIX E

MAYA CALENDRICAL LORDS OF THE NIGHT

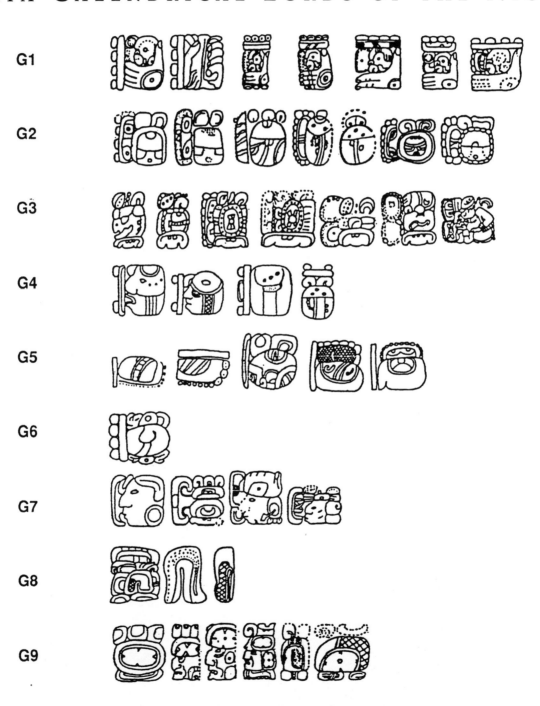

After Thompson 1971:fig. 34

APPENDIX F

CALCUATION TABLES FOR LONG COUNT AND CALENDAR ROUND DATES

Note: The spellings for Maya days and months used in these tables follows an earlier orthography. See lists below for equivalencies:

TABLE 1
Day Names and Positions

Imix	.1
Ik	.2
Akbal	.3
Kan	.4
Chicchan	.5
Cimi	.6
Manik	.7
Lamat	.8
Muluc	.9
Oc	.1
Chuen	.11
Eb	.12
Ben	.13
Ix	.14
Men	.15
Cib	.16
Caban	.17
Etznab	.18
Cauac	.19
Ahau	.0

TABLE 2
Month Names & Positions

0 Pop	.0	0
0 Uo	1.0	20
0 Zip	2.0	40
0 Zotz	3.0	60
0 Zec	4.0	80
0 Xul	5.0	100
0 Yaxkin	6.0	120
0 Mol	7.0	140
0 Chen	8.0	160
0 Yax	9.0	180
0 Zac	10.0	200
0 Ceh	11.0	220
0 Mac	12.0	240
0 Kankin	13.0	260
0 Muan	14.0	280
0 Pax	15.0	300
0 Kayab	16.0	320
0 Cumku	17.0	340
0 Uayeb	1.0.0	360

Months		Days	
Pop	Pohp	Imix	Imix
Uo	Wo	Ik	Ik'
Zip	Sip	Akbal	Ak'bal
Zotz	Sotz'	Kan	K'an
Zec	Sek	Chicchan	Chikchan
Xul	Xul	Cimi	Kimi
Yaxkin	Yaxk'in	Manik	Manik'
Mol	Mol	Lamat	Lamat
Chen	Chen	Muluc	Muluk
Yax	Yax	Oc	Ok
Zac	Sak	Chuen	Chuwen
Ceh	Keh	Eb	Eb
Mac	Mak	Ben	Ben
Kankin	K'ank'in	Ix	Ix
Muan	Muwan	Men	Men
Pax	Pax	Cib	Kib
Kayab	K'ayab	Caban	Kaban
Cumku	Kumk'u	Etznab	Erz'nab
Uayeb	Wayeb	Cauac	Kawak
		Ahau	Ahaw

TABLE 3

Base Dates	Cal Round
13.0.0.0.0	4 Ahau 8 Cumku
7.0.0.0.0	10 Ahau 18 Zac
8.0.0.0.0	9 Ahau 3 Zip
9.0.0.0.0	8 Ahau 13 Ceh
10.0.0.0.0	7 Ahau 18 Zip
11.0.0.0.0	6 Ahau 8 Mac
12.0.0.0.0	5 Ahau 13 Zotz

TABLE 4
Remainders in 13-day and 365-day Cycles

	Baktuns		Katuns		Tuns		Uinals		Kins	
	13	365	13	365	13	365	13	365	13	365
0	0	0	0	0	0	0	0	0	0	0
1	12	190	11	265	9	360	7	20	1	1
2	11	15	9	165	5	355	1	40	2	2
3	10	205	7	65	1	350	8	60	3	3
4	9	30	5	330	10	345	2	80	4	4
5	8	220	3	230	6	340	9	100	5	5
6	7	45	1	130	2	335	3	120	6	6
7	6	235	12	30	11	330	10	140	7	7
8	5	60	10	295	7	325	4	160	8	8
9	4	250	8	195	3	320	11	180	9	9
10	3	75	6	95	12	315	5	200	10	10
11	2	265	4	360	8	310	12	220	11	11
12	1	90	2	260	4	305	6	240	12	12
13	0	280	0	160	0	300	0	260	0	13
14	12	105	11	60	9	295	7	280	1	14
15	11	295	9	325	5	290	1	300	2	15
16	10	120	7	225	1	285	8	320	3	16
17	9	310	5	125	10	280	2	340	4	17
18	8	135	3	25	6	275			5	18
19	7	325	1	290	2	270			6	19

TABLE 5
Calendar Round Multiples & Remainders

CRs	Vague Yrs	Long Count	20	13
99	5148	13. 0.19. 9. 0		0
90	4680	11. 17. 5. 0. 0		0
81	4212	10. 13.10. 9. 0		0
72	3744	9. 9.16. 0. 0		0
63	3276	8. 6. 1. 9. 0		0
54	2808	7. 2. 7. 0. 0		0
45	2340	5. 18.12. 9. 0		0
36	1872	4. 14.18. 0. 0		0
27	1404	3. 11. 3. 9. 0		0
18	936	2. 7. 9. 0. 0		0
9	468	1. 3.14. 9. 0		0
8	416	1. 1. 1.14. 0		0
7	364	18. 9. 1. 0		0
6	312	15.16. 6. 0		0
5	260	13. 3.11. 0		0
4	208	10.10.16. 0		0
3	156	7.18. 3. 0		0
2	104	5. 5. 8. 0		0
1	52	2.12.13. 0		0 <---
	48	2. 8.12. 0		9
	44	2. 4.11. 0		5
	40	2. 0.10. 0		1
	36	1.16. 9. 0		10
	32	1.12. 8. 0		6
	28	1. 8. 7. 0		2
	24	1. 4. 6. 0		11
	20	1. 0. 5. 0		7
	16	16. 4. 0		3
	12	12. 3. 0		12
	8	8. 2. 0		8
	4	4. 1. 0		4
	3	3. 0.15		3
	2	2. 0.10		2
	1	1. 0. 5		1

APPENDIX G

LONG COUNT EXAMPLE ONE

Find the Calendar Round Position for the Long Count

9.12.10.5.12

STEP 1

	9.	12.	10.	5.	12				
	9.	0.	0.	0.	0	(8	Ahaw	13	Keh)
		12.	10.	5.	12				
					Eb				

STEP 2

	13	365
12 K'atuns	2	260
10 Tuns	12	315
5 Winals	9	100
12 Kins	12	12
	35	687

STEP 3

	8	233	Base Date Positions
	35	687	Remainders
	43	920	Sum

13   365

43 / 13 = 3 R 4   920 / 365 = 2 R 190

4   Eb   10   Yax

APPENDIX H

LONG COUNT EXAMPLE TWO

Find the Calendar Round Position for the Long Count

9.12.15.13.7

STEP 1

9.	12.	15.	13.	7
9.	0.	0.	0.	0

(8 **Ahaw** 13 **Keh**)

12.	15.	13.	7

Manik'

STEP 2

		13		365
12	K'atuns	2		260
15	Tuns	5		290
13	Winals	0		260
7	Kins	7		7
		14		817

STEP 3

8	233	Base Date Positions
14	817	Remainders
22	1050	Sum

13   365

22 / 13 = 1 R **9**   1050 / 365 = 2 R **320**

9 Manik' 0 K'ayab

APPENDIX I

TABLE OF *Tun* Endings

8.1.15 12	.8 6	.1 13	.14 7	.7 1	9.0.0 8	.13 2	.6 9	.19 3	.12 10	.5 4	.18 11	.11 5	Ahau 13 Ceh
.16 8	.9 2	.2 9	.15 3	.8 10	.1 4	.14 11	.7 5	9.11.0 12	.13 6	.6 13	.19 7	.12 1	Ahau 8 Ceh
.17 4	.10 11	.3 5	.16 12	.9 6	.2 13	.15 7	.8 1	.1 8	.14 2	.7 9	10.2.0 3	.13 10	Ahau 3 Ceh
.18 13	.11 7	.4 1	.17 8	.10 2	.3 9	.16 3	.9 10	.2 4	.15 11	.8 5	.1 12	.14 6	Ahau 18 Zac
.19 9	.12 3	.5 10	.18 4	.11 11	.4 5	.17 12	.10 6	.3 13	.16 7	.9 1	.2 8	.15 2	Ahau 13 Zac
8.2.0 5	.13 12	.6 6	.19 13	.12 7	.5 1	.18 8	.11 2	.4 9	.17 3	.10 10	.3 4	.16 11	Ahau 8 Zac
.1 1	.14 8	.7 2	8.13.0 9	.13 3	.6 10	.19 4	.12 11	.5 5	.18 12	.11 6	.4 13	.17 7	Ahau 3 Zac
.2 10	.15 4	.8 11	.1 5	.14 12	.7 6	9.4.0 13	.13 7	.6 1	.19 8	.12 2	.5 9	.18 3	Ahau 18 Yax
.3 6	.16 13	.9 7	.2 1	.15 8	.8 2	.1 9	.14 3	.7 10	9.15.0 4	.13 11	.6 5	.19 12	Ahau 13 Yax
.4 2	.17 9	.10 3	.3 10	.16 4	.9 11	.2 5	.15 12	.8 6	.1 13	.14 7	.7 1	10.6.0 8	Ahau 8 Yax
.5 11	.18 5	.11 12	.4 6	.17 13	.10 7	.3 1	.16 8	.9 2	.2 9	.15 3	.8 10	.1 4	Ahau 3 Yax
.6 7	.19 1	.12 8	.5 2	.18 9	.11 3	.4 10	.17 4	.10 11	.3 5	.16 12	.9 6	.2 13	Ahau 18 Chen
.7 3	8.6.0 10	.13 4	.6 11	.19 5	.12 12	.5 6	.18 13	.11 7	.4 1	.17 8	.10 2	.3 9	Ahau 13 Chen
.8 12	.1 6	.14 13	.7 7	8.17.0 1	.13 8	.6 2	.19 9	.12 3	.5 10	.18 4	.11 11	.4 5	Ahau 8 Chen
.9 8	.2 2	.15 9	.8 3	.1 10	.14 4	.7 11	9.8.0 5	.13 12	.6 6	.19 13	.12 7	.5 1	Ahau 3 Chen
.10 4	.3 11	.16 5	.9 12	.2 6	.15 13	.8 7	.1 1	.14 8	.7 2	9.19.0 9	.13 3	.6 10	Ahau 18 Mol
.11 13	.4 7	.17 1	.10 8	.3 2	.16 9	.9 3	.2 10	.15 4	.8 11	.1 5	.14 12	.7 6	Ahau 13 Mol
.12 9	.5 3	.18 10	.11 4	.4 11	.17 5	.10 12	.3 6	.16 13	.9 7	.2 1	.15 8	.8 2	Ahau 8 Mol
.13 5	.6 12	.19 6	.12 13	.5 7	.18 1	.11 8	.4 2	.17 9	.10 3	.3 10	.16 4	.9 11	Ahau 3 Mol
.14 1	.7 8	8.10.0 2	.13 9	.6 3	.19 10	.12 4	.5 11	.18 5	.11 12	.4 6	.17 13	.10 7	Ahau 18 Yaxkin
.15 10	.8 4	.1 11	.14 5	.7 12	9.1.0 6	.13 13	.6 7	.19 1	.12 8	.5 2	.18 9	.11 3	Ahau 13 Yaxkin
.16 6	.9 13	.2 7	.15 1	.8 8	.1 2	.14 9	.7 3	9.12.0 10	.13 4	.6 11	.19 5	.12 12	Ahau 8 Yaxkin
.17 2	.10 9	.3 3	.16 10	.9 4	.2 11	.15 5	.8 12	.1 6	.14 13	.7 7	10.3.0 1	.13 8	Ahau 3 Yaxkin
.18 11	.11 5	.4 12	.17 6	.10 13	.3 7	.16 1	.9 8	.2 2	.15 9	.8 3	.1 10	.14 4	Ahau 18 Xul
.19 7	.12 1	.5 8	.18 2	.11 9	.4 3	.17 10	.10 4	.3 11	.16 5	.9 12	.2 6	.15 13	Ahau 13 Xul
8.3.0 3	.13 10	.6 4	.19 11	.12 5	.5 12	.18 6	.11 13	.4 7	.17 1	.10 8	.3 2	.16 9	Ahau 8 Xul
.1 12	.14 6	.7 13	8.14.0 7	.13 1	.6 8	.19 2	.12 9	.5 3	.18 10	.11 4	.4 11	.17 5	Ahau 3 Xul
.2 8	.15 2	.8 9	.1 3	.14 10	.7 4	9.5.0 11	.13 5	.6 12	.19 6	.12 13	.5 7	.18 1	Ahau 18 Zec
.3 4	.16 11	.9 5	.2 12	.15 6	.8 13	.1 7	.14 1	.7 8	9.16.0 2	.13 9	.6 3	.19 10	Ahau 13 Zec
.4 13	.17 7	.10 1	.3 8	.16 2	.9 9	.2 3	.15 10	.8 4	.1 11	.14 5	.7 12	10.7.0 6	Ahau 8 Zec
.5 9	.18 3	.11 10	.4 4	.17 11	.10 5	.3 12	.16 6	.9 13	.2 7	.15 1	.8 8	.1 2	Ahau 3 Zec
.6 5	.19 12	.12 6	.5 13	.18 7	.11 1	.4 8	.17 2	.10 9	.3 3	.16 10	.9 4	.2 11	Ahau 18 Zotz
.7 1	8.7.0 8	.13 2	.6 9	.19 3	.12 10	.5 4	.18 11	.11 5	.4 12	.17 6	.10 13	.3 7	Ahau 13 Zotz
.8 10	.1 4	.14 11	.7 5	8.18.0 12	.13 6	.6 13	.19 7	.12 1	.5 8	.18 2	.11 9	.4 3	Ahau 8 Zotz
.9 6	.2 13	.15 7	.8 1	.1 8	.14 2	.7 9	9.9.0 3	.13 10	.6 4	.19 11	.12 5	.5 12	Ahau 3 Zotz
.10 2	.3 9	.16 3	.9 10	.2 4	.15 11	.8 5	.1 12	.14 6	.7 13	10.0.0 7	.13 1	.6 8	Ahau 18 Zip
.11 11	.4 5	.17 12	.10 6	.3 13	.16 7	.9 1	.2 8	.15 2	.8 9	.1 3	.14 10	.7 4	Ahau 13 Zip
.12 7	.5 1	.18 8	.11 2	.4 9	.17 3	.10 10	.3 4	.16 11	.9 5	.2 12	.15 6	.8 13	Ahau 8 Zip
.13 3	.6 10	.19 4	.12 11	.5 5	.18 12	.11 6	.4 13	.17 7	.10 1	.3 8	.16 2	.9 9	Ahau 3 Zip
.14 12	.7 6	8.11.0 13	.13 7	.6 1	.19 8	.12 2	.5 9	.18 3	.11 10	.4 4	.17 11	.10 5	Ahau 18 Uo
.15 8	.8 2	.1 9	.14 3	.7 10	9.2.0 4	.13 11	.6 5	.19 12	.12 6	.5 13	.18 7	.11 1	Ahau 13 Uo
.16 4	.9 11	.2 5	.15 12	.8 6	.1 13	.14 7	.7 1	9.13.0 8	.13 2	.6 9	.19 3	.12 10	Ahau 8 Uo
.17 13	.10 7	.3 1	.16 8	.9 2	.2 9	.15 3	.8 10	.1 4	.14 11	.7 5	10.4.0 12	.13 6	Ahau 3 Uo
.18 9	.11 3	.4 10	.17 4	.10 11	.3 5	.16 12	.9 6	.2 13	.15 7	.8 1	.1 8	.14 2	Ahau 18 Pop
.19 5	.12 12	.5 6	.18 13	.11 7	.4 1	.17 8	.10 2	.3 9	.16 3	.9 10	.2 4	.15 11	Ahau 13 Pop
8.4.0 1	.13 8	.6 2	.19 9	.12 3	.5 10	.18 4	.11 11	.4 5	.17 12	.10 6	.3 13	.16 7	Ahau 8 Pop
.1 10	.14 4	.7 11	8.15.0 5	.13 12	.6 6	.19 13	.12 7	.5 1	.18 8	.11 2	.4 9	.17 3	Ahau 3 Pop
.2 6	.15 13	.8 7	.1 1	.14 8	.7 2	9.6.0 9	.13 3	.6 10	.19 4	.12 11	.5 5	.18 12	Ahau 3 Uayeb
.3 2	.16 9	.9 3	.2 10	.15 4	.8 11	.1 5	.14 12	.7 6	9.17.0 13	.13 7	.6 1	.19 8	Ahau 18 Cumku
.4 11	.17 5	.10 12	.3 6	.16 13	.9 7	.2 1	.15 8	.8 2	.1 9	.14 3	.7 10	10.8.0 4	Ahau 13 Cumku
.5 7	.18 1	.11 8	.4 2	.17 9	.10 3	.3 10	.16 4	.9 11	.2 5	.15 12	.8 6	.1 13	Ahau 8 Cumku
.6 3	.19 10	.12 4	.5 11	.18 5	.11 12	.4 6	.17 13	.10 7	.3 1	.16 8	.9 2	.2 9	Ahau 3 Cumku
.7 12	8.8.0 6	.13 13	.6 7	.19 1	.12 8	.5 2	.18 9	.11 3	.4 10	.17 4	.10 11	.3 5	Ahau 18 Kayab
.8 8	.1 2	.14 9	.7 3	8.19.0 10	.13 4	.6 11	.19 5	.12 12	.5 6	.18 13	.11 7	.4 1	Ahau 13 Kayab
.9 4	.2 11	.15 5	.8 12	.1 6	.14 13	.7 7	9.10.0 1	.13 8	.6 2	.19 9	.12 3	.5 10	Ahau 8 Kayab
.10 13	.3 7	.16 1	.9 8	.2 2	.15 9	.8 3	.1 10	.14 4	.7 11	10.1.0 5	.13 12	.6 6	Ahau 3 Kayab
.11 9	.4 3	.17 10	.10 4	.3 11	.16 5	.9 12	.2 6	.15 13	.8 7	.1 1	.14 8	.7 2	Ahau 18 Pax
.12 5	.5 12	.18 6	.11 13	.4 7	.17 1	.10 8	.3 2	.16 9	.9 3	.2 10	.15 4	.8 11	Ahau 13 Pax
.13 1	.6 8	.19 2	.12 9	.5 3	.18 10	.11 4	.4 11	.17 5	.10 12	.3 6	.16 13	.9 7	Ahau 8 Pax
.14 10	.7 4	8.12.0 11	.13 5	.6 12	.19 6	.12 13	.5 7	.18 1	.11 8	.4 2	.17 9	.10 3	Ahau 3 Pax
.15 6	.8 13	.1 7	.14 1	.7 8	9.3.0 2	.13 9	.6 3	.19 10	.12 4	.5 11	.18 5	.11 12	Ahau 18 Muan
.16 2	.9 9	.2 3	.15 10	.8 4	.1 11	.14 5	.7 12	9.14.0 6	.13 13	.6 7	.19 1	.12 8	Ahau 13 Muan
.17 11	.10 5	.3 12	.16 6	.9 13	.2 7	.15 1	.8 8	.1 2	.14 9	.7 3	10.5.0 10	.13 4	Ahau 8 Muan
.18 7	.11 1	.4 8	.17 2	.10 9	.3 3	.16 10	.9 4	.2 11	.15 5	.8 12	.1 6	.14 13	Ahau 3 Muan
.19 3	.12 10	.5 4	.18 11	.11 5	.4 12	.17 6	.10 13	.3 7	.16 1	.9 8	.2 2	.15 9	Ahau 18 Kankin
8.5.0 12	.13 6	.6 13	.19 7	.12 1	.5 8	.18 2	.11 9	.4 3	.17 10	.10 4	.3 11	.16 5	Ahau 13 Kankin
.1 8	.14 2	.7 9	8.16.0 3	.13 10	.6 4	.19 11	.12 5	.5 12	.18 6	.11 13	.4 7	.17 1	Ahau 8 Kankin
.2 4	.15 11	.8 5	.1 12	.14 6	.7 13	9.7.0 7	.13 1	.6 8	.19 2	.12 9	.5 3	.18 10	Ahau 3 Kankin
.3 13	.16 7	.9 1	.2 8	.15 2	.8 9	.1 3	.14 10	.7 4	9.18.0 11	.13 5	.6 12	.19 6	Ahau 18 Mac
.4 9	.17 3	.10 10	.3 4	.16 11	.9 5	.2 12	.15 6	.8 13	.1 7	.14 1	.7 8	10.9.0 2	Ahau 13 Mac
.5 5	.18 12	.11 6	.4 13	.17 7	.10 1	.3 8	.16 2	.9 9	.2 3	.15 10	.8 4	.1 11	Ahau 8 Mac
.6 1	.19 8	.12 2	.5 9	.18 3	.11 10	.4 4	.17 11	.10 5	.3 12	.16 6	.9 13	.2 7	Ahau 3 Mac
.7 10	8.9.0 4	.13 11	.6 5	.19 12	.12 6	.5 13	.18 7	.11 1	.4 8	.17 2	.10 9	.3 3	Ahau 18 Ceh

APPENDIX J

CALENDAR ROUND TO LONG COUNT EXAMPLE

Find a Long Count near 9. 15. 0. 0. 0   which corresponds to

3 **Lamat**   6 **Pax**

Lamat occurs on the eighth day; i. e., x. x. x. x. 8 in any Long Count (see Table 1) To get to the nearest **Ahaw** day, just subtract 8 (**Ahaw** is   x. x. x. x. 0). This affects the CR date as follows:

$$\begin{array}{ll} 3 \textbf{ Lamat} & 6 \textbf{ Pax} \\ \underline{-8} & \underline{-8} \\ 8 \textbf{ Ahau} & 18 \textbf{ Muan} \end{array}$$

Scan the right column of the Table of **Tun** Endings for 8 <u>**Ahaw** 18 **Muwan**</u> (it's near the bottom). Now move to the left in the same row until you find the Day Number **8**. The **tun** position is <u>.7</u>. This position corresponds to a **tun** ending between 8. 19. 0. 0. 0 and 9. 0. 0. 0. 0 . Therefore, one *possible* **tun** ending for 8 **Ahaw** 18 **Muwan** is:

8. 19. 7. 0. 0.

This is not within our desired range. This date must be increased to around 9. 15. 0. 0 . 0 (about 15 1/2 **k'atuns**). Using Table 5, we find that six calendar rounds correspond to 15. 16. 6. 0. Adding these amounts to our **tun** ending should get us in the proper range.

$$\begin{array}{l} 8. 19. \ 7. 0. 0 \\ \underline{+ \quad 15.16. 6. 0} \\ 9. 15. \ 3. 6. 0 \end{array}$$

Now these dates must be increased by 8 days (since we decreased the original by 8 to get to the Ahau Day Name).

$$\begin{array}{l} 9. 15. \ 3. 6. 0 \\ \underline{\qquad + 8} \\ 9. 15. \ 3. 6. 8 = 3 \textbf{ Lamat} 6 \textbf{ Pax} \end{array}$$

APPENDIX K

CALCULATION OF PLANETARY ELONGATIONS

In Chapter 7, "Glyphs and Astronomy," the key parameter for defining the positions of Venus and other planets with respect to the sun, was *elongation*. The generally available basic source for deriving elongations is the so-called Tuckerman Tables, whose more complete title is "Planetary, Lunar, and Solar Positions, A.D. 2 to A.D. 1649, at Five-day and Ten-day Intervals" (Tuckerman 1964). The calculations were done for the location of Baghdad, but the corrections for other places on the earth are small enough for the sun and for the planets with which we will be concerned, that they can be ignored. For our purposes, the pertinent entries in the tables are longitudes (unfortunately elongations were not calculated!), which are given for five- or ten-day intervals. If the date we are interested in does not correspond exactly to one of the given dates, a simple extrapolation is necessary.

The desired elongation of a planet, for example, Venus, for a given date, can be derived from its longitude because elongation is defined as the longitude of the planet minus the longitude of the sun:

Elongation of Venus =
Longitude of Venus -Longitude of the Sun

Let's look at Table 7:1, entry (4), which concerns the "War-on-Seibal" event. The Long Count date for this event is 9.15.4.6.4. To use values from the Tuckerman Tables we must convert this date to the Julian date, because the Tuckerman Tables are based on the Julian calendar.[1] The Julian date for 9.15.4.6.4 is November 29, A.D. 735. Now look at Figure K:1. The longitude entries for Venus are given at five-day intervals, so the dates of interest to us are November 25 and November 30. The values for Venus in degrees on those dates are:

Longitude of Venus on Nov. 25 = 253.09°
Longitude of Venus on Nov. 30 = 259.37°
Difference = 6.28°

Because our date is November 29, the correct longitude will be that for November 25 + 4/5 of the difference between the values for November 25 and 30:

Longitude of Venus on Nov. 29 = 253.09° + 4/5(6.28°)
= 253.09° + 5.02°
= 258.11°

For the sun, the longitude values are given at ten-day intervals, so the values we need are for November 20 and November 30:

Longitude of the sun on Nov. 20 = 241.77°
Longitude of the sun on Nov. 30 = 251.96°
Difference = 10.19°

For November 29, the correct value of the sun's longitude will be that for November 20 + 9/10 of the difference between the values for November 20 and November 30:

Longitude of the sun on Nov. 29 = 241.77° + 9/10(10.19°)
= 241.77° + 9.17°
= 250.94°

Now we can get the elongation for Venus for November 29 735, from the equation:

Elongation of Venus =
Longitude of Venus - Longitude of the Sun

Elongation of Venus on Nov. 29 =
258.11° - 250.94° = +7.17°

The value is plus, so Venus is an evening star, but from the value itself, we don't know whether Venus has just appeared as an evening star, or whether it is on the verge of disappearing, that is, whether it is at first appearance or last

SATURN LONG.	LAT.	JUPITER LONG.	LAT.	MARS LONG.	LAT.	SUN LONG.	JULIAN 16.00U	MOON LONG.	LAT.	VENUS LONG.	LAT.	MERCURY LONG.	LAT.
734							**734**						**734**
							JA 4	227.7	5.2	266.43	0.25	265.45	2.57
30.80	-2.36	123.03	0.93	304.78	-1.10	293.22	9JA14	288.4 353.9	1.9-3.7	272.67 278.91	0.03-0.19	268.23 272.76	1.71 0.85
31.11	-2.31	121.71	0.95	312.69	-1.08	303.35	19JA24	64.2 135.3	-4.8 0.5	285.14 291.38	-0.40-0.59	278.40 284.79	0.06-0.63
31.59	-2.26	120.41	0.97	320.57	-1.05	313.44	29// 3	199.7 259.5	5.0 4.1	297.61 303.84	-0.77-0.93	291.74 299.17	-1.21-1.67
32.24	-2.21	119.21	0.97	328.43	-1.01	323.49	8FE13	322.9 32.5	-1.2-5.2	310.07 316.29	-1.08-1.20	307.04 315.36	-1.98-2.13
33.04	-2.17	118.21	0.97	336.24	-0.96	333.48	18FE23	103.1 170.1	-2.3 3.4	322.51 328.73	-1.30-1.37	324.14 333.41	-2.10-1.87
33.97	-2.13	117.46	0.97	344.00	-0.89	343.41	28FE	231.6	5.1	334.94	-1.42	343.17	-1.42
							MR 5	291.8	1.5	341.14	-1.44	353.28	-0.74
35.00	-2.10	117.00	0.96	351.69	-0.82	353.29	10MR15	359.2 71.9	-4.0-4.3	347.34 353.53	-1.43-1.40	3.44 13.03	0.14 1.12
36.13	-2.07	116.85	0.95	359.32	-0.74	3.11	20MR25	140.3 203.6	1.1 4.9	359.72 5.91	-1.34-1.25	21.32 27.68	2.02 2.70
37.33	-2.05	117.02	0.94	6.87	-0.66	12.87	30// 4	263.4 325.6	3.5-1.6	12.08 18.25	-1.15-1.02	31.79 33.49	3.00 2.83
38.58	-2.03	117.48	0.93	14.33	-0.57	22.58	9AP14	37.4 110.4	-5.0-1.3	24.42 30.58	-0.87-0.71	32.89 30.54	2.12 0.95
39.87	-2.01	118.23	0.91	21.71	-0.47	32.24	19AP24	175.6 236.4	3.9 4.7	36.74 42.89	-0.53-0.35	27.52 25.12	-0.46-1.80
41.17	-2.00	119.23	0.90	29.00	-0.37	41.86	29AP	295.9	0.7	49.03	-0.15	24.24	-2.81
							MY 4	1.4	-4.2	55.17	0.05	25.20	-3.40
42.47	-2.00	120.46	0.89	36.21	-0.27	51.45	9MY14	76.3 147.2	-3.7 2.1	61.31 67.44	0.25 0.45	27.96 32.33	-3.59-3.41
43.75	-2.00	121.89	0.88	43.32	-0.17	61.00	19MY24	209.5 268.9	5.1 2.8	73.57 79.70	0.64 0.83	38.11 45.20	-2.95-2.24
45.00	-2.00	123.49	0.87	50.34	-0.06	70.54	29// 3	329.9 39.3	-2.4-5.1	85.82 91.94	1.00 1.15	53.52 62.99	-1.37-0.42
46.19	-2.01	125.24	0.87	57.26	0.05	80.06	8JN13	114.5 181.9	-0.6 4.6	98.05 104.16	1.29 1.40	73.36 84.17	0.50 1.23
47.31	-2.03	127.11	0.87	64.10	0.16	89.59	18JN23	242.2 302.1	4.0-4.2	110.26 116.36	1.49 1.55	94.86 105.02	1.70 1.86
48.34	-2.04	129.08	0.86	70.86	0.27	99.12	28JN	6.0	-4.8	122.45	1.59	114.48	1.75
							JL 3	78.2	-3.5	128.54	1.59	123.19	1.40
49.27	-2.06	131.14	0.87	77.52	0.38	108.67	8JL13	151.1 215.1	2.7 5.3	134.62 140.69	1.57 1.51	131.17 138.41	0.88 0.20
50.07	-2.09	133.25	0.87	84.09	0.50	118.25	18JL23	274.6 336.7	2.3-3.2	146.75 152.80	1.42 1.30	144.86 150.41	-0.58-1.44
50.74	-2.11	135.40	0.88	90.58	0.61	127.86	28// 2	44.3 116.7	-5.1-0.3	158.84 164.87	1.15 0.98	154.85 157.85	-2.34-3.21
51.25	-2.14	137.57	0.89	96.98	0.72	137.51	7AU12	168.9 247.2	4.8 4.2	170.89 176.89	0.77 0.54	158.93 157.61	-3.94-4.34
51.59	-2.17	139.74	0.90	103.29	0.84	147.21	17AU22	307.5 13.3	-0.7-5.0	182.88 188.84	0.29 0.02	153.84 148.85	-4.14-3.15
51.75	-2.20	141.90	0.91	109.50	0.96	156.96	27AU	83.6	-3.1	194.80	-0.27	145.23	-1.61
							SE 1	153.9	2.9	200.73	-0.57	145.15	-0.05
51.74	-2.24	144.01	0.93	115.61	1.08	166.76	6SE11	219.1 278.8	5.0 1.8	206.63 212.52	-0.87-1.18	148.95 155.57	1.11 1.74
51.53	-2.26	146.06	0.95	121.61	1.20	176.63	16SE21	341.6 51.8	-3.5-4.6	218.37 224.19	-1.49-1.79	163.69 172.33	1.93 1.80
51.16	-2.29	148.02	0.97	127.49	1.33	186.55	26// 1	122.4 189.4	0.4 4.8	229.98 235.73	-2.07-2.34	181.01 189.51	1.46 1.00
50.62	-2.31	149.88	1.00	133.23	1.46	196.53	6OC11	251.2 310.8	3.6-1.3	241.43 247.07	-2.58-2.79	197.80 205.88	0.48-0.08
49.96	-2.32	151.59	1.03	138.81	1.60	206.56	16OC21	17.6 91.0	-5.0-2.0	252.65 258.15	-2.97-3.10	213.77 221.52	-0.62-1.15
49.20	-2.32	153.14	1.07	144.21	1.74	216.65	26OC31	159.9 223.3	3.6 4.7	263.56 268.87	-3.19-3.22	229.14 236.64	-1.62-2.01
48.39	-2.32	154.50	1.11	149.40	1.90	226.77	5NO10	282.9 344.1	0.9-3.9	274.05 279.07	-3.19-3.09	243.96 250.98	-2.29-2.40
47.56	-2.30	155.63	1.15	154.33	2.06	236.93	15NO20	55.2 129.4	-4.3 1.5	283.91 288.53	-2.91-2.65	257.38 262.50	-2.28-1.82
46.78	-2.28	156.50	1.19	158.95	2.24	247.11	25NO30	195.5 256.1	5.1 3.0	292.87 296.88	-2.29-1.83	265.10 263.55	-0.88 0.59
46.09	-2.25	157.09	1.24	163.18	2.43	257.31	5DE10	315.3 19.5	-2.1-5.2	300.48 303.58	-1.25-0.56	257.80 251.64	2.19 3.11
45.52	-2.21	157.38	1.29	166.94	2.64	267.51	15DE20	93.6 166.2	-1.6 4.3	306.06 307.81	0.27 1.24	248.96 250.06	3.11 2.58
45.10	-2.16	157.35	1.34	170.11	2.86	277.71	25DE30	229.2 288.5	4.7 0.2	308.68 308.56	2.34 3.54	253.73 258.91	1.84 1.06
735							**735**						**735**
44.87	-2.12	156.99	1.39	172.56	3.09	287.89	4JA 9	349.3 56.9	-4.5-4.3	307.40 305.27	4.78 5.97	265.02 271.72	0.32-0.36
44.81	-2.07	156.34	1.43	174.11	3.34	298.04	14JA19	131.6 201.0	1.8 5.3	302.43 299.34	6.97 7.66	278.87 286.39	-0.94-1.43
44.95	-2.02	155.42	1.47	174.57	3.58	308.15	24JA29	261.7 321.4	2.6-2.7	296.50 294.37	7.98 7.95	294.27 302.52	-1.79-2.02
45.28	-1.97	154.29	1.50	173.80	3.78	318.22	3FE 8	25.3 95.5	-5.2-1.4	293.20 293.05	7.62 7.09	311.16 320.22	-2.08-1.96
45.78	-1.93	153.03	1.52	171.75	3.92	328.24	13FE18	168.5 234.1	4.4 4.3	293.87 295.54	6.44 5.73	329.69 339.48	-1.62-1.03
46.44	-1.88	151.74	1.53	168.59	3.94	338.21	23FE28	293.5 355.7	-0.3-4.7	297.93 300.91	4.99 4.26	349.28 358.50	-0.21 0.79
47.25	-1.84	150.49	1.53	164.80	3.80	348.12	5MR10	63.4 134.3	-3.7 2.2	304.38 308.25	3.54 2.85	6.26 11.78	1.83 2.71
48.11	-1.81	149.38	1.51	161.07	3.51	357.97	15MR20	203.9 266.0	5.0 1.9	312.44 316.89	2.19 1.58	14.54 14.48	3.24 3.23
49.23	-1.77	148.48	1.49	158.08	3.11	7.76	25MR30	325.8 31.9	-3.1-4.8	321.57 326.43	1.00 0.48	12.12 8.67	2.61 1.45
50.36	-1.75	147.84	1.47	156.26	2.66	17.50	4AP 9	102.5 172.2	-0.4 4.6	331.45 336.59	-0.00-0.43	5.68 4.26	0.07-1.22
51.57	-1.72	147.50	1.44	155.74	2.20	27.19	14AP19	237.6 297.5	3.7-1.1	341.84 347.18	-0.81-1.14	4.82 7.24	-2.21-2.86
52.83	-1.70	147.45	1.40	156.48	1.77	36.83	24AP29	359.5 69.8	-4.9-2.8	352.61 358.10	-1.43-1.66	11.25 16.61	-3.16-3.16
54.12	-1.69	147.71	1.37	158.31	1.38	46.43	4MY 9	141.5 208.4	3.1 4.9	3.66 9.26	-1.85-1.99	23.13 30.73	-2.87-2.34
55.42	-1.67	148.25	1.34	161.05	1.03	56.00	14MY19	270.2 329.5	1.1-3.8	14.92 20.61	-2.08-2.13	39.35 48.97	-1.61-0.75
56.73	-1.67	149.07	1.30	164.55	0.72	65.54	24MY29	35.0 108.6	-4.8 0.6	26.35 32.12	-2.14-2.11	59.42 70.33	0.16 0.98
58.02	-1.66	150.12	1.27	168.66	0.45	75.08	3JN 8	179.3 242.8	5.1 3.3	37.92 43.75	-2.04-1.94	81.15 91.44	1.58 1.89
59.27	-1.66	151.39	1.25	173.28	0.20	84.60	13JN18	302.3 3.0	-1.8-5.2	49.60 55.49	-1.81-1.66	100.96 109.65	1.90 1.66
60.47	-1.66	152.86	1.22	178.33	-0.02	94.13	23JN28	72.3 147.3	-2.6 3.8	61.40 67.33	-1.48-1.28	117.51 124.50	1.18 0.51
61.59	-1.67	154.49	1.20	183.75	-0.22	103.67	3JL 8	215.1 275.7	4.9 0.6	73.29 79.27	-1.07-0.84	130.56 135.55	-0.31-1.25
62.63	-1.68	156.26	1.18	189.49	-0.40	113.23	13JL18	335.0 38.4	-4.2-4.7	85.27 91.30	-0.61-0.38	139.21 141.22	-2.26-3.26
63.56	-1.69	158.15	1.17	195.51	-0.56	122.82	23JL28	107.7 184.6	0.8 5.2	97.35 103.42	-0.14 0.08	141.17 138.84	-4.13-4.62
64.37	-1.71	160.14	1.16	201.77	-0.70	132.45	2AU 7	248.9 308.2	2.8-2.3	109.51 115.62	0.31 0.51	134.74 130.51	-4.45-3.52
65.04	-1.72	162.20	1.15	208.26	-0.83	142.12	12AU17	9.1 75.6	-5.2-2.2	121.76 127.91	0.71 0.89	128.32 129.53	-2.07-0.56
65.55	-1.74	164.32	1.14	214.94	-0.94	151.84	22AU27	149.3 220.0	3.8 4.4	134.08 140.26	1.04 1.17	134.18 141.41	0.68 1.47
65.89	-1.76	166.47	1.14	221.82	-1.04	161.62	1SE 6	281.2 341.0	-0.1-4.4	146.46 152.68	1.28 1.36	150.03 159.12	1.82 1.82
66.05	-1.78	168.64	1.15	228.85	-1.12	171.45	11SE16	45.1 114.2	-4.1 1.4	158.91 165.15	1.42 1.45	168.17 176.96	1.58 1.18
66.03	-1.80	170.80	1.15	236.05	-1.19	181.35	21SE26	186.9 253.3	5.0 2.0	171.40 177.66	1.45 1.42	185.45 193.64	0.68 0.13
65.82	-1.82	172.93	1.16	243.37	-1.24	191.29	1OC 6	312.9 15.1	-3.0-4.9	183.93 190.20	1.36 1.28	201.57 209.27	-0.43-0.98
65.43	-1.83	175.02	1.18	250.82	-1.28	201.30	11OC16	83.3 153.3	-1.1 4.3	196.48 202.77	1.18 1.05	216.76 224.02	-1.50-1.96
64.89	-1.84	177.03	1.19	258.38	-1.31	211.36	21OC26	222.7 285.3	4.0-1.0	209.05 215.34	0.91 0.74	231.01 237.56	-2.33-2.55
64.21	-1.85	178.95	1.22	266.02	-1.32	221.46	31OC	345.0	-4.8	221.64	0.57	243.33	-2.55
							NO 5	50.8	-3.5	227.93	0.38	247.65	-2.23
63.45	-1.84	180.74	1.24	273.74	-1.31	231.60	10NO15	121.8 191.5	2.5 5.1	234.22 240.51	0.19-0.01	249.30 246.79	-1.41-0.01
62.63	-1.83	182.37	1.27	281.52	-1.29	241.73	20NO25	256.7 316.8	1.5-3.6	246.80 253.09	-0.21-0.41	240.45 234.78	1.64 2.72
61.80	-1.82	183.83	1.30	289.35	-1.26	251.96	30// 5	18.1 87.9	-5.1-0.4	259.37 265.66	-0.60-0.78	233.05 235.13	2.92 2.55
61.02	-1.79	185.08	1.34	297.19	-1.22	262.16	10DE15	160.9 227.9	4.9 3.7	271.94 278.22	-0.94-1.09	233.59 245.38	1.94 1.24
60.33	-1.76	186.08	1.38	305.05	-1.17	272.36	20DE25	289.4 348.6	-1.5-5.1	284.49 290.76	-1.23-1.34	251.91 258.90	0.55-0.11
59.77	-1.73	186.82	1.42	312.90	-1.10	282.55	30DE	52.7	-3.4	297.02	-1.43	266.22	-0.70

Figure K:1   *Page 385 of the Tuckerman Tables.*

appearance as evening star. To determine which, we must determine the elongation of Venus for a day just before or just after November 29. This will tell us whether the elongation is increasing or decreasing; if it is increasing, it's a first appearance; if it is decreasing, it's a last appearance as evening star. The calculation is carried out exactly as just described. It turns out that in this case Venus is at a first appearance as evening star.

There are computer programs available that will calculate and print out the planetary, solar, and lunar data given in the Tuckerman Tables, as well as the elongations. Some of the programs also calculate the data for specific sites and for specific times of day. Such programs offer a decided advantage because they can easily give the data for a sequence of days on either side of the date in question. As we have just seen, this additional data is useful in determining whether a planet is just appearing or is about to disappear. One such program, Ka'an, has been developed by Jorge Orejel at the University of Texas at Austin in conjunction with Linda Schele. Figures K:2 and K:3 are printouts from this program of the longitudes and elongations calculated for all the visible planets, the sun, and the moon for fifteen days before and fifteen days after November 29, 735 (9.15.4.6.4), the date we have just looked at above with the Tuckerman Tables. A glance at the elongations shows that Venus was at a first appearance as evening star, since the values on the days immediately preceding November 29 are smaller.

Let's consider another example in which Venus is at or near a maximum elongation as evening star. This is entry (6) from Table 7:1, and the verb is a star-over-shell event, possibly a war-related event. It is recorded on Throne 1 of Piedras Negras, and the date is 9.17.10.6.1—March 29 781 (Fig. K:4). Again, since this date is not one for which longitude values are actually given in the tables, extrapolation will be necessary. The date falls between March 28 and April 2:

Longitude of Venus on March 28 = 56.67°
Longitude of Venus on April 2 = 60.91°
Difference = 4.24°

The value we need is that for March 28 plus 1/5 of the difference between the two dates:

$$\text{Longitude of Venus on March 29} = 56.67° + 1/5(4.24°)$$
$$= 56.67° + 0.85°$$
$$= 57.52°$$

For the sun, the value we want falls between the values for March 23 and April 2:

Longitude of the sun on March 23 = 6.65°
Longitude of the sun on April 2 = 16.39°
Difference = 9.74°

Because March 29 is 6 days after March 23, the longitude value we want is:

$$\text{Longitude of the sun on March 29} = 6.65° + 6/10(9.74°)$$
$$= 6.65° + 5.84°$$
$$= 12.49°$$

Again we get the elongation of Venus from the equation:

$$\text{Elongation of Venus} = \text{Longitude of Venus - Longitude of the Sun}$$

$$\text{Elongation of Venus on March 29} = 57.52° - 12.49° = +45.03°$$

This value is plus, thus Venus is an evening star and in the discussion above, the value is in the range of maximum elongation as evening star. In order to tell whether the value is precisely at, before, or after the date of maximum elongation, it is necessary to examine several dates on either side of 29 March 781. As indicated above, the easy way to do this is with one of the available computer programs. Figure K:5 is a printout of the elongations for fifteen days on either side of 29 March. The array of data shows that Venus was actually thirteen days past the precise maximum elongation, which had occurred on March 16, but the change was rather small, only 0.7 of a degree. We don't know how precise the Maya were in their astronomical measurements, so whether this small movement from the exact maximum elongation was significant to them is not clear.

NOTES

1. Tables are available that give Christian dates, both Gregorian and Julian, for Maya dates. They may also be calculated by hand (Chapter 2), but most people who work with Maya inscriptions now use one of several computer or hand calculator programs that will perform these and other conversions pertaining to Maya calendrics.

month	day	Sun	Moon	Mercury	Venus	Mars	Jupiter	Saturn
nov	14	235.9570	181.9058	247.4209	239.6117	277.0811	181.4523	63.1029
nov	15	236.9744	195.5193	246.5001	240.8700	277.8590	181.6166	63.0208
nov	16	237.9920	208.9433	245.4189	242.1283	278.6375	181.7792	62.9384
nov	17	239.0100	222.1519	244.2036	243.3866	279.4165	181.9402	62.8557
nov	18	240.0282	235.1238	242.8896	244.6448	280.1960	182.0994	62.7729
nov	19	241.0466	247.8470	241.5191	245.9031	280.9760	182.2568	62.6900
nov	20	242.0653	260.3238	240.1381	247.1612	281.7564	182.4124	62.6070
nov	21	243.0841	272.5722	238.7936	248.4193	282.5373	182.5663	62.5239
nov	22	244.1031	284.6259	237.5293	249.6774	283.3186	182.7182	62.4409
nov	23	245.1222	296.5336	236.3828	250.9353	284.1002	182.8682	62.3580
nov	24	246.1415	308.3564	235.3835	252.1931	284.8822	183.0163	62.2752
nov	25	247.1608	320.1658	234.5518	253.4509	285.6646	183.1625	62.1926
nov	26	248.1802	332.0412	233.8994	254.7085	286.4472	183.3067	62.1103
nov	27	249.1996	344.0669	233.4301	255.9659	287.2301	183.4488	62.0282
nov	28	250.2191	-3.6733	233.1416	257.2233	288.0133	183.5890	61.9464
nov	29	[251.2387]	8.8975	233.0268	[258.4805]	288.7967	183.7271	61.8650
nov	30	252.2582	21.8403	233.0756	259.7376	289.5804	183.8630	61.7841
dec	1	253.2779	35.1912	233.2760	260.9946	290.3642	183.9969	61.7036
dec	2	254.2975	48.9537	233.6150	262.2514	291.1483	184.1287	61.6236
dec	3	255.3172	63.0950	234.0797	263.5081	291.9325	184.2582	61.5442
dec	4	256.3370	77.5469	234.6574	264.7647	292.7169	184.3856	61.4653
dec	5	257.3568	92.2130	235.3363	266.0211	293.5014	184.5108	61.3871
dec	6	258.3767	106.9801	236.1053	267.2775	294.2862	184.6337	61.3096
dec	7	259.3967	121.7323	236.9544	268.5337	295.0710	184.7543	61.2329
dec	8	260.4167	136.3651	237.8746	269.7899	295.8560	184.8726	61.1569
dec	9	261.4368	150.7954	238.8578	271.0459	296.6412	184.9885	61.0817
dec	10	262.4570	164.9680	239.8969	272.3018	297.4264	185.1021	61.0073
dec	11	263.4772	178.8548	240.9856	273.5577	298.2118	185.2133	60.9339
dec	12	264.4975	192.4508	242.1184	274.8135	298.9973	185.3220	60.8614
dec	13	265.5179	205.7667	243.2904	276.0691	299.7829	185.4283	60.7899

Figure K:2   Printout of planetary, solar, and lunar longitudes for fifteen days before and fifteen days after 29 November A.D. 735. Calculated with Ka'an.

month	day	Sun	Moon	Mercury	Venus	Mars	Jupiter	Saturn
nov	14	0.0000	-54.0512	11.4639	3.6547	41.1241	-54.5048	-172.8541
nov	15	0.0000	-41.4551	9.5258	3.8956	40.8847	-55.3578	-173.9536
nov	16	0.0000	-29.0487	7.4269	4.1363	40.6455	-56.2128	-175.0537
nov	17	0.0000	-16.8580	5.1936	4.3766	40.4066	-57.0698	-176.1542
nov	18	0.0000	-4.9044	2.8614	4.6167	40.1678	-57.9288	-177.2553
nov	19	0.0000	6.8004	0.4725	4.8564	39.9294	-58.7898	-178.3567
nov	20	0.0000	18.2586	-1.9272	5.0960	39.6912	-59.6528	-179.4583
nov	21	0.0000	29.4881	-4.2905	5.3352	39.4532	-60.5179	179.4398
nov	22	0.0000	40.5228	-6.5738	5.5743	39.2155	-61.3849	178.3378
nov	23	0.0000	51.4114	-8.7395	5.8131	38.9780	-62.2540	177.2358
nov	24	0.0000	62.2150	-10.7580	6.0517	38.7408	-63.1251	176.1338
nov	25	0.0000	73.0050	-12.6089	6.2901	38.5038	-63.9983	175.0319
nov	26	0.0000	83.8610	-14.2807	6.5283	38.2670	-64.8735	173.9301
nov	27	0.0000	94.8672	-15.7695	6.7663	38.0305	-65.7508	172.8286
nov	28	0.0000	106.1076	-17.0775	7.0042	37.7942	-66.6301	171.7273
nov	29	0.0000	117.6589	-18.2118	[7.2419]	37.5581	-67.5116	170.6264
nov	30	0.0000	129.5821	-19.1826	7.4794	37.3221	-68.3952	169.5258
dec	1	0.0000	141.9133	-20.0019	7.7167	37.0864	-69.2809	168.4257
dec	2	0.0000	154.6562	-20.6825	7.9539	36.8507	-70.1689	167.3261
dec	3	0.0000	167.7777	-21.2375	8.1908	36.6153	-71.0590	166.2269
dec	4	0.0000	-178.7901	-21.6796	8.4277	36.3799	-71.9514	165.1283
dec	5	0.0000	-165.1438	-22.0205	8.6643	36.1446	-72.8461	164.0303
dec	6	0.0000	-151.3966	-22.2714	8.9008	35.9095	-73.7430	162.9329
dec	7	0.0000	-137.6643	-22.4423	9.1370	35.6744	-74.6424	161.8362
dec	8	0.0000	-124.0516	-22.5421	9.3732	35.4393	-75.5441	160.7402
dec	9	0.0000	-110.6414	-22.5790	9.6091	35.2044	-76.4483	159.6449
dec	10	0.0000	-97.4890	-22.5601	9.8449	34.9695	-77.3549	158.5504
dec	11	0.0000	-84.6225	-22.4916	10.0805	34.7346	-78.2639	157.4567
dec	12	0.0000	-72.0468	-22.3792	10.3159	34.4998	-79.1755	156.3639
dec	13	0.0000	-59.7511	-22.2275	10.5512	34.2650	-80.0896	155.2720

Figure K:3   Printout of planetary, solar, and lunar elongations for fifteen days before and fifteen days after 29 November, A.D. 735. Calculated with Ka'an.

SATURN		JUPITER		MARS		SUN	JULIAN	MOON		VENUS		MERCURY	
LONG.	LAT.	LONG.	LAT.	LONG.	LAT.	LONG.	16.00U	LONG.	LAT.	LONG.	LAT.	LONG.	LAT.
780							**780**						**780**
248.08	1.49	71.76	-0.26	131.34	4.36	292.02	JA 3	197.6	-4.4	240.17	3.44	266.06	2.90
248.98	1.50	71.14	-0.23	127.68	4.54	302.16	8JA13	260.4 319.8	-4.5 0.1	245.45 250.84	3.26 3.03	267.77 271.62	2.08 1.21
249.77	1.51	70.85	-0.20	123.72	4.55	312.26	18JA23	20.3 89.0	4.6 4.0	256.34 261.91	2.77 2.48	276.82 282.90	0.38 -0.36
250.44	1.52	70.90	-0.18	120.20	4.39	322.32	28// 2	164.4 232.8	-2.2 -5.3	267.56 273.26	2.17 1.84	289.61 296.84	-0.99 -1.50
250.97	1.53	71.27	-0.15	117.68	4.11	332.32	7FE12	293.2 352.7	-2.3 2.9	279.02 284.82	1.51 1.17	304.52 312.64	-1.87 -2.09
251.35	1.55	71.95	-0.13	116.44	3.75	342.27	17FE22	56.1 127.4	5.2 1.1	290.65 296.51	0.83 0.50	321.22 330.28	-2.14 -2.00
							27FE	201.2	-4.6	302.40	0.18	339.83	-1.64
251.57	1.56	72.90	-0.10	116.47	3.38	352.16	MR 3	266.1	-4.2	308.32	-0.12	349.82	-1.05
251.62	1.58	74.11	-0.08	117.64	3.02	1.99	8MR13	325.4 27.0	0.6 4.8	314.25 320.20	-0.40 -0.66	0.03 9.96	-0.25 0.70
251.51	1.59	75.54	-0.06	119.77	2.68	11.76	18MR23	93.8 166.1	3.6 -2.4	326.17 332.14	-0.89 -1.10	18.92 26.19	1.65 2.44
251.24	1.60	77.16	-0.04	122.68	2.38	21.48	28// 2	236.4 298.1	-5.0 -1.7	338.13 344.13	-1.28 -1.42	31.34 34.13	2.92 2.95
250.84	1.61	78.93	-0.02	126.23	2.10	31.16	7AP12	358.0 63.2	3.3 4.8	350.14 356.16	-1.54 -1.62	34.54 32.88	2.48 1.49
250.30	1.62	80.84	-0.00	130.29	1.84	40.78	17AP22	132.9 203.8	-0.3 -4.6	2.18 8.21	-1.66 -1.68	30.02 27.21	0.14 -1.27
							27AP	269.9	-3.6	14.25	-1.67	25.56	-2.45
249.67	1.62	82.86	0.01	134.77	1.61	50.37	MY 2	329.7	1.3	20.29	-1.62	25.67	-3.22
248.97	1.61	84.97	0.03	139.60	1.39	59.93	7MY12	31.9 101.2	4.9 2.7	26.34 32.39	-1.55 -1.45	27.64 31.29	-3.57 -3.54
248.24	1.60	87.14	0.05	144.72	1.19	69.47	17MY22	172.0 239.9	-3.2 -3.8	38.45 44.52	-1.33 -1.18	36.45 42.96	-3.19 -2.57
247.51	1.59	89.35	0.06	150.10	1.01	79.00	27// 1	302.1 1.7	-0.9 3.9	50.60 56.68	-1.02 -0.84	50.74 59.72	-1.76 -0.83
246.82	1.57	91.59	0.08	155.70	0.83	88.53	6JN11	67.7 140.2	4.6 -0.0	64.75 68.87	-0.65 -0.46	69.75 80.43	0.12 0.95
246.21	1.54	93.83	0.10	161.50	0.67	98.06	16JN21	210.0 274.2	-5.1 -3.1	74.97 81.09	-0.25 -0.05	91.24 101.66	1.54 1.82
							26JN	334.0	2.1	87.22	0.16	111.43	1.82
245.70	1.51	96.06	0.11	167.49	0.51	107.61	JL 1	35.1	5.2	93.35	0.35	120.47	1.57
245.32	1.48	98.25	0.13	173.64	0.36	117.18	6JL11	105.1 179.1	2.2 -4.0	99.50 105.65	0.54 0.72	128.77 136.34	1.11 0.50
245.09	1.45	100.40	0.15	179.95	0.22	126.78	16JL21	246.2 307.2	-4.8 -0.3	111.82 117.99	0.88 1.02	143.15 149.12	-0.24 -1.07
245.01	1.42	102.47	0.17	186.41	0.08	136.42	26JL31	6.4 70.2	4.4 4.6	124.17 130.36	1.15 1.25	154.09 157.78	-1.96 -2.84
245.09	1.38	104.45	0.19	193.01	-0.05	146.11	5AU10	143.6 216.6	-1.2 -5.3	136.56 142.77	1.33 1.38	159.79 159.60	-3.65 -4.22
245.34	1.35	106.31	0.21	199.75	-0.17	155.85	15AU20	280.3 339.6	-2.6 2.6	148.98 155.20	1.41 1.41	156.86 152.14	-4.31 -3.66
							25AU30	40.1 107.2	5.2 2.0	161.42 167.65	1.38 1.33	147.55 145.74	-2.30 -0.68
245.73	1.32	108.02	0.23	206.63	-0.29	165.64	4SE 9	182.1 252.2	-4.1 -4.3	173.88 180.12	1.25 1.14	147.89 153.43	0.68 1.54
246.28	1.28	109.56	0.25	213.63	-0.41	175.49	14SE19	312.9 12.5	0.3 4.6	186.36 192.59	1.01 0.87	161.03 169.52	1.90 1.89
246.96	1.25	110.89	0.28	220.75	-0.51	185.40	24SE29	75.7 145.5	4.1 -1.5	198.83 205.07	0.70 0.52	178.21 186.79	1.62 1.21
247.77	1.23	112.00	0.31	227.99	-0.61	195.37	4OC 9	219.5 285.5	-5.0 -1.8	211.31 217.54	0.32 0.11	195.17 203.33	0.70 0.16
248.67	1.20	112.84	0.34	235.34	-0.70	205.39	14OC19	344.9 46.7	3.1 4.9	223.78 230.01	-0.10 -0.31	211.30 219.11	-0.40 -0.93
249.67	1.18	113.38	0.37	242.80	-0.79	215.46	24OC29	113.2 184.4	1.1 -4.3	236.24 242.47	-0.52 -0.73	226.79 234.34	-1.43 -1.86
250.74	1.16	113.62	0.40	250.35	-0.86	225.58	3NO 8	255.1 317.4	-3.8 1.2	248.70 254.92	-0.93 -1.12	241.76 248.94	-2.19 -2.38
251.87	1.15	113.52	0.43	257.99	-0.93	235.73	13NO18	17.2 82.5	4.8 3.3	261.14 267.35	-1.29 -1.44	255.68 261.49	-2.37 -2.06
253.01	1.13	113.10	0.47	265.70	-0.98	245.91	23NO28	152.1 222.5	-2.5 -5.0	273.56 279.75	-1.57 -1.68	265.40 265.86	-1.34 -0.08
254.20	1.12	112.37	0.50	273.48	-1.03	256.11	3DE 8	288.7 348.4	-1.2 3.8	285.94 292.12	-1.75 -1.80	261.73 255.13	1.55 2.84
255.37	1.11	111.37	0.53	281.31	-1.06	266.31	13DE18	50.5 119.9	4.9 0.1	298.29 304.44	-1.81 -1.79	250.67 250.22	3.21 2.85
256.52	1.11	110.17	0.56	289.18	-1.08	276.51	23DE28	191.3 258.9	-4.9 -3.5	310.57 316.68	-1.74 -1.64	252.90 257.50	2.17 1.39
781							**781**						**781**
257.62	1.10	108.86	0.58	297.07	-1.10	286.69	2JA 7	321.2 20.6	1.8 5.2	322.76 328.82	-1.52 -1.35	263.24 269.71	0.63 -0.08
258.66	1.10	107.53	0.61	304.48	-1.09	296.85	12JA17	85.3 158.4	3.1 -3.2	334.85 340.84	-1.16 -0.93	276.67 284.03	-0.71 -1.24
259.63	1.10	106.28	0.62	312.89	-1.08	306.97	22JA27	229.5 293.3	-5.0 -0.7	346.79 352.70	-0.66 -0.37	291.75 299.84	-1.66 -1.95
260.49	1.10	105.21	0.63	320.78	-1.06	317.05	1FE 6	353.2 53.6	4.2 4.9	358.55 4.35	-0.06 0.28	308.30 317.18	-2.08 -2.04
261.24	1.11	104.37	0.64	328.64	-1.02	327.08	11FE16	121.9 197.1	-0.1 -5.1	10.08 15.73	0.64 1.01	326.48 336.16	-1.79 -1.31
261.86	1.11	103.82	0.64	336.45	-0.98	337.06	21FE26	265.6 326.4	-3.0 2.3	21.30 26.78	1.40 1.78	346.02 355.60	-0.59 0.35
262.34	1.12	103.58	0.65	344.22	-0.92	346.98	3MR 8	25.8 88.4	5.1 2.7	32.15 37.39	2.17 2.55	4.12 10.72	1.39 2.36
262.66	1.13	103.66	0.64	351.93	-0.85	356.84	13MR18	160.0 234.7	-3.3 -4.6	42.49 47.43	2.92 3.27	14.75 15.94	3.06 3.30
262.83	1.13	104.06	0.64	359.57	-0.78	**6.65**	23MR28	299.6 358.9	0.1 4.4	52.16 **56.67**	3.60 3.89	14.51 11.37	2.94 1.98
262.83	1.14	104.74	0.64	7.13	-0.70	**16.39**	2AP 7	59.6 125.1	4.3 -0.7	**60.91** 64.82	4.13 4.32	8.01 5.79	0.66 -0.71
262.67	1.14	105.69	0.64	14.61	-0.61	26.09	12AP17	198.0 270.3	-5.0 -2.2	68.35 71.38	4.44 4.47	5.45 7.05	-1.85 -2.64
262.36	1.15	106.88	0.64	22.00	-0.52	35.74	22AP27	332.1 31.8	3.0 5.0	73.85 75.63	4.40 4.20	10.38 15.15	-3.09 -3.21
261.91	1.15	108.27	0.64	29.30	-0.42	45.35	2MY 7	95.0 163.7	1.7 -3.9	76.61 76.66	3.85 3.32	21.16 28.29	-3.03 -2.60
261.34	1.15	109.85	0.64	36.52	-0.32	54.92	12MY17	239.3 304.0	-4.2 1.0	75.72 73.82	2.58 1.65	36.46 45.65	-1.95 -1.13
260.68	1.14	111.58	0.64	43.63	-0.21	64.47	22MY27	4.0 65.6	4.9 3.7	71.15 68.06	0.56 -0.61	55.77 66.53	-0.22 0.65
259.97	1.13	113.45	0.64	50.66	-0.10	74.01	1JN 6	132.3 203.1	-1.8 -5.2	65.05 62.56	-1.74 -2.73	77.46 88.02	1.36 1.79
259.24	1.12	115.41	0.65	57.60	0.01	83.53	11JN16	273.2 336.3	-1.7 3.7	60.91 60.54	-3.53 -4.11	97.89 106.95	1.93 1.79
258.52	1.10	117.47	0.65	64.44	0.12	93.06	21JN26	36.2 100.8	5.1 1.0	60.54 61.72	-4.50 -4.72	115.17 122.55	1.40 0.81
257.85	1.08	119.58	0.66	71.19	0.23	102.59	1JL 6	171.2 241.7	-4.6 -4.1	63.67 66.26	-4.79 -4.75	129.04 134.53	0.05 -0.84
257.27	1.06	121.74	0.67	77.84	0.35	112.15	11JL16	307.6 8.2	1.4 5.1	69.38 72.95	-4.62 -4.42	138.83 141.63	-1.82 -2.84
256.80	1.03	123.93	0.68	84.41	0.47	121.74	21JL26	69.2 137.8	3.6 -2.3	76.89 81.13	-4.16 -3.85	142.55 141.24	-3.79 -4.47
256.46	1.01	126.11	0.69	90.88	0.58	131.36	31// 5	210.7 278.4	-5.2 -1.2	85.63 90.34	-3.51 -3.15	137.79 133.34	-4.62 -4.01
256.27	0.98	128.29	0.71	97.25	0.71	141.02	10AU15	340.6 40.2	3.9 4.9	95.25 100.32	-2.76 -2.36	129.99 129.60	-2.73 -1.18
256.25	0.95	130.43	0.73	103.52	0.83	150.73	20AU25	103.5 176.3	0.7 -4.7	105.52 110.85	-1.96 -1.55	132.79 139.02	0.20 1.19
256.38	0.92	132.51	0.75	109.69	0.95	160.50	30AU	249.0	-3.4	116.29	-1.15	147.16	1.72
256.68	0.89	134.52	0.77	115.74	1.08	170.32	SE 4	313.1	2.0	121.83	-0.77	156.12	1.86
257.13	0.87	136.43	0.80	121.66	1.21	180.20	9SE14	13.2 73.1	5.0 3.0	127.45 133.16	-0.39 -0.04	165.22 174.13	1.71 1.36
257.72	0.84	138.20	0.83	127.45	1.35	190.14	19SE24	139.7 215.2	-2.6 -4.8	138.93 144.76	0.29 0.60	182.75 191.06	0.90 0.37
258.45	0.82	139.83	0.86	133.07	1.50	200.13	29// 4	285.1 346.3	-0.2 4.3	150.66 156.60	0.87 1.11	199.10 206.90	-0.19 -0.75
259.29	0.80	141.27	0.89	138.52	1.65	210.18	9OC14	45.9 107.6	4.4 -0.1	162.59 168.62	1.32 1.49	214.48 221.85	-1.29 -1.78
260.24	0.78	142.49	0.93	143.74	1.81	220.28	19OC24	177.7 252.9	-4.8 -2.7	174.69 180.79	1.63 1.72	228.97 235.75	-2.19 -2.47
							29OC	319.1	2.9	186.92	1.78	241.93	-2.58
261.27	0.76	143.47	0.97	148.71	1.99	230.41	NO 3	18.9	5.1	193.08	1.81	247.02	-2.41
262.36	0.74	144.18	1.02	153.36	2.17	240.58	8NO13	79.4 144.1	2.1 -3.3	199.25 205.44	1.80 1.76	250.04 249.51	-1.82 -0.67
263.51	0.73	144.59	1.06	157.64	2.38	250.77	18NO23	216.5 288.7	-4.7 0.5	211.65 217.87	1.68 1.58	244.60 237.98	0.96 2.38
264.67	0.71	144.68	1.11	161.45	2.60	260.97	28// 3	351.6 51.3	4.9 4.1	224.11 230.35	1.45 1.29	234.31 234.87	2.93 2.76
265.85	0.70	144.45	1.16	164.67	2.84	271.17	8DE13	114.5 182.7	-1.1 -5.2	236.59 242.84	1.12 0.93	238.44 243.72	2.22 1.54
267.02	0.69	143.90	1.20	167.17	3.09	281.36	18DE23	254.7 322.6	-2.5 3.4	249.09 255.35	0.73 0.52	249.96 256.77	0.84 0.16
							28DE	23.3	5.2	261.60	0.31	263.95	-0.46

Figure K:4   *Page 408 of the Tuckerman Tables.*

month	day	Sun	Moon	Mercury	Venus	Mars	Jupiter	Saturn	
mar	14	0.0000	-178.5110	17.2183	45.6765	-5.2026	105.5676	-95.4447	
mar	15	0.0000	-164.2402	16.5538	45.6863	-5.4185	104.6153	-96.4049	
mar	16	0.0000	-150.1857	15.7754	45.6894	-5.6346	103.6666	-97.3663	Maximum elongation as evening star
mar	17	0.0000	-136.4927	14.8850	45.6856	-5.8509	102.7216	-98.3287	
mar	18	0.0000	-123.2580	13.8854	45.6747	-6.0673	101.7801	-99.2921	
mar	19	0.0000	-110.5219	12.7806	45.6564	-6.2839	100.8420	-100.2568	
mar	20	0.0000	-98.2715	11.5757	45.6306	-6.5007	99.9075	-101.2225	
mar	21	0.0000	-86.4529	10.2772	45.5969	-6.7177	98.9764	-102.1894	
mar	22	0.0000	-74.9879	8.8929	45.5552	-6.9350	98.0488	-103.1574	
mar	23	0.0000	-63.7909	7.4315	45.5050	-7.1526	97.1246	-104.1266	
mar	24	0.0000	-52.7803	5.9035	45.4462	-7.3703	96.2037	-105.0970	
mar	25	0.0000	-41.8849	4.3199	45.3784	-7.5884	95.2863	-106.0685	
mar	26	0.0000	-31.0448	2.6929	45.3013	-7.8067	94.3722	-107.0412	
mar	27	0.0000	-20.2102	1.0353	45.2146	-8.0252	93.4615	-108.0149	
mar	28	0.0000	-9.3394	-0.6400	45.1179	-8.2441	92.5541	-108.9899	
mar	29	0.0000	1.6023	-2.3197	45.0109	-8.4632	91.6501	-109.9659	
mar	30	0.0000	12.6425	-3.9910	44.8931	-8.6825	90.7493	-110.9430	
mar	31	0.0000	23.8030	-5.6419	44.7642	-8.9021	89.8519	-111.9212	
apr	1	0.0000	35.1027	-7.2606	44.6236	-9.1220	88.9578	-112.9005	
apr	2	0.0000	46.5620	-8.8368	44.4710	-9.3422	88.0670	-113.8807	
apr	3	0.0000	58.2096	-10.3615	44.3058	-9.5626	87.1794	-114.8621	
apr	4	0.0000	70.0860	-11.8267	44.1275	-9.7833	86.2950	-115.8444	
apr	5	0.0000	82.2428	-13.2258	43.9355	-10.0043	85.4138	-116.8277	
apr	6	0.0000	94.7353	-14.5536	43.7294	-10.2255	84.5358	-117.8121	
apr	7	0.0000	107.6088	-15.8063	43.5085	-10.4471	83.6609	-118.7974	
apr	8	0.0000	120.8815	-16.9809	43.2722	-10.6689	82.7891	-119.7837	
apr	9	0.0000	134.5293	-18.0757	43.0199	-10.8911	81.9203	-120.7711	
apr	10	0.0000	148.4782	-19.0900	42.7509	-11.1136	81.0545	-121.7594	
apr	11	0.0000	162.6065	-20.0236	42.4646	-11.3364	80.1916	-122.7488	
apr	12	0.0000	176.7591	-20.8773	42.1602	-11.5596	79.3315	-123.7392	

Figure K:5   Printout of planetary, solar, and lunar elongations for fifteen days before and fifteen days after 29 March, A.D. 781. Calculated with Ka'an.

APPENDIX L

TESTING MAYA DATES FOR RETROGRADE MOTION OF PLANETS

In Chapter 7, the dates of several Maya events related to the occurrence of second stationary positions of the planet Jupiter were discussed. The terms first and second stationary positions refer to the starting and ending points, respectively, of the phenomenon known as "retrograde motion" of the planets. This appendix presents a method for determining whether retrograde motion of a planet of interest may be occurring near the date of an event of importance to the Maya.

A simple way to determine whether a date of interest falls during, or close to, a retrograde motion episode is to consult the Tuckerman Tables, which were discussed in Appendix K. For the detection of retrograde motion, we are interested in longitude values, not elongation, since retrograde motion is measured against the fixed star background. Because the Tuckerman Tables are tabulated in Julian dates, the Maya date must be converted to the Julian calendar (see endnote 1 in Appendix K). With the Julian date in hand, look in the tables for the appropriate date and scan the longitude values for several time intervals before and after the date in question. The usual motion of a planet against the background of fixed stars as seen from the earth is eastward—toward the point on the eastern horizon where the sun rises. By convention, the longitude increases as a planet moves in an eastward direction, and the values in the Tuckerman Tables reflect this. As the first stationary position is approached, the intervals of increase in longitude become smaller and smaller, and eventually the planet comes to a temporary standstill—the first stationary position. The planet then begins to move in a westward direction—the retrograde motion—and the longitude values become smaller during this episode. Eventually the decreases begin to become smaller, and the planet again comes to a standstill—the second stationary position. The longitude values start to increase again as the planet resumes its eastward path through the heavens.

Let's look at the appropriate page in the Tuckerman Tables (Fig. L:1) for the 2 Kib 14 Mol event tabulated in Table 7:3 (entry 3). The date was 9.12.18.5.16, or July 20, A.D. 690 (Julian). If we look at the top of the column of longitude values for Jupiter for A.D. 690, we see that the values increase as we go down the column until we come to the entry for March 1, after which a reversal begins. This is approximately the first stationary position, and the beginning of retrograde motion. The longitude decreases during the retrograde phase until July 9 (approximately the second stationary position), when another reversal begins, and the regular eastward movement of Jupiter resumes. The retrograde episode lasted about four months.

To get the exact dates of the stationary positions, the longitudes for each day must be calculated by extrapolation for the days between 1 March and 11 March 690, for the first stationary position, and for the days between 29 June and 9 July, for the second stationary position. As mentioned in Appendix K, this process can be handily done with the aid of computer programs, which can compute daily longitude values for any date range desired. The exact dates in this case are March 4, 690, for the first stationary position, and July 5, 690, for the second. The 2 Kib 14 Mol event occurred fifteen days later, on July 20, 690.

As was mentioned in the discussion of retrograde motion in Chapter 7, this process occurs for Jupiter about every thirteen months, so a second retrograde episode is evident in Figure L:1. Two retrograde episodes for Saturn and one for Mars also appear. See if you can find them.

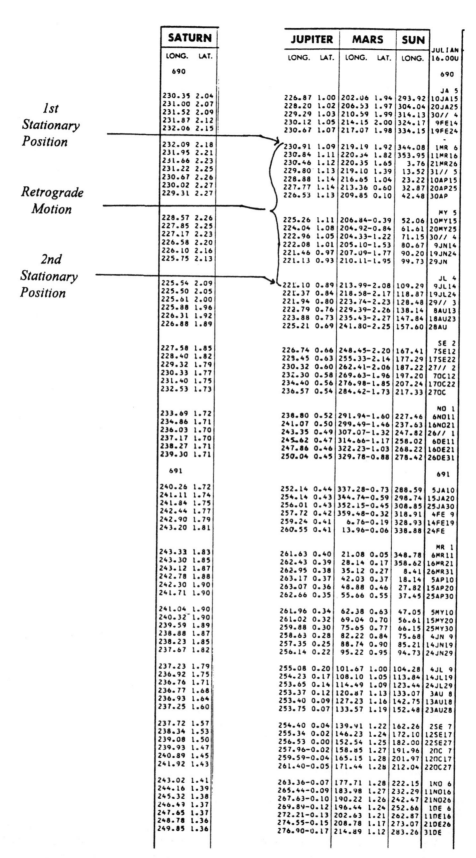

Figure L:1   Retrograde episode of Jupiter. See if you can find the two retrograde episodes for Saturn and the one for Mars in this table. (Tuckerman Tables, page 363).

REFERENCES AND RESOURCE BIBLIOGRAPHY

For those who wish to pursue additional study of the Maya hieroglyphic writing system, there are several useful publications. Two classic works by J. Eric Thompson contain much general information, some of which is now out of date, but each contains tables of hieroglyphs: *Maya Hieroglyphic Writing* (1960) and *A Catalog of Maya Hieroglyphics* (1962). David Kelley's *Deciphering the Maya Script* (1976), although also somewhat out of date, is still quite helpful. For a short overview of glyph studies, Stephen Houston's *Maya Glyphs* (1989), is recommended. For more information on the grammatical aspects of the writing system, we suggest Linda Schele's *Maya Glyphs: The Verbs* (1982) and Victoria Bricker's *A Grammar of Mayan Hieroglyphs* (1986). An excellent history of the decipherment of Maya hieroglyphs is available in Michael Coe's *Breaking the Maya Code* (1992). *A Resource Bibliography for the Decipherment of Maya Hieroglyphs* and *New Hieroglyph Readings*, by John Harris (1994) contains an extensive bibliography of recent publications in English on decipherment of Maya hieroglyphs.

For the latest decipherments, the following publications are recommended:

(1) *Research Reports on Ancient Maya Writing*
     The Center for Maya Research
     P.O. Box 65760
     Washington, D.C. 20035-57650

(2) *Notebooks for the Maya Hieroglyphic Workshops at Texas*, by Linda Schele and coauthors.
     The Maya Workshop Foundation
     P.O. Box 5645
     Austin, Texas 78705

(3) *Copan Notes*, Copan Mosaics Project and the Instituto Hondureno de Antropologia e Historia.
     Kinko's Copies
     2901-C Medical Arts Street
     Austin, Texas 78705

(4) *Texas Notes*, Center of the History and Art of Ancient American Culture of the Art Department of the University of Texas at Austin.
     Kinko's Copies
     2901-C Medical Arts Street
     Austin, Texas 78705

(5) *The Palenque Round Table (Mesa Redonda) Proceedings*, Merle Greene Robertson, general editor.
     Pre-Columbian Art Research Institute
     1100 Sacramento Street
     San Francisco, California 94108

(6) Two supplements to *Understanding Maya Inscriptions* (Harris, 1993, 1994).
     Unversity of Pennsylvania Museum
     Philadelphia, PA 19104

•••

Adams, Richard E. W.
  1977 Comments on the Glyphic Texts of the 'Altar Vase'. In *Social Process in Maya Prehistory: Studies in Honor of Sir Eric Thompson*, ed. Norman Hammond, pp. 409-420. London: Academic Press.
  1984 *Rio Azul Project Reports, No. 1, Final 1983 Report*. San Antonio: Center for Archaeological Research, The University of Texas at San Antonio.
  1990 Archaeological Research at the Lowland Maya City of Rio Azul. *Latin American Antiquity* 1(1): 23–41.

Adams, Richard E. W., and Robert C. Aldrich
  1980 A Reevaluation of the Bonampak Murals: A Preliminary Statement on the Paintings and Texts. In *Third Palenque Round Table, 1978, Vol. V*, ed. Merle Greene Robertson, pp. 45–59. Austin: University of Texas Press.

Alexander, Helen
1992   Celestial Links to the Ancestors: A Pattern of Celestial Events on Twelve Dates Recorded on Tikal Stela 31. *U Mut Maya IV*, eds. Tom and Carolyn Jones, pp. 48–60. Arcata, California: Tom and Carolyn Jones.

Alexander, Helen, Cal Tolman, Laura Lee Crumley, and Leroy Cleal
1988   The Early Stelae of Copan. *U Mut Maya*, eds. Tom Jones and Carolyn Young, pp. 31–35. Arcata, California: Tom Jones.

Anderson, Lloyd, and Janis Indrikis
1988   Some Miscellaneous Notes on Copan Inscriptions, Including Readings of Stelae 6 and 1. *U Mut Maya*, eds. Tom Jones and Carolyn Young, pp. 41–45. Arcata, California: Tom Jones.

Attanasi, John J.
1973   *Lak T'an: A Grammar of the Chol (Mayan) Word*. Ph.D. dissertation, Department of Linguistics, University of Chicago. [Includes a Chol-English dictionary.]

Aulie, H. Wilbur, and Evelyn W. de Aulie
1978   *Diccionario Ch'ol-Espanol Espanol-Ch'ol*. Serie de Vocabularios y Diccionarios Indigenas "Mariano Silva y Aceves," No. 21. Mexico City: Instituto Linguistico de Verano.

Aveni, Anthony
1980   The Mathematical and Astronomical Content of the Mesoamerican Inscriptions. Chapter IV of *Skywatchers of Ancient Mexico*, pp. 133–217. Austin: University of Texas Press.
1991   The Real Venus-Kukulcan in the Maya Inscriptions and Alignments. In *Sixth Palenque Round Table, 1986, Vol. VIII*, ed. Virginia M. Fields, pp. 309–321. Norman: University of Oklahoma Press.
1992a   The Moon and the Venus Table: An Example of Commensuration in the Maya Calendar. In *The Sky in Mayan Literature*, ed. Anthony F. Aveni, pp. 87–101. New York: Oxford University Press.
1992b   *The Sky in Mayan Literature*. New York: Oxford University Press.

Aveni, Anthony F., and Lorren D. Hotaling
1994   Monumental Inscriptions and the Observational Basis of Maya Planetary Astronomy. *Archaeoastronomy* 19: 21–54.
1996   Monumental Inscriptions and the Observational Basis of Mayan Planetary Astronomy. In *Eighth Palenque Round Table, 1993, Vol. X*, eds. Martha J. Macri and Jan McHargue, pp. 357–367. San Francisco: Pre-Columbian Art Research Institute.

Bardsley, Sandra Noble
1989a   The Panels of Temple 11 (Copan): A Chronology Summary. *U Mut Maya II*, eds. Tom Jones and Carolyn Young, pp. 37–39. Arcata, California: Tom Jones and Carolyn Young.
1989b   Copan: A Compilation of Known and Tentative Data. *U Mut Maya II*, eds. Tom Jones and Carolyn Young, pp. 47–58. Arcata, California: Tom Jones and Carolyn Young.
1992   So Many Kings…So Few Katuns: The Middle Era of Tikal's History. *U Mut Maya IV*, eds. Tom and Carolyn Jones, pp. 77–86. Arcata, California: Tom and Carolyn Jones.
1994   Rewriting History at Yaxchilan: Inaugural Art of Bird Jaguar IV. In *Seventh Palenque Round Table, 1989, Vol. 9*, ed. Virginia M. Fields, pp. 87–94. San Francisco: Pre-Columbian Art Research Institute.
1996   Benches, Brothers, and Lineage Lords of Copan. In *Eighth Palenque Round Table, 1993, Vol. X*, eds. Martha J. Macri and Jan McHargue, pp. 195–201. San Francisco: Pre-Columbian Art Research Institute.

Barnhart, Ed
1994   The Pakal-GI Connection. *U Mut Maya V*, eds. Carolyn and Tom Jones, pp. 30–35. Arcata, California: Tom and Carolyn Jones.
1995   Groups of Four and Five Day Names in the Dresden Codex Almanacs: The First Twenty-three Pages. *Texas Note 72*. Austin: Center of the History and Art of Ancient American Culture, University of Texas at Austin.

Barrera Vasquez, Alfredo
1980   *Diccionario Maya Cordemex. Maya-Espanol, Espanol-Maya*. Merida: Ediciones Cordemex.

Barrett, Rusty, and Kam Manahan
1991   A New Luk' at Two Stuccoes from Temple XVIII (It's at Palenque). *Texas Note 26*. Austin: Center of the History and Art of Ancient American Culture, University of Texas at Austin.

Barthel, Thomas S.
1977   A Tubingen Key to Maya Glyphs. *Tribus* 26: 97–102.

Bassie-Sweet, Karen
1991   *From the Mouth of the Dark Cave*. Norman: University of Oklahoma Press.
1996   *At the Edge of the World: Caves and Late Classic Maya World View*. Norman: University of Oklahoma Press.

Baudez, Claude F.
1996   The Cross Group at Palenque. In *Eighth Palenque Round Table, 1993, Vol. X*, eds. Martha J. Macri and Jan McHargue, pp. 121–128. San Francisco: Pre-Columbian Art Research Institute.

Baudez, Claude F., and Peter Mathews
1979   Capture and Sacrifice at Palenque. In *Tercera Mesa Redonda de Palenque, 1978, Vol. IV*, eds. Merle Greene Robertson and Donnan C. Jeffers, pp. 31–40. Palenque, Chiapas, Mexico: Pre-Columbian Art Research Institute.

Beetz, Carl P., and Linton Satterthwaite
1981   *The Monuments and Inscriptions of Caracol, Belize*. University Museum Monograph 45. Philadelphia: The University of Pennsylvania Museum.

Benson, Elizabeth P., ed.
1973   *Mesoamerican Writing Systems*. Washington, D.C.: Dumbarton Oaks.

Benson, Elizabeth P., and Gillett G. Griffin, eds.
1988   *Maya Iconography*. Princeton: Princeton University Press.

Berlin, Heinrich
1951   El Templo de las Inscripciones—VI—de Tikal. *Antropologia e Historia de Guatemala* 3: 33–55.
1958   El glifo 'emblema' en las inscripciones Maya. *Journal de le Société des Américanistes*, n.s., 47: 111–119. Paris. [Translated into English by Khristaan D. Villela as Texas Note 36 (1993).] Austin: Center of the History and Art of Ancient American Culture, University of Texas at Austin.
1959   Glifos nominales en el sarcofago de Palenque. *Humanidades* 2(10): 1–8. Guatemala City: Universidad de San Carlos. [Translated into English by Khristaan D. Villela as Texas Note 37 (1993).] Austin: Center of the History and Art of Ancient American Culture, University of Texas at Austin.
1963   The Palenque Triad. *Journal de la Société des Américanistes*, n.s., 52: 91–99. Paris.
1965   The Inscription of the Temple of the Cross at Palenque. *American Antiquity* 30: 330–342.
1968a   Estudios Epigraphicos II. *Antropologia e Historia de Guatemala* XX(1): 13–24.
1968b   The Tablet of the 96 Glyphs at Palenque, Chiapas, Mexico. In *Archaeological Studies in Middle America*. New Orleans: Middle American Research Institute, Tulane University. Publ. 26: 135–150.
1973   Beitrage zum Verständnis der Inschriften von Naranjo. *Bulletin de la Société Suisse des Américanistes* 37: 7–14.

Berlin, Heinrich, and David H. Kelley
1961   The 819–Day Count and Color-Direction Symbolism Among the Classic Maya. In *Archaeological Studies in Middle America*. New Orleans: Middle American Research Institute, Tulane University. Publ. 26: 9–20.

Bernal-Garcia, Maria Elena
1988   A Paraphrase of the Text of Dresden 61–69. *U Mut Maya*, eds, Tom Jones and Carolyn Young, pp. 95–99. Arcata, California: Tom Jones.

Berlo, Janet Catherine
1989   Early Writing in Central Mexico: In Tlilli, In Tlapalli before A.D. 1000. In *Mesoamerica after the Decline of Teotihuacan A.D. 700–900*, eds. Richard A. Diehl and Janet Catherine Berlo, pp. 19–47. Washington, D.C.: Dumbarton Oaks.

Bernal-Garcia, Maria Elena, James B. Buchanan, Donald H. Green, and Richard E Johnson
1988   The Dresden Codex Pages 61–69: The Serpent Numbers, Multiplication Tables and Almanacs. *U Mut Maya*, eds. Tom Jones and Carolyn Young, pp. 83–94. Arcata, California: Tom Jones.

Beyer, Hermann
1926   Los Dos Estelas Mayas de Tila, Chias. *El Mexico Antiguo* II(10): 235–250. Mexico, D.F.
1937   *Studies on the Inscriptions of Chichen Itza*. Contributions to American Archaeology, No. 21. Washington, D.C.: Carnegie Institution of Washington. Publ. 483.

Bolles, David
1990   The Mayan Calendar: The Solar-Agricultural Year, and Correlation Questions. *Mexicon* XII(5): 85–89.

Bolles, John S.
1977   *Las Monjas: A Major Pre-Mexican Architectural Complex at Chichen Itza*. Norman: University of Oklahoma Press.

Bowen, Sharon, and Lloyd Anderson
1994   The Palenque Emblem Bird Mat and Matawil. *U Mut Maya V*, eds. Carolyn and Tom Jones, pp. 37–71. Arcata, California: Tom and Carolyn Jones.

Braunstein, Mannetta
1989   An Analysis of the Texts and Iconography of

Selected Ceramics from the Early Classic Period at Tikal. *U Mut Maya II*, eds. Tom Jones and Carolyn Young, pp. 75–90. Arcata, California: Tom Jones and Carolyn Young.

Brenner, Edgar H.
1996   The Corpus of Maya Hieroglyphic Inscriptions Project: Initiated in 1967 by the Stella and Charles Guttman Foundation. In *Eighth Palenque Round Table, 1993, Vol. X*, eds. Martha J. Macri and Jan McHargue, pp. 321–324. San Francisco: Pre-Columbian Art Research Institute.

Bricker, Harvey M.
1996   Nightly Variation in the Characteristics of Venus Near Times of Greatest Elongation. In *Eighth Palenque Round Table, 1993, Vol. X*, eds. Martha J. Macri and Jan McHargue, pp. 369–377. San Francisco: Pre-Columbian Art Research Institute.

Bricker, Harvey M., and Victoria R. Bricker
1983   Classic Maya Prediction of Solar Eclipses. *Current Anthropology* 24(1): 1–23.
1992   Zodiacal References in the Maya Codices. In *The Sky in Mayan Literature*, ed. Anthony F. Aveni, pp. 148–183. New York: Oxford University Press.

Bricker, Victoria R.
1983   Directional Glyphs in Maya Inscriptions and Codices. *American Antiquity* 48(2): 347–353.
1985a   A Morphosyntactic Interpretation of Some Accession Compounds and Other Verbs in the Mayan Hieroglyphs. In *Fourth Palenque Round Table, 1980, Vol. VI*, ed. Elizabeth P. Benson, pp. 67–85. San Francisco: Pre-Columbian Art Research Institute.
1985b   Notes on Classic Maya Metrology. In *Fifth Palenque Round Table, 1983, Vol. VII*, ed. Virginia M. Fields, pp. 189–192. San Francisco: Pre-Columbian Art Research Institute.
1985c   Noun Incorporation in the Dresden Codex. *Anthropological Linguistics* 27(4): 413–423.
1986   *A Grammar of Mayan Hieroglyphs*. New Orleans: Middle American Research Institute, Tulane University. Publ. 56.
1987a   Abbreviation Conventions in the Maya Inscriptions and Books of Chilam Balam. *Anthropological Linguistics* 29(4): 425–438.
1987b   Landa's Second Grapheme for u. *Research Reports on Ancient Maya Writing* 9. Washington, D.C.: Center for Maya Research.
1988a   Astronomical Syntax in the Dresden Codex. *Journal of Mayan Linguistics* 6: 55–78.
1988b   A Phonetic Glyph for Zenith: Reply to Closs. *American Antiquity* 53(2): 394–400.

1988c   The Relationship between the Venus Table and an Almanac in the Dresden Codex. In *New Directions in American Archaeoastronomy*, ed. Anthony F. Aveni, pp. 81–103. Oxford: BAR International Series 454.
1989   The Last Gasp of Maya Hieroglyphic Writing in the Books of Chilam Balam of Chumayel and Chan Kan. In *Word and Image in Maya Culture*, eds. William F. Hanks and Don S. Rice, pp. 39–50. Salt Lake City: University of Utah Press.
1991   Faunal Offerings in the Dresden Codex. In *Sixth Palenque Round Table, 1986, Vol. VIII*, ed. Virginia M. Fields, pp. 285–292. Norman: University of Oklahoma Press.
1992a   Noun and Verb Morphology in the Maya Script. In *Supplement to the Handbook of Middle American Indians*, Vol. 5, Epigraphy, ed. Victoria R. Bricker, pp. 70–81. Austin: University of Texas Press.
1992b   A Reading for the 'Penis-Mannikin' Glyph and Its Variants. *Research Reports on Ancient Maya Writing* 38. Washington, D.C.: Center for Maya Research.
1992c   *Supplement to the Handbook of Middle American Indians Vol. 5, Epigraphy*. Austin: University of Texas Press.
1995   Advances in Maya Epigraphy. *Annual Review of Anthropology* 24:215–235.

Bricker, Victoria R., and Cassandra R. Bill
1994   Mortuary Practices in the Madrid Codex. In *Seventh Palenque Round Table, 1989, Vol. 9*, ed. Virginia M. Fields, pp. 195–200. San Francisco: Pre-Columbian Art Research Institute.

Bricker, Victoria R., and Harvey M. Bricker
1986a   Archaeoastronomical Implications of an Agricultural Almanac in the Dresden Codex. *Mexicon* VIII(2): 29–35.
1986b   The Mars Table in the Dresden Codex. In Research and Reflections in Archaeology and History: Essays in Honor of Doris Stone, ed. E. Wyllys Andrews V, pp. 51–80. New Orleans: Middle American Research Institute, Tulane University. Publ. 57.
1988   The Seasonal Table in the Dresden Codex and Related Almanacs. *Archaeoastronomy* (Supplement to the *Journal for the History of Astronomy* 19) 12: S1–S62.
1989   Astronomical References in the Table on Pages 61–69 of the Dresden Codex. In *World Archaeoastronomy*, ed. Anthony F. Aveni, pp. 232–245. Cambridge University Press.
1992   A Method for Cross-Dating Almanacs with Tables in the Dresden Codex. In *The Sky in Mayan Literature*, ed. Anthony F. Aveni, pp. 43–86. New York: Oxford University Press.

1995   An Astronomical Text from Chichen Itza, Yucatan, Mexico. *Human Mosaic* 28(2): 91–105.

Bricker, Victoria R., and Gabrielle Vail, eds.
1997   *Papers on the Madrid Codex*. New Orleans: Middle American Research Institute, Tulane University. [in press]

Brisko, Jo Ann Roman
1989   The Reign of Smoke-Imix-God-K: Copan Altar H. *U Mut Maya II*, eds. Tom Jones and Carolyn Young, pp. 9–11. Arcata, California: Tom Jones and Carolyn Young.
1990a   Two Yaxchilan Mysteries. *U Mut Maya III*, eds. Tom and Carolyn Jones, pp. 65–70. Arcata, California: Tom and Carolyn Jones.
1990b   Yaxchilan Structure 44 and the Hieroglyphic Stairway. *U Mut Maya III*, eds. Tom and Carolyn Jones, pp. 71–82. Arcata, California: Tom and Carolyn Jones.
1992a   The Mystery Woman of Naranjo. *U Mut Maya IV*, eds. Tom and Carolyn Jones, pp. 1–8. Arcata, California: Tom and Carolyn Jones.
1992b   The Puzzle of the Sibling's Wife. *U Mut Maya IV*, eds. Tom and Carolyn Jones, pp. 9–12. Arcata, California: Tom and Carolyn Jones.
1994   Maya Goddesses: By What Name Do We Call Them? *U Mut Maya V*, eds. Carolyn and Tom Jones, pp. 197–206. Arcata, California: Tom and Carolyn Jones.

Brown, Cecil H.
1991   Hieroglyphic Literacy in Ancient Mayaland: Inferences from Linguistic Data. *Current Anthropology* 32(4): 489–496.

Campbell, Lyle
1984a   The Implications of Mayan Historical Linguistics for Glyphic Research. In *Phoneticism in Mayan Hieroglyphic Writing*, eds. John S. Justeson and Lyle Campbell, pp. 1–16. Albany: Institute for Mesoamerican Studies, State University of New York at Albany. Publ. 9.
1984b   Linguistic Orthographies. In *Phoneticism in Mayan Hieroglyphic Writing*, eds. John S. Justeson and Lyle Campbell, Appendix E, pp. 371. Albany. Institute for Mesoamerican Studies, State University of New York at Albany. Publ. 9.

Campbell, Paul D.
1992a   *The Humboldt Celt: The Key to the Lost Olmec World*. Laguna Hills: Aegean Park Press.
1992b   *Astronomy and the Maya Calendar Correlation*. Laguna Hills: Aegean Park Press.

Campillo, Jose Miguel Garcia
1991   Nuevas Inscripciones en el Area de Calcehtok, Yucatan, Mexiko. *Mexicon* XIII(6): 112–115.
1995   Nuevos Monumentos Esculpidos en el Norte de la Region Puuc: Kuxub y Xburrotunich. *Mexicon* XVII(6): 106–111.

Carlson, John B.
1977   Copan Altar Q: The Maya Astronomical Congress of A.D. 763? In *Native American Astronomy*, ed. Anthony F. Aveni, pp. 100–109. Austin: University of Texas Press.
1980   On Classic Maya Monumental Recorded History. In *Third Palenque Round Table, 1978, Vol. V*, ed. Merle Greene Robertson, pp. 199–203. Austin: University of Texas Press.
1983   The Grolier Codex: A Preliminary Report on the Content and Authenticity of a Thirteenth Century Maya Venus Almanac. In *Calendars in Mesoamerica and Peru: Native American Computations of Time*, ed. Anthony F. Aveni, pp. 27–57. Oxford: BAR International Series 174.

Carrasco, Ramon V.
1985   La Senora Cimi Senora de La Familia de La Luna en Las Inscripciones Tardias de Yaxchilan y Bonampak. In *Fifth Palenque Round Table, 1983, Vol VII*, ed. Virginia M. Fields, pp. 85–95. San Francisco: Pre-Columbian Art Research Institute.
1991   The Structure 8 Tablet and Development of the Great Plaza at Yaxchilan. In *Sixth Palenque Round Table, 1986, Vol. VIII*, ed. Virginia M. Fields, pp. 110–117. Norman: University of Oklahoma Press.
1994   The Rings from the Ball Court at Uxmal. In *Seventh Palenque Round Table, 1989, Vol. IX*, ed. Virginia M. Fields, pp. 49–52. San Francisco: Pre-Columbian Art Research Institute.
1996   Los Ultimos Gobernantes de Kabah. In *Eighth Palenque Round Table, 1993, Vol. X*, eds. Martha J. Macri and Jan McHargue, pp 297–307. San Francisco: Pre-Columbian Art Research Institute.

Caruso, Josie
1992   The Capture Record at Yaxchilan. *U Mut Maya IV*, eds. Tom and Carolyn Jones, pp. 243–274. Arcata, California: Tom and Carolyn Jones.

Caso, Alfonso
1928   Las Estelas Zapotecas. In *Monograficas del Museo Nacional de Arqueologica, Historia y Etnografia* 95. Publicasiones de la Secretaria de Educacional Publica, Mexico: Tellares Graficosde de la Nacion.

1947 Calendario y Escritura de las Antiguas Culturas de Monte Alban. In *Ombras Completas de Miguel Othon de Mendizabal*, vol. 1., fig. 16.

Chase, Arlen F.
1985 Troubled Times: Archaeology and Iconography of the Terminal Classic Southern Lowland Maya. In *Fifth Palenque Round Table, 1983, Vol. VII*, ed. Virginia M. Fields, pp. 103–114. San Francisco: Pre-Columbian Art Research Institute.

Chase, Arlen F., and Diane Z. Chase
1996 The Organization and Composition of Classic Lowland Maya Society: The View from Caracol. In *Eighth Palenque Round Table, 1993, Vol. X*, eds. Martha J. Macri and Jan McHargue, pp. 213–222. San Francisco: Pre-Columbian Art Research Institute.

Chase, Arlen F., Nikolai Grube, and Diane Z. Chase
1991 Three Terminal Classic Monuments from Caracol, Belize. *Research Reports on Ancient Maya Writing* 36. Washington, D.C.: Center for Maya Research.

Chase, Diane Z.
1985 Between Earth and Sky: Idols, Images, and Postclassic Cosmology. In *Fifth Palenque Round Table, 1983, Vol. VII*. ed. Virginia M. Fields, pp. 223–233. San Francisco: Pre-Columbian Art Research Institute.

Christie-Shults, Jessica Joyce
1992 The Hieroglyphic Stairway at Naranjo: Matching Some Pieces of the Puzzle. *U Mut Maya IV*, eds. Tom and Carolyn Jones, pp. 31–36. Arcata, California: Tom and Carolyn Jones.

Ciaramella, Mary A.
1994 The Lady with the Snake Headdress. *Seventh Palenque Round Table, 1989, Vol. IX*, ed. Virginia M. Fields, pp. 201–209. San Francisco: Pre-Columbian Art Research Institute.

Clancy, Flora S.
1986 Text and Image in the Tablets of the Cross Group at Palenque. *RES* 11: 17–32.

Closs, Michael P.
1977 The Date-Reaching Mechanism in the Venus Table of the Dresden Codex. In *Native American Astronomy*, ed. Anthony F. Aveni, pp. 89–99. Austin: University of Texas Press.
1978 The Initial Series on Stela 5 at Pixoy. *American Antiquity* 43(4): 690–694.
1979a An Important Maya Inscription from the Xcalumkin Area. *Mexicon* I(4): 44–46.

1979b Venus in the Maya World: Glyphs, Gods, and Associated Astronomical Phenomena. In *Tercera Mesa Redonda de Palenque, 1978, Vol. IV*, eds. Merle Greene Robertson and Donnan C. Jeffers, pp. 147–165. Palenque, Chiapas, Mexico: Pre-Columbian Art Research Institute.
1981 Venus Dates Revisited. *Archaeoastronomy* IV(4): 38–41.
1982 On a Classic Maya Accession Phrase and a Glyph for 'Rulership'. *Mexicon* IV(3): 47–50.
1983 A Truncated Initial Series from Xcalumkin. *American Antiquity* 48(1): 115–122.
1984a The Dynastic History of Naranjo: The Early Period. *Estudios de Cultura Maya* XV: 77–96.
1984b The Maya Glyph Batel, 'Warrior'. Mexicon VI(4): 50–52.
1985 The Dynastic History of Naranjo: The Middle Period. In *Fifth Palenque Round Table, 1983, Vol. VII*, ed. Virginia M. Fields, pp. 65–77. San Francisco: The Pre-Columbian Art Research Institute.
1986 Orthographic Conventions in Maya Writing: The Rule of Phonetic Complementation. *Anthropological Linguistics* 28(2): 229–252.
1987 Bilingual Glyphs. *Research Reports on Ancient Maya Writing* 12. Washington, D.C.: Center for Maya Research.
1988a The Hieroglyphic Text of Stela 9, Lamanai, Belize. *Research Reports on Ancient Maya Writing* 21. Washington, D.C.: Center for Maya Research.
1988b A Phonetic Version of the Maya Glyph for North. *American Antiquity* 53(2): 386–393.
1988c Response to Coggins and Bricker (Glyph for North). *American Antiquity* 53(2): 402–411.
1989a Cognitive Aspects of Ancient Maya Eclipse Theory. In *World Archaeoastronomy*, ed. Anthony F. Aveni, pp. 389–415. Cambridge: Cambridge University Press.
1989b The Dynastic History of Naranjo: The Late Period. In *Word and Image in Maya Culture*, eds. Wm. F. Hanks and Don S. Rice, pp. 244–254. Salt Lake City: University of Utah Press.
1992a I Am a kahal; My Parents Were Scribes. *Research Reports on Ancient Maya Writing* 39. Washington, D.C.: Center for Maya Research.
1992b Some Parallels in the Astronomical Events Recorded in the Maya Codices and Inscriptions. In *The Sky in Mayan Literature*, ed. Anthony F. Aveni, pp. 133–147. New York: Oxford University Press.
1994 A Glyph for Venus as Evening Star. In *Seventh Palenque Round Table, 1989, Vol. IX*, ed. Virginia M. Fields, pp. 229–236. San Francisco: Pre-Columbian Art Research Institute.

Closs, Michael P., A. F. Aveni, and B. Crowley
1984   The Planet Venus and Temple 22 at Copan. *Indiana* 9: 221–247.

Coe, Michael D.
1957   Cycle 7 Monuments in Middle America: A Reconsideration. *American Anthropologist* 59: 597–611.
1965   The Olmec Style and Its Distribution. In *Handbook of Middle American Indians* 3: 739–775.
1966   An Early Stone Pectoral from Southeastern Mexico. In *Studies in Pre-Columbian Art and Archaeology* 1. Washington, D.C: Dumbarton Oaks.
1973   *The Maya Scribe and His World*. New York: The Grolier Club.
1974   A Carved Wooden Box from the Classic Maya Civilization. In *Primera Mesa Redonda de Palenque, 1973, Part II*, ed. Merle Greene Robertson, pp. 51–58. Pebble Beach, California: Robert Louis Stevenson School.
1975   Native Astronomy in Mesoamerica. In *Archaeoastronomy in Pre-Columbian America*, ed. Anthony F. Aveni, pp. 3–31. Austin: University of Texas Press.
1976   Early Steps in the Evolution of Maya Writing. In *Origins of Religious Art and Iconography in Preclassic Mesoamerica*, ed. H. B. Nicholson, pp. 107–122. Los Angeles: UCLA Latin American Center.
1978   *Lords of the Underworld: Masterpieces of Classic Maya Ceramics*. Princeton: The Art Museum, Princeton University.
1989a   The Hero Twins: Myth and Image. In *The Maya Vase Book, Vol. 1* (by Justin Kerr), pp. 161–184. New York: Kerr Associates.
1989b   The Royal Fifth: Earliest Notices of Maya Writing. *Research Reports on Ancient Maya Writing* 28. Washington, D.C.: Center for Maya Research.
1992   *Breaking the Maya Code*. New York. Thames and Hudson, Inc.

Coe, Michael D., and Elizabeth P. Benson
1966   *Three Maya Relief Panels at Dumbarton Oaks*. Studies in Pre-Columbian Art and Archaeology, No. 2. Washington, D.C.: Dumbarton Oaks.

Coggins, Clemency Chase
1989   A New Sun at Chichen Itza. In *World Archaeoastronomy*, ed. Anthony F. Aveni, pp. 260–275. Cambridge: Cambridge University Press.
1990   The Birth of the Baktun at Tikal and Seibal. In *Vision and Revision in Maya Studies*, eds.

Flora S. Clancy and Peter D. Harrison, pp. 79–97. Albuquerque: University of New Mexico Press.
1992   Pure Language and Lapidary Prose. In *New Theories of the Ancient Maya*, eds. Elin C. Danien and Robert J. Sharer, pp. 99–107. Philadelphia: The University of Pennsylvania Museum.

Cohodas, Marvin
1989   Transformations: Relationships between Image and Text in the Ceramic Paintings of the Metropolitan Master. In *Word and Image in Maya Culture*, eds. William F. Hanks and Don S. Rice, pp. 198–232. Salt Lake City: University of Utah Press.
1991   Ballgame Imagery of the Maya Lowlands: History and Iconography. In *The Mesoamerican Ballgame*, eds. Vernon L. Scarborough and David R. Wilcox, pp. 251–288. Tucson: The University of Arizona Press.

Collea, Beth A.
1981   The Celestial Bands in Maya Hieroglyphic Writing. In *Archaeoastronomy in the Americas*, ed. Ray A Williamson, pp. 215–231. Los Altos, California: Ballena Press.

Copan Notes
See complete numerical listing beginning page **XXX**.

Covarrubias, Miguel
1946   *Mexico South: the Isthmus of Tehuantepec*. New York: Alfred A. Knopf.

Crumley, Laura Lee
1989   Notes on the Tikal Wooden Tablets. *U Mut Maya II*, eds. Tom Jones and Carolyn Young, pp. 91–97. Arcata, California: Tom Jones and Carolyn Young.
1992   Peering Through Time: A Reading of Naranjo Altar 1. *U Mut Maya IV*, eds. Tom and Carolyn Jones, pp. 13–30. Arcata, California: Tom and Carolyn Jones.

Crumley, Laura Lee, and Helen Alexander
1988   A Literary Reading of Copan Stela P. *U Mut Maya*, eds. Tom Jones and Carolyn Young, pp. 39–40. Arcata, California: Tom Jones.

Culbert, T. Patrick
1988   Political History and the Decipherment of Maya Glyphs. *Antiquity* 62(234): 135–152.
1991   *Classic Maya Political History: Hieroglyphic and Archaeological Evidence*. Cambridge: Cambridge University Press/School of American Research.

Davoust, Michel
1980   Les premiers chefs Maya de Chichen Itza. *Mexicon* II(1): 25–29.
1983   Estudios de los Glifos Locativos en la Epi-grafia Maya. In *Contributions to Maya Hieroglyphic Decipherment, I*, ed. Stephen D. Houston, pp. 1–12. New Haven: Human Relations Area Files, Inc.
1991   Nueva Lectura de las Inscripciones de Xcalumkin, Campeche, Mexico. *Mesoamerica* 12(22): 249–276.
1994a   The Glyphic Names for Some Maya Scribes and Sculptors of the Classic Period. *Seventh Palenque Round Table, 1989, Vol. 9*, ed. Virginia M. Fields, pp. 105–111. San Francisco: Pre-Columbian Art Research Institute.
1994b   A New Phonetic Reading of the Nominal Glyphs for the First Yaxchilan Rulers and Their Guests (translated by Michel Quenon). *U Mut Maya V*, eds. Carolyn and Tom Jones, pp. 109–132. Arcata, California: Tom and Carolyn Jones.
1995   *L'Ecriture Maya et Son Dechiffrement*. Paris: Centre National de la Recherche Scientifique.

Dienhart, John M.
1986   The Mayan Hieroglyph for Cotton. *Mexicon* VIII(3): 52–56.

Dillon, Brian D.
1978   A Tenth Cycle Sculpture from Alta Verapaz, Guatemala. In *Contributions of the University of California Research Facility* 36, pp. 39–46. Berkeley: Archaeological Research Facility, Department of Anthropology, University of California.
1987   The Highland-Lowland Maya Frontier: Archaeological Evidence from Alta Verapaz, Guatemala. In *The Periphery of the Southeastern Classic Maya Realm*, ed. Gary W. Pahl, pp. 135–143. Los Angeles: UCLA Latin American Center Publications, University of California, Los Angeles.

Drucker, Philip
1952   *La Venta, Tabasco: A Study of Olmec Ceramics and Art*. Smithsonian Institution, Bureau of American Ethnology, Bulletin 153. Washington, D.C.: Smithsonian Institution.

Dunning, Nicholas P., and Jeff Karl Kowalski
1994   Lord of the Hills: Classic Maya Settlement Patterns and Political Iconography in the Puuc Region, Mexico. *Ancient Mesoamerica* 5(1): 63–95.

Dütting, Dieter
1978   'Bats' in the Usumacinta Valley: Remarks on Inscriptions of Bonampak and Neighboring Sites in Chiapas, Mexico. *Zeitschrift für Ethnologie* 103: 1–56.
1979   Birth, Inauguration, and Death in the Inscriptions of Palenque, Chiapas, Mexico. In *Tercera Mesa Redonda de Palenque, 1978, Vol. IV*, eds. Merle Greene Robertson and Donnan C. Jeffers, pp. 183–214. Palenque, Chiapas, Mexico: Pre-Columbian Art Research Institute.
1981   Zum Character der Maya-Schrift und den Schwierigkeiten ihrer Entzifferung. *Mexicon* III(3): 45–48.
1982   The 2 Cib 14 Mol Event in the Inscriptions of Palenque, Chiapas, Mexico. *Zeitschrift für Ethnologie* 107: 233–258.
1984   Venus, the Moon, and the Gods of the Palenque Triad. *Zeitschrift für Ethnologie* 109: 7–74.
1985a   On the Astronomical Background of Mayan Historical Events. In *Fifth Palenque Round Table, 1983, Vol. VII*, ed. Virginia M. Fields, pp. 261–274. San Francisco: Pre-Columbian Art Research Institute.
1985b   On the Context-Dependent Use of Bi-and Polyvalent Graphemes in Mayan Hieroglyphic Writing. In *Fourth Palenque Round Table, 1980, Vol. VI*, ed. Elizabeth P. Benson, pp. 103–114. San Francisco: Pre-Columbian Art Research Institute.
1986a   Lunar Periods and the Quest for Rebirth in the Mayan Hieroglyphic Inscriptions. *Estudios de Cultura Maya* XVI: 113–147.
1986b   The Vase of the Eighty-eight Glyphs: Implications for the Decipherment of the Maya Script. *Tribus* 35: 83–103.
1987   Two Early Classic Maya Jade Plaques and the Meaning of the God K Insignia. *Latin American Indian Literatures Journal* 3(2): 196–224.
1991   Aspects of Polyvalency in Maya Writing: Affixes T12, T229, and T110. In *Sixth Palenque Round Table, 1986, Vol. VIII*, ed. Virginia M. Fields, pp. 273–284. Norman: University of Oklahoma Press.

Edmonson, Munro S.
1965   *Quiche-English Dictionary*. New Orleans: Middle American Research Institute, Tulane University. Publ. 30.

Escobedo A., Hector L., and Federico Fahsen
1995   Decipherment of the Puerto Barrios Altar. *Mexicon* XVII (5): 92–95.

Fahsen, Federico
1984   Notes for a Sequence of Rulers of Machaquila. *American Antiquity* 49(1): 94–104.

1987 A Glyph for Self Sacrifice in Several Maya Inscriptions. *Research Reports on Ancient Maya Writing* 11. Washington, D.C.: Center for Maya Research.

1988 A New Early Classic Text from Tikal. *Research Reports on Ancient Maya Writing* 17. Washington, D.C.: Center for Maya Research.

1990 A Logograph in Maya Writing for the Verb 'to Record'. *Ancient Mesoamerica* 1(1): 91–95.

1992 A Toponym in Waxaktun. *Texas Note 35.* Austin: Center of the History and Art of Ancient American Culture, University of Texas at Austin.

1995 La Transicion Preclasico Tardio - Clasico Temprano: El Desarrollo de los Estados Mayas y la Escritura. In *The Emergence of Lowland Maya Civilization: The Transition from the Precalssic to the Early Classic*, ed. Nikolai Grube, pp. 151–162: Mockmuhl: Verlag Anton Saurwein.

Fahsen, Federico, and Linda Schele
1991a Curl-Snout under Scrutiny, Again. *Texas Note 13*. Austin: Center of the History and Art of Ancient American Culture, University of Texas at Austin.

1991b A Proposed Reading for the 'Penis Perforation' Glyph. *Texas Note 8*. Austin: Center of the History and Art of Ancient American Culture, University of Texas at Austin Austin.

Fash, William L., Jr
1988 A New Look at Maya Statecraft from Copan, Honduras. *Antiquity* 62(234):157–169.

Fash, William L., and David Stuart
1991 Dynastic History and Cultural Evolution at Copan, Honduras. In *Classic Maya Political History*, ed. T. Patrick Culbert, pp. 147–179. Cambridge: Cambridge University Press/ School of American Research.

Fash, William L., Richard V. Williamson, Carlos Rudy Larios, and Joel Palka
1992 The Hieroglyphic Stairway and its Ancestors: Investigations of Copan Structure 10L-26. *Ancient Mesoamerica* 3(1): 105–115.

Flannery, Kent V., and Joyce Marcus
1983 The Growth of Site Hierarchies in the Valley of Oaxaca: pt. I. In *The Cloud People: Divergent Evolution of Zapotec and Mixtec Civilization*, pp. 53–65. New York: Academic Press.

Folan, William J., Joyce Marcus, Sophia Pincemin, Maria del Rosario Dominguez Carrasco, Laraine Fletcher, and Abel Morales Lopez
1995 Calakmul: New Data from an Ancient Maya Capital in Campeche, Mexico. *Latin American Antiquity* 6(4): 310–334.

Forstemann, Ernst W.
1906 Commentary on the Maya Manuscript in the Royal Public Library of Dresden. *Papers of the Peabody Museum of American Archaeology and Ethnology* 4(2): 182–215. Cambridge, Mass.: Harvard University.

Foster, Lynn, and Linnea Wren
1996 World Creator and World Sustainer: God N at Chichen Itza. In *Eighth Palenque Round Table, 1993, Vol. X*, Martha J. Macri and Jan McHargue, pp. 259–269. San Francisco: Pre-Columbian Art Research Institute.

Fought, John G.
1965 A Phonetic and Morphological Interpretation of Zimmerman's Affix 61 in the Maya Hieroglyphic Codices. *Estudios de Cultura Maya* 5: 253–280.

Fox, James A., and John S. Justeson
1978 A Mayan Planetary Observation. In *Contributions of the University of California Archaeological Research Facility* 36, pp. 55–59. Berkeley: Department of Anthropology, University of California.

1980 Mayan Hieroglyphs as Linguistic Evidence. In *The Third Palenque Round Table, 1978, Vol. V*, ed. Merle Greene Robertson, pp. 204–216. Austin: University of Texas Press.

1984a Conventions for the Transliteration of Mayan Hieroglyphs. In *Phoneticism in Mayan Hieroglyphic Writing*, eds. John S. Justeson and Lyle Campbell, Appendix C, pp. 363–366. Albany: Institute for Mesoamerican Studies, State University of New York at Albany. Publ. 9.

1984b Polyvalence in Mayan Hieroglyphic Writing. In *Phoneticism in Mayan Hieroglyphic Writing*, eds. John S. Justeson and Lyle Campbell, pp. 17–76. Albany: Institute for Mesoamerican Studies, State University of New York at Albany. Publ. 9.

1986 Classic Maya Dynastic Alliance and Succession. In *Supplement to the Handbook of Middle American Indians, Vol. 4: Ethnohistory*, ed. Ronald Spores, pp. 7–34. Austin: University of Texas Press.

Freidel, David
1979 Cultural Areas and Interaction Spheres: Contrasting Approaches to the Emergence of Civilization in the Maya Lowlands. *American Antiquity* 44: 36–54.

1988   Discourse Patterns in Maya Art and Architecture of the Late Preclassic Lowlands: Antecedents for Classic Period Texts and Images. *Journal of Mayan Linguistics* 6: 23–46.

1992   The Trees of Life: Ahau as Idea and Artifact in Classic Lowland Maya Civilization. In *Ideology and Pre-Columbian Civilizations*, eds. A. A. Demarest and G. W. Conrad, pp. 115–133. Santa Fe: School of American Research Press.

Freidel, David A., and Linda Schele
1988a   Kingship in the Late Preclassic Maya Lowlands: The Instruments and Places of Ritual Power. *American Anthropologist* 90: 546–567.

1988b   Symbol and Power: A History of the Lowland Maya Cosmogram. In *Maya Iconography*, eds. Elizabeth P. Benson and Gillett G. Griffin, pp. 44–93. Princeton: Princeton University Press.

1989   Dead Kings and Living Temples: Dedication and Termination Rituals among the Ancient Maya. In *Word and Image in Maya Culture*, eds. Wm. F. Hanks and Don S. Rice, pp. 233–243. Salt Lake City: University of Utah Press.

Freidel, David, Linda Schele, and Joy Parker
1993   *Maya Cosmos: Three Thousand Years on the Shaman's Path*. New York: William Morrow and Company.

Frumker, Bruce
1990   Remarks on the Temple of the Cross (Palenque). *U Mut Maya III*, eds. Tom and Carolyn Jones, pp. 7–12. Arcata, California: Tom and Carolyn Jones.

1992   Curl Snout and the 4th Lord of the Night. *U Mut Maya IV*, eds. Tom and Carolyn Jones, pp. 37–39. Arcata, California: Tom and Carolyn Jones.

1993   Wuk Ah, the Fourth Lord of the Night. *Texas Note 51*. Austin: Center of the History and Art of Ancient American Culture, University of Texas at Austin.

Frumker, Bruce, Martha Mentch, Dennis Tedlock, and Loa Traxler
1990   An Oral Recitation of the Tablet of the Cross (Palenque). *U Mut Maya III*, eds. Tom and Carolyn Jones, pp. 5–6. Arcata, California: Tom and Carolyn Jones.

Gates, William E.
1978   *An Outline Dictionary of Maya Glyphs*. New York: Dover Publications, Inc.

Girard, Rafael
1962   Los Mayas Eternos. In *Antigua Libreria Robredo*. Mexico.

Graham, Ian
1967   *Archaeological Explorations in El Peten, Guatemala*. New Orleans: Middle American Research Institute, Tulane University. Publ. 33.

1970   The Ruins of La Florida, Peten, Guatemala. In *Monographs and Papers in Maya Archaeology*, ed. W. R. Bullard, pp. 425–455. Peabody Museum Papers No. 61. Cambridge, Mass.: Harvard University.

1988   Homeless Hieroglyphs. *Antiquity* 62(234): 122–126.

Graham, Ian, Eric von Euw, and Peter Mathews
1975–1996   *Corpus of Maya Hieroglyphic Inscriptions, Vols. 1–7*. Peabody Museum of American Archaeology and Ethnology. Cambridge, Mass.: Harvard University.

Graham, John A.
1971   Non-Classic Inscriptions and Sculptures at Seibal. In *Contributions of the University of California Archaeological Research Facility* 13, pp. 143–153. Berkeley: Department of Anthropology, University of California.

1972   *The Hieroglyphic Inscriptions and Monumental Art of Altar de Sacrificios*. Papers of the Peabody Museum of Archaeology and Ethnology, Vol. 64, No. 2. Cambridge, Mass.: Harvard University.

1990   *Excavations at Seibal: Number 1: Monumental Sculpture and Hieroglyphic Inscriptions*. Cambridge, Mass: Peabody Museum, Harvard University.

Graham, John A., and James Porter
1989   A Cycle 6 Initial Series? A Maya Boulder Inscription of the First Millenium B.C. from Abaj Takalik. *Mexicon* XI(3): 46–49.

Griffin, Gillett G., Michael Guillen, and Jim Langley
1988   A Prose Reading of the Tablet of the 96 Glyphs (Palenque). *U Mut Maya*, eds. Tom Jones and Carolyn Young, pp. 27–29. Arcata, California: Tom Jones.

Grove, David C.
1970   Olmec Paintings of Oxtotitlan Cave, Guerrero. In *Studies in Pre-Columbian Art and Iconography* 6. Washington, D.C.: Dumbarton Oaks.

Grube, Nikolai
1981   Die Mayahieroglyph fur 'Vollendung' and 'Halbe Periode'. *Mexicon* II(6): 93–95.

1985 Altar 1 aus Hotzuc, Yukatan, Mexiko. *Mexicon* VII(3): 41–43.

1986 Die Hieroglyphenplattform von Kabah, Yukatan, Mexiko. *Mexicon* VIII(1): 13–17.

1987 Notes on the Reading of Affix T142. *Research Reports on Ancient Maya Writing* 4. Washington, D.C.: Center for Maya Research.

1990a The Primary Standard Sequence in Chochola Style Ceramics. In *The Maya Vase Book, Vol. 2* (by Justin Kerr), pp, 320–330. New York: Kerr Associates.

1990b *Die Entwicklung der Mayaschrift.* Acta Mesoamericana, Vol. 3. Berlin: Verlag von Flemming.

1991 An Investigation of the Primary Standard Sequence on Classic Maya Ceramics. In *Sixth Palenque Round Table, 1986, Vol. VIII,* ed. Virginia M. Fields, pp. 223–232. Norman: University of Oklahoma Press.

1992 Classic Maya Dance: Evidence from Hieroglyphs and Iconography. *Ancient Mesoamerica* 3(2): 201–218.

1994a Epigraphic Research at Caracol, Belize. In *Studies in the Archaeology of Caracol, Belize,* eds. Diane Z. Chase and Arlen F. Chase, pp. 83–122. San Francisco: Pre-Columbian Art Research Institute, Monograph 7.

1994b A Hieroglyphic Panel in the Emiliano Zapata Museum, Tabasco. *Mexicon* XVI(1): 2.

1994c Observations on the History of Maya Hieroglyphic Writing. In *Seventh Palenque Round Table, 1989, Vol. IX,* ed. Virginia M. Fields, pp. 177–186. San Francisco: Pre-Columbian Art Research Institute.

1994d Hieroglyphic Sources for the History of Northwest Yucatan. In *Hidden among the Hills: Maya Archaeology of the Northwest Yucatan Penninsula.* Acta Mesoamericana, Vol. 7, ed. Hanns J. Prem, pp. 316–358. Mockmohl: Verlag von Flemming.

1994e A Preliminary Report on the Monuments and Inscriptions of La Milpa, Orange Walk, Belize. *Baessler-Archiv, Neue Folge* XLII: 217–238.

1995 *The Emergence of Lowland Maya Civilization: The Transition from the Preclassic to the Early Classic.* Acta Mesoamericana Vol. 8. Mockmuhl: Verlag Anton Saurwein.

1996 Palenque in the Maya World. In *Eighth Palenque Round Table, 1993, Vol. X,* eds. Martha J. Macri and Jan McHargue, pp. 1–13. San Francisco: Pre-Columbian Art Research Institute.

Grube, Nikolai, Ekkehardt-Wolke Hasse, and Mareike Sattler
1990 Vier neue archaeologische Fundorte im nordwestlichen Peten. *Mexicon* XII(3): 46–49.

Grube, Nikolai, and Barbara MacLeod
1990 The Wing That Doesn't Fly: Problems and Possibilities Concerning the Reading of the "Wing" Sign. *U Mut Maya III,* eds. Tom and Carolyn Jones, pp. 167–177. Arcata, California: Tom and Carolyn Jones.

Grube, Nikolai, and Werner Nahm
1990 A Sign for the Syllable mi. *Research Reports on Ancient Maya Writing* 33. Washington, D.C.: Center for Maya Research.

1994 A Census of Xibalba: A Complete Inventory of *Way* Characters on Maya Ceramics. In *The Maya Vase Book, Vol. 4,* eds. Barbara Kerr and Justin Kerr, pp. 686–715. New York: Kerr Associates.

Grube, Nikolai, and Linda Schele
1991 Tzuk in the Classic Maya Inscriptions. *Texas Note 14.* Austin: Center of the History and Art of Ancient American Culture, University of Texas at Austin.

1993a Naranjo Altar 1 and Rituals of Death and Burials. *Texas Note 54.* Austin: Center of the History and Art of Ancient American Culture, University of Texas at Austin.

1993b Un Verbo Nakwa para "Batallar o Conquistar." *Texas Note 55.* Austin: Center of the History and Art of Ancient American Culture, University of Texas at Austin.

1994a Kuy, the Owl of Omen and War. Mexicon XVI(1): 10–17.

1994b Tikal Altar 5. *Texas Note 66.* Austin: Center of the History and Art of Ancient American Culture, University of Texas at Austin.

1996 New Observations on the Loltun Relief. *Mexicon* XVIII (1): 11–14.

Grube, Nikolai, Linda Schele, and Federico Fahsen
1991 Odds and Ends from the Inscriptions of Quirigua. *Mexicon* XIII(6): 106–112.

Grube, Nikolai, and David Stuart
1987 Observations on T110 as the Syllable ko. *Research Reports on Ancient Maya Writing* 8. Washington, D.C.: Center for Maya Research.

Gutierrez, Mary Ellen
1990 The Maya Ballgame as a Metaphor for Warfare. *Mexicon* XII(6): 105–108.

1993a Caracol, Altar 21: A Reconsideration of the Chronological Framework and Implications for the Middle Classic Dynastic Sequence. *Mexicon* XV(2): 28–33.

1993b Ballcourts: The Chasms of Creation. Texas Note 53. Austin: Center of the History and Art of Ancient American Culture, University of Texas at Austin.

Hales, Donald, John Harris, and Robert Williams
1988   An Analysis of Three Inscribed Monuments at Quirigua—or Quirigua: The Mouse That Roared. *U Mut Maya*, eds. Tom Jones and Carolyn Young, pp. 67–82. Arcata, California: Tom Jones.

Hammond, Norman
1982   Pom for the Ancestors: A Reexamination of Piedras Negras Stela 40. *Mexicon* 3(5): 77–79.
1987   The Sun Also Rises: Iconographic Syntax of the Pomona Flare. *Research Reports on Ancient Maya Writing* 7. Washington, D.C.: Center for Maya Research.

Hammond, Norman, David H. Kelley, and Peter Mathews
1975   A Maya 'Pocket Stela?' In *Contributions of the University of California Archaeological Research Facility* 27, pp. 17–31. Berkeley: Department of Anthropology, University of California.

Hanks, William F., and Don S. Rice, eds.
1989   *Word and Image in Maya Culture: Explorations in Language, Writing, and Representation.* Salt Lake City: University of Utah Press.

Hansen, Richard D
1991   An Early Maya Text from El Mirador, Guatemala. *Research Reports on Ancient Maya Writing* 37. Washington, D.C.: Center for Maya Research.

Harris, John F.
1989a   The Inscription on Lintel 3 of Tikal Temple I. *U Mut Maya II*, eds. Tom Jones and Carolyn Young, pp. 111–120. Arcata, California: Tom Jones.
1989b   Late Tikal Inscriptions. *U Mut Maya II*, eds. Tom Jones and Carolyn Young, pp. 131–138. Arcata, California: Tom Jones and Carolyn Young.
1989c   Possible Significance of Positions of Venus and Mercury for Late Tikal Dates and Events. *U Mut Maya II*, eds. Tom Jones and Carolyn Young, pp. 139–144. Arcata, California: Tom Jones and Carolyn Young.
1990a   The Inscriptions of Shield Jaguar I of Yaxchilan. *U Mut Maya III*, eds. Tom and Carolyn Jones, pp. 39–63. Arcata, California: Tom and Carolyn Jones.
1990b   The Inscription on Stela 18 of Yaxchilan. *U Mut Maya III*, eds. Tom and Carolyn Jones, pp. 121–133. Arcata, California: Tom and Carolyn Jones.
1992   A Summary of Caracol Dates and Astronomy. *U Mut Maya IV*, eds. Tom and Carolyn Jones, pp. 149–159. Arcata, California: Tom and Carolyn Jones.
1993   *New and Recent Maya Hieroglyph Readings: A Supplement to Understanding Maya Inscriptions.* Philadelphia: The University of Pennsylvania Museum.
1994   *A Resource Bibliography for the Decipherment of Maya Hieroglyphs and New Maya Hieroglyph Readings.* Philadelphia: The University of Pennsylvania Museum.

Harris, John F., and Stephen K. Stearns
1992   *Understanding Maya Inscriptions.* Philadelphia: The University of Pennsylvania Museum.

Harrison, William F.
1990   The Role of Gods 7 and 9 in the Iconography and Epigraphy of Stela D at Copan. *U Mut Maya III*, eds. Tom and Carolyn Jones, pp. 25–38. Arcata, California: Tom and Carolyn Jones.

Hartig, Helga-Maria
1980   The Astronomical Background of Stela 5 at Pixoy, Campeche. *Mexicon* I(6): 81–82.

Healy, Paul F.
1990   An Early Classic Maya Monument at Pacbitun, Belize. *Mexicon* XII(6): 109–110.

Henderson, John S.
1981   *The World of the Ancient Maya.* Ithaca, New York: Cornell University Press.

Henricksen, Joan E.
1992a   A Review of the Enigmas of K'an Boar. *U Mut Maya IV*, eds. Tom and Carolyn Jones, pp. 61–67. Arcata, California: Tom and Carolyn Jones.
1992b   Yaxun Balam of Yaxchilan: His "Count of Captives" Title and Prisoner Ah Uk. *U Mut Maya IV*, eds. Tom and Carolyn Jones, pp. 201–207. Arcata, California: Tom and Carolyn Jones.

Hernandez, Alfonso Arellano
1996   Algunas Notas Sobre Tortuguero, Tabasco. In *Eighth Palenque Round Table, 1993, Vol. X*, eds. Martha J. Macri and Jan McHargue, pp. 135–142. San Francisco: Pre-Columbian Art Research Institute.

Hoffman, Patricia
1990   The Temple of the Sun at Palenque. *U Mut Maya III*, eds. Tom and Carolyn Jones, pp. 15–16. Arcata, California: Tom and Carolyn Jones.

Hofling, Charles A.
1988   Venus and the Miscellaneous Almanacs in the Dresden Codex. *Journal of Mayan Linguistics* 6: 79–102.
1989   The Morphosyntactic Basis of Discourse Structure in Glyphic Texts in the Dresden Codex. In *Word and Image in Maya Culture*, eds. William F. Hanks and Don S. Rice, pp. 51–72. Salt Lake City: University of Utah Press.

Hofling, Charles A., and Thomas O'Neil
1992   Eclipse Cycles in the Moon Goddess Almanacs in the Dresden Codex. In *The Sky in Mayan Literature*, ed. Anthony F. Aveni, pp. 102–132. New York: Oxford University Press.

Hopkins, Nicholas A.
1968   A Method for the Investigation of Glyph Syntax. *Estudios de Cultura Maya* 7: 79–83.
1985   On the History of the Chol Language. In *Fifth Palenque Round Table, 1983, Vol. VII*, ed. Virginia M. Fields, pp. 1–5. San Francisco: Pre-Columbian Art Research institute.
1991   Classic and Modern Relationship Terms and the 'Child of Mother' Glyph (T1:606.23). In *Sixth Palenque Round Table, 1986, Vol. VIII*, ed. Virginia M. Fields, pp. 255–265. Norman: University of Oklahoma Press.

Hoppan, Jean-Michel
1994   Nuevos Datos Sobre Las Inscripciones de Comalcalco. *U Mut Maya V*, eds Carolyn and Tom Jones, pp. 78–86. Arcata, California: Tom and Carolyn Jones.
1996   Nuevos Datos Sobre Las Inscriptiones de Comalcalco. In *Eighth Palenque Round Table, 1993, Vol. X*, eds. Martha J. Macri and Jan McHargue, pp. 153–158. San Francisco: Pre-Columbian Art Research Institute.

Hotaling, Lorren
1995   A Reply to Werner Nahm: Maya Warfare and the Venus Year. *Mexicon* XVII(2): 32–37.

Houston, Stephen D.
1983a   Ballgame Glyphs in Classic Maya Texts. In *Contributions to Maya Hieroglyphic Decipherment, I*, ed. Stephen D. Houston, pp. 26–30. New Haven: Human Relations Area Files, Inc.
1983b   *Contributions to Maya Hieroglyphic Decipherment, I*, ed. Stephen D. Houston. New Haven: Human Relations Area Files, Inc.
1983c   A Reading for the Flint-Shield Glyph. In *Contributions to Maya Hieroglyphic Decipherment, I*, ed. Stephen D. Houston, pp. 13–25. New Haven: Human Relations Area Files, Inc.

1983d   On "Ruler 6" at Piedras Negras, Guatemala. *Mexicon* V(5): 84–86.
1983e   Warfare between Naranjo and Ucanal. In *Contributions to Maya Hieroglyphic Decipherment, I*, ed. Stephen D. Houston, pp. 31–39. New Haven: Human Relations Area Files, Inc.
1983f   Unprovenanced Inscriptions: An Album of Drawings. In *Contributions to Maya Decipherment, I*, ed. Stephen D. Houston, pp. 104–109. New Haven: Human Relations Area Files, Inc.
1984a   Another Example of a 'Truncated' Initial Series. *American Antiquity* 49(2): 401–403.
1984b   An Example of Homophony in Maya Script. *American Antiquity* 49(4): 790–805.
1986   Problematic Emblem Glyphs: Examples from Altar de Sacrificios, El Chorro, Rio Azul, and Xultun. *Research Reports on Ancient Maya Writing* 3. Washington, D.C.: Center for Maya Research.
1987   Notes on Caracol Epigraphy and Its Significance. In *Investigations at the Classic Maya City of Caracol, Belize: 1985–1987* (by Arlen F. Chase and Diane Z. Chase), pp. 85–100. San Francisco: Pre-Columbian Art Research Institute. Monograph 3.
1988   The Phonetic Decipherment of Mayan Glyphs. *Antiquity* 62(234): 126–135.
1989a   Archaeology and Maya Writing. *Journal of World Prehistory* 3(1): 1–32.
1989b   *Maya Glyphs*. Berkeley: University of California Press.
1991   Caracol Altar 21. In *Sixth Palenque Round Table, 1986, Vol. VIII*, ed. Virginia M. Fields, pp. 38–42. Norman: University of Oklahoma Press.
1992a   Classic Maya History and Politics at Dos Pilas, Guatemala. In *Supplement to the Handbook of Middle American Indians, Vol. 5, Epigraphy*, ed. Victoria R. Bricker, pp. 110–127. Austin: University of Texas Press.
1992b   Classic Maya Politics. In *New Theories on the Ancient Maya*, eds. Elin C. Danien and Robert J. Sharer, pp. 65–69. Philadelphia: The University Museum, University of Pennsylvania.
1992c   A Name Glyph for Classic Maya Dwarfs. In *The Maya Vase Book, Vol. 3* (by Justin Kerr), pp. 526–531. New York: Kerr Associates.
1993   *Hieroglyphs and History at Dos Pilas: Dynastic Politics of the Classic Maya*. Austin: University of Texas Press.

Houston, Stephen, and Paul Amaroli
1988   The Lake Guija Plaque. *Research Reports on Ancient Maya Writing* 15. Washington, D.C.: Center for Maya Research.

Houston, Stephen D., and Peter Mathews
1985 *The Dynastic Sequence of Dos Pilas, Guatemala*. San Francisco: Pre-Columbian Art Research Institute. Monograph 1.

Houston, Stephen D., and David Stuart
1989 The *Way* Glyph: Evidence for 'Co-Essences' among the Classic Maya. *Research Reports on Ancient Maya Writing* 30. Washington, D.C.: Center for Maya Research.
1992 On Maya Hieroglyphic Literacy. *Current Anthropology* 33(5): 589–593.
1996 Of Gods, Glyphs and Kings: Divinity and Rulership among the Classic Maya. *Antiquity* 70: 289–312.

Houston, Stephen D., David Stuart, and Karl Taube
1989 Folk Classification of Classic Maya Pottery. *American Anthropologist* 91(3): 720–726.
1992 Image and Text on the 'Jauncy Vase'. In *The Maya Vase Book, Vol. 3* (by Justin Kerr), pp. 499–512. New York: Kerr Associates.

Houston, Stephen D, and Karl A. Taube
1987 'Name-tagging' in Classic Mayan Script: Implications for Native Classifications of Ceramics and Jade Ornaments. *Mexicon* 9(2): 38–41.

Johnson, Richard E.
1988 Dresden 65–69: The Glyphic Text Identified by T-Number and Paraphrased. *U Mut Maya*, eds. Tom Jones and Carolyn Young, pp. 101–107. Arcata, California: Tom Jones.
1989a The Inscriptions of Chichen Itza. *U Mut Maya II*, eds. Tom Jones and Carolyn Young, pp. 145–156. Arcata, California: Tom Jones and Carolyn Young.
1989b Chichen Itza Dates and Planetary Events. *U Mut Maya II*, eds. Tom Jones and Carolyn Young, pp. 157–168. Arcata, California: Tom and Carolyn Jones.

Johnson, Richard E., and Michel Quenon
1994 A Maya Zodiac: Comments on the Paris Codex Pages 23 and 24. *U Mut Maya V*, eds. Carolyn and Tom Jones, pp. 207–228. Arcata, California: Tom and Carolyn Jones.

Johnston, Kevin
1985 Maya Dynastic Territorial Expansion: Glyphic Evidence from Classic Centers of the Pasion River, Guatemala. In *Fifth Palenque Round Table, 1983, Vol. VII*, ed. Virginia M. Fields, pp. 49–56. San Francisco: Pre-Columbian Art Research Institute.

Jones, Carolyn, and Tom Jones, eds.
1995 *U Mut Maya V*. Arcata, California: Tom and Carolyn Jones.

Jones, Carolyn, and Cheyenne Spetzler
1992 Where Have All the Fathers Gone? An Analysis of Site Q Altar 1. *U Mut Maya IV*, eds. Tom and Carolyn Jones, pp. 104–116. Arcata, California: Tom and Carolyn Jones.

Jones, Christopher
1977 Inauguration Dates of 3 Late Classic Rulers of Tikal, Guatemala. *American Antiquity* 42(1): 28–60.
1983a Monument 26, Quirigua, Guatemala. In *Quirigua Reports II*, eds. Robert J. Sharer, Edward M. Shortman, and Patricia A. Urban, pp. 118–128. Philadelphia: The University of Pennsylvania Museum.
1983b New Drawings of Monuments 23 and 24, Quirigua, Guatemala. In *Quirigua Reports II*, eds. Robert J. Sharer, Edward M. Shortman, and Patricia A. Urban, pp. 137–140. Philadelphia: The University Museum, University of Pennsylvania.
1984 *Deciphering Maya Hieroglyphs*. Philadelphia: The University of Pennsylvania Museum.
1985 Maya Hieroglyphs: A History of Decipherment. *Expedition* 27(3): 20–25.

Jones, Christopher, and Linton Satterthwaite
1982 *The Monuments and Inscriptions of Tikal: The Carved Monuments*. Tikal Report No. 33, Part A. University Museum Monograph 44. Philadelphia: The University of Pennsylvania Museum.

Jones, Tom
1985 The *Xoc*, the *Sharke*, and the Sea Dogs: An Historical Encounter. In *Fifth Palenque Round Table, 1983, Vol. VII*, ed. Virginia M. Fields, pp. 211–222. San Francisco: Pre-Columbian Art Research Institute.
1989a 18-Rabbit and the Game That Never Was. *U Mut Maya II*, eds. Tom Jones and Carolyn Young, pp. 27–35. Arcata, California: {pub}.
1989b The 'Serpent Segment' Glyph: Its Sound and Sense. *U Mut Maya II*, eds. Tom Jones and Carolyn Young, pp. 179–185. Arcata, California: Tom Jones and Carolyn Young.
1990a Empowering the Flint and Shield: A Motive for the Vision Serpent Rite of Yaxchilan Structure 23. *U Mut Maya III*, eds. Tom and Carolyn Jones, pp. 83–98. Arcata, California: Tom and Carolyn Jones.
1990b PAY: A Proposed Reading for the 'God N' Verb. *U Mut Maya III*, eds. Tom and Carolyn Jones, pp. 115–119. Arcata, California: Tom

and Carolyn Jones.

1991   Jaws II: Return of the Xoc. In *Sixth Palenque Round Table, 1986, Vol. VIII*, ed. Virginia M. Fields, pp. 246–254. Norman: University of Oklahoma Press.

1992a   Evidence for the Ch'ak Reading of the 'Axe-Verb' as Found in the Madrid Codex. *U Mut Maya IV*, eds. Tom and Carolyn Jones, pp. 133–142. Arcata, California: Tom and Carolyn Jones.

1992b   Two Armed Sky and the G-Glyph of Quirigua Stela E. *U Mut Maya IV*, eds. Tom and Carolyn Jones, pp. 41–47. Arcata, California: Tom and Carolyn Jones.

1994a   Of Blood and Scars: A Phonetic Rendering of the 'Penis Title.' *Seventh Palenque Round Table, 1989, Vol. 9*, ed. Virginia M. Fields, pp. 79–86. San Francisco: Pre-Columbian Art Research Institute.

1994b   Notes on an Unprovenanced Lowland Maya Relief Panel. *U Mut Maya V*, eds. Carolyn and Tom Jones, pp. 247–251. Arcata, California: Tom and Carolyn Jones.

1996   Polyvalency in the 'Xoc'-glyph: Phonetic u and a Morphemic Patronym. In *Eighth Palenque Round Table, 1993, Vol. X*, eds. Martha J. Macri and Jan McHargue, pp. 325–342. San Francisco: Pre-Columbian Art Research Institute.

Jones, Tom, and Carolyn Jones

1992   The *Xok-Balam* Connection Revisited: A Re-examination of the Text of Yaxchilan Lintel *23*. *U Mut Maya IV*, eds. Tom and Carolyn Jones, pp. 169–200. Arcata, California: Tom and Carolyn Jones.

1994   Yaxchilan's *Hok' Balam*: Uncle or Brother? *U Mut Maya V*, eds. Carolyn and Tom Jones, pp. 133–140. Arcata, California: Tom and Carolyn Jones.

Jones, Tom, and Carolyn Jones, eds.

1990   *U Mut Maya III*. Arcata, California: Tom and Carolyn Jones.

1992   *U Mut Maya IV*. Arcata, California: Tom and Carolyn Jones.

Jones, Tom, Carolyn Jones, and Randa Marhenke

1990   Blood Cousins: The *Xok-Balam* Connection at Yaxchilan. *U Mut Maya III*, eds. Tom and Carolyn Jones, pp. 99–114. Arcata, California: Tom and Carolyn Jones.

Jones, Tom, and Cheyenne Spetzler

1994   A Phonetic Possibility for the Bonampak Emblem Glyph. *U Mut Maya V*, eds. Carolyn and Tom Jones, pp. 87–108. Arcata, California: Tom and Carolyn Jones.

Jones, Tom, and Carolyn Young, eds.

1988   *U Mut Maya*. Arcata, California: Tom Jones.

1989   *U Mut Maya II*. Arcata, California: Tom Jones and Carolyn Young.

Joralemon, David

1974   Ritual Blood-Sacrifice among the Ancient Maya: Part 1. In *Primera Mesa Redonda de Palenque, 1973, Part II*, ed. Merle Greene Robertson, pp. 59–75. Pebble Beach, Calif.: Robert Louis Stevenson School.

Josserand, J. Kathryn

1975   Archaeological and Linguistic Correlations for Maya Prehistory. In *Actas del XLI Congresso Internacional de Americanistes* 1: 501–510. Mexico: Instituto Nacional de Anthropologia e Historia.

1991   The Narrative Structure of Hieroglyphic Texts at Palenque. In *Sixth Palenque Round Table, 1986, Vol. VIII*, ed. Virginia M. Fields, pp. 12–31. Norman: University of Oklahoma Press.

Josserand, J. Kathryn, Linda Schele, and Nicholas A. Hopkins

1985   Linguistic Data on Mayan Inscriptions: The *Ti* Constructions. In *Fourth Palenque Round Table, 1980, Vol. VI*, ed. Elizabeth P. Benson, pp. 87–102. San Francisco: Pre-Columbian Art Research Institute.

Junell, Cathy, and Brian Stross

1994   The Deer As Western Sun. *U Mut Maya V*, eds. Carolyn and Tom Jones, pp. 237–246. Arcata, California: Tom and Carolyn Jones.

Justeson, John S.

1975   The Identification of the Emblem Glyph of Yaxha, El Peten. In *Contributions of the University of California Faculty* 27 pp. 123–129. Berkeley: Archaeological Research Facility, Department of Anthropology.

1983   Mayan Hieroglyphic 'Name-Tagging' of a Pair of Jade Plaques from Xcalumkin. In *Contributions to Maya Hieroglyphic Decipherment, I*, ed. Stephen D. Houston, pp. 40–43. New Haven: Human Relations Area Files, Inc.

1984a   Interpretations of Mayan Hieroglyphs. In *Phoneticism in Mayan Hieroglyphic Writing*, eds. John S. Justeson and Lyle Campbell, Appendix B, pp. 315–362. Albany: Institute for Mesoamerican Studies, State University of New York at Albany. Publ. 9.

1984b   Subscript Designations for Mayan Hieroglyphs. In *Phoneticism in Mayan Hieroglyphic Writing*, eds. John S. Justeson and Lyle Campbell, Appendix D, pp. 367–370. Albany:

Institute for Mesoamerican Studies, State University of New York at Albany. Publ. 9.

1985 Hieroglyphic Evidence for Lowland Maya Linguistic History. *International Journal of American Linguistics* 51: 429–471.

1986 The Origin of Writing Systems: Preclassic Mesoamerica. *World Archaeology* 17(3): 437–458.

1988 The Non-Maya Calendars of Southern Veracruz-Tabasco and the Antiquity of the Civil and Agricultural Years. *Journal of Mayan Linguistics* 6: 1–22.

1989a Ancient Maya Ethnoastronomy: An Overview of Hieroglyphic Sources. In *World Archaeoastronomy*, ed. Anthony F. Aveni, pp. 76–129. Cambridge: Cambridge University Press.

1989b The Representational Conventions of Mayan Hieroglyphic Writing. In *Word and Image in Maya Culture*, eds. Wm. F. Hanks and Don S. Rice, pp. 25–38. Salt Lake City: University of Utah Press.

Justeson, John S., and Lyle Campbell, eds.
1984 *Phoneticism in Mayan Hieroglyphic Writing*. Albany: Institute for Mesoamerican Studies, State University of New York at Albany. Publ. 9.

Justeson, John S., and Terrance Kaufman
1993 A Decipherment of Epi-Olmec Hieroglyphic Writing. *Science* 259(5102): 1703–1711.

Justeson, John S., and Peter Mathews
1983 The Seating of the *Tun*: Further Evidence Concerning a Late Preclassic Lowland Maya Stela Cult. *American Antiquity* 48(3): 586–593.

1990 Evolutionary Trends in Mesoamerican Hieroglyphic Writing. *Visible Language* 29(1): 89–132.

Justeson, John S., Wm. M. Norman, Lyle Campbell, and Terrance Kaufman
1985a *The Foreign Impact on Lowland Mayan Language and Script*. New Orleans: Middle American Research Institute, Tulane University. Publ. 53.

1985b The Origin of Mesoamerican Writing. In *The Foreign Impact on Lowland Mayan Language and Script*, eds. John S. Justeson, Wm. M. Norman, Lyle Campbell, and Terrance Kaufman, pp. 31–37. New Orleans: Middle American Research Institute, Tulane University, Publ. 53.

Justeson, John S., William M. Norman, and Norman Hammond
1988 The Pomona Flare: A Preclassic Maya Hiero-

glyphic Text. In *Maya Iconography*, eds. Elizabeth P. Benson and Gillett G. Griffin, pp. 94–151. Princeton: Princeton University Press.

Kahn, Anna Lee
1994 Some Themes Concerning the Icon of Woman in Maya Vessel Painting. *U Mut Maya V*, eds. Carolyn and Tom Jones, pp. 141–158. Arcata, California: Tom and Carolyn Jones.

Kaufman, Terrence S., and William M. Norman
1984 An Outline of Proto-Cholan Phonology, Morphology, and Vocabulary. In *Phoneticism in Mayan Hieroglyphic Writing*, eds. John S. Justeson and Lyle Campbell, pp. 77–166. Albany: Institute for Mesoamerican Studies, State University of New York at Albany. Publ. 9.

Keeler, Peter, Rafael Hilt-Nelson, and Bette Royce
1989 Early Copan Texts. *U Mut Maya II*, eds. Tom Jones and Carolyn Young, pp. 3–5. Arcata, California: Tom Jones and Carolyn Young.

Kelley, David H.
1962a Glyphic Evidence for a Dynastic Sequence at Quirigua, Guatemala. *American Antiquity* 27: 323–335.

1962b A History of Decipherment of Maya Script. *Anthropological Linguistics* 4(8): 1–48.

1965 The Birth of the Gods at Palenque. *Estudios de Cultura Maya* 5: 93–134.

1968a Kakupacal and the Itzas. *Estudios de Cultura Maya* 7: 255–268.

1968b Mayan Fire Glyphs. *Estudios de Cultura Maya* 7: 141–157.

1972 The Nine Lords of the Night. In *Contributions of the University of California Archaeological Research Facility* 16: 53–68. Berkeley: Department of Anthropology, University of California.

1975 Planetary Data on Caracol Stela 3. In *Archaeoastronomy in Pre-Columbian America*, ed. Anthony F. Aveni, pp. 257–262. Austin: University of Texas Press.

1976 *Deciphering the Maya Script*. Austin: University of Texas Press.

1977a Maya Astronomical Tables and Inscriptions. In *Native American Astronomy*, ed. Anthony F. Aveni, pp. 57–73. Austin: University of Texas Press.

1977b A Possible Maya Eclipse Record. In *Social Process in Maya Prehistory*, ed. Norman Hammond, pp. 405–408. New York: Academic Press.

1982 Notes on Puuc Inscriptions and History. In *The Puuc: New Perspectives: Papers Pre-

sented at the Puuc Symposium, Central College, May, 1977, Supplement, ed. Lawrence Mills. Pella, Iowa: Central College.
1985 The Lords of Palenque and the Lords of Heaven. In *Fifth Palenque Round Table, 1983, Vol. VII*, ed. Virginia M. Fields, pp. 235–239. San Francisco: Pre-Columbian Art Research Institute.

Kelley, David H., and K. Ann Kerr
1973 Mayan Astronomy and Astronomical Glyphs. In *Mesoamerican Writing Systems*, ed. Elizabeth P. Benson, pp. 179–215. Washington, D.C.: Dumbarton Oaks.

Kerr, Barbara, and Justin Kerr
1994 *The Maya Vase Book, Vol. 4*. New York: Kerr Associates.

Kerr, Justin
1989 *The Maya Vase Book, Vol. 1*. New York: Kerr Associates.
1990 *The Maya Vase Book, Vol. 2*. New York: Kerr Associates.
1992a *The Maya Vase Book, Vol. 3*. New York: Kerr Associates.
1992b The Myth of the Popol Vuh as an Instrument of Power. In *New Theories on the Ancient Maya*, eds. Elin C. Danien and Robert J. Sharer, pp. 109–121. Philadelphia: The University of Pennsylvania Museum.
1994 *The Maya Vase Book*, Vol. 4. New York: Kerr Associates.

Kerr, Justin, and Joanne M. Spero
1989 Animal Titles on Classic Maya Vases. *U Mut Maya II*, eds. Tom Jones and Carolyn Young, pp. 63–74. Arcata, California: Tom Jones and Carolyn Young.

Knorozov, Yuri V.
1955 Writing System of the Ancient Maya. *Sovetskaya Etnografiya* 1955(1): 94–125.
1956 New Data on the Maya Written Language. *Journal de la Société des Américanistes (N.S.)* 45: 209–217.
1958a New Data on the Maya Written Language. *Proceedings of the 32nd International Congress of Americanists* 1956: 467–475. Copenhagen.
1958b The Problem of the Study of Maya Hieroglyph Writing. *American Antiquity* 23: 284–291. [Translated by Sophie Coe]
1967 *Selected Chapters from the Writing of the Maya Indians*. Russian Translation Series of the Peabody Museum of American Archaeology and Ethnology, Vol. 4. Cambridge, Mass: Harvard University.

1982 *Maya Hieroglyphic Codices*. Albany: Institute for Mesoamerican Studies, State University of New York at Albany. Publ. 8. (Translated by Sophie Coe)

Koontz, Rex
1995 The Three Stones of Maya Creation at Quirigua. *Mexicon* XVII(2): 24–30.

Koontz, Rex, Erik Boot, and Linnea Wren
1994 A Group of Related Titles from Structure 6E1 at Chichen Itza. *U Mut Maya V*, eds. Carolyn and Tom Jones, pp. 191–195. Arcata, California: {pub}.

Koontz, Rex, and Issac Cux Garcia
1993 K'awil in the Maya Highlands. *Texas Note 38*. Austin: Center of the History and Art of Ancient American Culture, University of Texas at Austin.

Kowalski, Jeff Karl
1985a A Historical Interpretation of the Inscriptions of Uxmal. In *Fourth Palenque Round Table, 1980, Vol. VI*, ed. Elizabeth P. Benson, pp. 235–247. San Francisco: Pre-Columbian Art Research Institute.
1985b Lords of the Northern Maya: Dynastic History in the Inscriptions of Uxmal and Chichen Itza. *Expedition* 27(3): 50–60.
1986 Some Comments on Uxmal Inscriptions. *Mexicon* VIII(5): 93–95.
1989a The Mythological Identity of the Figure on the La Esperanza ('Chinkultic') Ball Court Marker. *Research Reports on Ancient Maya Writing* 27. Washington, D.C.: Center for Maya Research.
1989b Who Am I among the Itza?: Links between Northern Yucatan and the Western Maya Lowlands and Highlands. In *Mesoamerica after the Decline of Teotihuacan A.D. 700–900*, eds. R. A. Diehl and J. C. Berlo, pp. 173–185. Washington, D.C.: Dumbarton Oaks Research Library and Collection.
1994 The Puuc as Seen from Uxmal. In *Hidden among the Hills: Maya Archaeology of the Northwest Yucatan Peninsula. Acta Mesoamericana, Vol. 7*, ed. Hanns J. Prem, pp. 93–120. Mockmuhl: Verlag von Flemming.

Kowalski, Jeff Karl, Alfredo Barrera Rubio, Heber Ojeda Mas, and Jose Huchim Herrera
1996 Archaeological Excavations of a Round Temple at Uxmal: Summary Discussion and Implications for Northern Maya Culture History. In *Eighth Palenque Round Table, 1993, Vol. X*, eds. Martha J. Macri and Jan McHargue, pp. 281–296. San Francisco: Pre-Columbian Art Research Institute.

Kremer, Jurgen, and Fausto UC Flores
1996   The Ritual Suicide of Maya Rulers. In *Eighth Palenque Round Table, 1993, Vol. X*, Martha J. Macri and Jan McHargue, pp. 79–91. San Francisco: Pre-Columbian Art Research Institute.

Krochock, Ruth
1988   *The Hieroglyphic Inscriptions and Iconography of the Temple of the Four Lintels and Related Monuments, Chichen Itza, Yucatan, Mexico.* (M.A. Thesis). Austin: University of Texas.
1989   Hieroglyphic Inscriptions at Chichen Itza, Yucatan, Mexico: The Temples of the Initial Series, the One Lintel, the Three Lintels, and the Four Lintels. *Research Reports on Ancient Maya Writing*, 23. Washington, D.C.: Center for Maya Research.
1991   Dedication Ceremonies at Chichen Itza: The Glyphic Evidence. In *Sixth Palenque Round Table, 1986, Vol. VIII*, ed. Virginia M. Fields, pp. 43–50. Norman: University of Oklahoma Press.

Krochock, Ruth, and David A. Freidel
1994   Ballcourts and the Evolution of Political Rhetoric at Chichen Itza. In *Hidden among the Hills: Maya Archaeology of the Northwest Yucatan Peninsula. Acta Mesoamericana, Vol. 7*, ed. Hanns J. Prem, pp. 359–375. Mockmuhl: Verlag von Flemming.

Kubler, George
1973   The Clauses of Maya Inscriptions. In *Mesoamerican Writing Systems*, ed. Elizabeth P. Benson, pp. 145–164. Washington, D.C.: Dumbarton Oaks.
1974   Mythological Ancestries in Classic Maya Inscriptions. In *Primera Mesa Redonda de Palenque, 1973, Part II*, ed. Merle Greene Robertson, pp. 23–43. Pebble Beach, Calif.: The Robert Louis Stevenson School.
1976   Mythological Dates at Palenque and the Ring Numbers in the Dresden Codex. In *The Art, Iconography & Dynastic History of Palenque Part III (Proceedings of the Segunda Mesa Redonda de Palenque)*, ed. Merle Greene Robertson. pp. 225–230. Pebble Beach, Calif.: Robert Louis Stevenson School.

Kurbjuhn, Kornelia, ed.
1989   *The Complete Catalogue of Glyph Readings*. Kassel: Schneider and Weber.

Landa, Friar Diego de
1978   *Yucatan Before and After the Conquest.* Translated with notes by William Gates. New York: Dover Publications, Inc.

Langley, J. C.
1990   Some Notes on Copan Stela 6. *U Mut Maya III*, eds. Tom and Carolyn Jones, pp. 17–23. Arcata, California: Tom and Carolyn Jones.

Laporte, Juan Pedro, and Vilma Fialko
1995   Un Reencuentro con Mundo Perdido, Tikal, Guatemala. *Ancient Mesoamerica* 6(1):41–94.

Larios, Rudy V., William L. Fash, and David Stuart
1994   Architectural Stratigraphy and Epigraphic Dating of Copan Structure 10L-22: An Exercise in the Conjunctive Approach. *Seventh Palenque Round Table, 1989, Vol. 9*, ed. Virginia M. Fields, pp. 69–77. San Francisco: Pre-Columbian Art Research Institute.

Laughlin, Robert N.
1988   *The Great Tzotzil Dictionary of Santo Domingo Zinacantan, Vol. I: Tzotzil-English.* Smithsonian Contributions to Anthropology 31. Washington, D.C.: Smithsonian Institution Press.

Le Fort, Genevieve, and Robert Wald
1995   Large Numbers on Naranjo Stela 32. *Mexicon* XVII (6): 112–114.

Linden, John H.
1986   Glyph X of the Maya Lunar Series: An Eighteen-Month Lunar Synodic Calendar. *American Antiquity* 51(1): 122–136.
1996   The Deity Head Variants of Glyph C. In *Eighth Palenque Round Table, 1993, Vol. X*, eds. Martha J. Macri and Jan McHargue, pp. 343–356. San Francisco: Pre-Columbian Art Research Institute.

Lipp, Frank J.
1985   Mixe Ritual: An Ethnographic and Epigraphical Comparison. *Mexicon* VII(5): 83–87.

Looper, Matthew G.
1991a   Observations on the Glyph for 'Manikin'. *Texas Note 7.* Austin: Center of the History and Art of Ancient American Culture, University of Texas at Austin
1991b   The Peccaries Above and Below Us. *Texas Note 10.* Austin: Center of the History and Art of Ancient American Culture, University of Texas at Austin.
1991c   A Reinterpretation of the Wooden Box from Tortuguero. *Texas Note 11.* Austin: Center of the History and Art of Ancient American Culture, University of Texas at Austin.
1991d   The Name of Copan and of a Dance at Yaxchilan. *Copan Note 95.* Copan Mosaics Pro-

ject and the Instituto Hondureno de Antropologia e Historia.

1992a Creation Mythology at Naranjo. *Texas Note 30.* Austin: Center of the History and Art of Ancient American Culture, University of Texas at Austin.

1992b The 'Canoe Gods'. *Texas Note 31.* Austin: Center of the History and Art of Ancient American Culture, University of Texas at Austin.

1992c The Parentage of 'Smoking-Squirrel' of Naranjo. *Texas Note 32.* Austin: Center of the History and Art of Ancient American Culture, University of Texas at Austin.

1993 Observations on the Morphology of Sprouts in Olmec Art. *Texas Note 58.* Austin: Center of the History and Art of Ancient American Culture, University of Texas at Austin.

1995 The Three Stones of Maya Creation Mythology at Quirigua. *Mexicon* XVII(2): 24–30.

Looper, Matthew G., and Linda Schele
1991 A War at Palenque during the Reign of Ah-K'an. *Texas Note 25.* Austin: Center of the History and Art of Ancient American Culture, University of Texas at Austin.

Lounsbury, Floyd G.
1973 On the Derivation and Reading of the 'ben-ich' Prefix. In *Mesoamerican Writing Systems*, ed. Elizabeth P. Benson, pp. 99–144. Washington, D.C.: Dumbarton Oaks.

1974 The Inscription of the Sarcophagus Lid at Palenque. In *Primera Mesa Redonda de Palenque, 1973, Part II*, ed. Merle Greene Robertson, pp. 5–20. Pebble Beach, Calif.: Robert Louis Stevenson School.

1976 A Rationale for the Initial Date of the Temple of the Cross at Palenque. In *The Art, Iconography, and Dynastic History of Palenque, Part III: (Proceedings of the Segunda Mesa Redonda de Palenque. 1974)*, ed. Merle Greene Robertson, pp. 211–224. Pebble Beach, Calif.: Robert Louis Stevenson School.

1978 Maya Numeration, Compution, and Calendrical Astronomy. In *Dictionary of Scientific Biography*, Vol. 15, ed. Charles C. Gillispie, pp. 759–818. New York: Charles Scribner's Sons.

1980 Some Problems in the Interpretation of the Mythological Portion of the Hieroglyphic Text of the Temple of the Cross at Palenque. In *Third Palenque Round Table, 1978, Vol. V*, ed. Merle Greene Robertson, pp. 99–115. Austin: University of Texas Press.

1982 Astronomical Knowledge and Its Uses at Bonampak, Mexico. In *Archaeoastronomy in the New World*, ed. Anthony F. Aveni, pp. 143–169. Cambridge: Cambridge University Press.

1983a The Base of the Venus Table of the Dresden Codex, and Its Significance in the Calendar-Correlation Problem. In *Calendars in Mesoamerica and Peru: Native American Computation of Time*, eds. Anthony F. Aveni and Gordon Brotherston, pp. 1–26. Oxford: BAR International Series 174.

1983b Glyph Values: T:99, 155, 279, 280. In *Contributions to Maya Hieroglyphic Decipherment, I*, ed. Stephen D. Houston, pp. 44–49. New Haven: Human Relations Area Files, Inc.

1984 Glyphic Substitutions: Homophonic and Synonymic. In *Phoneticism in Mayan Hieroglyphic Writing*, eds. John S. Justeson and Lyle Campbell, pp. 167–184. Albany: Institute for Mesoamerican Studies, State University of New York at Albany. Publ. 9.

1985 The Identities of the Mythological Figures in the Cross Group Inscriptions of Palenque. In *Fourth Palenque Round Table, 1980, Vol. VI*, ed. Elizabeth Benson, pp. 45–58. San Francisco: Pre-Columbian Art Research Institute.

1989a The Ancient Writing of Middle America. In *The Origins of Writing*, ed. Wayne M. Senner, pp. 203–237. Lincoln: University of Nebraska Press.

1989b The Names of a King: Hieroglyphic Variants as a Key to Decipherment. In *Word and Image in Maya Culture*, eds. Wm. F. Hanks and Don S. Rice, pp. 73–91. Salt Lake City: University of Utah Press.

1989c A Palenque King and the Planet Jupiter. In *World Archaeoastronomy*, ed. Anthony F. Aveni, pp. 246–259. Cambridge: Cambridge University Press.

1991 Recent Work in the Decipherment of Palenque's Hieroglyphic Inscriptions. *American Anthropologist* 93: 809–825.

1992a A Derivation of the Mayan-to-Julian Calendar Correlation from the Dresden Codex Venus Chronology. In *The Sky in Mayan Literature*, ed. Anthony F. Aveni, pp. 184–206. New York: Oxford University Press.

1992b A Solution for the Number 1.5.5.0 of the Mayan Venus Table. In *The Sky in Mayan Literature*, ed. Anthony F. Aveni, pp. 207–215. New York: Oxford University Press.

Lounsbury, Floyd G., and Michael D. Coe
1968 Linguistic and Ethnographic Data Pertinent to the 'Cage' Glyph of Dresden 36C. *Estudios de Cultura Maya VII*: 269–284.

Love, Bruce
1987 Glyph T93 and Maya 'Hand-Scattering' Events. *Research Reports on Ancient Maya*

Writing 5. Washington, D.C.: Center for Maya Research.

1988   The Human Hand as Power Object in Yucatec Ritual. *Journal of Mayan Linguistics* 6: 103–113.

1989a   The Hieroglyphic Lintels of Yula, Yucatan, Mexico. *Research Reports on Ancient Maya Writing* 24. Washington, D.C.: Center for Maya Research.

1989b   Yucatec Sacred Breads Through Time. In *Word and Image in Maya Culture*, eds. Wm. F. Hanks and Don S. Rice, pp. 336–350. Salt Lake City: University of Utah Press.

1991   A Text from the Dresden New Year Pages. In *Sixth Palenque Round Table, 1986, Vol. VIII*, ed. Virginia M. Fields, pp. 293–302. Norman: University of Oklahoma Press.

1992   Divination and Prophecy in Yucatan. In *New Theories on the Ancient Maya*, eds. Elin C. Danien and Robert J. Sharer, pp. 205–216. Philadelphia: The University of Pennsylvania Museum.

1992a   Another Glyph for *Na. Texas Note 28*. Austin: Center of the History and Art of Ancient American Culture, University of Texas at Austin.

1994   *The Paris Codex: Handbook for a Maya Priest*. Austin: University of Texas Press.

1995   A Dresden Codex Mars Table? Latin American *Antiquity* 6(4): 350–361.

Lowe, Gareth W.
1962   Algunos Resultados de la Temporada 1961 en Chiapa de Corzo, Chiapas. *Estudios de Cultura Maya* 2: 185–196.

Mack, John
1989   A Chronology of 'Smoke-Imix-God-K' of Copan. *U Mut Maya II*, eds. Tom Jones and Carolyn Young, pp. 7–8. Arcata, California: Tom Jones and Carolyn Young.

MacLeod, Barbara
1983   Remembrances of Cycles Past: T669b in Palenque Katun Histories. In *Contributions to Maya Hieroglyphic Decipherment, I*, ed. Stephen D. Houston, pp. 50–59. New Haven: Human Relations Area Files, Inc.

1984   Cholan and Yucatec Verb Morphology and Glyphic Verbal Affixes in the Inscriptions. In *Phoneticism in Mayan Hieroglyphic Writing*, eds. John S. Justeson and Lyle Campbell, pp. 233–262. Albany: Institute for Mesoamerican Studies, State University of New York at Albany. Publ. 9.

1987   *An Epigrapher's Annotated Index to Cholan and Yucatecan Verb Morphology*. University of Missouri Monographs in Anthropology 9. Columbia, Mo.: Department of Anthropology, University of Missouri-Columbia.

1989a   The 819-Day-Count: A Soulful Mechanism. In *Word and Image in Maya Culture*, eds. Wm. F. Hanks and Don S. Rice, pp. 112–126. Salt Lake City: University of Utah Press.

1989b   Writing on the Curved Page: A Reading for the Manik Collocation in the Primary Standard Sequence. *Mexicon* XI(2): 27–31.

1990   The God N/Step Set in the Primary Standard Sequence. In *The Maya Vase Book, Vol. 2* (by Justin Kerr), pp. 331–347. New York: Kerr Associates.

1993   Musings about Rare Variants of Glyph A of the Lunar Series. *Texas Note 33*. Austin: Center of the History and Art of Ancient American Culture, University of Texas at Austin.

Macleod, Barbara, and Dorie Reents-Budet
1994   The Art of Caligraphy: Image and Meaning. In *Painting the Maya Universe: Royal Ceramics of the Classic Period*, ed. Dorie Reents-Budet, pp. 106–163. Durham, N.C.: Duke University Press.

MacLeod, Barbara, and Andrea Stone
1995   The Hieroglyphic Inscriptions of Naj Tunich. Chapter 7 in *Images from the Underworld: Naj Tunich and the Tradition of Maya Cave Painting* (by Andrea Stone). Austin: University of Texas Press.

MacLeod, Barbara, and Brian Stross
1990   The Wing-Quincunx. *Journal of Mayan Linguistics* 7: 14–32.

Macri, Martha J.
1991   Prepositions and Complementizers in the Classic Maya Inscriptions. In *Sixth Palenque Round Table, 1986, Vol. VIII*, ed. Virginia M. Fields, pp. 266–272. Norman: University of Oklahoma Press.

1994   The Five-Door Temples at Piedras Negras and Palenque. *Mexicon* XVI(5): 100–102.

Macri, Martha J., and L. Furbee
1985   Velar and Alveopalatal Consonants in the Maya Hieroglyphs. *International Journal of Linguistics* 51: 412–416.

Macri, Martha J., and Laura M. Stark
1993   *A Sign Catalog of the La Mojarra Script*. San Francisco: Pre-Columbian Art Research Institute, Monograph 5.

Marcus, Joyce
1973   Territorial Organization of the Lowland Classic Maya. *Science* 180: 911–916.

1976a   *Emblem and State in the Classic Maya Low-*

lands. Washington, D.C.: Dumbarton Oaks.

1976b   The Origins of Mesoamerican Writing. Ann. Rev. *Anthropology* 5: 35–67.

1983   The First Appearance of Zapotec Writing and Calendrics. In *The Cloud People: Divergent Evolution of the Zapotec and Mixtec Civilizations*, eds. Kent V. Flannery and Joyce Marcus, pp. 91–96. New York: Academic Press.

1984   Monumentos Mayas en el museo 'Rufino Tamayo,' Oaxaca. *Estudios de Cultura Maya XV: 97–115.*

1987   *The Inscriptions of Calakmul: Royal Marriage at a Maya City in Campeche, Mexico.* University of Michigan Museum of Anthropology, Technical Report 21. Ann Arbor: University of Michigan.

1992a   *Mesoamerican Writing Systems: Propaganda, Myth, and History in Four Ancient Civilizations.* Princeton: Princeton University Press.

1992b   Royal Families, Royal Texts: Examples from the Zapotec and Maya. In *Mesoamerican Elites: An Archaeological Assessment*, eds. Diane Z. Chase and Arlen F. Chase, pp. 221–241. Norman: University of Oklahoma Press.

1992c   The Evolutionary Context of Early Writing. In *Mesoamerican Writing Systems: Propaganda, Myth and History in Four Ancient Civilizations.* Princeton: Princeton University Press.

Marhenke, Randa

1988   Copan Stela 11: A Monument to Yax Pac's Death? (Copan). *U Mut Maya*, eds. Tom Jones and Carolyn Young, pp. 61–65. Arcata, California: Tom Jones.

1989a   "18-Rabbit" Name Phrases. *U Mut Maya II*, eds. Tom Jones and Carolyn Young, pp. 17–19. Arcata, California: Tom Jones and Carolyn Young.

1989b   A Note on the 'ADI-Title" Glyph. *U Mut Maya II*, eds. Tom Jones and Carolyn Young, pp. 59–61. Arcata, California: Tom Jones and Carolyn Young.

1994   Ah Sul, The Flayer. *U Mut Maya V*, eds. Carolyn and Tom Jones, pp. 73–77. Arcata, California: Tom and Carolyn Jones.

Martin, Frederick

1993   A Dresden Codex Eclipse Sequence: Projections for the Years 1970–1972. *Latin American Antiquity* 4(1): 74–93.

Martin, Simon

1996   Tikal's "Star War" Against Naranjo. In *Eighth Palenque Round Table, 1993, Vol. X*, eds. Martha J. Macri and Jan McHargue, pp.

223–236. San Francisco: Pre-Columbian Art Research Institute.

Martin, Simon, and Nikolai Grube

1995   Maya Superstates. *Archaeology* 48(6): 41–46.

Martinez Hernandez, Juan

1929   *Diccionario de Motul, Maya-Espanol.* Merida: La Compania Tipografica Yucateca.

Mathews, Paul

1994   Ch'akah U Tz'ibal: The Axing of History at Seibal. *Texas Note 65.* Austin: Center of the History and Art of Ancient American Culture, University of Texas at Austin.

Mathews, Peter

1977   The Inscription on the Back of Stela 8, Dos Pilas, Guatemala. Paper presented at the International Conference on Maya Art, Architecture, Archaeology, and Hieroglyphic Writing, Guatemala City, May 13, 1977.

1979   The Glyphs on the Ear Ornaments from Tomb A-1/1. In *Excavations at Altun Ha, Belize, 1964–1970*, ed. David M. Pendergast, Vol. 1, pp. 79–80. Toronto: Royal Ontario Museum.

1980   Notes on the Dynastic Sequence of Bonampak, Part I. In *Third Palenque Round Table, 1978, Part 2*, ed. Merle Greene Robertson, pp. 60–73. Austin: University of Texas Press.

1982   The Dynastic Sequence of Tonina, Chiapas, Mexico. In *Tonina, un Cité Maya du Chiapas, Vol. 2*, eds. Pierre Becquelin and Claude Baudez, pp. 894–902. Paris: Mission Archéologique et Ethnologique Française au Mexique.

1984   A Maya Hieroglyphic Syllabary. In *Phoneticism in Mayan Hieroglyphic Writing*, eds. John S. Justeson and Lyle Campbell, Appendix A, pp. 311–314. Albany: Institute for Mesoamerican Studies, State University of New York at Albany. Publ. 9.

1985   Maya Early Classic Monuments and Inscriptions. In *A Consideration of the Early Classic Period in the Maya Lowlands*, eds. Gordon R. Willey and Peter Mathews, pp. 5–54. Albany: Institute for Mesoamerican Studies, State University of New York at Albany. Publ. 10.

1988   *The Sculpture of Yaxchilan* (Ph.D. Dissertation). New Haven: Yale University.

1990   *Notebook for the Maya Hieroglyphic Weekend at Cleveland State University*, Cleveland, October 27–28, 1990.

1991   Classic Maya Emblem Glyphs. In *Classic Maya Political History*, ed. T. Patrick Culbert, pp. 19–29. Cambridge: Cambridge University Press/School of American Research.

1993a   The 'Bee Man' of Tonina. *Texas Note 46*. Austin: Center of the History and Art of Ancient American Culture, University of Texas at Austin.

1993b   The Emblem Glyph of Bonampak, Chiapas, Mexico. *Texas Note 44*. Austin: Center of the History and Art of Ancient American Culture, University of Texas at Austin.

1993c   A Painted Capstone at Becan, Campeche. *Texas Note 45*. Austin: Center of the History and Art of Ancient American Culture, University of Texas at Austin.

1993d   The Stucco Text Above the Piers of the Temple of the Inscriptions at Palenque. *Texas Note 49*. Austin: Center of the History and Art of Ancient American Culture, University of Texas at Austin.

1993e   Tonina Dates I: A Glyph for the Period of 260 Days? *Texas Note 47*. Austin: Center of the History and Art of Ancient American Culture, University of Texas at Austin.

1993f   Tonina Dates II: The Date of Tonina F.35. *Texas Note 48*. Austin: Center of the History and Art of Ancient American Culture, University of Texas at Austin.

1994   On the Glyphs 'West' and 'Mah k'ina.' *Texas Note 61*. Austin: Center of the History and Art of Ancient American Culture, University of Texas at Austin.

Mathews, Peter, and John S. Justeson
1984   Patterns of Sign Substitution in Mayan Hieroglyphic Writing: 'the Affix Cluster'. In *Phoneticism in Mayan Hieroglyphic Writing*, eds. John S. Justeson and Lyle Campbell, pp. 185–231. Albany: Institute for Mesoamerican Studies, State University of New York at Albany. Publ. 9.

Mathews, Peter, and David H. Pendergast
1979   The Altun Ha Jade Plaque: Deciphering the Inscription. In *Contributions of the University of California Archaeological Research Facility*, Vol. 41, pp. 197–214. Berkeley: Department of Anthropology, University of California.

Mathews, Peter, and Merle Greene Robertson
1985   Notes on the Olvidado, Palenque, Chiapas, Mexico. In *Fifth Palenque Round Table, 1983, Vol. VII*, ed. Virginia M. Fields, pp. 7–17. San Francisco: Pre-Columbian Art Research Institute.

Mathews, Peter, and Linda Schele
1974   Lords of Palenque: The Glyphic Evidence. *In Primera Mesa Redonda de Palenque, Part I*, ed. Merle Greene Robertson, pp. 63–76. Peb-

ble Beach, Calif.: The Robert Louis Stevenson School.

Mathews, Peter, and Gordon Willey
1991   Prehistoric Polities of the Pasion Region: Hieroglyphic Texts and Their Archaeological Settings. In *Classic Maya Political History*, ed. T. Patrick Culbert, pp. 30–71. Cambridge: Cambridge University Press/School of American Research.

Maudslay, Alfred P.
1889–1902   *Archaeology. Biologia Centrali-Americana*. 5 vols. London: R.H. Porter and Dulau & Co.

Maxwell, Judith M.
1988   The Temple of the Cross Main Panels: A Reading. *U Mut Maya*, eds. Tom Jones and Carolyn Young, pp. 15–23. Arcata, California: Tom Jones.

Mayer, Karl Herbert
1990   *The Stelae and Inscriptions of Sacul, Guatemala*. Mexicon Occasional Publications No. 1. Berlin: Verlag von Flemming.

1991   Maya Monuments: Sculptures of Unknown Provenance, Supplement 3. Berlin: Verlag von Flemming.

1994   *Maya Inscriptions from Hobomo, Campeche, Mexico*. Mexicon Occassional Publications No. 2. Mochmuhl: Verlag Anton Saurwein.

1995   A Unique Maya Glyphic Panel in Guatemala. *Mexicon* XVII(1): 3.

Mayer, Karl Herbert, and Berthold Riese
1983   Monument 134 aus Tonina, Chiapas, Mexiko. Eine neue Inschrift zu Herrscher III. *Mexicon* V(5): 87–90.

McGee, R. Jon
1993   Palenque and Lacandon Maya Cosmology. *Texas Note 52*. Austin: Center of the History and Art of Ancient American Culture, University of Texas at Austin.

1996   Lacandon Maya Oral Performance and the Inscriptions of Palenque. In *Eighth Palenque Round Table, 1993, Vol. X*, eds. Martha J. Macri and Jan McHargue, pp. 129–134. San Francisco: Pre-Columbian Art Research Institute.

McHargue, Jan
1996   A Carving Sequence for Stela 1, Copan, Honduras. In *Eighth Palenque Round Table, 1993, Vol. X*, eds. Martha J. Macri and Jan McHargue, pp. 177–182. San Francisco: Pre-Columbian Art Research Institute.

Meluzin, Sylvia
1987   The Tuxtla Statuette: An Internal Analysis of Its Writing System. In *The Periphery of the South-eastern Classic Maya Realm*, ed. Gary W. Pahl, pp. 67–113. Los Angeles: UCLA Latin American Studies, Vol. 61, UCLA Latin American Center.
1992   The Tuxtla Script: Steps toward Decipherment of La Mojarra Stela 1. *Latin American Antiquity* 3(4): 283–297.
1995   *Further Investigations of the Tuxtla Script: An Inscribed Mask and La Mojarra Stela 1.* Papers of the New World Archaeological Foundation, No. 65. Provo: Brigham Young University.

Meyerson, Sylvia
1994   La Mojarra Stela 1: The Pyramid Outline and the Reverse Images. *U Mut Maya V*, eds. Carolyn and Tom Jones, pp. 229–236. Arcata, California: Tom and Carolyn Jones.

Milbrath, Susan
1981   Astronomical Imagery in the Serpent Sequence of the Madrid Codex. In *Archaeoastronomy in the Americas*, ed. Ray A. Williamson, pp. 263–284. Los Altos, Calif.: Ballena Press.
1996   Postclassic Maya Metaphors for Lunar Motion. In *Eighth Palenque Round Table, 1993, Vol. X*, eds. Martha J. Macri and Jan McHargue, pp. 379–391. San Francisco: Pre-Columbian Art Research Institute.

Miles, Suzanne W.
1965   Sculpture of the Guatemala-Chiapas Highlands and Pacific Slopes, and Associated Hieroglyphs. In *Handbook of Middle American Indians, Vol. 2, Pt. 1*, ed. Gordon R. Willey, pp. 237–275. Austin: University of Texas Press.

Miller, Arthur
1989   Comparing Maya Image and Text. In *Word and Image in Maya Culture*, eds. Wm. F. Hanks and Don S. Rice, pp. 176–188. Salt Lake City: University of Utah Press.

Miller, Jeffrey H.
1974   Notes on a Stelae Pair Probably from Calakmul, Campeche, Mexico. In *Primera Mesa Redonda de Palenque, Part I*, ed. Merle Greene Roberetson, pp. 149–161. Pebble Beach, Calif.: Robert Louis Stevenson School.

Miller, Mary Ellen
1983   Some Observations on Structure 44, Yaxchilan. In *Contributions to Maya Hieroglyphic Decipherment, I*, ed. Stephen D. Houston, pp. 62–99. New Haven: Human Relations Area Files, Inc.
1984   Four Maya Reliefs. *Appolo* CXIX (266): 17–20.
1986   *The Murals of Bonampak.* Princeton: Princeton University Press.
1993   On the Eve of the Collapse: Maya Art of the Eighth Century. In *Lowland Maya Civililization in the Eighth Century A.D.*, eds. Jeremy A. Sabloff and John S. Henderson, pp. 355–413. Washington, D.C.: Dumbarton Oaks.

Miller, Mary Ellen, and Stephen D. Houston
1987   The Classic Maya Ballgame and Its Architectural Setting. *RES* 14: 46–65.

Miller, Mary Ellen, and David S. Stuart
1981   Dumbarton Oaks Relief Panel 4. *Estudios de Cultura Maya 13*: 197–204.

Miller, Mary Ellen, and Karl Taube
1993   *The Gods and Symbols of Ancient Mexico and the Maya.* London: Thames and Hudson, Ltd.

Miram, Helga-Maria
1994   The Role of the Books of Chilam Balam in Deciphering Maya Hieroglyphs: New Material and New Considerations. In *Seventh Palenque Round Table, 1989, Vol. IX*, ed. Virginia M. Fields, pp. 211–216. San Francisco: Pre-Columbian Art Research Institute.

Miram, Helga-Maria, and Victoria R. Bricker
1996   Relating Time to Space: The Maya Calendar Compasses. In *Eighth Palenque Round Table, 1993, Vol. X*, eds. Martha J. Macri and Jan McHargue, pp. 393–402. San Francisco: Pre-Columbian Art Research Institute.

Montgomery, John
1989a   The Protagonist of Tikal Stela 8. *U Mut Maya II*, eds. Tom Jones and Carolyn Young, pp. 99–103. Arcata, California: Tom Jones and Carolyn Young.
1989b   Drawings of Selected Maya Monuments and Inscriptions. Appendix E in *U Mut Maya II*, eds. Tom Jones and Carolyn Young, pp. 211–217. Arcata, California: Tom Jones and Carolyn Young.
1990a   A Glyph for Jaguar Paw on Piedras Negras Throne 1. *U Mut Maya III*, eds. Tom and Carolyn Jones, pp. 135–137. Arcata, California: Tom and Carolyn Jones.
1990b   A Note on the Date of Piedras Negras Lintel 3. *U Mut Maya III*, eds. Tom and Carolyn

Jones, pp. 139. Arcata, California: Tom and Carolyn Jones.

1990c   Observations on Name Clauses at Chichen Itza: Part I. *U Mut Maya III*, eds. Tom and Carolyn Jones, pp. 141–146. Arcata, California: Tom and Carolyn Jones.

1990d   Drawings of Selected Maya Monuments and Inscriptions. *U Mut Maya III*, eds. Tom and Carolyn Jones, pp. 179–188. Arcata, California: Tom and Carolyn Jones.

1992   Drawings of Maya Monuments and Inscriptions. *U Mut Maya IV*, eds. Tom and Carolyn Jones, pp. 283–290. Arcata, California: Tom and Carolyn Jones.

Moore, Dan R.
1989   A Phonetic Reading of Xaman in the Maya Inscriptions. *U Mut Maya II*, eds. Tom Jones and Carolyn Young, pp. 171–174. Arcata, California: Tom Jones and Carolyn Young.

Moran, Francisco
1935   *Arte y Diccionario en Lengua Cholti*. Baltimore: The Maya Society. Publ. 9.

Morley, Frances R., and Sylvanus G. Morley.
1938   *The Age and Provenance of the Leyden Plate*. Contributions to Anerican Anthropology and History 5(24). Washington, D.C.: Carnegie Institution of Washington, Publ. 509.

Morley, Sylvanus G.
1915   *An Introduction to the Study of Maya Hieroglyphs*. Washington D.C.: Smithsonian Institution, Bureau of American Ethnology. Bulletin 57.

1920   *The Inscriptions of Copan*. Washington, D.C.: Carnegie Institution of Washington. Publ. 219.

1937–1938   *The Inscriptions of Peten*. 5 vols. Washington D.C.: Carnegie Institution of Washington. Publ. 437.

1946   *The Ancient Maya*. Stanford: Stanford University Press.

Nahm, Werner
1994   Maya Warfare and the Venus Year. *Mexicon* XVI(1): 6–10.

Newsome, Elizabeth A.
1996   Precious Stones of Grace: A Theory of the Origin and Meaning of the Classic Maya Stela Cult. In *Eighth Palenque Round Table, 1993, Vol. X*, eds. Martha J. Macri and Jan McHargue, pp. 183–193. San Francisco: Pre-Columbian Art Research Institute.

Orejel, Jorge L.
1990   The 'Axe/Comb' Glyph as ch'ak. *Research Reports on Ancient Maya Writing* 31. Washington, D.C.: Center for Maya Research.

1991   Artificial Intelligence Meets Maya Epigraphy. In *Sixth Palenque Round Table, 1986, Vol. VIII*, ed. Virginia M. Fields, pp. 322–332. Norman: University of Oklahoma Press.

1996   A Collocation Denoting a 'Substitute' Relationship in Classic Maya Inscriptions. In *Eighth Palenque Round Table, 1993, Vol. X*, eds. Martha J. Macri and Jan McHargue, pp. 63–77. San Francisco: Pre-Columbian Art Research Institute.

Owen, Nancy Kelley
1975   The Use of Eclipse Data to Determine the Maya Correlation Number. In *Archaeoastronomy in Pre-Columbian America*, ed. Anthony F. Aveni, pp. 237–246. Austin: University of Texas Press.

1989   The Parallel Passages of Copan Stelas 12 and 2. *U Mut Maya II*, eds. Tom Jones and Carolyn Young, pp. 13–16. Arcata, California: Tom Jones and Carolyn Young.

Pahl, Gary W.
1976   A Successor-Relationship Complex and Associated Signs. In *The Art, Iconography & Dynastic History of Palenque Part III (Segunda Mesa Redonda de Palenque)*, ed. Merle Greene Robertson, pp. 35–44. Pebble Beach Calif.: The Robert Louis Stevenson School.

1977   The Inscriptions of Rio Amarillo and Los Higos: Secondary Centers of the Southeastern Maya Frontier. *Journal of Latin American Lore* 3: 133–154.

1978   An Inscribed Monument from the Ocosingo Valley. *Estudios de Cultura Maya* 11: pp. 181–186.

Paisa, Marina Besada, Michel Davoust, and Michel Quenon
1992   A New Phonetic Reading of the Inscription on Lintel 3 of Tikal Temple I. *U Mut Maya IV*, eds. Tom and Carolyn Jones, pp. 87–103. Arcata, California: Tom and Carolyn Jones.

Paxton, Merideth
1992   The Books of Chilam Balam: Astronomical Content and the Paris Codex. In *The Sky in Mayan Literature*, ed. Anthony F. Aveni, pp. 216–246. New York: Oxford University Press.

Perry, Steven S.
1981   The Glyphic Texts at Aguateca. *Estudios de Cultura Maya* XIII: 187–195.

Porter, James B.
1994 The Palace Intaglios: A Composite Stairway Throne at Palenque. In *Seventh Palenque Round Table, 1989, Vol. IX*, ed. Virginia M. Fields, pp. 11–18. San Francisco: Pre-Columbian Art Research Institute.

Prouskouriakoff, Tatiana
1950 *A Study of Maya Sculpture*. Washington, D.C.: Carnegie Institution of Washington, Publ. 593.
1960 Historical Implications of a Pattern of Dates at Piedras Negras, Guatemala. *American Antiquity* 25(4): 454–475.
1961a The Lords of the Maya Realm. *Expedition* 4(1): 14–21.
1961b Portraits of Women in Maya Art. In *Essays in Pre-Columbian Art and Archaeology*, eds. Samuel K. Lothrop et al., pp. 81–99. Cambridge, Mass: Harvard University Press.
1963 Historical Data in the Inscriptions of Yaxchilan, Part I. *Estudios de Cultura Maya* 3: 149–167.
1964 Historical Data in the Inscriptions of Yaxchilan, Part II. *Estudios de Cultura Maya* 4: 177–201.
1970 On Two Inscriptions at Chichen Itza. In *Monographs and Papers in Maya Archaeology*, ed. W. R. Bullard, pp. 457–467. Peabody Museum Papers 61. Cambridge, Mass.: Harvard University.
1973 The Hand-Grasping-Fish and Associated Glyphs on Classic Maya Monuments. In *Mesoamerican Writing Systems*, ed. Elizabeth P. Benson, pp. 165–178. Washington, D.C.: Dumbarton Oaks.
1978 Olmec Gods and Maya God Glyphs. In *Codex Wauchope*, eds. M. Giardino, B. Edmonson, and W. Creamer, pp. 112–117. New Orleans: Tulane University.

Quirarte, Jacinto
1979 The Representation of Place, Location and Direction on a Classic Maya Vase. In *Tercera Mesa Redonda de Palenque, 1978, Vol. IV*, eds. Merle Greene Robertson and Donnan C. Jeffers, pp. 99–110. Palenque, Chiapas, Mexico: Pre-Columbian Art Research Institute.

Reents, Dorie J., and Ronald L. Bishop
1985 History and Ritual Events on a Petexbatun Classic Maya Polychrome Vessel. In *Fifth Palenque Round Table, 1983, Vol. VII*, ed. Virginia M. Fields, pp. 57–63. San Francisco: Pre-Columbian Art Research Institute.

Reents-Budet, Dorie
1986 Inter-Site Dynastic Relations Recorded on a Plate from Holmul, Guatemala. *Estudios de Cultura Maya* XVI: 149–166.
1987 The Discovery of a Ceramic Artist and Royal Patron among the Classic Maya. *Mexicon* IX(6): 123–126.
1988 The Iconography of Lamanai Stela 9. *Research Reports on Ancient Maya Writing* 22. Washington, D.C.: Center for Maya Research.
1989 Narrative in Classic Maya Art. In *Word and Image in Maya Culture*, eds. William F Hanks and Don S. Rice, pp. 189–197. Salt Lake City: University of Utah Press.
1991 The 'Holmul Dancer' Theme in Maya Art. In *Sixth Palenque Round Table, 1986, Vol. VIII*, ed. Virginia M. Fields, pp. 217–222. Norman: University of Oklahoma Press.
1994 *Painting the Maya Universe: Royal Ceramics of the Classic Period*. Durham, NC: Duke University Press.

Reents-Budet, Dorie, Ronald L. Bishop, and Barbara MacLeod
1994 Painting Styles, Workshop Locations, and Pottery Production. In *Painting the Maya Universe: Royal Ceramics of the Classic Period*, pp. 164–233. Durham, NC: Duke University Press.

Reilly, F. Kent, III
1996 The Lazy-S: A Formative Period Iconographic Loan to Maya Hieroglyphic Writing. In *Eighth Palenque Round Table, 1993, Vol. X*, eds. Martha J. Macri and Jan McHargue, pp. 413–424. San Francisco: Pre-Columbian Art Research Institute.

Riese, Berthold
1978 La Inscripcion del Monumento 6 de Tortuguero. *Estudios de Cultura Maya* 11: 187–198.
1980 Katun-Altersangaben in Klassichen Maya-Inschriften. *Baessler-Archiv, Neue Folge Band* XXVIII: 155–180.
1984a Hel Hieroglyphs. In *Phoneticism in Mayan Hieroglyphic Writing*, eds. John S. Justeson and Lyle Campbell, pp. 263–286. Albany: Institute for Mesoamerican Studies, State University of New York at Albany. Publ. 9.
1984b Kriegsberichte der Klassichen Maya. *Baessler-Archiv* (n.f.) 30: 255–321.
1984c Dynastiegeschichtliche und Kalendarische Beobachtungen an den Maya-Inschriften von Machaquila, Peten, Guatemala. *Tribus* 33: 149–154.
1986 Late Classsic Relationship between Copan and Quirigua: Some Epigraphic Evidence. In *The Southeast Maya Periphery*, eds. Patricia

A. Urban and Edward M. Shortman, pp. 94–101. Austin: University of Texas Press.

1988a   Epigraphy of the Southeast Zone in Relation to Other Parts of Mesoamerica. In *The Southeast Classic Maya Zone*, eds. Elizabeth Boone and Gordon Willey, pp. 67–94. Washington, D.C.: Dumbarton Oaks.

1988b   The Po Throne Panel: A Classic Maya Stone Relief. *Journal of Mayan Linguistics* 6: 47–54.

1989   The Inscription on the Sculptured Bench of the House of the Bacabs. In *The House of the Bacabs, Copan, Honduras, Studies in Precolumbian Art and Archaeology 29*, ed. David Webster, pp. 82–88. Washington, D.C.: Dumbarton Oaks.

1992   The Copan Dynasty. In *Supplement to the Handbook of Middle American Indians, Vol. 5, Epigraphy*, ed. Victoria R. Bricker, pp. 128–153. Austin: University of Texas Press.

Riese, Berthold, and Karl H. Mayer

1984   Altar 10 von Uxmal, Yukatan, Mexico. *Mexicon* VI(5): 70–73.

Ringle, William M.

1985   Notes on Two Tablets of Unknown Provenance. In *Fifth Palenque Round Table, 1983, Vol. VII*, ed. Virginia M. Fields, pp. 151–158. San Francisco: Pre-Columbian Art Research Institute.

1988   Of Mice and Monkeys: The Value and Meaning of T1016, the God C Hieroglyph. *Research Reports on Ancient Maya Writing* 18. Washington, D.C.: Center for Maya Research.

1990   Who Was Who in Ninth-Century Chichen Itza? *Ancient Mesoamerica* 1(2): 233–243.

1996   Birds of a Feather: The Fallen Stucco Inscription of Temple XVIII, Palenque, Chiapas. In *Eighth Palenque Round Table, 1993, Vol. X*, eds. Martha J. Macri and Jan McHargue, pp. 45–61. San Francisco: Pre-Columbian Art Research Institute.

Ringle, William M., and Thomas C. Smith-Stark

1996   *A Concordance to the Hieroglyphs of Palenque, Chiapas, Mexico*. New Orleans: Middle American Research Institute, Tulane University (in press).

Robicsek, Francis, and Donald M. Hales

1981   *The Maya Book of the Dead: The Ceramic Codex*. Charlottesville: The University of Virginia Art Museum.

de Rosny, Leon

1876   *Essai sur le Dechiffrement de l'Ecriture Hieratique de l'Amerique Centrale*. Paris: Maisonneuve et Cie.

Royce, Betty, Jo Ann Roman Brisko, Barbara Hinton, Inga Calvin, and Steve Stearns

1988   Temple of the Inscriptions (Palenque). *U Mut Maya*, eds. Tom Jones and Carolyn Young, pp. 1–13. Arcata, California: {pub}.

Satterthwaite, Linton

1965   Calendrics of the Maya Lowlands. In *Handbook of Middle American Indians Vol. 3*, vol. ed. Gordon R. Willey, gen. ed. Robert Wauchope, pp. 603–631. Austin: University of Texas Press.

1979   Quirigua Altar L (Monument 12). In *Quirigua Reports I*, eds. Robert J. Sharer and Wendy Ashmore, pp. 39–43. Philadelphia: The University of Pennsylvania Museum.

Schele, Linda

1974   Observations on the Cross Motif at Palenque. In *Primera Mesa Redonda de Palenque, Part I*, ed. Merle Greene Roberetson, pp. 41–62. Pebble Beach, Calif.: Robert Louis Stevenson School.

1976   Accession Iconography of Chan-Bahlum in the Group of the Cross at Palenque. In *The Art, Iconography & Dynastic History of Palenque, Part III (Segunda Mesa Redonda de Palenque, 1974)*, ed. Merle Greene Robertson, pp. 9–34. Pebble Beach, Calif.: The Robert Louis Stevenson School.

1977   Palenque: The House of the Dying Sun. In *Native American Astronomy*, ed. Anthony F. Aveni, pp. 42–56. Austin: University of Texas Press.

1979   Genealogical Documentation on the Tri-Figure Panels at Palenque. In *Tercera Mesa Redonda de Palenque, 1978, Vol. IV*, eds. Merle Greene Robertson and Donnan C. Jeffers, pp. 41–70. Palenque, Chiapas, Mexico: Pre-Columbian Art Research Institute.

1981   Sacred Site and World View at Palenque. In *Mesoamerican Sites and World Views*, ed. Elizabeth P. Benson, pp. 87–117. Washington, D.C.: Dumbarton Oaks.

1982   *Maya Glyphs: The Verbs*. Austin: University of Texas Press.

1984a   Human Sacrifice among the Classic Maya. In *Ritual Human Sacrifice in Mesoamerica*, ed. Elizabeth P. Benson, pp. 7–48. Washington, D.C.: Dumbarton Oaks.

1984b   Some Suggested Readings of the Event and Office of Heir-Designate at Palenque. In *Phoneticism in Mayan Hieroglyphic Writing*, eds. John S. Justeson and Lyle Campbell, pp. 287–307. Albany: Institute for Mesoamerican Studies, State University of New York at Albany. Publ. 9.

1985a   Balan-Ahau: A Possible Reading of the Tikal

Emblem Glyph and a Title at Palenque. In *Fourth Palenque Round Table, 1980, Vol. VI*, ed. Elizabeth P. Benson, pp. 59–65. San Francisco: Pre-Columbian Art Research Institute.

1985b The Hauberg Stela: Bloodletting and the Mythos of Maya Rulership. In *Fifth Palenque Round Table, 1983, Vol. VII*, ed. Virginia M Fields, pp. 135–149. San Francisco: The Pre-Columbian Art Research Institute.

1986 *Notebook for the Maya Hieroglyphic Writing Workshop at Texas*. Austin: Institute of Latin American Studies, University of Texas at Austin.

1987 *Notebook for the Maya Hieroglyphic Writing Workshop at Texas*. Austin: The University of Texas at Austin.

1988a *Notebook for the Maya Hieroglyphic Writing Workshop at Texas*. Austin: The University of Texas at Austin.

1988b The Xibalba Shuffle: A Dance after Death. In *Maya Iconography*, eds. Elizabeth P. Benson and Gillett G. Griffin, pp. 294–317. Princeton: Princeton University Press.

1989a A Brief Note on the Name of the Vision Serpent. In *The Maya Vase Book, Vol. 1* (by Justin Kerr), pp. 146–148. New York: Kerr Associates.

1989b *Notebook for the XIIIth Maya Hieroglyphic Workshop at Texas*. Austin: Art Department, University of Texas at Austin.

1990a Ba as 'First' in Classic Period Titles. *Texas Note 5*. Austin: Center of the History and Art of Ancient American Culture, University of Texas at Austin.

1990b House Names and Dedication Rituals at Palenque. In *Vision and Revision in Maya Studies*, eds. Flora S. Clancy and Peter D. Harrison, pp. 143–157. Albuquerque: University of New Mexico Press.

1990c *Notebook for the XIVth Maya Hieroglyphic Workshop at Texas*. Austin: Art Department, University of Texas at Austin.

1990d The Palenque War Panel: Commentary on the Inscription. *Texas Note 2*. Austin: Center of the History and Art of Ancient American Culture, University of Texas at Austin.

1991a The Demotion of Chac-Zutz': Lineage Compounds and Subsidiary Lords at Palenque. In *Sixth Palenque Round Table, 1986, Vol. VIII*, ed. Virginia M. Fields, pp. 6–11. Norman: University of Oklahoma Press.

1991b An Epigraphic History of the Western Maya Region. In *Classic Maya Political History*, ed. T. Patrick Culbert, pp. 72–101. Cambridge: Cambridge University Press/School of American Research.

1991c Further Adventures with T128 ch'a. *Texas Note 9*. Austin: Center of the History and Art of Ancient American Culture, University of Texas at Austin.

1991d *Notebook for the XVth Maya Hieroglyphic Workshop at Texas*. Austin: Art Department, University of Texas at Austin.

1991e A Proposed Name for Rio Azul and a Glyph for 'Water'. *Texas Note 19*. Austin: Center of the History and Art of Ancient American Culture, University of Texas at Austin.

1991f Some Observations on the War Expressions at Tikal. *Texas Note 16*. Austin: Center of the History and Art of Ancient American Culture, University of Texas at Austin.

1992a The Founders of Lineages at Copan and Other Maya Sites. *Ancient Mesoamerica* 3(1): 135–144.

1992b A New Look at the Dynastic History of Palenque. In *Supplement to the Handbook of Middle American Indians, Vol. 5, Epigraphy*, ed. Victoria R. Bricker, pp. 82–109. Austin: University of Texas Press.

1992c *Notebook for the XVIth Maya Hieroglyphic Workshop at Texas*. Austin: Department of Art and Art History and the Institute of Latin American Studies, University of Texas at Austin.

1992d The Proceedings of the Maya Hieroglyphic Workshop, March 14–15, 1992. Transcribed and edited by Phil Wanyerka.

1993 Creation and the Ritual of the Bakabs. *Texas Note 57*. Austin: Center of the History and Art of Ancient American Culture, University of Texas at Austin.

1994a Some Thoughts on the Inscriptions of House C. *Seventh Palenque Round Table, 1989, Vol. 9*, ed. Virginia M. Fields, pp. 1–10. San Francisco: Pre-Columbian Art Research Institute.

1994b New Observations on the Oval Palace Tablet at Palenque. *Texas Note 71*. Austin: Center of the History and Art of Ancient American Culture, University of Texas at Austin.

1995a An Alternative Reading for the Sky-Penis Title. *Texas Note 69*. Austin: Center of the History and Art of Ancient American Culture, University of Texas at Austin.

1995b Sprouts and the Early Symbolism of Rulers in Mesoamerica. In *The Emergence of Lowland Maya Civilization: The Transition from the Preclassic to the Early Classic*, ed. Nikolai Grube, pp 117–135: Mockmuhl: Verlag Anton Sauerwein.

Schele, Linda, and Federico Fahsen
1991 A Substitution Pattern in Curl-Snout's Name. *Texas Note 12*. Austin: Center of the History and Art of Ancient American Culture, University of Texas at Austin.

Schele, Linda, Federico Fahsen, and Nikolai Grube
1992   El Zapote and the Dynasty of Tikal. *Texas Note 34*. Austin: Center of the History and Art of Ancient American Culture, University of Texas at Austin.

Schele, Linda, and David A. Freidel
1990   *A Forest of Kings: The Untold Story of the Ancient Maya*. New York: William Morrow and Company.
1991   The Courts of Creation: Ballcourts, Ballgames, and Portals to the Maya Otherworld. In *The Mesoamerican Ballgame*, eds. Vernon L. Scarborough and David R. Wilcox, pp. 289–315. Tucson: The University of Arizona Press.

Schele, Linda, and Nikolai Grube
1993   *Pi* as "Bundle." *Texas Note 56*. Austin: Center of the History and Art of Ancient American Culture, University of Texas at Austin.
1994a   *Notebook for the XVIIIth Maya Hieroglyphic Workshop at Texas*. Austin: Department of Art and Art History, The College of Fine Arts, The Center for Mexican Studies, and The Institute of Latin American Studies, University of Texas at Austin.
1994b   *The Proceedings of the Maya Hieroglyphic Workshop: Tlaloc-Venus Warfare, March 12–13, 1994*. Transcribed and edited by Phil Wanyerka.
1994c   Some Revision to Tikal's Dynasty of Kings. *Texas Note 67*. Austin: Center of the History and Art of Ancient American Culture, University of Texas at Austin.
1994d   Notes on the Chronology of Piedras Negras Stela 12. *Texas Note 70*. Austin: Center of the History and Art of Ancient American Culture, University of Texas at Austin.
1995a   *Notebook for the XIXth Maya Hieroglyphic Workshop at Texas*. Austin: Department of Art and Art History, The College of Fine Arts, and The Institute of Latin American Studies, University of Texas at Austin.
1995b   *Proceedings of the Maya Hieroglyphic Workshop: Late Classic and Terminal Classic Warfare, March 11–12, 1995*. Transcribed and edited by Phil Wanyerka.

Schele, Linda, Nikolai Grube, and Federico Fahsen
1992   The Lunar Series in Classic Maya Inscriptions: New Observations and Interpretations. *Texas Note 29*. Austin: Center of the History and Art of Ancient American Culture, University of Texas at Austin.

Schele, Linda, and Rudi Larios
1991   Some Venus Dates on the Hieroglyphic Stair at Copan. *Copan Note 99*. Copan, Honduras: Copan Mosaics Project and the Instituto Hondureno de Antropologia e Historia.

Schele, Linda and Matthew Looper
1996a   *Notebook for the XXth Maya Hieroglyphic Forum at Texas*. Austin: Department of Art and Art History, the College of Fine Arts, and the Institute of the Latin American Studies, University of Texas at Austin.
1996b   *Proceedings of the Maya Hieroglyphic Workshop: Copan and Quirigua, March 9–11,1996*. Transcribed and edited by Phil Wanyerka.

Schele, Linda, and Paul Mathews
1994   The Last Kings of Seibal. *Texas Note 68*. Austin: Center of the History and Art of Ancient American Culture, University of Texas at Austin.

Schele, Linda, and Peter Mathews
1979   *The Bodega of Palenque, Chiapas, Mexico*. Washington, D.C.: Dumbarton Oaks.
1983   Parentage Statements in Classic Maya Inscriptions. Unpublished manuscript.
1990   A Proposed Decipherment for Portions of Resbalon Stair 1. *Texas Note 3*. Austin: Center of the History and Art of Ancient American Culture, University of Texas at Austin.
1991   Royal Visits and Other Intersite Relationships among the Classic Maya. In *Classic Maya Political History*, ed. T. Patrick Culbert, pp. 226–252. Cambridge: Cambridge University Press/School of American Research.
1993   *Notebook for the XVIIth Maya Hieroglyphic Workshop at Texas*. Austin: The Department of Art and Art History, The College of Fine Arts, The College of Liberal Arts, and The Institute of Latin American Studies, University of Texas at Austin.

Schele, Linda, Peter Mathews, Nikolai Grube, Floyd Lounsbury, and David Kelley
1991   New Readings of Glyphs for the Month Kumk'u and Their Implications. *Texas Note 15*. Austin: Center of the History and Art of Ancient American Culture, University of Texas at Austin.

Schele, Linda, Peter Mathews, and Floyd Lounsbury
1990a   Redating the Hauberg Stela. *Texas Note 1*. Austin: Center of the History and Art of Ancient American Culture, University of Texas at Austin.

1990b Untying the Headband. *Texas Note 4*. Austin: Center of the History and Art of Ancient American Culture, University of Texas at Austin.

1990c The Nal Suffix at Palenque and Elsewhere. *Texas Note 6*. Austin: Center of the History and Art of Ancient American Culture, University of Texas at Austin.

Schele, Linda, and Jeffrey H. Miller
1983 *The Mirror, the Rabbit, and the Bundle: Accession Expressions from the Classic Maya Inscriptions*. Studies in Pre-Columbian Art and Arcaheology 25. Washington, D.C.: Dumbarton Oaks.

Schele, Linda, and Mary E. Miller
1986 *The Blood of Kings: Dynasty and Ritual in Maya Art*. Fort Worth: Kimbell Art Museum.

Schele, Linda, and Khristaan D. Villela
1991 Some New Ideas about the T713/757 'Accession' Phrases. *Texas Note 27*. Austin: Center of the History and Art of Ancient American Culture, University of Texas at Austin.

1994 The Helmet of the Chakte. *Texas Note 63*. Austin: Center of the History and Art of Ancient American Culture, University of Texas at Austin.

1996 Creation, Cosmos, and the Imagery of Palenque and Copan. In *Eighth Palenque Round Table, 1993, Vol. X*, eds. Martha J. Macri and Jan McHargue, pp. 15–30. San Francisco: Pre-Columbian Art Research Institute.

Schellhas, Paul
1904 *Representation of Deities of the Maya Manuscripts*. Papers of the Peabody Museum of Archaeology and Ethnology, Vol. 4, No. 1. Cambridge, Mass.: Harvard University.

Schlak, Arthur
1983 Moon-Ages with a Hand-Held Calculator. In *Contributions to Maya Hieroglyphic Decipherment, I*, ed. Stephen D. Houston, pp. 80–87. New Haven: Human Relations Area Files, Inc.

1989 Jaguar and Serpent Foot: Iconography as Astronomy. In *Word and Image in Maya Culture*, eds. Wm. F. Hanks and Don S. Rice, pp. 260–271. Salt Lake City: University of Utah Press.

Schuren, Ute
1992 The Yaxchilan Emblem Glyphs: Indicators of Political Change and Expansion of a Classic Maya Polity. *Mexicon* XIV(2): 30–38.

Sedat, W. David
1992 Preclassic Notation and the Development of Maya Writing. In *New Theories on the Ancient Maya*, eds. Elin C. Danien and Robert J. Sharer, pp. 81–90. Philadelphia: The University Museum, University of Pennsylvania.

Severin, G. M.
1981 *The Paris Codex: Deciphering an Astronomical Ephemeris*. Transactions of the American Philosophical Society, Vol. 71, Pt. 5. Philadelphia: American Philosophical Society.

Sharer, Robert J.
1985 Archaeology and Epigraphy Revisited: An Archaeological Enigma and the Origins of Maya Writing. *Expedition* 27(3): 16–19.

1989 The Preclassic Origins of Maya Writing: A Highland Perspective. In *Word and Image in Maya Culture*, eds. Wm. F. Hanks and Don S. Rice, pp. 165–175. Salt Lake City: University of Utah Press.

1990 *Quirigua: A Classic Maya Center & Its Sculptures*. Durham, N.C.: Carolina Academic Press.

Sharer, Robert J., and David W. Sedat
1973 Monument 1, El Porton, Guatemala, and the Development of Maya Calendrical and Writing Systems. *Contributions of the University of California Archaeological Research Facility* 18: 177–194. Berkeley: Department of Anthropology, University of California.

1987 *Archaeological Investigations in the Northern Maya Highlands, Guatemala*. Philadelphia: The University of Pennsylvania Museum.

Shook, Edwin M.
1960 Tikal Stela 29. *Expedition* 2(2): 28–35.

Simpson, Jon Erik
1976 The New York Relief Panel and Some Associations with Reliefs at Palenque and Elsewhere, Part I. In *The Art, Iconography and Dynastic History of Palenque, Part III (Segunda Mesa Redonda de Palenque, 1974)*, ed. Merle Greene Robertson, pp. 95–105. Pebble Beach, Calif.: The Robert Louis Stevenson School.

Sosa, John R., and Dorie J. Reentz
1980 Glyphic Evidence for Classic Maya Militarism. *Belizean Studies* 8(3): 2–11.

Spero, Joanne M.
1991 Beyond Rainstorms: The Kawak as an Ancestor, Warrior, and Patron of Witchcraft. In *Sixth Palenque Round Table, 1986, Vol. VIII*,

ed. Virginia M. Fields, pp. 184–193. Norman: University of Oklahoma Press.

Spero, Joanne M., and Justin Kerr
1994   Glyphic Names of Animals on Codex-Style Vases. In *Seventh Palenque Round Table, 1989, Vol. IX*, ed. Virginia M. Fields, pp. 145–155. San Francisco: Pre-Columbian Art Research Institute.

Spetzler, Cheyenne
1989a   The Maya Altar Ego. *U Mut Maya II*, eds. Tom Jones and Carolyn Young, pp. 105–109. Arcata, California: Tom Jones and Carolyn Young.
1989b   The Texts of Tikal's Ruler B: A Structure and Commentary. *U Mut Maya II*, eds. Tom Jones and Carolyn Young, pp. 121–130. Arcata, California: Tom Jones and Carolyn Young.

Spetzler, Cheyenne, and Carolyn Jones
1992   The Caracol Emblem Glyph. *U Mut Maya IV*, eds. Tom and Carolyn Jones, pp. 143–148. Arcata, California: Tom and Carolyn Jones.

Stearns, Steve
1989   How High the Moon - Yax Pac's Ephemeris for Copan. *U Mut Maya II*, eds. Tom Jones and Carolyn Young, pp. 41–45. Arcata, California: Tom Jones and Carolyn Young.

Stirling, Mathew W.
1940   An Initial Series from Tres Zapotes, Veracruz, Mexico. *Contributed Technical Papers Mexican Archaeological Series* 1(1). Washington, D.C.: National Geographic Society.

Stone, Andrea J.
1982   Recent Discoveries from Naj Tunich. *Mexicon* IV(5/6): 93–99.
1983   Epigraphic Patterns in the Inscriptions of Naj Tunich Cave. *Contributions to Maya Hieroglyphic Decipherment, I*, ed. Stephen D. Houston, pp. 88–103. New Haven: Human Relations Area Files, Inc.
1985   The Moon Goddess at Naj Tunich. *Mexicon* VII(2): 23–30.
1989   Disconnection, Foreign Insignia, and Political Expansion: Teotihuacan and the Warrior Stelae of Piedras Negras. In *Mesoamerica after the Decline of Teotihuacan A.D. 700–900*, eds. Richard A. Diehl and Janet Catherine Berlo, pp. 153–172. Washington, D.C.: Dumbarton Oaks.
1995   A Catalog of Naj Tunich Paintings and Petroglyphs. Chapter 8 in *Images from the Underworld: Naj Tunich and the Tradition of Maya Cave Painting* (by Andrea Stone). Austin: Uni-

versity of Texas Press.
1996   The Cleveland Plaque: Cloudy Places of the Maya Realm. In *Eighth Palenque Round Table, 1993, Vol. X*, eds. Martha J. Macri and Jan McHargue, pp. 403–412. San Francisco: Pre-Columbian Art Research Institute.

Stone, Andrea, Dorie Reents, and Robert Coffman
1985   Genealogical Documentation of the Middle Classic Dynasty of Caracol, El Cayo, Belize. In *Fourth Palenque Round Table, 1980, Vol. VI*, ed. Elizabeth P. Benson, pp. 267–275. San Francisco: Pre-Columbian Art Research Institute.

Stross, Brian
1986   Some Observations on T585(Quincunx) of the Maya Script. *Anthropological Linguistics* 28(3): 283–311.
1988   The Burden of Office: A Reading. *Mexicon* X(6): 118–121.
1992a   Genital Iconography in Landa's Alphabet. *U Mut Maya IV*, eds. Tom and Carolyn Jones, pp. 117–126. Arcata, California: Tom and Carolyn Jones.
1992b   Earflare in a Classic Maya Name. *U Mut Maya IV*, eds. Tom and Carolyn Jones, pp. 275–282. Arcata, California: Tom and Carolyn Jones.
1993   The Man in the *Maw*, an Olmec *Way* in the Sky. *Texas Note 43*. Austin.: Center of the History and Art of Ancient American Culture, University of Texas at Austin
1994a   Glyphs on Classic Maya Vessels: The Introductory Formula of the Primary Standard Sequence. In *Seventh Palenque Round Table, 1989, Vol. IX*, ed. Virginia M. Fields, pp. 187–193. San Francisco: Pre-Columbian Art Research Institute.
1994b   Maya Creation: A Shamanic Perspective. *U Mut Maya V*, eds. Carolyn and Tom Jones, pp. 159–170. Arcata, California: Tom and Carolyn Jones.

Stross, Brian, and Justin Kerr
1990   Notes on the Maya Vision Quest Through Enema. In *The Maya Vase Book*, Vol. 2 (by Justin Kerr), pp. 348–361. New York: Kerr Associates.

Stuart, David
1979   Some Thoughts on Certain Occurrences of the T565 Glyph Element at Palenque. In *Tercera Mesa Redonda de Palenque, 1978, Vol. IV*, eds. Merle Greene Robertson and Donnan C. Jeffers, pp. 167–171. Palenque, Chiapas, Mexico: Pre-Columbian Art Research Institute.

1984a   A Note on the 'Hand-Scattering' Glyph. In *Phoneticism in Mayan Hieroglyphic Writing*, eds. John S. Justeson and Lyle Campbell, pp. 307–310. Albany: Institute for Mesoamerican Studies, State University of New York at Albany. Publ. 9.

1984b   Royal Auto-Sacrifice among the Maya: A Study of Image and Meaning. *RES* 7/8: 6–20.

1985a   The 'Count-of-Captives' Epithet in Classic Maya Writing. In *Fifth Palenque Round Table, 1983, Vol. VII*, ed. Virginia M. Fields, pp. 97–101. San Francisco: Pre-Columbian Art Research Institute.

1985b   The Inscription on Four Shell Plaques from Piedras Negras, Guatemala. In *Fourth Palenque Round Table, 1980, Vol. VI*, ed. Elizabeth P. Benson, pp. 175–183. San Francisco: Pre-Columbian Art Research Institute.

1985c   A New Child-Father Relationship Glyph. *Research Reports on Ancient Maya Writing* 2. Washington, D.C.: Center for Maya Research.

1985d   The Yaxha Emblem Glyph as Yax-ha. *Research Reports on Ancient Maya Writing* 1. Washington, D.C.: Center for Maya Research.

1986   The 'Lu-bat' Glyph and Its Bearing on the Primary Standard Sequence. Presented at The Primer Simposio Mundial Sobre Epigrafia Maya, a conference held in Guatemala City, August, 1986.

1987a   Ten Phonetic Syllables. *Research Reports on Ancient Maya Writing* 14. Washington, D.C.: Center for Maya Research.

1987b   A Variant of the chak Sign. *Research Reports on Ancient Maya Writing* 10. Washington, D.C.: Center for Maya Research.

1988a   Blood Symbolism in Maya Iconography. In *Maya Iconography*, eds. Elizabeth P. Benson and Gillett G. Griffin, pp. 175–221. Princeton: Princeton University Press.

1988b   The Rio Azul Cacao Pot: Epigraphic Observation on the Function of a Maya Ceramic Vessel. *Antiquity* 62(234): 153–157.

1989a   Hieroglyphs on Maya Vessels. In *The Maya Vase Book*, Vol. 1 (by Justin Kerr), pp. 149–160. New York: Kerr Associates.

1989b   Kinship Terms in Maya Inscriptions. Paper presented at The Language of Maya Hieroglyphs, a conference held at the University of California at Santa Barbara, February 18–19, 1989

1989c   The Epigraphic Record of the Late Classic Maya. Talk given at Dumbarton Oaks, October 8, 1989.

1990a   The Decipherment of 'Directional Count Glyphs' in Maya Inscriptions. *Ancient Mesoamerica* 1(2): 213–224.

1990b   A New Carved Panel from the Palenque Area. *Research Reports on Ancient Maya Writing* 32. Washington, D.C.: Center for Maya Research.

1992   Hieroglyphs and Archaeology at Copan. *Ancient Mesoamerica* 3(1): 169–184.

1993   Historical Inscriptions and the Maya Collapse. In *Lowland Maya Civilization in the Eighth Century A.D.*, eds. Jeremy A. Sabloff and John S. Henderson, pp. 321–354. Washington, D.C.: Dumbarton Oaks.

Stuart, David, and Stephen Houston
1989   Maya Writing. *Scientific American*, August, 1989, pp. 82–89.

1994   Classic Maya Place Names. *Studies in Pre-Columbian Art and Archaeology*, No. 33. Washington, D.C.: Dumbarton Oaks.

Stuart, George
1988   Glyph Drawings from Landa's Relacion: A Caveat to the Investigator. *Research Reports on Ancient Maya Writing* 19. Washington, D.C.: Center for Maya Research.

1989a   The Beginning of Maya Hieroglyphic Study: Contributions of Constantine S. Rafinesque and James H. McCulloh, Jr. *Research Reports on Ancient Maya Writing* 29. Washington, D.C.: Center for Maya Research.

1989b   The Hieroglyphic Record of Chichen Itza and Its Neighbors. Introduction to *Research Reports on Ancient Maya Writing* 23–25. Washington, D.C.: Center for Maya Research.

1992   Quest for Decipherment: A Historical and Biographical Survey of Maya Hieroglyphic Investigation. In *New Theories on the Ancient Maya*, eds. Elin C. Danien and Robert J. Sharer, pp. 1–63. Philadelphia: The University of Pennsylvania Museum.

1993   The Carved Stela from La Mojarra, Veracruz, Mexico. *Science* 259(5102): 1700–1701.

Taack, George H.
1976   Accession Glyphs on Maya Monuments; A Linguistic Approach. *Anthropological Linguistics* 18(1); 29–52.

Tate, Carolyn
1985a   The Carved Ceramics Called Chochola. In *Fifth Palenque Round Table, 1983, Vol. VII*, ed. Virginia M. Fields, pp. 123–133. San Francisco: Pre-Columbian Art Research Institute.

1985b   Summer Solstice Ceremonies Performed by Bird Jaguar III of Yaxchilan, Chiapas, Mexico. *Estudios de Cultura Maya* XVI: 85–112.

1986   Maya Astronomical Rituals Recorded on Yaxchilan Structure 23. *The Rutgers Art Review* 7: 1–20.

1989The Use of Astronomy in Political Statements at Yaxchilan, Mexico. In *World Archaeoastronomy*, ed. Anthony F. Aveni, pp. 416–429. Cambridge: Cambridge University Press.

1991The Period-Ending Stelae of Yaxchilan. In *Sixth Palenque Round Table, 1986, Vol. VIII*, ed. Virginia M. Fields, pp. 102–109. Norman: University of Oklahoma Press.

1992*Yaxchilan: The Design of a Maya Ceremonial City*. Austin: University of Texas Press.

1994*Ah Ts'ib*: Scribal Hands and Sculpture Workshops at Yaxchilan. In *Seventh Palenque Round Table, 1989, Vol.9*, ed. Virginia M. Fields, pp. 95–103. San Francisco: Pre-Columbian Art Research Institute.

Taube, Karl
1985The Classic Maya Maize God: A Reappraisal. In *Fifth Palenque Round Table, 1983, Vol. VII*, ed. Virginia M. Fields, pp. 171–181. San Francisco: Pre-Columbian Art Research Institute.

1987A Representation of the Principal Bird Deity in the Paris Codex. *Research Reports on Ancient Maya Writing* 6. Washington, D.C.: Center for Maya Research.

1992*The Major Gods of Ancient Yucatan*. Studies in Pre-Columbian Art and Archaeology, No. 32. Washington, D.C.: Dumbarton Oaks.

1994The Birth Vase: Natal Imagery in Ancient Maya Myth and Ritual. In *The Maya Vase Book*, Vol. 4, eds. Barbara Kerr and Justin Kerr, pp. 650–685. New York: Kerr Associates.

Taube, Karl A., and Bonnie L. Bade
1991An Appearance of Xuihtecuhtli in the Dresden Venus Pages. Research *Reports on Ancient Maya Writing* 35. Washington D.C.: Center for Maya Research.

Taylor, Dicey
1992Toponyms for Plazas in Maya Cities. *U Mut Maya IV*, eds. Tom and Carolyn Jones, pp. 127–131. Arcata, California: Tom and Carolyn Jones.

Tedlock, Barbara
1992*Time and the Highland Maya* (Revised Edition). Albuquerque: University of New Mexico Press.

Tedlock, Dennis
1990Drums, Egrets, and the Mother of the Gods: Remarks on the Tablet of the Cross at Palenque. *U Mut Maya III*, eds. Tom and Carolyn Jones, pp. 13–14. Arcata, California: Tom and Carolyn Jones.

1992aMyth, Math, and the Problem of Correlation in Mayan Books. In *The Sky in Mayan Literature*, ed. Anthony F. Aveni, pp. 247–273. New York: Oxford University Press.

1992bOn Hieroglyphic Literacy in Ancient Mayaland: An Alternative Interpretation. *Current Anthropology* 33(2): 216–218.

1992cThe Popol Vuh as a Hieroglyphic Book. In *New Theories on the Ancient Maya*, eds. Elin C. Danien and Robert J. Sharer, pp. 229–240. Philadelphia: The University Museum, University of Pennsylvania.

Thomas, Cyrus
1892aKey to Mayan Hieroglyphs. *Science* 20: 44–46.

1892bIs the Maya Hieroglyphic Writing Phonetic? *Science* 20: 197–201.

1893Are the Maya Hieroglyphs Phonetic? *American Anthropologist* 6: 241–270.

1904Central American Hieroglyphic Writing. In *Smithsonian Institution Annual Report for 1903*: 705–721. Washington D.C.: Smithsonian Institution.

Thompson, J. Eric S.
1943aThe Initial Series of Stela 14, Piedras Negras, Guatemala, and a Date on Stela 19, Naranjo, Guatemala. In *Notes on Middle American Archaeology and Ethnology I*, pp. 113–116. Cambridge, Mass.: Carnegie Institution of Washington, Division of Historical Research.

1943bMaya Epigraphy: Directional Glyphs in Counting. In *Notes on Middle American Archaeology and Ethnology* 1: 122–126. Cambridge, Mass.: Carnegie Institution of Washington, Division of Historical Research.

1944The Fish as a Maya Symbol for Counting. In *Theoretical Approaches to Problems No. 2*. Cambridge, Mass.: Carnegie Institution of Washington, Division of Historical Research.

1945The Inscriptions on the Altar of Zoomorph O, Quirigua. In *Notes on Middle American Archaeology and Ethnology, 2*, pp. 189–199. Cambridge, Mass.: Carnegie Institution of Washington, Division of Historical Research.

1950*Maya Hieroglyphic Writing: An Introduction*. Washington, D.C.: Carnegie Institution of Washington. Publ. 589. [Reprinted in new editions, 1960, 1973, by the University of Oklahoma Press, Norman]

1959Systems of Hieroglyphic Writing in Middle America and Methods of Deciphering Them. *American Antiquity* 24(4): pp. 349–64.

1962*A Catalog of Maya Hieroglyphs*. Norman: University of Oklahoma Press.

1965Maya Hieroglyphic Writing. In *Handbook of Middle American Indians Volume 3*, vol. ed. Gordon R. Willey, gen. ed. Robert Wauchope, pp. 632–658. Austin: University of Texas Press.

1972a *A Commentary on the Dresden Codex.* Philadelphia: American Philosophical Society.
1972b *Maya Hieroglyphs Without Tears.* London: British Museum.

Tolman, Cal
1988 Linguistic Evidence for Pa Glyph Used in Groundbreaking and/or Construction Events. *U Mut Maya*, eds. Tom Jones and Carolyn Young, pp. 37. Arcata, California: Tom Jones.

Tozzer, Alfred M.
1941 *Landa's Relacion de la Cosas de Yucatan.* Papers of the Peabody Museum of American Archaeology and Ethnology, Vol. 18. Cambridge, Mass.: Harvard University.

Tuckerman, Bryant
1964 *Planetary, Lunar, and Solar Positions, A.D. 2 to A.D. 1649, at Five-Day and Ten-Day Intervals.* Philadelphia: The American Philosophical Society.

Turner, Paul, and Shirley Turner
1971 *Dictionary: Chontal to Spanish-English, Spanish to Chontal.* Tucson: The University of Arizona Press.

Ulrich, E. Matheo, and Rosemary D. de Ulrich
1976 *Diccionario Maya Mopan-Espanol/Espanol-Maya Mopan.* Guatemala: Instituto Linguistico de Verano.

Urban, Patricia A.
1992 A Partial Solution to the Dating Problem of Tikal Stela 10. *U Mut Maya IV*, eds. Tom and Carolyn Jones, pp. 69–75. Arcata, California: Tom and Carolyn Jones.

Urcid, Javier
1993 Bones and Epigraphy: The Accurate Versus the Fictitious? *Texas Note 42.* Austin: Center of the History and Art of Ancient American Culture, University of Texas at Austin.

Valdes, Juan Antonio, and Federico Fahsen
1995 *The Reigning Dynasty of Uaxactun During the Early Classic.* Ancient Mesoamerica 6(2): 197–219.

Van Akkeren, Ruud W.
1995 The Scorpion and the Turtle. *Texas Note 73.* Austin: Center of the History and Art of Ancient American Culture, University of Texas at Austin.

Villacorta C., J. Antonio, and Carlos A. Villacorta
1977 *Codices Mayas* (2nd ed.). Guatemala City: Tipografia Nacional.

Villela, Khristaan D.
1991a The Death of Lady Wak Chan Tzuk of Naranjo Recorded at Dos Pilas. *Texas Note 18.* Austin: Center of the History and Art of Ancient American Culture, University of Texas at Austin.
1991b Early Notices on the Maya Paddler Gods. *Texas Note 17.* Austin: Center of the History and Art of Ancient American Culture, University of Texas at Austin.
1993a A New Curl–Snout Event on the Hombre de Tikal. *Texas Note 39.* Austin: Center of the History and Art of Ancient American Culture, University of Texas at Austin.
1993b Parallel Throne Phrases at Tikal and Palenque. Texas Note 40. Austin: Center of the History and Art of Ancient American Culture, University of Texas at Austin.
1993c Quirigua Zoomorph P and Three 'Stones of Creation.' *Texas Note 59.* Austin: Center of the History and Art of Ancient American Culture, University of Texas at Austin.

Villela, Khristaan D., and Rex Koontz
1993 A Nose Piercing Ceremony in the North Temple of the Great Ballcourt at Chichen Itza. *Texas Note 41.* Austin: Center of the History and Art of Ancient American Culture, University of Texas at Austin.

Villela, Khristaan D., and Linda Schele
1996 Astronomy and the Iconography of Creation Among the Classic and Colonial Period Maya. In *Eighth Palenque Round Table, 1993, Vol. X*, eds. Martha J. Macri and Jan McHargue, pp. 31–44. San Francisco: Pre-Columbian Art Research Institute.

Von Winning, Hasso
1981 An Iconographic Link between Teotihuacan and Palenque. *Mexicon* III(2): 30–32.

Wagner, Elisabeth
1995 The Dates of the High Priest Grave ("Osario") Inscription, Chichen Itza, Yucatan. *Mexicon* XVII(1): 10–13.

Wald, Robert F.
1992 The Inheritance of Shield Jaguar I: The Program of Yaxchilan Structure 44. *U Mut Maya IV*, eds. Tom and Carolyn Jones, pp. 209–241. Arcata, California: Tom and Carolyn Jones.

Walker, Debra Selsor
  1990   The Primary Standard Sequence on a Sample of Maya Vessels. *U Mut Maya III*, eds. Tom and Carolyn Jones, pp. 147–166. Arcata, California: Tom and Carolyn Jones.

Wanyerka, Phil
  1990   The East Panel of the Temple of the Inscriptions. *U Mut Maya III*, eds. Tom and Carolyn Jones, pp. 1–4. Arcata, California: Tom and Carolyn Jones.
  1996   The Carved Monuments of Uxbenka, Toledo District, Belize. *Mexicon* XVIII(2): 29–36.

Webster, David
  1989   The Original Location, Date, and Possible Implications of Altar W'. In *The House of the Bacabs, Studies in Precolumbian Art and Archaeology* 29, ed. David Webster, pp. 108–111. Washington, D.C.: Dumbarton Oaks.

Weisbrod, Richard L.
  1987   Data Representation for a Maya Hieroglyphic Data Base System. In *The Periphery of the Southeastern Classic Maya Realm*, ed. Gary W. Pahl, pp. 115–133. Los Angeles: UCLA Latin American Studies, Vol. 61, UCLA Latin American Center.

Whittaker, Gordon
  1986   The Mexican Names of Three Venus Gods in the Dresden Codex. *Mexicon* VIII(3): 56–60.

Whorf, Benjamin L.
  1933   The Phonetic Value of Certain Characters in Maya Writing. In *Papers of the Peabody Museum of American Archaeology and Ethnology*, Vol. 13(2). Cambridge, Mass.: Harvard University.

Williamson, Richard
  1996   Excavations, Interpretations, and Implications of the Earliest Structures Beneath Structure 10L-26 at Copan, Honduras. In *Eighth Palenque Round Table, 1993, Vol. X*, eds. Martha J. Macri and Jan McHargue, pp. 169–175. San Francisco: Pre-Columbian Art Research Institute.

Wilson, R. W.
  1924   Astronomical Notes on the Maya Codices. In *Papers of the Peabody Museum of American Archaeology and Ethnology* 6(3). Cambridge, Mass.: Harvard University.

Winfield Capitaine, Fernando
  1988   La estela 1 de la Mojarra, Veracruz, Mexico. *Research Reports on Ancient Maya Writing* 16. Washington, D.C.: Center for Maya Research.

Winters, Diane
  1991   A Study of the Fish-in-Hand Glyph, T714: Part 1. In *Sixth Palenque Round Table, 1986, Vol. VIII*, ed. Virginia M. Fields, pp. 233–245. Norman: University of Oklahoma Press.

Wren, Linnea H.
  1991   The Great Ball Court Stone from Chichen Itza. In *Sixth Palenque Round Table, 1986, Vol. VIII*, ed. Virginia M. Fields, pp. 51–58. Norman: University of Oklahoma Press.

Wren, Linnea, and Lynn Foster
  1992   Familial and Titular Patterns in the Inscriptions of Chichen Itza. *U Mut Maya IV*, eds. Tom and Carolyn Jones, pp. 161–167. Arcata, California: Tom and Carolyn Jones.

Wren, Linnea, Ruth Krochock, Erik Boot, Lynn Foster, Peter Keeler, Rex Koontz, and Walter Wakefield
  1994   Maya Creation and Re-Creation in the Art, Architecture and Inscriptions of Chichen Itza. *U Mut Maya V*, eds. Carolyn and Tom Jones, pp. 171–189. Arcata, California: Tom and Carolyn Jones.

Wren, Linnea H., and Peter Schmidt
  1991   Elite Interaction During the Terminal Classic Period: New Evidence from Chichen Itza. In *Classic Maya Political History*, ed. T. Patrick Culbert, pp. 199–225. Cambridge: Cambridge University Press/School of American Research.

Wren, Linnea H., Peter Schmidt, and Ruth Krochock
  1989   The Great Ball Court Stone of Chichen Itza. *Research Reports on Ancient Maya Writing* 25. Washington, D.C.: Center for Maya Research.

Yaeger, Jason
  1988   A Report of the Research Done on the Tablet of the Foliated Cross. *U Mut Maya*, eds. Tom Jones and Carolyn Young, pp. 25–26. Arcata, California: Tom Jones.

Yasugi, Yoshiho, and Kenji Saito
  1991   Glyph Y of the Maya Supplementary Series. *Research Reports on Ancient Maya Writing* 34. Washington, D.C.: Center for Maya Research.

Young, Carolyn
  1988   The Titles of Yax Pac (Copan). *U Mut Maya*,

eds. Tom Jones and Carolyn Young, pp. 47–59. Arcata, California: Tom Jones.

COPAN NOTES

Copan Notes are a running series of commentaries and small reports deriving from the multidisciplinary research project currently being carried out at Copan. They are published by the Copan Acropolis Project and the Instituto Hondureno de Antropologia e Historia.

Copan Note 1
Te-Tun as the Glyph for "Stela," by Linda Schele and David Stuart (1986)

Copan Note 2
A Glyph for "Stone Incensario," by David Stuart (1986)

Copan Note 3
The Chronology of Altar U, by Linda Schele and David Stuart (1986)

Copan Note 4
The Hieroglyphic Name of Altar U, by David Stuart (1986)

Copan Note 5
Paraphrase of the Text of Altar U, by Linda Schele (1986)

Copan Note 6
Yax-K'uk'-Mo', the Founder of the Lineage of Copan, by David Stuart and Linda Schele (1986)

Copan Note 7
The "First Ruler" on Stela 24, by David Stuart (1989)

Copan Note 8
The Founders of Lineages at Copan and Other Maya Sites, by Linda Schele (1986)

Copan Note 9
Substitution in the Emblem Glyph of Copan, by David Stuart [in preparation]

Copan Note 10
The Protagonist of Altars G, U and T, by David Stuart [in preparation]

Copan Note 11
Thoughts on the Temple Inscription from Structure 26, by David Stuart (1986)

Copan Note 12
The Chronology of Stela 4 at Copan, by David Stuart (1986)

Copan Note 13
The Figures on the Central Marker of Ballcourt AIIb at Copan, by Linda Schele (1987)

Copan Note 14
Butz'-Chaan, the 11th Successor of the Yax-K'uk'-Mo' Lineage, by Linda Schele and David Stuart (1986)

Copan Note 15
Moon-Jaguar, the 10th Successor of the Lineage of Yax-K'uk'-Mo' of Copan, by Linda Schele (1986)

Copan Note 16
Waterlily-Jaguar, the Seventh Successor of the Lineage of Yax-K'uk'-Mo', by Linda Schele and David Stuart (1986)

Copan Note 17
Interim Report on the Hieroglyphic Stair of Structure 26, by David Stuart and Linda Schele (1986)

Copan Note 18
The Step Inscription of Temple 22 at Copan, by David Stuart (1986)

Copan Note 19
Interim Report on the Iconography of the Architectural Sculpture of Temple 22, by Linda Schele (1986)

Copan Note 20
The Brother of Yax-Pac, by Linda Schele and Nikolai Grube (1987)

Copan Note 21
U Cit-Tok, the Last King of Copan, by Nikolai Grube and Linda Schele (1987)

Copan Note 22
The Birth Monument of Butz'-Chaan, by Linda Schele and Nikolai Grube (1987)

Copan Note 23
The Date on the Bench from Structure 9N-82, Sepulturas, Copan, Honduras, by Nikolai Grube and Linda Schele (1987)

Copan Note 24
The Figures on the Legs of the Scribe's Bench, by Linda Schele (1987)

Copan Note 25
Some Ideas of the Protagonist and Dating of Stela E, by Linda Schele (1987)

Copan Note 26
A Possible Death Date for Smoke-Imix-God K, by Linda Schele (1987)

Copan Note 27
A Brief Commentary on a Hieroglyphic Cylinder from Copan, by Linda Schele (1987)

Copan Note 28
Wan, the "Standing-up" of Stela A, by Linda Schele (1987)

Copan Note 29
New Data on the Paddlers from Butz'-Chaan of Copan, by Linda Schele (1987)

Copan Note 30
Stela I and the Founding of the City of Copan, by Linda Schele (1987)

Copan Note 31
The Inscription on Stela 5 and Its Altar, by Linda Schele (1987)

Copan Note 32
The Reviewing Stand of Temple 11, by Linda Schele (1987)

Copan Note 33
The Surviving Fragments of Stela 9, by Linda Schele (1987)

Copan Note 34
A Cached Jade from Temple 26 and the World Tree at Copan, by Linda Schele (1987)

Copan Note 35
The Dedication of Structure 2 and a New Form of the God N Event, by Linda Schele (1987)

Copan Note 36
Two Altar Names at Copan, by Linda Schele (1987)

Copan Note 37
Notes on the Rio Amarillo Altars, by Linda Schele (1987)

Copan Note 38
New Fits on the North Panel of the West Doorway of Temple 11, by Linda Schele (1987)

Copan Note 39
The Father of Smoke-Shell, by Linda Schele and Nikolai Grube (1988)

Copan Note 40
Cu-Ix, the Fourth Ruler of Copan and His Monuments, by Nikolai Grube and Linda Schele (1988)

Copan Note 41
A Venus Title on Copan Stela F, by Nikolai Grube and Linda Schele (1988)

Copan Note 42
The Future Marker on a Hand Scattering Verb at Copan, by Linda Schele and Nikolai Grube (1988)

Copan Note 43
A Quadrant Tree at Copan, by Nikolai Grube and Linda Schele (1988)

Copan Note 44
Stela 13 and the East Quadrant of Copan, by Linda Schele and Nikolai Grube (1988)

Copan Note 45
Revisions to the Dynastic Chronology of Copan, by Linda Schele (1988)

Copan Note 46
Altar F' and the Structure 32, by Linda Schele (1988)

Copan Note 47
The 260-Day Periods on Stelae A and 3, by Helen Alexander (1988)

Copan Note 48
A Suggested Reading Order for Stela 6 at Copan, by Mary McCready, Barbara MacLeod, Vito Veliz, Peter Keeler, and Ruth Krochock (1988)

Copan Note 49
Renaming a Copan King: Phonetic Evidence for a More Accurate Rendering of the Name "Smoke-Imix-God K," by Barbara MacLeod (1988)

Copan Note 50
The "Ninth Child of the Lineage": An Alternative Dynastic Reference to Moon-Jaguar on Stela 9 at Copan, by Barbara MacLeod (1988)

Copan Note 51
A House Dedication on the Harvard Bench at Copan, by Linda Schele (1989)

Copan Note 52
The Text of Altar F': Further Considerations, by Barbara MacLeod (1989)

Copan Note 53
A New Glyph for "Five" on Stela E, by Linda Schele (1989)

Copan Note 54
A Note on the Copan Emblem Glyph, by Brian Stross (1989)

Copan Note 55
A Primary Standard Sequence on Copan Altar K, by Nikolai Grube and Barbara MacLeod (1989)

Copan Note 56
Stela 63, a New Monument from Copan, by David Stuart, Nikolai Grube, Linda Schele, and Floyd Lounsbury (1989)

Copan Note 57
A New Inscription from Temple 22a at Copan, by Linda Schele, David Stuart, Nikolai Grube, and Floyd Lounsbury (1989)

Copan Note 58
A Substitution Set for the "Ma Cuch/Batab" Title, by David Stuart, Nikolai Grube, and Linda Schele (1989)

Copan Note 59
The Date of Dedication of Ballcourt III at Copan, by Linda Schele, Nikolai Grube, and David Stuart (1989)

Copan Note 60
A Possible Death Reference for Yax-K'uk'-Mo', by Nikolai Grube, David Stuart, and Linda Schele (1989)

Copan Note 61
A New Alternative for the Date of the Sepulturas Bench, by David Stuart, Nikolai Grube, and Linda Schele (1989)

Copan Note 62
A Mention of 18 Rabbit on the Temple 11 Reviewing Stand, by David Stuart, Linda Schele, and Nikolai Grube (1989)

Copan Note 63
Comments on the Temple 22 Inscription, by David Stuart (1989)

Copan Note 64
A Commentary on the Restoration and Reading of the Glyphic Panels from Temple 11, by Linda Schele, David Stuart, and Nikolai Grube (1989)

Copan Note 65
The Numbered-Katun Titles of Yax-Pac, by Linda Schele (1989)

Copan Note 66
A Brief Commentary on the Top of Altar Q, by Linda Schele (1989)

Copan Note 67
Some Further Thoughts on the Quirigua-Copan Connection, by Linda Schele (1989)

Copan Note 68
A Reference to Water-Lily Jaguar on Caracol Stela 16, by Linda Schele (1990)

Copan Note 69
"End of" Expressions at Copan and Palenque, by Linda Schele (1990)

Copan Note 70
The Early Classic Dynastic History of Copan: Interim Report 1989, by Linda Schele (1990)

Copan Note 71
The Glyph of "Hole" and the Skeletal Maw of the Underworld, by Linda Schele (1990)

Copan Note 72
Preliminary Commentary on a New Altar from Structure 30, by Linda Schele (1990)

Copan Note 73
Further Comments on Stela 6, by Linda Schele (1990)

Copan Note 74
A New Fragment from Altar J', by Linda Schele (1990)

Copan Note 75
Early Quirigua and the Kings of Copan, by Linda Schele (1990)

Copan Note 76
The Dedication Stair of "Ante" Temple, by Alfonso Morales, Julie Miller, and Linda Schele (1990)

Copan Note 77
Brothers and Others: New Insights From "New" Incensarios, by Sandy Bardsley (1990)

Copan Note 78
A New Fragment from Structure 22-6th at Copan, Honduras, by Linda Schele and Alfonso Morales (1990)

Copan Note 79
Some Thoughts on Two Jade Pendants from the Termination Cache of "Ante" Structure at Copan, by Linda Schele and Alfonso Morales (1990)

Copan Note 80
Speculations from an Epigrapher on Things Archaeological in the Acropolis at Copan, by Linda Schele (1990)

Copan Note 81
Lounsbury's Contrived Numbers and Two 8 Eb Dates at Copan, by Linda Schele (1990)

Copan Note 82
Two Early Classic Monuments from Copan, by Nikolai Grube and Linda Schele (1990)

Copan Note 83
Six-Staired Ballcourts, by Linda Schele and Nikolai Grube (1990)

Copan Note 84
A Tentative Identification of the Second Successor of the Copan Dynasty, by Linda Schele and Nikolai Grube (1990)

Copan Note 85
A New Interpretation of the Temple 18 Jambs, by Nikolai Grube and Linda Schele (1990)

Copan Note 86
The Glyph for Plaza or Court, by Linda Schele and Nikolai Grube (1990)

Copan Note 87
Royal Gifts to Subordinate Lords, by Nikolai Grube and Linda Schele (1990)

Copan Note 88
A Suggested Reading Order for the West Side of Stela J, by Linda Schele and Nikolai Grube (1990)

Copan Note 89
Commentary on Altar G', by Linda Schele (1990)

Copan Note 90
A Possible Death Statement for 18-Rabbit, by Linda Schele (1990)

Copan Note 91
Two Examples of the Glyph for "Step" from the Hieroglyphic Stairs, by Nikolai Grube and Linda Schele (1990)

Copan Note 92
Building, Court, and Mountain Names in the Text of the Hieroglyphic Stairs, by Linda Schele and Nikolai Grube (1990)

Copan Note 93
A Preliminary Inventory of Place Names in the Copan Inscriptions, by Linda Schele and Nikolai Grube (1990)

Copan Note 94
A Scribe on Stela 63 at Copan, by Justin Kerr (1991)

Copan Note 95
The Name of Copan and of a Dance at Yaxchilan, by Matthew G. Looper (1991)

Copan Note 96
Taking the Headband at Copan, by Linda Schele and Elizabeth Newsome (1991)

Copan Note 97
A New Assessment of Smoke Monkey, the 14th Successor in the Line of Yax-K'uk'-Mo', by Linda Schele and Barbara Fash (1991)

Copan Note 98
A Commentary on the Inscriptions of Structure 10L-22A at Copan, by Linda Schele, David Stuart, and Nikolai Grube (1991)

Copan Note 99
Some Venus Dates on the Hieroglyphic Stairs at Copan, by Linda Schele and Rudi Larios (1991)

Copan Note 100
Venus and the Reign of Smoke-Monkey, by Linda Schele and Barbara Fash (1991)

Copan Note 101
Venus and the Monuments of Smoke-Imix-God K and Others in the Great Plaza, by Linda Schele (1991)

Copan Note 102
Speculations on Who Built the Temple Under 11, by Linda Schele and Nikolai Grube (1991)

Copan Note 103
Another Look at Stela 11, by Linda Schele (1991)

Copan Note 104
The Initial Series Dates on Stelae 2 and 12, by Linda Schele (1992)

Copan Note 105
New Information on the Earlier Date on the Ante Stair, by Linda Schele and Nikolai Grube (1992)

Copan Note 106
Yet Another Look at Stela 11, by Nikolai Grube and Linda Schele (1992)

Copan Note 107
The Founding Events at Copan, by Linda Schele and Nikolai Grube (1992)

Copan Note 108
Venus, the Great Plaza, and Recalling the Dead, by Linda Schele and Nikolai Grube (1992)

Copan Note 109
·*Ceiba Flower Titles at Copan*, by Khristaan D. Villela (1993)

Copan Note 110
Daughter of "Yet Another Look at Stela 11," by Barbara MacLeod (1993)

Copan Note 111
A Reexamination of U-Yak'-Chak, by Linda Schele (1993)

Copan Note 112
A Possible Birth Statement for Waxaklahun-U-Bah-K'awil, by Elisabeth Wagner (1994)

Copan Note 113
The Xukpi Stone: A Newly Discovered Early Classic Inscription from the Copan Acropolis, Pt. I: The Archaeology, by David W. Sedat and Robert J. Sharer (1994)

Copan Note 114
The Xukpi Stone: A Newly Discovered Early Classic Inscription from the Copan Acropolis, Pt. II: Commentary on the Text (Version 2), by Linda Schele, Nikolai Grube, and Federico Fahsen (1994)

Copan Note 115
The 9.17.0.0.0 Eclipse at Quirigua and Copan, by Linda Schele and Matthew Looper (1994)

Copan Note 116
Who was Popol-K'inich? A Re-evaluation of the Second Successor in the Line of Yax K'uk' Mo' in Light of New Archaeological Evidence, by Linda Schele and Nikolai Grube (1994)

Copan Note 117
The Floor Marker from Motmot, by Linda Schele, Federico Fahsen, and Nikolai Grube (1994)

Copan Note 118
The Texts of Group 10L-2: A New Interpretation, by Linda Schele (1993)